Dublin, 1910–1940

The making of Dublin City

SERIES EDITORS
Joseph Brady and Anngret Simms, Department of Geography,
University College Dublin

Dublin, 1910–1940

SHAPING THE CITY
& SUBURBS

Ruth McManus

FOUR COURTS PRESS

Set in 11 pt on 14 pt Garamond by
Carrigboy Typesetting Services, County Cork for
FOUR COURTS PRESS LTD
Fumbally Court, Fumbally Lane, Dublin 8, Ireland
e-mail: info@four-courts-press.ie
http://www.four-courts-press.ie
and in North America for
FOUR COURTS PRESS
c/o ISBS, 5824 N.E. Hassalo Street, Portland, OR 97213.

ISBN 1-85182-615-7 hbk
ISBN 1-85182-712-9 pbk

Printed in England
by MPG Books, Bodmin, Cornwall

Contents

Dublin City Public Libraries
Marino
Borrower Receipt

Customer name: Fitzsimons, William

Title: Dublin : A grand tour / Jacqueline O'Bri
ID: 02978322473016
Due: 11-11-21

Title: Dublin, 1910-1940 : shaping the city an
ID: 18518271298008
Due: 11-11-21

Total items. 2
21/10/2021 12:03
Checked out: 2
Overdue: 0
Hold requests: 0
Ready for pickup: 0

Thank you for using the Selfservice System.

K1

Abbreviations

CII	Civics Institute of Ireland (see HTPAI)
DADC	Dublin Artizans' Dwellings Company
DDHBA	Dublin and District Housebuilders' Association
DED	District Electoral Division (sometimes also termed 'ward')
DLGPH	Department of Local Government and Public Health
DUTC	Dublin United Tramway Company
ESB	Electricity Supply Board
FRIBA	Fellow, Royal Institute of British Architects
GAA	Gaelic Athletic Association
GPO	General Post Office (O'Connell Street, Dublin)
GSR	Great Southern Railway Company
HTPAI	Housing and Town Planning Association of Ireland (later became Civics Institute of Ireland)
ISSLT	Irish Sailors' and Soldiers' Land Trust
LCC	London County Council
LGB	Local Government Board
MP	Member of Parliament
OPW	Office of Public Works
PLV	Poor Law Valuation
PUS	Public Utility Society
RDC	Rural District Council
RDS	Royal Dublin Society
RFS	Registrar of Friendly Societies
RIAI	Royal Institute of the Architects of Ireland, founded 1839
SDAA	Small Dwellings Acquisition Act
TD	(Teachta Dála) member of Dáil Eireann, the lower house of the Irish parliament
UCD	University College Dublin
UDC	Urban District Council
VEC	Vocational Education Committee

Currency equivalences

The currency referred to in this text is the pre-decimal pound. This was divided into 20 shillings, each shilling containing 12 pence.

Pre-decimal £	Decimal £	euro €
£1=240*d.*	£1=100p	€1=£0.787564
6*d.*	2.5p	3.2 cent
1*s.*	5p	6.3 cent
2*s.* 6*d.*	12.5p	15.9 cent
10*s.*	50p	63.5 cent

Series editor's introduction

In the first volume of this series, we explored the growth and development of the city of Dublin from its origins to the beginning of the twentieth century. The thousand or so years encompassed in this time period were eventful for the city and its fortunes waxed and waned. By the beginning of the twentieth century it was a small and elegant city but no longer a capital city. It boasted many fine public and civic buildings but they were mostly the legacy of another era. Infrastructure and social provision had improved during the previous 100 years but there were still massive problems of poverty and inadequate housing to be dealt with. The twentieth century was going to pose many challenges to Dublin, particularly in relation to housing. Assessing how the city met these demands is the task that Ruth McManus takes up in the pages that follows. To set the scene, the next section offers a brief discussion of the forces that shaped the city, though the reader is referred to *Dublin through space and time* (2001) for a thorough discussion.

The geographical factors that initially brought the Vikings to Dublin had ceased to have any major significance by the beginning of the twentieth century. City defense had long ceased to be a consideration. It was over two hundred years since anyone had seriously suggested that Dublin ought to be fortified, though the Great South Wall had been provided with a gun battery. The Half Moon battery continued to appear on nineteenth-century Ordnance Survey maps. The Vikings had quickly turned to trade and the city developed as a port quite early on in its history. This has to be qualified, however, by the fact that Dublin was not a good natural port, despite appearances. The configuration of the bay promoted silting and Dublin could be a difficult and dangerous port to enter until the early years of the nineteenth century. The many shipwrecks in the bay are a testament to the violence of the storms in the bay and the impossibility of escape. Thereafter, the Great Walls provided the necessary scouring action and the port of Dublin developed throughout the nineteenth century until it had to reclaim land at the mouth of the Liffey for purpose-built docks. This need for this berthage indicated Dublin's integration into a national economy. As with most colonies, Ireland's economy fulfilled the dual role of provider of cheap primary products to Britain and consumer of her industrial goods. Whether this economic orientation was fortuitous or deliberate is beyond the scope of these short comments. Suffice it to say that if it was not the former, it could easily have become the latter.

Despite its importance as a port, Dublin lacked significant industries in the nineteenth century. True, there were extensive brewing and distilling complexes but beyond the food and textile sectors, there was little large-scale manufacturing industry. There were the limiting factors of geography without doubt; the raw materials of iron ore and coal were on the other side of the Irish Sea but Belfast managed to develop industrial manufacturing and ship building despite this limitation. Whatever the reason, the lack of industry denied Dublin the employment base that it so badly needed. It limited the capacity for civic building and public works funded by captains of industry. Despite this lack of employment opportunities for ordinary workers, especially the unskilled and semi-skilled, Dublin grew very substantially during the nineteenth century. Some 70,000 additional people were added to the city's population between 1800 and 1850 and the greater part of this growth was from migration. This might not seem such a large increase until one remembers that it added over one-third to the size of the city. Similar or greater increases were experienced in the industrial centres of Britain but here there was a demand for this labour. In fact, in Britain the demand for labour was insatiable. Industries were labour intensive but industrial work and city life was dangerous and the death rate in many cities was so high that it was only the continuous flow of migrants that keep population growing. The evidence is that many of those who ended up in Dublin had originally intended coming to the city only en-route to Liverpool and thence to Manchester and Birmingham but for whatever reason they stayed in Dublin. There was no insatiable demand for their labour in Dublin and so they settled into the demi-monde of the underemployed and marginal that was so much a feature of the city. This is not to say that an industrial sector would have been a panacea for the city's ills. It would have given the city additional wealth and spurred its development but it would not have eliminated poverty. Most Victorian industrialists paid the minimum that they could get away with but even that would have reduced the depth of poverty in Dublin and perhaps (and it is only perhaps) speeded the process of its elimination.

Matters were not enhanced by the unfortunate system of governance that Dublin had to endure. The Act for the Improvement of the City of Dublin in 1849 was an important landmark in streamlining the process of government within the city. It eliminated a number of competing and inefficient bodies and brought most matters under the control of Dublin Corporation. That body had itself been reformed by the Municipal Corporations (Ireland) Act of 1840 to become a more democratic body. But in its own way, this was the source of new problems in that it set up an opposition between the city authorities and the apparatus of the Crown as well as with the suburban townships. Dublin Corporation took on a strongly nationalist character in the second half of the century. One sign of this can be seen in the iconography of the city where the public statuary of the city reflected a growing nationalist confidence with statues to O'Connell, William Smith O'Brien and Parnell. In contrast, it was with the greatest reluctance that statues commemorating Queen Victoria and Prince Albert were erected. These were not given public locations on thoroughfares but cleverly they were given locations that were prominent, the grounds of the RDS, but not strictly public.

A growing difference between the city proper and the townships was a feature of the times. The drift of the better-off to the suburbs was a European-wide phenomenon and was driven both by a romantic idyll of country life and the desire to escape the smells and poverty of the industrial inner city. Improvements in roads and the development of the railways and omnibus services facilitated the process. While railway suburbs did develop in Dublin, the most successful suburbs were barely suburban in that they began just across the border of the city. These suburbs developed as independent township not under the jurisdiction of the Corporation. The most successful were the Pembroke township and the Rathmines/Rathgar township, both south of the Grand Canal. North of the Royal Canal, the Drumcondra and Clontarf townships achieved a measure of success but had not reached a critical mass by the time they were absorbed into the city at the beginning of the twentieth century.

It was an odd way for suburbs to develop but it was not unusual for the period. They were truly independent with their own government, a system of commissioners, their own services and their own rating system and the loss of these rates was a blow to economy of the area under the control of the Corporation. The townships' independence allowed them to dictate the character of their suburbs. Thus Pembroke used the leases it granted to ensure an upper middle class character for its township though it had a working-class population in Irishtown that it had 'inherited'. The Rathmines/Rathgar township was less exclusive but it too concentrated on the middle classes and so ensured a relatively small working-class population. They developed into enclaves of relative privilege, sundered from and different to the city of Dublin which was within walking distance. The physical distance might have been small but the social and political distance between these two townships and the city proper was considerable. As Dublin Corporation came to be more nationalist, the townships came to be a haven for those of a unionist persuasion. Thus the people who had money and who had it within their power to do much to alleviate the problems of the city, if they could be so persuaded, were increasingly alienated from the government of that city. This is not to say that they abandoned the city of Dublin. It was where they did business, where they shopped, where they entertained themselves but it was not where they lived and had an emotional attachment. The persistence of the townships until 1930 reflects their unwillingness to be a part of the city of Dublin. In 1900, the smaller townships of Drumcondra, Clontarf and Kilmainham were absorbed into the city. They were unable to resist incorporation because they did not have the resources needed to ensure the future development of their suburbs. However both Pembroke and Rathmines successfully resisted the attempts of Dublin Corporation to have them incorporated. The Corporation admitted that they would have been the jewel in their Crown but the population of the townships, for a variety of reasons, political and financial, did not wish it. Had Dublin Corporation been less nationalist and less at odds with Dublin Castle, its will might have prevailed. Pembroke and Rathmines continued to develop separately to the remainder of the city until 1930 and by then, the social geography of the southern city had been determined. There had developed a higher social status sector in the south-east, leaving only the south-west to be developed for social housing and producing the west-east social gradient that is still a feature of this part of the city. Interestingly no such gradient exists north of the city where social areas are less spatially extensive and differentiated.

The existence and persistence of the townships made the work of Dublin Corporation somewhat more difficult but not impossible. Dublin did well during the nineteenth century and much was achieved in infrastructural improvements. It hosted two international exhibitions as well as Royal visits. The city was a successful urban centre, a focus of business and commerce with shopping streets that were both elegant and costly. The Corporation slowly came to the view that it needed to be involved in solving the social problems of the city. It was a slow realization. The Housing Inquiry of 1913, published in 1914, had some hard words for at least some of the then members of the Corporation and it drew particular attention to the property owned by Alderman G. O'Reilly, Alderman Corrigan and Councillor Crozier. Moreover they noted that the Corporation had not used effectively the powers at their disposal to improve the quality of housing and they further stated that 'the want of a firm administration has created a number of owners with but little sense of their responsibilities of landlords, and that it has helped much in the demoralization of a number of the working classes and increased the number of inefficient workers in the city' (p. 14). This would suggest that a social conscience was not one of the stronger aspects of the ethos of the Corporation despite their nationalism.

Some efforts were made and it would be churlish not to recognize them. The selection of a modest number of unhealthy areas by Dr Mapother, the city's first medical officer of health, in his report of 1876 for clearance may be considered the opening move in the municipality's mammoth task of tackling the city's housing and public health problems. Seven of the twelve areas were in the old Liberties – Meath Market, McClean's Lane, Elbow Lane, Plunket Street, Patrick's Close, Wood Street and Liberty Lane. Also on the south side there was Chatham Row, and the Boyne Street area east of Trinity College. On the north side Bow Street, Fisher's Lane and the Ormond Market, three distinct though nearby areas, were chosen. These areas were reduced to two – the Coombe and Boyne Street. A provisional order enabling schemes in these two areas was issued and confirmed by Parliament in 1877, at an estimated cost of £20,000. However, the £20,000 borrowed from the Commissioners of Public Works in Ireland was found to be sufficient only for purchasing and clearing the Coombe property, and the Boyne Street plans were shelved. The Corporation did not undertake the work itself but rather developed a public-private partnership with a private company, the Dublin Artizan's Dwelling Company (DADC).

The scheme at Gray Street was a success, at least in its own terms. It comprised 120 houses of four different classes: one-storey cottages, containing one living-room and one or two bedrooms; and two-storey houses, containing one or two living rooms and two bedrooms. There were also four houses of three storeys, used as shops. They were solidly built with good sanitation and remain desirable today. This scheme was followed in 1879 by another at Plunket Street, a notorious blackspot. The site was more irregular than in the Coombe but here also two-storey (and a few single-storey) houses were built along 'wide', 'healthful' roads such as John Dillon Street, Dean Swift Square and Thomas Davis Street, while single-storey cottages faced on to small but open areas, such as Power Square, Dillon Place, and Francis Square. The dwellings proposed for the Plunket Street site were to reflect the best sanitary practices, an advance even on the Coombe scheme, as the building conditions spelt out. Both schemes represented an important step for Dublin Corporation – direct intervention in the housing of the poor though not the poorest classes. However they proved to be hugely expensive, costing far more than had been expected, due largely to the often inflated compensation that the owners of the compulsorily-acquired property were able to obtain. It seemed that they were far better able to use the system than was the Corporation. The costs undoubtedly put a brake on the Corporation's enthusiasm for further projects. Moreover these schemes did nothing for the very poor. These could not afford the rents charged by the DADC and to add insult to injury these were the very people displaced during development. The Corporation was not insensible to the problem but was at a loss at what to do. The idea of providing accommodation cheaply to this class of people had not taken hold and it would be many years before there was a complete acceptance of relating rents to ability to pay. These were not the only attempts at working class housing. The Corporation experimented with blocks rather than individual houses such as on Benburb Street. This scheme was a disaster, proving more insanitary than speculative housing. There were others who contributed to the relief of the poor. The Iveagh Trust, for example, constructed block buildings on Kevin Street and Patrick Street. In the latter case, they are complemented by a Corporation development on Nicholas Street. The Iveagh Trust is of interest because it did not limit its activities to housing but also sought to improve its tenants by providing access to bathing facilities as well as education and training. However, though architecturally striking and important in the story of the housing of the working classes in Ireland, their impact on the problem was slight.

If they could not build, the Corporation had acquired powers to regulate private housing. The Medical Officer for Health, Dr Cameron had a staff at his disposal and they worked hard inspecting and cleansing sewers, privies, water closets, dwellings, and yards. Inspections were also undertaken of bakeries, slaughterhouses and dairy yards, while the disinfecting of articles and the serving of notices and summonses for sanitary offences were also key matters. They inspected houses and had the power to close dwellings which they found unfit. The total number of houses closed and de-tenanted as unfit for human habitation from 31 August 1879 to 31 December 1882 was 1345, with 389 cellars and 'several hundreds of rooms' also closed. By 1886 a further 721 houses had been closed. In a review of progress to 1893 Dr Cameron noted that while the number of sanitary defects in that year had been up to the average, on the whole they were not of as serious a nature as had been the case in previous years. In general, he felt that conditions were improving due, in no small measure, to the activities of his staff. He claimed that during the previous twelve years that 2700 houses had been de-tenanted. About 350 of these houses had been demolished, never to be rebuilt since their site and situation was unsuitable. Some hundreds more had been demolished but were likely to re-appear. The remainder had been improved sufficiently to permit their use again.

On the whole, he took satisfaction that the tenements of Dublin were in at least as good order as those of London and other large towns.

And so it continued into the twentieth century. Dublin Corporation, the DADC and the Iveagh Trust made important, but small scale, contributions to the housing problem. But they never did more than chip at the margins and at the next, inevitable, housing inquiry in 1913, the magnitude of the problem was manifest.

We should close this section by assessing how well the Corporation did. On the face of it, they did not do very well. Almost three-quarters of the nineteenth century passed before they became actively involved and even then it was only on a small scale. Their defenders will point to the difficult circumstances under which they worked. Their rateable base was small, in consequence of drift of the middle classes to the townships, while the number of the poor was large. The legislation under which they had to operate was cumbersome. The need to compensate property owners made clearance schemes ruinously expensive. However, as we have seen, some at least, of the Corporation did rather well out of the housing crisis.

This is the point at which Ruth McManus begins her discussion. The compact city of the nineteenth century was about to grow dramatically. The middle classes were already suburbanites and this continued as the twentieth century developed. There were to be joined by the working classes whose housing provision was effected by an interesting and complex public- private relationship.

It is worth recalling at this point just how far reaching these changes were going to be. Dublin is often called an eighteenth-century city in deference to its heritage of Georgian architecture that gives much of the city centre its distinctive character. The more prosaic reality is that the city is a twentieth-century creation. The greatest land-use in Dublin, as in any city, is its residential areas and these were created by the processes that were begun in the period of this book. Less than 15 per cent of the housing stock of the present-day city pre-dates 1919 and much of this is concentrated in the former townships. The creation of the suburbs was not a smooth process, as the text makes clear. Much planning was *ad hoc* and reactive despite the attempts of many to develop a town-plan for the city. There were lengthy policy debates and policy shifts about the nature and location of social housing. State policy was also an important influence. The system of grants and loans determined how developments were undertaken while an encouragement of home ownership as a desirable social goal drove many policies.

Moreover suburban development was a sophisticated business with complex relationships between city authorities and private builders. The distinction between public and private enterprise was quite blurred and public-private partnerships, to use the current buzz-phrase, were an essential element. It is quite clear from Ruth McManus' work that both speculative builders and Dublin Corporation needed each other and this can be seen in spatial terms in the housing developments that resulted.

Dublin did not develop in an international vacuum. Despite our island status, the people who built Dublin were very much aware of what was happening on the continent of Europe. Both Corporation and private builders borrowed the best (usually!) of what was being tried elsewhere and improved on it where they could. Ruth McManus has provided an appendix in which she describes this context and the people that were important.

We are geographers and in a book such as this we are attempting to reveal the processes that created the spatial environment of the city. With such an emphasis on the built environment, the visual medium is of vital importance. We speak of the crucial geographical skill as 'having an eye for landscape'. There are many illustrations in this book and we hope that these will help the reader to 'see' the places that are discussed. Maps are essential geographical tool and many are reproduced in the text. A brief guide to the maps of Dublin is provided by the editors in an appendix and this should be read in conjunction with a similar guide in volume 1.

A final appendix offers a perspective on what was happening to the city centre. The focus of this book is on the suburbs and suburban growth and it would not have been possible to provide a detailed look at the heart of the city without detracting from this. However, to carry on the story of the city centre from volume 1 we have provided a short guide to what happened to the places that were talked about in that volume.

We continue to be very grateful to our university, University College Dublin, for the help and encouragement which we are given and particularly for the financial assistance provided to produce these volumes. Thanks are also due to Ordnance Survey Ireland for permission to reprint the many map extracts that appear in this book (permit no. MP006702).

This introduction was begun by commending the reader to the first volume in this series and it seems appropriate to end by a reminder that there will be future volumes in this series which we hope will give as much pleasure as we believe this book will.

JOSEPH BRADY

Preface

'The story of a nation is written in the stones of its cities.' These words of Horace Tennyson O'Rourke, the City Architect of Dublin from 1922 to 1944 seem an appropriate introduction to a piece of work which considers the development of Dublin city through a turbulent period in political, economic and social terms. The physical transformation of the city from 1910 to 1940 reflects changing thinking on the nature of cities, appropriate forms of housing, slum clearance and modern town planning. The change not only encompasses the rapid growth of suburbanization for all social classes, but also the process whereby the very poorest members of the working classes began to be 'ghettoised' in Dublin Corporation's central area flat schemes. While some space is given to the redevelopment of the city centre following the destruction of 1916 and the Civil War, the main focus of the book is on the way in which Dublin's suburbs were constructed at this time. It explores the nature of the new and idealistic schemes built at Marino, Crumlin and elsewhere on behalf of the local authority, as well as the way in which individual private builders had a major impact on the layout and style of the suburbs which they constructed. For the first time in an Irish context, the extent of the interaction between the State, local authorities, public utility societies and private speculators is explored, showing that the general perception of a clear divide between public and private housing is largely unfounded. The book also considers ways in which the modern town planning movement and evolving ideas about citizenship in the new State impacted on the shaping of the city. Importantly, many of the formative decisions that came to shape the modern low-rise, low-density city were taken at this time.

This book has grown from my doctorate, undertaken in the UCD Geography Department under the supervision of Dr Joe Brady, to whom I owe a great debt of gratitude. The work would not have been possible without assistance from a wide variety of people. I would particularly like to thank Mary Clark, Dublin City Archivist, for her help. Staff at the National Archives, Gilbert Library, National Library, UCD Architecture Library and Trinity College Dublin library also gave welcome assistance. Deirdre Ellis-King, Chief Librarian, Dublin City and County Libraries, gave permission for reproduction of the photograph which appears as figure 97.

The quality of the illustrations which appear in this volume is the result of hard work, perseverance and technical know-how of Joe Brady, who also generously supplied illustrations from his private collection. Stephen Hannon lent his cartographic expertise in redrawing the maps. I would also like to thank my Dad, Derry McManus, who helped in the taking of many of the photographs.

The late Mrs Christina Hughes told me of her own experiences of life in a Capel Street tenement before moving out to 'the country' to Marino. I would also like to thank Mr and Mrs Caird who remembered Mr Strain and the early years of the Cremore estate.

In addition to the direct help provided by the librarians and archivists of the institutions I have mentioned, I would also like to thank my colleagues in UCD, Dundalk Institute of Technology, NUI Maynooth, Trinity College Dublin and most recently St Patrick's College, Drumcondra, for their support throughout the lengthy gestation of this work. I also received moral support from friends both near and far, including Marcie, Martin, Bertrand, Edel, Aisling, Shane, Edmund, Niamh and the Tarpey family. Particular thanks to my parents for their constant support and encouragment, and to my extended family of aunts, uncles and cousins who provided inspiration, motivation and assistance, often in very practical ways.

I am grateful to the St Patrick's College Research Committee for a generous subvention towards publication costs.

A final word of thanks must go to the series editors, Dr Joe Brady and Professor Anngret Simms, both of whom have been friends and colleagues since my time as a student in the UCD Geography Department. Their commitment to this project has ensured its fruition despite many difficulties along the way.

Many thanks to all of those mentioned. Of course, all errors and omissions are my own responsibility. They would doubtless have been more numerous were it not for the assistance received from those mentioned above.

Planning the city: the beginnings

Introduction

This is a story of hope amid despair, of optimism and rebirth at a time of incredible hardship. In many ways the Dublin of less than a hundred years ago has receded into the recesses of our collective memory, given the huge economic and social changes which have taken place since then. Yet it is to the workers and visionaries of the early decades of the twentieth century that we must turn, if we wish to understand fully the nature of the city as it is today. It was at this time that many of the formative decisions were taken which came to shape the modern low-rise, low-density city. Decisions intended to alleviate the poor housing conditions of the working population came to have enormous, sometimes unforeseen, outcomes for the whole population. This is the story, too, of an interesting relationship between public and private interests, between the State, the local authorities and their officials and the many private contractors who contributed to the building of the city. While one of the catch phrases of today is public-private partnership, touted as a new way of funding public projects, in fact it is not *that* new, and was the basis of much of Dublin's development, as we shall see. In particular, Dublin's Corporation, the local authority which governed the area within the city boundaries, relied quite extensively on semi-private organizations known as public utility societies to assist in completing its schemes. Although their nature and scale of operation varied, these public utility societies shared a common object of providing quality housing for tenants or more often tenant-purchasers at reasonable prices. They were aided by State measures as well as by the local authorities, who provided cheap sites on serviced land as well as rates remissions and other forms of assistance.

Dublin's physical area grew extensively during the early twentieth century, as illustrated by Horner (1985), as low-density suburbs were built around the city. We shall see that, although the middle classes had already begun to move out of the city into newly developed suburbs by the mid-nineteenth century, the pace and scale of suburbanization increased rapidly in the first half of the twentieth century, setting the tone for the city we know today. This suburban development owed much to the influence of the garden city ideas and the

town planning movement, which promoted low-density planned development as an alternative to the evils of city centre slums. This was the time when
attempts were being made to solve the problems of the slum city, so well
described by Prunty (1998) and others. A combination of ideas and influences
was to lead to the adoption of a policy of planned suburbanization of the
working classes. While some flats were built in the city, particularly in the
1930s, the desirable norm was perceived (by the authorities at least) as the
individual house with its own garden, built at a density of no more than 12
houses to the acre (c.30 per ha). The decision to build high-quality, low-
density housing also influenced the type of housing being provided by private
speculators, who aimed at least to match the type of offering provided by the
local authority. In many cases, private builders added particular features to
distinguish their houses from the 'Corporation type', including bay windows
or stained glass surrounds in doorways.

In this book we will explore the development of housing in Dublin,
looking at the process of private speculative building as well as the planned
efforts of the State sector. We will see that the period from 1913 to 1939 marked
a shift in the way in which housing was provided. By 1913, the neglect of
working-class housing in the city had reached such a level that a formal
inquiry was undertaken to determine the causes and identify possible
solutions to 'the housing problem'. It found that 60,000 people urgently
required rehousing, a huge task made more difficult by the political turmoil
of the time. As time moved on, the State increasingly acknowledged its role in
supplying adequate housing for those who could not otherwise afford it.
Slums were cleared and the aspirations of the middle-class legislators were
reflected in the building of low-density suburban housing, sometimes termed
'garden suburbs', to rehouse those displaced from the slums and tenements of
the city centre. Many of the local authority houses built in this way in the
1920s were sold under tenant purchase schemes to their occupants. Despite
the fact that high quality accommodation was provided both the Government
and Dublin Corporation were heavily criticized at this time for the failure to
tackle the roots of the housing problem. With a renewed phase of slum
clearance from 1932, greater efforts were made to provide housing for the very
poorest classes, generally in city centre flats. In tandem with this flat provision,
there was a continuation of suburban house building, but increasingly these
houses were built for rental rather than tenant purchase.

At the opposite end of the spectrum, private speculative development saw
a contrasting trend in the period from before 1914 to 1940. We shall see that

the building of investment property that was then made available for letting was a far more common practice prior to World War I, whereas the tendency in the 1920s and increasingly in the 1930s was to build housing directly for sale. Although such houses were generally sold to owner occupiers, in some cases individual builders operated their own version of tenant purchase schemes. While levels of planning in the private speculative market were minimal, there was an increase in the amount of local authority influence over private building during the 1930s. It will also become clear that the divisions between what is perceived as 'public' housing and that which was built for the 'private' market were rather less clear-cut than might have previously been believed. In this respect, the development of public utility societies from the 1920s is particularly significant.

The nature and form of housing development in Dublin prior to 1940 offers many lessons for the planners and citizens of today. False economies, social segregation, manipulation and evasion will inevitably be seen, the result of ill-conceived policies or human nature. But by the same token we shall see that drive, determination, citizenship and goodwill could achieve much, even where only a handful of individuals was involved.

The 1913 Housing Inquiry and its aftermath

> On one thing I am perfectly clear, and that is that this report cannot be allowed to rest, as so many other reports have done, in the pigeon holes of offices … In fact, there is a moderation of tone in the report which only adds to its value, and there can be no mistake that the state of things which now exists is horrible and intolerable.
>
> (Chief Secretary for Ireland and President of the Local Government Board for Ireland, Mr Augustine Birrell, quoted in Report 35/1916, p. 349)

Our story begins in 1913, a memorable year for the city of Dublin. This was the year of great labour unrest which culminated in a lock-out of workers who were members of the Irish Transport and General Workers Union (ITGWU). Indeed, the success of Jim Larkin's union was said by many to relate to the impoverished conditions of the workers. In a letter to the *Irish Times* at the height of the lockout, E.A. Aston eloquently expressed this view:

> Twenty thousand families – one third of the people of Dublin – live in one-room tenements. How many of our federated employers after 12

months of life under such conditions would think of abstract considerations of citizenship or industrial prosperity? Are they sure that their
children would not learn to throw bottles at the police if society had
condemned them to the reeking nursery of the tenement house.

(E.A. Aston, letter to the Irish Times, 3 September 1913)

As we shall see, Aston was an important player in housing and town
planning affairs in early-twentieth-century Dublin. He was a founder member
of the Housing and Town Planning Association of Ireland, for four years
honorary secretary of the Dublin Citizens' Association and a contributor of
influential articles to the *Irish Builder and Engineer* under the pseudonym
'Artifex'.

Even the conservative *Irish Times* acknowledged the appalling social
conditions that contributed to Larkin's following among the slum-dwellers. In
an editorial following the deaths of seven people in the Church Street
tenement collapse, it noted that members of the ITGWU lived 'for the most
part in slums like Church Street' and that 'the condition of the Dublin slums
is responsible not only for disease and crime but for much of our industrial
unrest … The workers, whose only escape from these wretched homes lies in
the public house, would not be human beings if they did not turn a ready ear
to anybody who promises to improve their lot.' The writer concluded that 'if
every unskilled labourer in Dublin were the tenant of a decent cottage of three
or even two rooms, the city would not be divided into two hostile camps.'
(*Irish Times*, 4 September 1913, p. 6). Thus there was a perceived link between
the provision of good housing and social order.

During 1913, increased public awareness of deteriorating housing
conditions in the city gave rise to calls for 'something to be done'. The huge
public outcry following the collapse of 66 and 67 Church Street on
2 September was probably the final straw leading to the establishment of a
housing inquiry. The Local Government Board for Ireland appointed a
Committee to Inquire into the Housing Conditions of the Working Classes
in the City of Dublin which heard evidence from 76 people over 17 days. The
evidence stated the nature and scale of the problem, providing information on
the state of the city's housing, the quality and rents paid in existing tenements
and the incomes of their inhabitants. It also detailed the financial balance
sheet of existing Corporation schemes and the costs of undertaking the
necessary re-housing schemes. The report of the inquiry, published in 1914,
suggested that housing problem was getting worse.

1 Poole Street at the end of the nineteenth century. (Postcard.)

In common with other British cities, a number of attempts had been made to deal with Dublin's slum problem on philanthropic lines in the Victorian period. Among the most notable achievements were those of the Dublin Artizans' Dwellings Company (DADC), founded in 1876, and the Guinness (later Iveagh) Trust, which have been researched by Aalen (1984, 1985). The DADC provided about 3300 working-class dwellings in the period prior to 1913, which was more than twice what Dublin Corporation had achieved during the same period. The work of the Guinness Trust, the only major housing trust to operate in Dublin, is described in detail by Aalen (1990). It began its first flat schemes in 1891. In themselves, however, such organizations could only scratch the surface of an enormous problem. Although profits were kept to a minimum, the very poor could not afford to rent the new accommodation, while the scale of building was too small to contribute much to central renewal. Indeed accusations were often leveled that these enterprises merely exacerbated the problem, because it was impossible to re-house all those displaced by their schemes. Therefore, despite some small-scale efforts at improvement, the condition of the housing of the working classes of Dublin remained an enormous problem well into the twentieth century.

Dublin of 1913 has been well described in *Divided City* (1978), while the first book of this series illustrated the many issues facing Dublin in the first decade of the twentieth century. In the nineteenth century the city was bounded by the two canals, with much of the suitable land already built upon. By the second half of the century, therefore, development had flowed beyond the canal, particularly to the south of the fashionable Merrion Square area. The move to the suburbs in Dublin was initiated by the professional and upper middle classes who were seeking new residences which would be physically removed from a city characterized by disrepair and physical dereliction as well as a distressed and unhealthy population. This was a common phenomenon in western cities from the mid-nineteenth century. By moving to healthier surroundings they also left the city for independently governed 'townships' and avoided the financial costs of the city's workhouse, hospitals and police which were borne by the ratepayers. The savings were often considerable, given that rates could account for more than 25 per cent of the rent in the case of some properties within the city boundaries. The townships provided an administrative framework within which development could take place with all the benefits of services such as good roads, sewerage and lighting. North of the Royal Canal, the former townships of Glasnevin, Drumcondra, Clonliffe and Clontarf had been absorbed by Dublin Corporation in 1900, along with Kilmainham to the south-west of the city. To the south, where the majority of middle-class suburbanization had occurred, independent townships of Pembroke, Rathmines and Rathgar retained their independence under the control of separate Urban District Councils until their eventual absorption into the city in 1930. The existence of these independent entities, with their separate political and social agendas, tended to hinder the orderly develop- ment of the city which was so desired by the early town planning movement.

The move to the suburbs had further implications apart from a reduction in the Corporation's revenues. The former houses of the upper and middle classes could be let at high rents to the working classes. Georgian-style houses which had been built for single-family occupation were subdivided into tenements housing several families. Because the demand for accommodation was so acute, and the poor were willing (or had no choice but) to accept overcrowding, the site value was such that the landlord was given little or no incentive to rebuild the property. Thus the city authority, Dublin Corporation, found itself in an increasingly difficult situation, lacking the financial means to cope with a worsening housing crisis.

By the final quarter of the nineteenth century there was a gulf between city and suburbs in terms of both religion and social status, with a suburban pre- dominance among the members of the professional, employer and managerial classes, as well as a high relative proportion of domestic servants. In self-governing townships like Rathmines and Pembroke, developers were creating fine residential environments, where the 'Protestant and unionist Dublin middle-class could evade the unpleasant reality that they were a minority which was increasingly losing political control in both Ireland and in the city of Dublin' (Daly, 1988, p. 123). For example, Rathmines Township was unashamedly hostile to the city's nationalist Corporation, which would undoubtedly have appealed to many Protestant families who felt increasingly alienated from Dublin's Catholicism and nationalism. Mary Daly (1984) has described how the location, indigenous population, and development policies of their respective landowners and builders, gave rise to diverse religious and occupational patterns within the various townships adjoining the city. More than half of all suburban residents lived in the neighbouring townships of Rathmines and Pembroke, compared to just over 12 per cent in the comparable suburbs of Clontarf and Drumcondra to the north of the city. The northern areas were slower to grow for a number of reasons, including land ownership, proximity to the increasingly unfashionable north-eastern quadrant of the city with its red-light tenement district ('Monto') and to urban blight associated with the expanding docks and railway stations, as well as poorly-drained land less suited to building than the southern suburbs. New Kilmainham owed its growth more to the state of local industry than to suburban expansion and was almost exclusively working class.

Improvements in public transport contributed to the growth of the suburbs. The city's tramlines serviced a wide area, enabling people to work in the city while living in the suburbs, while there was an excellent train service from Kingstown (now Dún Laoghaire) to the city centre. Areas such as Monkstown and Blackrock became fashionable due to their access to fresh sea air as well as the possibility of having large and elegant gardens. Other attractions of the suburbs to the south of the city proper included relative closeness to the sea, to the mountains and leisure pursuits such as golfing, hunting and racing.

Although the majority of people rented their homes, it was also possible to purchase houses in the new townships. In 1913 a seven-roomed house on Appian Way could be bought for £350 through James H. North & Co., on a 900-year lease with a ground rent of £5. In the same year, the building firm of Crampton, Ballsbridge, was offering 'a new semi-detached villa, No. 18 Herbert Park, for Sale', while the high-quality rental opportunities included an eight-roomed house on Anglesea Road for £75 per annum, a house on Upper Mount Street for £12 monthly, or a furnished house on Waterloo Road with five bedrooms, two sitting rooms and a bath for eight guineas monthly.

2a Advertisement – Autocars of Chatham Street.

The wealthy investor could have purchased a north-side tenement house with stable, in good order, for just £75 (*Irish Times*, 5 July 1913). The net annual profit on this investment was £40, while the lease was for 42 years. Others preferred to spend their money on the new motor cars which were coming into vogue. The Rover Company Limited, Lord Edward Street, advertised a 12-horsepower Rover in a two-seater version for £300, or a four-seater for £315. Elswick cycles were available in Dixon's of Suffolk Street from £7 12s. 6d., while second-hand cycles cost from £2. Foreign travel was becoming more common, with Thomas Cook and Sons offering trips to Lugano (with excursions, travel, hotel and 'conductor' included) for just £9 9s.

In the summer sales of 1913, the well-dressed lady could purchase a smart linen costume for 29*s*. 6*d*. at Coventry's, 3 Grafton Street, reduced from the usual price of two guineas, while trimmed and untrimmed hats were available from 1*s*. 11*d*. Royal Worcester corsets cost from 4*s*. to 12*s*. at Pim Bros Ltd. of South Great George's Street. In McGuire's of Merrion Row, ladies two-button chamois gloves worth 2*s*. 6*d*. were on special offer, while Clery's sale offered sun umbrellas to protect that delicate skin at 6*s*. 11*d*.

At the other end of the social spectrum, one of the main sources of employment for working-class women was in domestic service. Male servants were less common and highly prestigious, commanding good wages. A butler valet could earn £40 to £50 per annum, while a Dublin household which kept six servants could afford a footman at £25 per annum. A second

AVRO *Corsetry*
(REGD.)
for Health and Beauty

MORE than ever the Modern Foundation garment is the deciding factor in a well dressed appearance, that is the well designed, expertly cut and skilfully finished Foundation. The choice of a garment too has become a responsibility instead of the haphazard business that it used to be. And the many figure types and problems—how are they to be provided for ? . . . . only by such a comprehensive range to select from as **AVRO** regd. **Health and Beauty Corsetry.** From the schoolgirl to Matron—every age and figure type has an **AVRO** garment specially designed to take care of it.

YOU CANNOT DO BETTER THAN CHOOSE AVRO !

AVRO BIAS BINDING

carded and in 72 yard rolls. Write for samples and shade card.

2b Advertisement – Catering to every need.

gardener 'good in and out' required for Somerville, Clontarf Castle could expect '17*s*., lodge, two ton coal'. Among the female servants, there were many degrees of work. Conditions varied, depending on the employer and on the number of servants employed, while wages were also related to levels of expertise (Luddy, 1995). Some households kept a single general servant, who was generally required to do cooking and washing. The 'smart general' required for Auburn Villa, Howth Road, Dublin, was also expected to milk a cow, for which she could hope to receive £14 a year. A family of three at 43 Rathmines Road was prepared to pay just £10 for a 'smart tidy girl' who was also an early riser. On average, the wages of female domestic servants were higher in households which employed a greater number of servants. Many households engaged their servants through agencies such as Morton's Registry, 30 Dawson Street, which offered good cooks at £18 to £30, or Blackwood's of 41 Lower Mount Street, where rates for cooks varied from £25 to £30. Often the advertisements specified the preferred religious persuasion of their staff, while many also expressed a preference for workers from the country: 'Wanted for Foxrock. Cook, good bread maker and early riser, wages £18. Country girl preferred'. The lowest female on the servants' pecking order was the scullery maid, who could expect to earn up to £10 a year. Moving up the scale, Kennedy's of 68 Sackville Street advertised kitchen maids at £14 to £24, while Blackwood's had offers for housemaids at £25 and parlour maids at £22 and £25. More educated women, perhaps reduced to genteel poverty, could hope to be engaged through Madame Bois' Ladies Employment Bureau, 40 Westland Row, as nursery governesses for perhaps £35 a year.

Yet despite the considerable wealth in Dublin and its developing suburbs (Brady, 2001), and the obvious ability to pay for luxury goods and engage quality servants, poverty was very evident throughout the city. 'No inconsiderable number of the poor get out of their beds, or substitutes for them, without knowing when they are to get their breakfast, for the simple reason that they have neither money nor credit. They must starve if they have got nothing which would be taken in pawn.' (Cameron, 1913, p. 166). Much of this poverty was linked to the weakness of Dublin's industrial sector which is reflected in the occupational structure of the city. The Census of 1911 shows that, of a total population of 304,000, almost 55,000 males were in the industrial class and just under 21,000 in the commercial class. A full third of the working population was classed as unskilled labourers. Some 53,000 males were classified in the 'Indefinite and Non-productive Class'. Children under 15 years comprised a large proportion of this category but child labour was an important source of income for many poor families. The housing question was linked, therefore, with a need to improve industrial conditions in Dublin, where there were so many casual and seasonal workers. Because of this dependence on casual labour, low rent-paying capacity was an obstacle to housing improvements. The bulk of Dublin's population lived in tenements or in tiny cottages in courts and alleys behind the main streets. In his 1913 volume of reminiscences, Sir Charles Cameron, Dublin's Medical Officer of Health, discussed the plight of the tenement dwellers:

> In the case of one-room tenements, the occupants are usually very poor, and unable to pay for more accommodation. The wages of unskilled labourers are rarely more than £1 per week; many earn only from 15s. to 18s. weekly. Even when the labourer is a sober man, and has a small family, he cannot enjoy much comfort on the higher rate of

wages. When he is of the inferior order, has a large family, and pre-
carious employment, it is easy to imagine his deplorable condition.

(Cameron, 1913, p. 166)

Poor living conditions were not restricted to the general labouring classes.
Cameron noted that many thousands of families had weekly incomes not
exceeding 15s., while in some cases the income was as low as 10s.

A family, man and wife, resides in Dame Court. His occupation is that
of a tailor, but he can only earn 10s. a week. His rent is 2s. 6d., which
leaves 7s. 6d. for food, fuel, light, clothes, bedding, etc. Their breakfast
consists of dry bread and tea. They have only another meal, dinner and
supper combined: it consists of dry bread and tea and herrings, occasionally porridge. It may appear strange that a tradesman could earn only 10s.
per week; but such is often the case owing to irregular employment and
the poor payment for the making of the cheaper kind of clothes.

(Cameron, 1913, p. 168)

When, in 1918, the Housing Committee of Dublin Corporation undertook
a survey of housing conditions on the north side of the city, they found that
over one quarter of the 161,551 people living in the area occupied tenement
houses, paying average weekly rents of 2s. to 3s. for a single room, 2s. 6d. to 4s.
6d. for two-room lettings, 4s. to 6s. for three or more rooms (Report 13/1918).
Many families were eking out an existence on less than 10s. per week, managing to survive due to assistance from the Poor Law Union and other charitable
organizations. The Corporation faced the huge difficulty of providing these
people with accommodation at rents which they would be able to pay.

The majority of the labouring class, and a substantial proportion of the artizan
class, lived in Dublin's slums in 1913. Indeed, 87,000 Dubliners (29 per cent of
the city's population) lived in slums. A third of these dwellings were described as
being unfit for human habitation, while the rest were either 'structurally sound
but not in good repair' or 'so decayed as are soon like to be unfit for habitation'.

One of the characteristics of Dublin's slums was that they were not
geographically distinct in their location, but were widespread throughout the
city: 'In most cities the purlieus are in a limited number of districts, but in
Dublin they are to be met with everywhere' (Cameron, 1904, p. 2). A further
feature of the problem was the high proportion of people living in single
rooms. Of the 25,822 families living in tenement houses in 1913, over 20,000

(78 per cent) occupied one room only. This situation had persisted for some time. For example, in a 1908 report describing conditions in the United Kingdom's principal towns, Dublin was singled out as a city of one-room tenements, while again in 1911, it was shown that one third of all tenements consisted of one room. In terms of the city's population as a whole, it was also clear that a far greater proportion of the population of Dublin City was living in one-room tenements (22.9 per cent) than was the case in other cities of the United Kingdom. The only large centres of population approaching Dublin in this respect were Finsbury in London (14.8 per cent) and Glasgow (13.2 per cent). The implications of the preponderance of one-room tenements were disturbing. This unhealthy overcrowding was one of the main explanations for high death rates in the city, as suggested as far back as 1904 by Sir Charles Cameron, Dublin's Medical Officer of Health.

Table 1 Tenement conditions in 1913.

	Classification	*Number*	*Families*	*Persons*
First Class	'structurally sound, capable of being put in good repair'	1516 tenements	8295	27,052
Second Class	'decayed or so badly constructed', approaching 'the border line of unfit for habitation'	2288 houses	10,696	37,552
Third Class	'unfit for habitation and incapable of being rendered fit'	1518 tenements	6831	22,701
	Small houses		1136	

(*Source*: Housing Inquiry, 1914, p. 3, para 8.)

The table shows that 60,000 people in the city (all of those in third-class accommodation, and the majority of those in second-class housing) needed to be rehoused. However, the inquiry also recognized that to have condemned and closed these dwellings would, on its own, simply have led to further overcrowding (Housing Inquiry, 1914, 2, pp 18–25). There was nowhere else for the people to go. The condition of this 'unfit' housing was sometimes incredibly bad. At a Corporation meeting in 1921, Mr Lyons gave a startling account of the conditions of dwellings in the Boyne Street area. 'Walls, he said, were propped up by sticks and beams to prevent people falling into the street, and he was aware of one case of a lady of 'avoir-dupois pattern' exchanging apartments with another lady for fear she might fall through' (*Irish Builder and Engineer*, 19 November 1921, p. 749).

Conditions in the tenements were quite shocking. Out of a total of 5322 tenements, over one fifth (1159) had only one closet for every 20 to 40 people. The diet of the labourers, hawkers and other tenement dwellers in a similar social position was generally very poor and insufficient, relying heavily on bread and tea. According to Cameron (1913), beef and mutton were seldom seen on the tables of the poor, and then generally only for the breadwinner of the family. They were fried or boiled, as there was no way of roasting them. Crubeens, or pig's feet, and boiled bacon with cabbage were also consumed. Few vegetables, except potatoes and cabbage, were used, while fruit was uncommon. Often the milk used was condensed skim milk, purchased at 1*d.* to 3*d.* per tin (Cameron, 1913).

Although 57,000 pupils were enrolled in Dublin's primary schools, education was an impossible luxury and truancy was rife. In 1920, average daily attendance was just 50 per cent (Humphreys, 1966).

One of the most controversial aspects of the inquiry was the exposure of serious negligence on the part of Dublin Corporation. Many commentators had already implied that members of the Corporation were actually contributing to the housing problem through their outside interests. Now those suspicions were verified, as the report exposed conflict of interest in respect of 14 members of Dublin Corporation who were found to be owners of tenement properties or small cottages. Although the overwhelming majority owned from one to three houses, three owners between them held a total of 61 properties. When the President of the Inquiry, Mr C.H. O'Connor, made an inspection of some of these tenements, he noted that some had been recently cleaned and painted, probably since the opening of the inquiry, in what he suggested was a clear attempt to cover up the worst cases. The properties owned by Alderman Corrigan, Councillor Crozier and Alderman O'Reilly were virtually all in poor repair, being officially classified as unfit for human habitation. Despite this, all had received rates rebates ostensibly for improvements carried out. Arising out of this finding, it was alleged that Sir Charles Cameron, Dublin Medical Officer of Health and a Freeman of the City of Dublin, had passed as fit some unfit housing belonging to Aldermen, and had abused his powers in granting a rent rebate where none was justified by Corporation regulations.

Table 2 Diet of a sample of the poor in Dublin in the early years of the twentieth century.

No. in family	Food Used			Vegetables – if any	Name of Street	Occupation of Tenant	Rent per Week	Weekly Wages	Employment
	Breakfast	Dinner	Supper or Tea						
6–4 children, father & mother	Tea, bread, and sometimes butter on Sundays	Fish, usually meat	Oatmeal stirabout and buttermilk	Cabbage and scallions	Phibsboro' Road	Labourer	1s. 6d.	16s.	
5	Bread, butter and tea	Meat and vegetables	Bread, butter and tea	Cabbage and potatoes	Hackett's Court	Labourer	3s.	20s.	Very irregular
7 - father, mother and 5 children	Bread, butter and tea	Week-days – bread, butter and tea. Sundays – Bacon	Bread, butter and tea	Cabbage and potatoes (on Sunday)	Cottage at rere of 122 Townsend Street	Labourer	1s. 6d.	Average of 14s.	
5	Tea, bread and butter, with occasionally eggs or fish	Bacon, potatoes and cabbage	Bread, butter and tea	Cabbage and potatoes	151 North King Street	Cattle drover (and other jobs)	2s. 6d.	10s.	Irregular
3 children, father, mother and mother-in-law	Bread, butter, and tea	Bacon and cabbage, herrings (occasionally) and bread	Bread and tea	Cabbage	Belmont Place	Van driver	2s. 6d.	15s.	Constant
5	Bread, butter and tea	Bread, tea and herrings	Bread and tea	Potatoes, cabbage and onions	5 Johnston's Court	Casual labourer	2s.	Irregular (uncertain)	Irregular
6	Bread, butter and tea	Bacon, potatoes and cabbage, steak and fish occasionally	Bread, butter and tea	Potatoes	10 and 11 Denmark Place	Coal porter	2s. 6d	18s.	Irregular
3	Bread, butter and tea	Fish, meat	Bread, butter and tea	Potatoes	Lamb Alley, off Francis Street	Dealer in sawdust	2s.	Average 12s. 6d.	Irregular
4	Bread, butter and tea	Potatoes and meat	Bread, butter and tea	Potatoes	Francis Street	Labourer	2s.	Average 14s.	Irregular
5	Bread, butter and tea	Fish, bread and tea	Bread, butter and tea	Potatoes	30 Lower Mayor Street.	Labourer	2s.	17s.	Irregular
4 – husband, wife and 2 children	Bread, butter and tea at all meals	Meat & potatoes occasionally	Sometimes 'stew' consisting of potatoes & meat is made	Potatoes	4 Ball's Yard	Grocer's porter	2s. 6d.	18s.	Irregular

(Cameron, 1913, pp 172–3.)

Overall, the report was seriously critical of Dublin Corporation and suggested that their appeal for additional powers would have had more force 'if it were supported by evidence of a rigid administration of their existing powers' (Housing Inquiry, 1914, p. 12, para. 28). However, the Dublin Corporation Public Health Committee firmly rebutted the allegations against Cameron and claimed that the Corporation had been unfairly treated in the Report having 'done our best according to our means' (Report 120/1914, p. 177).

In 'doing its best', Dublin Corporation had succeeded in rehousing a total of 1385 families in the 30 years since its first scheme began. The 12 schemes which had been undertaken had provided dwellings for about 7600 people, with capital expenditure amounting to £354,215 19s. 0d. Indeed, the Corporation had housed about 2.5 per cent of the population by 1913, a proportion which, a spokesman claimed, was greater than in any other UK city. Even Glasgow, seen as a pioneer of working-class housing, did not achieve Dublin's level (Allan, 1965). The combined efforts of Dublin Corporation and various philanthropic groups and individuals had provided 5271 dwellings by 1913, amounting to almost 19 per cent of the city's housing stock. However this was insufficient to meet the city's needs, and those in greatest need were not the beneficiaries. Dublin still needed to house 60,000 people. The inquiry found that a further £3½ million would be required to provide a total of 14,000 houses which were urgently needed to relieve congestion and to close tenements which were unfit for habitation.

In order to solve the existing housing problem, the inquiry found that it would be necessary to build a substantial number of new housing units. Even a massive renovation programme of existing tenements, assuming that all the first and second class tenement houses did in fact lend themselves to being remodelled, would only house 13,000 families. Already 7967 families living in third class tenements and small houses required new accommodation, while the remodelling of better class tenements would result in a displacement of 5991 families to be rehoused elsewhere. Based on these calculations, a minimum of 13,958 new dwellings was required.

One of the main questions raised by the inquiry, therefore, was where these 14,000 or so new dwellings were to be built. Overall, the Committee of Inquiry came out strongly in favour of suburban housing, although it did recognize that some workers employed on the quays would require housing within a convenient distance of their work: 'What is required is decentralization' (p. 31). The Committee went so far as to 'deprecate much work being undertaken at the start in the heart of the City, and would rather see

Table 3 Dwellings completed by Dublin Corporation and rentals.

Area	Dwellings	Type	Weekly Rent
Benburb Street	139	Shops	10s.
		Three-room dwellings	From 4s. 6d. to 5s.
		Two-room dwellings	From 3s. to 4s.
		One-room dwellings	From 1s. 6d. to 2s.
Bow Lane	86	Shops	From 5s. to 5s. 6d.
		Three-room dwellings	From 4s. to 4s. 6d.
		Two-room dwellings	From 2s. to 3s. 6d.
Blackhall Place	81	4-room self-contained houses	7s. 6d.
		Shops	6s. 6d.
		Two-room dwellings	3s. to 4s.
Clontarf	57	4-room houses	4s. 6d.
		3-room	3s. 6d.
		2-room	2s. 6d.
Bride's Alley	172	3-room dwellings	4s. 6d. to 6s. 6d.
		2-room dwellings	3s 6d. to 4s.
St Joseph's Place	80	3-room self-contained cottages with scullery and WC	4s.
Elizabeth Street	14	3-room cottages	5s. 6d.
Donnycarney	8	3-room cottages	2s.
Foley Street	460	Single rooms	1s. to 1s. 6d.
		2-room	3s. to 3s. 6d.
		3-room	4s. 6d.
Inchicore	228	4-room cottages	5s. 6d.
		3-room	3s. to 4s.
Townsend Street	20	Shops	7s. 6d.
		2-room	3s. 6d.
Cook Street	45	3-room cottages	4s. 6d.

(Housing Inquiry (1914), Appendix XI.)

such houses as may be built erected on virgin soil in suitable sites on the outskirts' (p. 31, para. 68). In relation to the availability of 'virgin soil', the Borough Surveyor had told the inquiry that 1146 acres (c.460 ha) of land under grass or tillage were available for building within the City Boundary.

A number of other influential witnesses to the inquiry also favoured suburbanization. The City Architect, Charles MacCarthy, argued strongly for suburban building and against renovation of existing houses which would 'become ruins in a few years' (Housing Inquiry, 1914, p. 40, para. 955), while the Dublin Citizens' Association stated that its ideal was 'the suburban house for the working man', taking the form of self-contained cottages close to tram-lines. Although everything should be done to provide good, healthy housing in the centre city for those people 'whose work and means will not allow them to live outside', this was clearly seen as a consolation prize (Housing Inquiry, 1914, p. 160, para. 4200).

The need for town planning was recognized by a number of witnesses to the inquiry: 'Putting buildings up in a permanent way without town planning is preparing slums for the future' (Evidence of Geddes, Housing Inquiry, 1914, p. 209, para. 5637). Some of the most radical proposals made to the inquiry came from E.A. Aston, who stated that there was a huge need for a town plan for Dublin, since no attempt had been made by the Corporation to formulate any general plan of city development. Aston was also critical of Dublin's housing authorities for their haphazard methods:

> Block tenements of cottages have been planted – in response to the pressure of Ward Committees and representatives – without reference to any of the larger considerations of healthy surroundings, future industrial developments, or even obvious traffic facilities. Architectural incongruities – such as building red brick cottages beside the Four Courts – have been sanctioned. New streets – as in the case of the Cook Street scheme – have been constructed which are obviously dangerous either for vehicular or pedestrian traffic. Such instances of a patch-work policy could be multiplied almost indefinitely.
>
> (Housing Inquiry, 1914, p. 213, para. 5687)

Despite these criticisms, Aston believed that the Municipality should acquire every acre of land and every building in the city, in order to prevent its unordered and uneconomic physical development. He also included several radical suggestions in relation to the acquisition of derelict sites. Aston was very much in favour of suburbanization, but recognized that a civic survey was essential, to highlight important topographical, geological, and sociological considerations in the development of virgin territory. Development should be seen in a much broader context, so that garden suburbs would have to be related not only to the city itself and its immediate environs, but to the larger surrounding region. He recognized that the formulation of a plan for the City of Dublin would be useless without considering its surrounding townships. In order to achieve coherent development, Aston suggested that a joint Housing Authority should deal with housing and related matters in the City, the adjacent townships and in Dublin County. This would enable the plans to embrace the 'entire natural community of Dublin', including 100,000 people who had moved southwards outside the city boundary. This idea of an integrated plan following on from a civic survey was one which was to recur from this point, gradually gaining momentum until the *Dublin Civic Survey* was actually undertaken in the early 1920s.

Aston made particularly interesting suggestions for the location and nature of the 10,000 local authority dwellings which he estimated would be required. About half would be located in what was termed 'the middle circle', on unbuilt suburban and rural land within the then city boundaries in easily serviced areas such as Clontarf, Glasnevin, Drumcondra, Kilmainham, Inchicore and Dolphin's Barn. This housing would be built at densities of 20 cottages to the acre (50 cottages per ha). Meanwhile, he suggested the development of 'plantations' for city workers in convenient rural areas within six miles (*c.*10 km) of the GPO, such as Raheny, Clontarf, Chapelizod, Inchicore, Dundrum, Stillorgan and Blackrock. All the suggested areas were convenient to tramway and rail services. These would be totally different in cost and character from the garden-suburb schemes in the middle circle, with families living a 'semi rural life' at densities of not more than four houses to the acre (10 houses per ha).

Scottish town planner, ecologist, philosopher and social thinker Patrick Geddes (1854–1932) gave evidence to the inquiry on behalf of the Women's National Health Association. The organization was committed to the eradication of tuberculosis and other diseases, and had formed one of the deputations which demanded Government assistance for housing and supported the demands made by the Association of Municipal Representatives in the months prior to the opening of the Housing Inquiry. Geddes, like Aston, stressed the need for town planning and argued for extended powers to be achieved by means of a Town Planning Act. For him, town planning was 'not an expensive luxury', but 'at once practical and economical', 'it pays its way'. Geddes thought that public authorities and private organizations and individuals could co-operate, with an emphasis on self help, to solve the housing problems of the poor. Indeed, the preparation of a town plan was not just a matter for experts but a very large undertaking involving 'the entire community'. He paid particular attention to the importance of citizen participation, especially of the poor who were all too often treated 'as if they were mere passive creatures to be housed like cattle'. There was much truth in these words, as will be seen in the eventual outcomes of the attempts to solve the housing problem. Geddes also stressed that, given the urgency of Dublin's problem, the making of a plan should not be used as an excuse to procrastinate further on dealing with the crisis. Instead, during the preparation of a town plan much useful work could proceed 'subject to criticisms'.

Stressing that improvements in living conditions would enable people to help overcome their impoverishment, Geddes argued that: 'The people will not injure the houses you give them, provided these houses are sufficiently good to enable them to live in decency and comfort'. He argued for a social mix and against segregation, noting that the practice of erecting rows of two-roomed dwellings segregated from three-roomed and larger dwellings, was 'not only mistaken, wasteful, and costly, but even injurious' and inevitably created future slums, like the then recent development in Foley Street. Both economically and morally, it was important to combine as many types and scales of dwelling as practicable in each scheme and for each neighbourhood. He pointed out the 'very greatest value' of the garden village and suburb, for which he saw a great number and variety of sites in the vicinity of Dublin. Overall, Geddes foresaw the suburban expansion of working-class housing, but without central depopulation, because in the centre good houses would replace bad ones.

The Housing Inquiry, and in particular the evidence of Geddes and Aston, reflected current thinking. In its findings, the inquiry suggested that large-scale perimeter housing developments were needed to relieve central congestion, in addition to some central city schemes. These schemes should receive State finance, although there was also a role for private enterprise in housing. One of the members of the Committee of Inquiry, Mr J.F. MacCabe, voiced his reservations to the general findings of the inquiry in a separate memorandum. Although in general agreement with his colleagues regarding future building operations in Dublin, MacCabe felt that they did not go sufficiently far concerning one vital point:

> If even the areas which have already been acquired are built upon before a Civic Survey is completed, I shall look upon it as a grave misfortune. A Civic Survey embraces all the factors hitherto left out of consideration – the topography, the means of communication, the industries (past, present and future) and the movements, needs, and occupations of the population of Dublin and its surroundings, and without such information no Town Plan can be provided. To build without a Town Plan in the old City will prevent effectually Dublin ever becoming what it should be – as beautiful as its own surroundings.
>
> (Housing Inquiry, 1914, p. 30)

Thus the message of the need for survey and plan was gradually being diffused.

Unfortunately, the inquiry, while providing detailed and accurate evidence of the scale of the housing problem and financial requirements for its solution, was not in a position to make political suggestions for financing such a scheme. While Dublin Corporation emerged as seriously negligent, the role of the Local Government Board as the supervising agency was not examined. This is not surprising, since the Committee of Inquiry had been appointed by that body. The overall recommendations did not actually commit the Government to new forms of expenditure, and were rather vague in their admission of the State's obligations to provide housing. The Report was also quite unrealistic in its suggestion that the problem of housing the working classes would be solved by stringent local enforcement of sanitary legislation, combined with a considerable amount of private housing development.

The practical consequences of the inquiry were limited, particularly due to the Government's refusal to provide preferential interest rates, such as applied to agricultural cottages, to the urban working-class housing in Ireland. This was on the grounds that similar concessions would be sought by other cities in the United Kingdom, whereas Ireland's rural housing problem was held to be unique. However, many of the suggestions made at the inquiry were at least considered over the next decade, and the perceived importance of town planning increased. One of the most important outcomes was the decision that suburban housing for the working-classes was to be the preferred means of easing the housing problem, an approach which was reflected in Corporation housing policy throughout the 1920s.

Funding problems for Corporation housing, 1900–22

Although Dublin Corporation was judged seriously negligent during the 1913 Housing Inquiry, the problems experienced by that body in providing working-class accommodation should not be overlooked. While the Corporation frequently came in for sharp, often well-deserved, criticism regarding its policies and operating methods, it also encountered severe impediments to any more efficient approach, the most important of which was lack of adequate finance. The significance of funding to the success of any scheme was widely recognized: 'Finance is the most important single factor, and the greatest obstacle in the path of a speedy solution of the slum problem' (Citizens' Housing Council, 1937, p. 11).

Compared with other European countries, Ireland was in the unusual situation that the first large public housing programmes undertaken were located in rural areas. These late-nineteenth-century interventions were associated with major land reforms (Aalen, 1987). As a result, by 1914 Ireland's rural labourers were among the best housed of their class in Western Europe, while there had been almost no improvement in the plight of the urban slum dwellers. Although the first legislation empowering urban local authorities to provide working-class housing was introduced in 1890 (the Housing of the Working Classes Act, 1890), little activity was undertaken. The first subsidy for urban housing was provided in 1908 under the Housing (Ireland) Act, but it was insufficient to meet the numerous demands for new housing schemes. Thus, little had been achieved in Dublin by the time of the 1913 Housing Inquiry, at least in part for reasons which were outside the control of the Dublin Corporation. As late as 1921, it was reported that 48,000 cottages had been provided in rural Ireland since 1883, with a total expenditure of £8½ million, whereas under the Urban Housing Acts only £2½ million had been spent and just 10,000 houses built. Thus, when the new Free State Government took over responsibility for housing the urban poor, it was left with a very meagre legacy in terms of existing housing stock (*Irish Builder and Engineer*, 1921, p. 325).

The first direct State assistance for working class-housing in Irish urban areas was the Irish Housing Fund, established in 1908. Income from the £180,000 Fund was used to pay grants to local authorities for houses built. In addition, the Act improved the conditions under which local authorities could borrow money from the Local Government Board for the erection of working-class housing. Annual sums were payable to urban authorities proportionate to the amount of loan charges incurred. For example, the Dublin County Borough's share in the income of the Irish Housing Fund amounted to £2,658 9s. 8d. for the year ended March 1926, calculated on the basis of the housing charge for that year (Report 147/1927). However, the income of the Fund was comparatively small; the *total* amount available for distribution in 1939 was under £5,000.

With the outbreak of World War I, a bleak situation was to become even worse, as funds for housing dried up completely and building materials became unobtainable.

Another factor which impeded the successful implementation of a local authority housing policy for Dublin was the apparently antagonistic attitude of the Local Government Board for Ireland to any Corporation endeavours.

This was probably politically motivated, with the representatives of the Crown (the Local Government Board) opposed to Dublin Corporation's staunchly Nationalistic stance. The information provided in a 1920 Housing Committee Report (110/1920) relating to the Fairbrother's Fields area (described variously in reports as Fairbrother's and Fairbrothers' Fields) illustrates this point.

The Fairbrother's Fields scheme had been initiated as far back as December 1912, but construction had yet to begin in late 1920. Plans had run into difficulties at an early stage when negotiations for site purchase were unsuccessful. Due to delays in acquiring compulsory purchase powers, an arbitrator was not appointed by the Local Government Board to settle compensation claims until March 1915. However, in May of that year a circular had been received from the Board restricting borrowing by local authorities. Because the Housing Committee of the Corporation considered the work to be of 'pressing necessity for reasons of public health' and therefore exempt from borrowing restrictions, it continued with the negotiations. By the time that the Committee was informed that it was not exempt it was already 'irretrievably committed' to purchasing the site. In December 1915, the Chancellor of the Exchequer stepped in, intimating that the Treasury intended to advance the acquisition loans, but that no advance for building work would be made. However, the Board of Works then refused to approve these loans, saying that they should be obtained from a private source, and it was not until December 1916, a full year later, that the Board of Works finally advanced the money to acquire the lands.

Once the land was acquired, the Corporation had to search for some means of paying for the building work at Fairbrother's Fields. During 1914 and 1915, the Housing Committee 'made every effort to secure an advance under the Housing (No. 2) Act, 1914 (which became law in August 1914, and operated for one year) and which purported to appropriate £4 million out of the Consolidated Fund for housing purposes in Great Britain and Ireland' (Report 110/1920, p. 364). Having furnished the necessary information to the Local Government Board on 24 March 1915, and not having received a reply, the Housing Committee pressed for a decision, only to be informed on 10 September 1915 that the Act was no longer in force. On requesting clarification from the Treasury it was discovered that the case of Dublin had never been submitted to them, suggesting that someone on the Local Government Board had obstructed the proposals. 'The foregoing circumstances will give some idea of the vexatious methods with which the Committee had to contend in their efforts to carry on their pressing work' (Report 110/1920, p. 364).

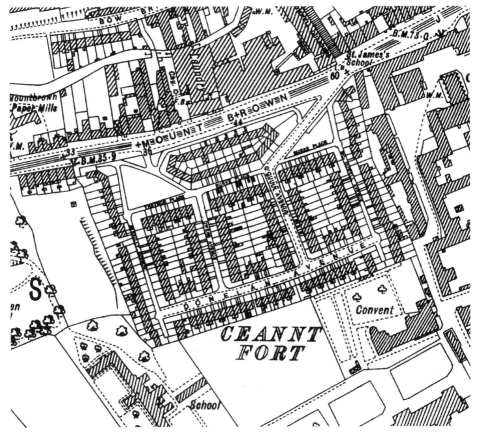

3 St James' Walk (Ceannt Fort) development.
(Ordnance Survey 1:2500 plan, Sheet 18 X, Dublin, 1943 revision.)

The poorer citizens in thousands pine away and die in surroundings which give them no fighting chance of life. Delay to them is death, and are they to be told that the State has no time and no money to bother about them?

(Report 35/1916, p. 351)

In a desperate plea in late 1915, a 'digest of the case for immediate housing loans for Dublin', summarized the appalling condition of the poor in the City of Dublin. It was argued that delays in dealing with the situation should be avoided, echoing the social order arguments for good housing as follows: 'if, on humanitarian grounds, their tragic appeal will not be listened to, passions may be aroused of menace to those in happier circumstances who turn a deaf ear to their clamour to be allowed to live under decent conditions'. The report continued by referring to the 'countless millions' of pounds being spent 'on the prosecution of a war to which Dublin alone has sent some 14,000 men to fight the Empire's battle'. 'Are they to find the Empire's gratitude on their return represented in the refusal of the Government to allow the Corporation to lift their wives and children from the horrors of life in dilapidated tenement houses or cellar dwellings into the atmosphere of light and life in a sanitary, self-contained, comfortable home?' In addition to this passionate entreaty, Alderman Thomas Kelly, Chairman of the Housing Committee, suggested that good housing was a principal weapon in fighting tuberculosis. He stated that an advance of at least £300,000 for Housing Purposes was required within the next 18 months.

Although in September 1916, the Committee was informed that there was a possibility of obtaining money from American sources under the provisions of the Finance Act, 1916, negotiations fell through due to the prohibitive rates of interest demanded (Report 103/1917). Needless to say, none of the Irish banks showed a disposition to give quotations for housing loans. Thus, 'every conceivable source was tapped with a view to obtaining funds for building, but without success, so that a hopeless deadlock was then created' (Report 110/1920, p. 364).

It was not until April 1917, when Chief Secretary Mr Duke inspected the housing areas for which schemes had been prepared and was impressed with the distressing conditions he saw, that immediate arrangements were made with the Chancellor of the Exchequer to advance the necessary money. This was to provide for Spitalfields (1st section), McCaffrey Estate, St James' Walk (figure 3), Fairbrother's Fields and Crabbe Lane. While Spitalfields was completed in 1918, and McCaffrey and St James's Walk were in the hands of contractors, it was not until December 1918 that the Local Government Board sanctioned the loan to build on Fairbrother's Fields.

By late 1918, grave concern was expressed by the Corporation regarding the differential treatment received by Irish local authorities compared to their counterparts in England with reference to financial aid for housing schemes As a last resort, the Lord Mayor of Dublin, Laurence O'Neill, wrote to the Prime Minister, Lloyd George, appealing for assurance that substantial aid would be forthcoming from the Treasury to enable the Corporation to grapple with the housing question (Report 18/1919).

Thus it can be seen that the Corporation's apparent inaction following the 1913 Housing Inquiry was not entirely of its own making. While that body

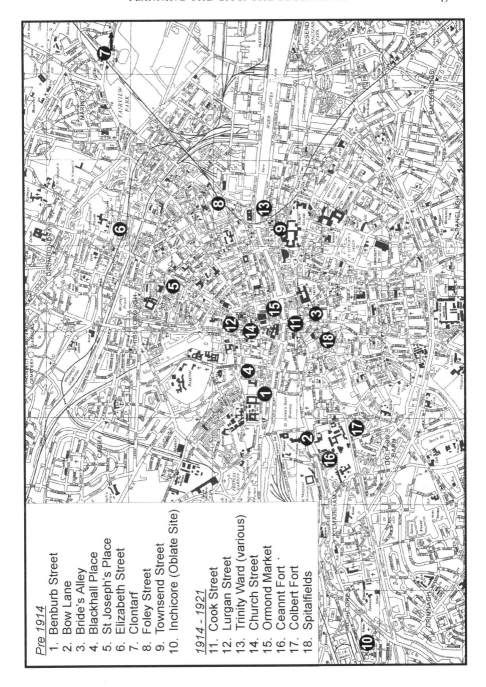

Pre 1914
1. Benburb Street
2. Bow Lane
3. Bride's Alley
4. Blackhall Place
5. St Joseph's Place
6. Elizabeth Street
7. Clontarf
8. Foley Street
9. Townsend Street
10. Inchicore (Oblate Site)

1914 - 1921
11. Cook Street
12. Lurgan Street
13. Trinity Ward (various)
14. Church Street
15. Ormond Market
16. Ceannt Fort
17. Colbert Fort
18. Spitalfields

4 Location of early Corporation developments.

had to shoulder the blame for the deteriorating slum situation in Dublin, it becomes apparent, from the evidence provided in the reports of the Corporation that financial concerns beyond the scope of that body rendered it almost impossible for any work to be carried out. Much of the responsibility thus lies with the Local Government Board for Ireland and the British Government of the time, which persistently refused to come to the aid of a beleaguered city.

Following the outbreak of the World War I, little local authority building was undertaken due to increased costs and shortages, but some schemes in hand in 1914 were completed. The number of working-class dwellings required to meet the housing emergency was continually increasing, as in-migration compounded the city's problems, and by 1918 it was estimated that some 50,000 houses were urgently required (Cowan, 1918). The 1919 Addison Act, more properly known as the 1919 Housing Act (England and Wales) which has been described as the beginning of large-scale central government inter-vention in the housing market (Pooley, 1992), did not apply in Ireland, where the Housing (Ireland) Act of the same year aimed specifically to compel the Irish local authorities to build with direct State subsidies, a measure intended to curb unrest.

The 1919 Housing Act marked a change of attitude from the mid-nineteenth century *laissez-faire* approach. Indeed, the obligations of the State to provide housing were increasingly recognized at this time: 'The provision of decent housing … is one of the first duties of any government' (McKenna, 1919, p. 279). The 1919 Act was a much-needed piece of legislation, particularly because since 1914, of the 4150 families who had to leave following the closure of 1000 tenements, 3563 'have gone to intensify the congestion of the still standing 6735 tenement houses, or have been packed into small single houses throughout the city' (McKenna, 1919, p. 283). The Housing (Ireland) Act, 1919, extended the Housing of the Working Classes (Ireland) Acts, 1890 to 1908, and also amended the Small Dwellings Acquisition Act, 1899. This 1919 Act marked a new epoch in housing provision by closing the era of permissive legislation and for the first time placing the responsibility to provide adequate housing squarely on the shoulders of the local authorities. It now became the duty of every urban district council and body of town commissioners to consider the needs of their district or town with regard to working class housing provision, and to prepare and submit to the Local Government Board schemes for providing house accommodation to be carried out within a specified time limit. The Board was empowered to recoup the losses incurred by a local authority in carrying out such a scheme, by providing an annual subsidy. In addition, the compensation payable under compulsory land acquisition was reduced and the powers to acquire land compulsorily for housing purposes were increased. The laying out of open spaces and the lease or sale of land to persons prepared to build working-class dwellings on modern lines thereon was now authorized. Building bylaws were to be relaxed for housing schemes of this nature, while the Local Authority would also have powers to make bylaws with respect to houses in order to improve the health and well-being, both physical and moral (!) of working class families. Local authorities were also empowered to promote and assist any public utility society (of which more later) which aimed to provide houses for the working classes, and to provide loans to owners for the reconstruction, enlargement and improvement of houses or buildings capable of being made suitable for occupation by the working classes. However, due to the difficult political situation, only 800 houses were built in the country under the Act by 1921.

Also in 1919, the Housing (Additional Powers) Act was introduced with the intention to encourage the building of houses by private owners on a large scale following World War I. However, within the municipal area of Dublin only 70 houses were erected, at a total subsidy value of £16,276. 'The provisions of this Act were liberal, and would, no doubt, have been availed of to a much greater extent but for the political situation and unsettled conditions of the building trade' (Civics Institute of Ireland, 1925, p. 63).

As we have seen, the funding for local authority housing under the Housing of the Working Classes Acts was made available under the Local Government Board for Ireland (LGB), a body with which the Corporation had a rather difficult relationship. In 1920, the underground Dáil Eireann, formed by successful Sinn Féin candidates in the 1918 General Election, set up a Local Government Department which assumed the functions of a central authority with William T. Cosgrave acting as Minister. This new 'Department' competed with the existing Local Government Board, which was still active and at least nominally in control of affairs, for the allegiance of the Irish local authorities. The LGB announced in July 1920 that all financial assistance would be withdrawn if the authority of the British Government was not accepted and the LGB recognized. This helps to account for the lack of activity under the 1919 Housing Act in Dublin. However, a majority of the local authorities quickly recognized the new Dáil department and broke with the Local Government Board. In April 1922, the Ministry of Local Government of the newly independent Free State took over the central administration and in 1924 the Department of Local Government and Public Health was established.

Town Planning and Dublin

> As far as we know, nothing in the nature of a systematic or organized
> scheme of town extension has ever been adopted in these countries,
> suburban additions to the large cities have been left in practically every
> instance to the meagre instincts of the speculative builder. The result
> has in too many cases been the reverse of pleasant.
>
> (*Irish Builder and Engineer*, 1 July 1905, p. 457)

As we have seen, the concept of town planning was considered by many
people to offer an alternative to the existing nature of the city. In particular, it
seemed to offer some hope in the light of the apparent disorder which
threatened to overwhelm the city in the late-nineteenth century. Reformers
hoped that proper planning would mitigate the evils of the slums and reduce
the high death rates prevalent in the city, while aesthetes believed that
planning would allow for the greater beautification of urban areas. Although
the British Housing and Town Planning Act (1909) did not apply to Ireland,
and no serious attempt was made to found an Irish garden city, Irish people
would have been aware of international developments in planning, partly due
to the frequency of articles in the *Irish Builder and Engineer*, which kept its
readers up to date on developments in Britain and Continental Europe in the
first decade of the twentieth century. One reason for the great interest in the
town-planning movement stemmed from the realization that the garden-city
concept might offer a practical solution to the persistent housing problems of
Ireland's cities.

However, there was also a strand of pragmatism as commentators, such as
the *Irish Builder and Engineer*, and the Corporation itself, recognized that
many of the ideals of the planning movement were at present out of reach. At
best, they sought a means of regulating growth so that 'everything should not
be sacrificed to the mere desire of planting as many dwellings as possible in a
given area' (*Irish Builder and Engineer*, 1 July 1905, p. 457). The article
continues as follows: 'These are days when there is talk of garden cities, village
colonies, and other schemes for brightening the lives of those whose lot it is
to work in towns, but these things are difficult of achievement, and the day
when they will be carried out on any large scale is still distant. The existing
centres of population have on the other hand, been growing, and will
continue to grow, and if this growth were only intelligently directed suburban
dreariness would be very considerably alleviated'.

Certainly, from the middle of the first decade of the twentieth century, there was a surge of interest in town planning in Dublin, as documented by Michael Bannon (1985). In 1910, Dublin Corporation established a separate Housing Committee for the first time. It also invited the Royal Institute of Public Health to hold its 1911 Annual Congress in Dublin. James Walter offered to sell his farm at Marino as the site for a miniature Garden City in 1910, in response to a delegation from local residents. Early in 1911, Corporation representatives visited Birmingham, where they were impressed by the city's approach to working-class housing provision, and by the direct influence of German town planning on their thinking. In January 1911 the *Irish Architect and Craftsman*, edited by H.T. O'Rourke, was launched. Horace Tennyson O'Rourke, LRIBA (1880–1963), was appointed as Permanent Assistant in the City Architect's Office in March 1916, having begun work in Dublin Corporation in March 1914 as Clerk of Works, Lisburn Street, subsequently being transferred to the City Architect's Department. In April 1918 he was appointed Assistant City Architect and on 13 January 1922, he became City Architect (Report 90/1922), a post he held until 1944. He influenced the rebuilding of O'Connell Street in the 1920s and was largely responsible for the preparation of the Dublin Civic Survey (see later discussion). From 24 May to 7 June 1911, Geddes' City and Town Planning Exhibition was held at the RDS, Ballsbridge, Dublin, at the invitation of Lord and Lady Aberdeen, and was attended by 160,000 people. The Annual Congress of the Royal Institute of Public Health, which took place on 15–21 August 1911, included a section dealing with 'Housing of the Working Classes, Town Planning etc.'. At the end of September 1911, in what might be seen as a culmination of these events, the Housing and Town Planning Association of Ireland (HTPAI) was formed, with Lady Aberdeen as President. The HTPAI was responsible for the organization of a conference on Housing and Town Development in October 1912, with delegates from urban districts and other councils.

Despite physical inaction on the housing front in the aftermath of the 1913 Housing Inquiry, there was a continued interest in town planning throughout 1914. Among the events to take place in Dublin in that year were a series of lectures on the re-planning of Dublin, with several international speakers including Henry Long (Boston), John Nolen (Cambridge, Mass.) and Raymond Unwin, the Civic Week and Exhibition, Annual Conference of the Association of Municipal Authorities, the Dublin Summer School of Civics, the Geddes/Unwin report and the Dublin Town Planning Competition.

The Civic Exhibition held in Dublin in the summer of 1914 has been described as 'one of the most hectic and exciting periods of planning promotion ever witnessed in Ireland' (Bannon, 1985, p. 214). In order to ensure representation from all interested parties, the HTPAI called a conference of interested organizations, following which a broadly based Civic Exhibition Committee was set up to organize the exhibition. Organizations involved included the Housing and Town Planning Association of Ireland, the Women's National Health Association of Ireland, the Association of Municipal Authorities of Ireland, the Royal Institute of Architects in Ireland, the Architectural Association of Ireland, the Institute of Civil Engineers of Ireland, the Dublin Chamber of Commerce, the Royal Irish Academy, the Dublin Industrial Development Authority. The Lord Lieutenant was President while the Dublin Lord Mayor was one of the Treasurers, and Dr John Nolen, Professor of City Planning at Cambridge, Massachusetts, was appointed manager of the project.

The Civic Exhibition was held in the Linenhall Buildings and the grounds of the King's Inns from 15 July to 31 August, attracting 9000 visitors on its opening day (Bannon, 1985). It was both a social and financial success. In addition to the exhibition, there was a programme of lectures and several field trips, while various events were scheduled to run concurrently with the exhibition, including the annual Conference of the Association of Municipal Authorities and Geddes' Dublin Summer School of Civics.

The Civics Institute of Ireland, which formally took over the functions of the HTPAI from 30 June 1916, became an umbrella organization, centralizing the efforts of all movements sponsoring housing and town planning improvements. Thus the importance of public participation in planning, which had been emphasized by Geddes in his evidence to the Housing Inquiry, became a recurring theme.

Geddes and Unwin as consultants

Apart from the various lectures and exhibitions which were taking place at this time, something intensely practical was to happen in September 1914. As has been seen from the evidence to the Housing Inquiry, it was repeatedly argued at this time that town planning matters were closely linked to the housing problem and, indeed, that proceeding with housing schemes in the absence of a town planning approach was likely to lead to future slums. In this climate of uncertainty as to the desirability of proposed Corporation housing schemes, and the general lack of direction in city development, the Citizen's Housing League, a body formed in April 1914 with the aim of pressurizing the Government into acting on the recommendations of the housing inquiry (see Fraser, 1996), offered to place the advice of two well-known British planners, Raymond Unwin and Patrick Geddes, at the disposal of the Corporation. In particular, the two men were asked to formulate recommendations, alterations and suggestions in connection with the Beresford Street, Church Street, Ormond Market and Trinity Ward schemes which had been prepared by the City Architect in compliance with the policy of slum clearance and high-density housing development. Their report also provided a general consideration of Dublin housing and suburbanization, and a report of inspection of 13 city areas, with detailed recommendations on two sites. This report marks the first foray by recognized modern town planners into the field of planning for the city of Dublin. Many of the ideas presented in the report had been raised during the Housing Inquiry of the previous year, while many were to recur in later years, particularly in Abercrombie's prize-winning town plan of 1914/22. As Appendix I illustrates, Unwin's ideas at Letchworth and Hampstead were extremely influential in shaping the image of the 'garden city' and 'garden suburb' internationally.

Unwin and Geddes inspected 13 sites where new housing was in the course of construction or which were scheduled for housing, and were generally well pleased although they did express a desire for lower densities and more play space in many of the schemes. For example, a reduced density was suggested on the 22–acre (9 ha) Fairbrother's Fields site, where 694 three-room dwellings housing 2470 people had been planned (that is, a density of over 30 houses to the acre, or 75 per ha), with the area laid out on the lines of a garden suburb and having regard to the future growth of the south-western sector of the city. The Fassaugh Lane area at Cabra was judged an excellent situation, while the Marino site was considered ideal with regard to accessibility, economy and beauty, and was the subject of a separate memorandum entitled 'Garden Suburbs'. The consultants actually held negotiations with the Christian Brothers concerning the acquisition of adjacent land to overcome boundary irregularities which would militate against good planning, and prepared a preliminary layout for the Walter's estate part of Marino.

In their report on the plans for Beresford Street/Church Street and Ormond Market, Geddes and Unwin stressed the significance of these centre-city sites within an overall perspective of civic improvement. At the Beresford Street/ Church Street site, as with the Fairbrother's Fields scheme, the consultants recommended a lower density, a layout 'on garden suburb lines' with common back gardens and forecourts, and with less space used for roads. It was felt that the Ormond Market site, which had been acquired and cleared by the Corporation in 1912 with the intention of erecting 100 small artisan houses, was incongruous in its location beside the grandeur of the Four Courts. They suggested that the location would be more suitable for a new Roman Catholic cathedral. The sites should be seen within a town-planning framework which opened up the centre, relieving congestion and pulling the city centre back towards the west. With this aim in mind, two north-south routes were urged (probably reflecting Geddes' influence). A 'Via Practica' would run south from Constitution Hill along Church Street to Bridge Street on the south side, while a 'Via Sacra' linking the three cathedrals would run from St Patrick's Cathedral via Beresford Street to the Broadstone Station. In addition, they foresaw the need for improved east-west routes from Nelson's Pillar. Unwin and Geddes were well aware that they might be providing a lead for the forthcoming Dublin plan competition, and indeed the Via Sacra duly appeared in the winning entry, together with a full range of satellite suburbs.

The consultants also drew up proposals for a general development policy, calling for additional powers to deal with derelict sites and to facilitate the preparation of town planning schemes. They suggested that Dublin's primary need was for an ample supply of good housing which would be erected within the context of comprehensive schemes designed to improve communications and amenities. Once again, a policy of suburbanization was favoured, since low-density schemes on plentiful and relatively cheap land outside the central area would provide healthier surroundings for those who moved out. Importantly, the garden suburbs should be of adequate size to support their own social, recreational and cultural centres. It was argued that building on small plots of vacant inner city land would not solve the housing crisis and was likely to increase land values. Through the implementation of a suburban policy, those remaining in the city would filter up into the best of the houses which had been vacated, and central population densities would be reduced, in turn causing a reduction in the death rate (much as Ebenezer Howard had suggested, see Appendix I). Short-term measures for improving conditions in the existing habitable tenements were also proposed, involving the novel suggestion of adding pre-fabricated bathroom towers to existing tenements. The consultants urged that nothing should deflect the Corporation from providing good housing.

Although the report of the consultants was relatively well received, the proposals for a garden-suburb type development were rejected by the Housing

Committee as being too idealistic for the job in hand. Geddes and Unwin were accused by the City Treasurer, with some justification, of artificially separating the problem of poverty from the physical housing plan. Whereas only a few, well-off tenants would benefit from the ideal and artistic suburban-style houses, many more poorly-paid workers would be accommodated in simple self-contained cottages at uniform rents under excellent and healthy city conditions. Ironically, by the late 1920s the Corporation was to be accused by critics of making this very mistake. Most of the recommendations for congested areas were thus considered irrelevant to the existing problem, and the schemes were proceeded with as originally planned, 'due to the urgency of the housing problem' (Report 78/1915, p. 707).

The City Architect, Charles MacCarthy, was also unconvinced of the advantages of redesigning his schemes, stating that the proposed modifications were typical of English Garden Suburb planning, and impractical in a large and congested city. The use of culs-de-sac was also opposed as contravening the Public Health Acts to no justifiable purpose, a criticism also to be levelled at Unwin during his preparation of material for the 1918 Tudor Walters Report in Britain (Miller, 1985). The Report, which is discussed later, was that of a committee which had inquired into working-class housing provision in Britain and recommended construction and design standards.

However, despite the lack of immediate attention given to the consultants' report, its application of new approaches and concepts to the Dublin problem was to prove significant. The inner-city schemes criticized by Unwin and Geddes were in fact the last major developments to be undertaken inside the canals for almost two decades, while the new ex-urban developments closely followed the garden suburb model, and culs-de-sac were used in schemes such as Drumcondra. During this time, little was done to improve the living conditions of the considerable proportion of the population which remained in the centre. Unwin's garden suburb rather than Geddes' conservative surgery was the ideal vision which came to be applied in Dublin. Planned suburbanization came to be emphasized until the 1930s, although not without some opposition. Developments such as Marino displayed the very faults that had been identified by Corporation officials in 1914. While the scheme was attractive, it could only cater for a relatively small number of families, and only those who could afford the weekly minimum purchase-rent of 16 shillings were to benefit from this model development.

The Dublin Town Planning Competition

While in Dublin in 1914, Patrick Geddes pressurized the Lord Lieutenant into offering a £500 prize for the winning entry in an international Dublin Town Planning Competition to be held in connection with the Civics Exhibition. Promoted by the Civics Institute of Ireland, the competition's planning proposals were to relate to a Greater Dublin area which stretched from Howth to Dalkey and inland from Glasnevin and Ashtown to Dundrum. Three main headings were to be covered:

- *Communications:* Road, rail and canal systems; existing and proposed industrial locations and main existing and proposed streets and thoroughfares.
- *Housing:* Existing tenements, number, location and types of dwellings required, housing densities, phasing of developments, open space in every development using the American standard of ten per cent open space, and the relocation of institutions from centre city to suburbs.
- *Metropolitan improvements:* Better use of city's situation including the rivers and bay, preservation or expansion needs of public buildings (e.g. administration buildings, new art gallery, cathedral etc.), provision of parkways and park system.

Eight entries were received from Ireland, England and America. Judging was delayed due to the outbreak of war, but the three assessors, Patrick Geddes, John Nolen and Charles MacCarthy, finally met in late 1916 and were unanimous in their choice of the winning entry, submitted by Patrick Abercrombie, with Sydney A. Kelly and Arthur Kelly. Abercrombie was soon to be appointed Lever Professor of Civic Design at the University of Liverpool, while the Kellys were Liverpool surveyors. This plan is of particular interest for several reasons. Firstly, the plan marked the start of Abercrombie's long association with Dublin, culminating in his appointment (together with Sydney Kelly) as town planning consultant to the City Council in 1936 and preparation of the 1941 *Dublin Sketch Development Plan*. In addition, it was Abercrombie's first applied planning work, the success of which marked his entry into the leading ranks of the young planning profession, drawing national and international attention to him. Even more importantly for Dublin, as the only existing modern plan for the city, it was inevitable that this winning entry was to influence Corporation thinking for the next decade or more.

A City Plan is not a grandiose scheme for immediate and costly civic improvements. On the contrary, as opposed to the present planless and haphazard growth, squalor and extravagance, a City Plan would mean a well-reasoned scheme, outlining an economic system of scientific, artistic and hygienic municipal reconstruction and development, providing specially for the conservation of citizen life and natural resources, and the total abolition of slum conditions.

(Foreword to the published plan, *Dublin of the Future,* 1922, p. v)

Like Geddes, the Civics Institute believed in the importance of a well-informed citizenship 'for the proper correction of the defects of community life', and expressed the hope that the plan would be of educational value, securing popular support for the general principles of 'City Planning'. The Institute hoped to arouse civic pride in the populace, and 'to revive that native genius which will place Dublin in its proper position as one of the World's best Capital Cities' (Abercrombie, 1922, p. vi). It called for the appointment of a permanent, well-funded planning commission to conduct a civic survey, following which a plan could be prepared. Abercrombie too hoped for a comprehensive plan which would make it impossible for the citizens to sanction 'piecemeal tinkerings which have been allowed in the past', and expressed the hope that his plan would serve as a starting point, and possibly as a quarry of ideas, from which the final plan would be built.

The housing problem was described as 'a scandal of the worst character' and it was noted that, while some work had been done, this was counteracted by the rate at which houses were falling into an insanitary condition, while some of the 'improvements' were unsound, being of a 'nodular type', that is, small areas pulled down and rebuilt at high-density without any reference whatever to communications: 'such schemes tend to become new slums within old ones' (Abercrombie, 1922, p. vii). The adjudicators favoured a policy of suburbanization, stating that, despite the 'too popular misconception', working people *could* be economically housed in suburban areas, in conjunction with improved transport facilities or by the decentralization of industry. They cited the example of the port of Antwerp, where workers cultivated allotments when not required for dock work.

Dublin of the Future

Before discussing the town plan for Dublin which won the 1914 competition, it is worth remembering that the competitive circumstances under which the scheme was prepared led to a certain tendency to produce flamboyant, rather than practical, suggestions. Abercrombie freely admitted that 'the spectacular is impossible to avoid when competing against others – it is necessary to arrest the eye with features whose boldness are perhaps more evident than their practicability. Nor is sufficient research possible to reinforce every suggestion that is made' (Abercrombie, 1922, p. x). Some wild claims were also made in the plan – Abercrombie saw Dublin with a population of one to two million in the near future! However, despite these reservations, the Civics Institute of Ireland decided to publish the winning plan, supplementing it with drawings, additional data and revisions to take subsequent developments into account.

The proposals covered a comprehensive range of issues, but the focus here will be on suggested housing and civic improvements. Among the other suggestions were major improvements and additions to the road system as well as an underground rail system. Parts of Dublin Bay were to be reclaimed, while a huge power station, the 'Power Citadel', would replace the existing one at Pigeon House Fort.

> Dublin is a city of magnificent possibilities, containing features of the first order, but loosely co-related and often marred by the juxtaposition of incongruities and squalor.
>
> (Abercrombie, 1922, p. 3)

Abercrombie intended to remodel the city, with due reference to architectural effect, traffic convenience, hygienic housing and adequate park provision, to compose a city 'worthy to be the capital of a modern country'. His plan was divided into three stages of urgency, allowing redevelopment to begin with absolute necessities. The housing schemes for 64,000 people living in unfit conditions would be foremost among the undertakings of extreme urgency, although Abercrombie emphasized that the housing question was intimately bound up and reacted upon by general urban improvements, so that to consider either separately would be disastrous. The next two salient features were a new city centre and a scheme for land reclamation from Dublin Bay.

In relation to redeveloping the city centre, reference was made to the work of the Wide Streets Commissioners, whose 'enlightened re-modelling, extending over a period of 50 years, should now, after a lapse of a century, be carried on in the same spirit of boldness and economic foresight' (Abercrombie, 1922, p. 36). Architecturally, Abercrombie considered that the plain brick buildings of the Georgian era could not be improved upon, while the new public buildings proposed should follow the Custom House and the Four Courts in terms of their simplicity and restraint. In his opinion, the central improvements would affect the north bank of the Liffey much more than the south, given the considerable amount of derelict property there and 'the commercial desirability of the improvement of many strangulated streets'. He planned to move the central focus of the city westwards and to remove several institutions to the countryside.

A balanced river-front arrangement was conceived, with its centre at the new traffic focus close to the Four Courts and its extremes at the entrance to the Phoenix Park and the new Custom House Circus. The Phoenix Park Mall would provide a parallel thoroughfare leading to a much improved Abbey Street, relieving Mary, Henry, North Earl and Talbot Streets of traffic congestion.

O'Connell Street would have a new role, taking 'its rightful place' as the central section of a monumental route from the National Theatre and Auditorium to the north (at Parnell Square), across O'Connell Bridge and down Westmoreland Street to the new Houses of Parliament and Trinity College. A new approach to the Phoenix Park was considered to be one of the most notable improvements which Dublin could initiate. Abercrombie referred to Gandon's suggestion that the Wellington Monument should take the form of a triumphal arch at the entrance to the Phoenix Park, which would have given Dublin a rival to the Arc de Triomphe in Paris. The wide approach to the park from the central square was orientated on the axis of this obelisk, in order to bring it into due relation with the city. There would thus be a new route from the Custom House, complete with full circus and without the impediment of the Loop Line Bridge, to the Phoenix Park, the grandeur of which was lovingly described by Abercrombie in his imagined movement towards the park. The crossing of O'Connell Street would open the vista beyond the Nelson Pillar towards the National Theatre, while the new Roman Catholic cathedral would face down Capel Street, with its 'single lofty round tower' serving as 'the spiritual emblem of the city' (Abercrombie, 1922, p. 38). The road would widen to a new Central Square, with the Four Courts to the left and the tower of Christ Church cathedral visible across the river. The wide tree-lined mall dominated by the obelisk would lead past the busy market-place and the tree enclosed Art Gallery (the vacated Royal Barracks), ending up at the entrance of the central *allée* of the park.

Abercrombie's proposals clearly relate to the tradition of monumental city design and indeed both Paris and Vienna are referred to in the text of the competition plan. Certainly, the suggestion of vistas and long straight tree-lined boulevards is strongly reminiscent of Haussmann's Paris. By contrast, the proposals for the new housing areas, complete with their geometric layouts, relate to Unwin's garden suburb plans which evolved from a different strand of planning thought.

Housing formed an important element in the plan. 'Independent housing, however good it may be in itself, cannot be said to be well carried out unless it is combined with town planning: it can only be likened to putting a valuable jewel into an ill-designed setting' (Abercrombie, 1922, p. 27).

Picking up on the point stressed by Aston in evidence to the Housing Inquiry, Abercrombie recognized that the existing city boundaries were arbitrary in nature. Instead of following these boundaries, he marked out 'a real and natural area of intra-urban Dublin, which may be described as one in which full town conditions prevail' (Abercrombie, 1922, p. 19). This would be delineated to the south mainly by the canal, although Beggar's Bush Barracks and Irishtown to the east would be included, as would a line of the Circular Road as far as the Phoenix Park to the west. On the north the boundary was not so apparent, but would be taken just outside the North Circular Road to the west, then following the North Wall branch and Clonliffe Road, to the mouth of the Tolka River. The urban area which he defined covered 4200 acres (c.1700 ha) and had a population of approximately 275,000. The 'normal urban acreage' available for housing purposes housed 95.8 persons per acre (c.240 persons per ha), rather than the 75 persons per normal urban acre (c.188 persons per ha) advocated for health purposes. Therefore, he calculated that a surplus population of 59,750 must be moved from the centre to extra-urban areas, with the remaining 4450 people requiring new houses to be rehoused within the urban area. Three studies, including the 1914 Housing Inquiry and a survey by the Citizens' Housing League, were used in the examination of housing density in order to indicate the lines upon which action should be taken.

The old-fashioned solution would have been to fill the 300 acres (c.120 ha) of unoccupied or derelict lands within the urban area, retaining the existing population density, though more evenly distributed and modernly housed. Instead, it was suggested that these derelict sites, together with the vacated institutions, could serve an important future role. Whereas a new tenement problem might arise following an anticipated wave of prosperity as commercial pressure on residential streets forced some families to find room in already occupied houses, the 300 acres (c.120 ha) would provide additional

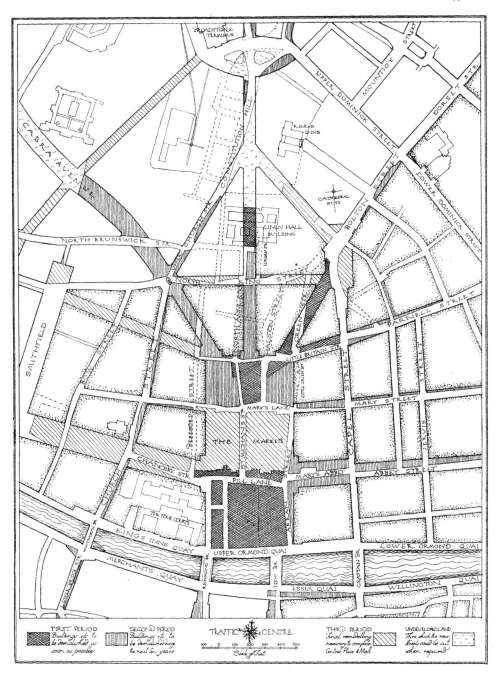

5 Abercrombie's plan for a new traffic centre. (Abercrombie, 1922.)

leeway, allowing for the shifting of the intra-urban population without exceeding the standard of 75 persons per acre (*c.*188 persons per ha).

A large proportion of the population occupied over-crowded and insanitary dwellings due to the scarcity of suitable accommodation at a reasonable rent. The supply, whether by public authorities, public utility societies, or private enterprise was very much less than the demand, while the high cost of land, rates, and local bylaws militated against the supply being maintained. Abercrombie considered the conclusions of the Parliamentary Land Enquiry Committee, and the recommendations which follow, to be 'entirely applicable' to the city of Dublin:

- *That* as a result of a complete survey of their district, a local authority shall prepare a scheme for the provision of the necessary housing accom-modation for the population likely to be permanently resident within this area;
- *That* where cheap sites are not availing, transit schemes should be promoted and undeveloped areas town-planned, and congested areas replanned;
- *That* public utility societies should be assisted financially to enable them to provide such accommodation;
- *That* insanitary property should be improved and adapted to modern conditions in order to mitigate the hardships of the present closing order procedure.

The plan favoured refurbishment of the first-class tenement houses, as proposed in a recent Architectural Society competition, by knocking three of the large old houses into one, retaining the central staircase and converting the two side staircases into sanitary blocks. However, Abercrombie saw this as a temporary solution as he anticipated that industrial prosperity and progress in the reorganized and enlightened Dublin which would cause all such property to be used for business and semi-business purposes, as was the case in Liverpool. Unfortunately, Abercrombie's optimism was misplaced. Few of the tenements were refurbished either privately or by the Corporation, and few were to be used for business purposes for many years to come.

In order to provide for those who must live in the central area, and to supplement the shortage resulting from the immediate demolition of second and third class tenements, Abercrombie proposed a 'composite tenement scheme' for the Townsend Street area. The proposed Townsend Street scheme,

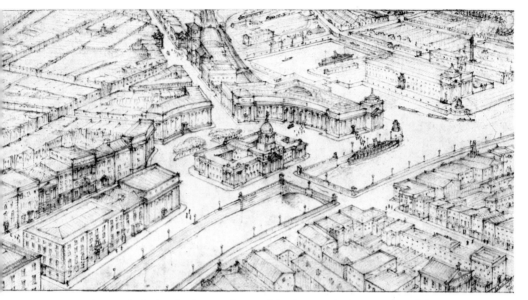

6 Abercrombie's plan for the completion of the Custom House environs and the development of the passenger port of Dublin. (Abercrombie, 1922.)

largely seen as a sort of clearing house during the immense operations of re-housing, would house 3698 people in a 28 acre (*c.*11 hectare) area which would include 166 self-contained houses as well as 444 purpose-built tenements. A total of 13 acres (*c.*5 ha) would be devoted to open spaces, recreation or children's playing areas in front of the flats, being intended to offer 'some compensation to those workers who, by reason of their occupation and the limitations of their income, are forced to live near to the locality of their employment' (Abercrombie, 1922, p. 25). However, if the provision of new houses and adequate transport facilities were to keep pace with the removal of the slums, it was suggested that this scheme might not be necessary. It was also suggested that the remaining 752 people (of the 4450 to be housed within the city) should be housed on one of the vacant sites within the city, in order to set an example for infilling projects.

However, Abercrombie considered suburban housing with adequate transit schemes to be 'the essence of the solution of the housing difficulty'. Apart from anything else, high-quality, well-planned local authority suburbs would set an example which would have to be followed by private builders: 'The moral and exemplary effect of these large tracts of suburban planning on the most up-to-date lines would be incalculable. The fashion for the future growth of Dublin would have been set' (Abercrombie, 1922, p. 23). Suburban re-housing was seen as a 'bolder course, which is alone possible in conjunction with radical town planning' (Abercrombie, 1922, p. 22). Intra-urban sites would be more expensive, more difficult to acquire and treat due to their scattered nature, whereas large extra-urban tracts could be bought cheaply in bulk, and portions could be sold off at an increased value once development had been initiated. Indeed, the Housing Inquiry had shown that land in the city centre cost an average of £4070 per acre (£10,175 per ha), mainly on account of compensation paid to owners, in contrast to Abercrombie's figures for land in Crumlin at £300 per acre (£750 per ha). In addition, well-planned suburban schemes would set a good example for future growth. Whereas, in central areas it would only be practicable to build four – and perhaps five-storeyed flat blocks to ensure a moderate rental, 'such tenements are not desirable for the better class workman, who prefers a self-contained cottage'. Abercrombie was firm in his conviction 'that the future generation must be reared under better conditions than city tenement dwellings can offer' (Abercrombie, 1922, p. 26).

In accordance with the conditions of the competition, in the extra-urban area a norm of 12 houses per acre (30 houses per ha), or 14.4 houses per 'normal extra-urban acre' (c.36 houses per ha) (including house plots, streets, sites of public buildings, small local playgrounds, ordinary dispersed commercial premises, and gardens or allotments) would be used. Thus the re-housing of 59,750 people would require, at the rate of 60 persons per acre (150 persons per ha), 996 acres (403 ha), to be located at three points:

Crumlin	430 acres (c.170 ha)
Cabra	400 acres (c.160 ha)
Drumcondra	166 acres (c.67 ha)

In developing such suburban schemes, Abercrombie suggested that communications and recreation were two essential factors. It was considered imperative that rapid and cheap tramway facilities with the centre would be provided, linking the three new areas of Crumlin, Cabra and Drumcondra with the centre, since it was expected that the majority of these rehoused people would have their occupations and interests to begin with, at any rate, near the centre of the city. Over time it was expected that the development of the Crumlin industrial area (another of the plan's proposals) would provide employment in the area, and that the town would more rapidly grow in this direction than Cabra. Meanwhile, the private development of Clontarf would provide housing for the population that would spring up following the

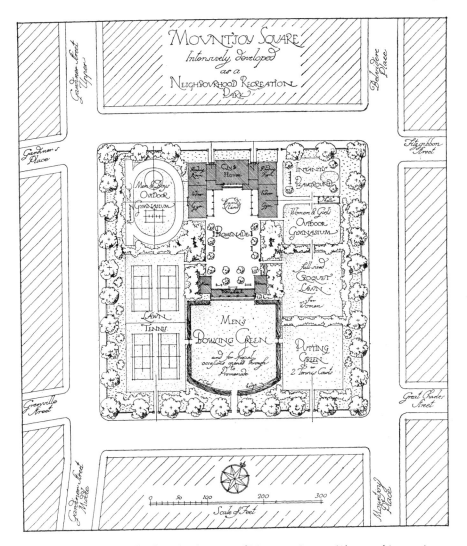

7 Abercrombie's plan for the redevelopment of Mountjoy Square. (Abercrombie, 1922.)

industrial and dock development of reclaimed lands in the port area. A light footbridge over the river Tolka would bring this area of suitable housing land into immediate use, checking the building of houses near or on ground required for commercial purposes.

Suggestions were also made for a 'suburban house type' which differed from the urban type, with a through-lit living room plan to suit any site aspect. Abercrombie also included illustrations for a 'Neighbourhood Centre', which should be just off, but close by, a main traffic route, and near a neighbourhood park or parkway. The site for such centres would be carefully selected and reserved, and Abercrombie noted that the sale of the sites, particularly for shops, would be of material assistance to the Corporation in carrying out their housing schemes.

A variety of garden sizes was proposed, ranging from moderate-sized gardens, to small front gardens, yard space and allotments. There were similar to the arrangement at Port Sunlight, the model village, near Liverpool, built by Lever for his workers (Hubbard and Shippobottom, 1988). One acre in ten would be given over to allotments, the same rate as park provision. Shallow plots would back on to a green, used either as a children's playground, or possibly a bowling green. Abercrombie also suggested that for the smallest size of house the rows, instead of facing the traffic streets, should be set at right angles to them, approached by narrow walks between long gardens widening out at the centre to a small children's playground. This style of planning, reminiscent of Hampstead Garden Suburb, was applied in part of the Corporation's Drumcondra Housing Scheme (see Figure 36), and is also found in London County Council schemes of the same period, including Becontree.

Despite the evident influence of early garden suburbs on Abercrombie's proposals, he was critical of the architecture of these schemes. He suggested that Dublin had 'the most architectural slums in Europe', possessing all those characteristics which were missed in the typical Garden Village: spacious rooms, simple architecture, dignified doorways, ample sash windows. He called for the same spirit to be carried into the new suburbs, 'avoiding the machine-made monotony and harshness of the bylaw suburb, on the one hand, and the fussy picturesqueness of the early garden suburb, on the other' (Abercrombie, 1922, p. 39). In particular he was critical of Dublin Corporation's Inchicore scheme, with its dreary rows of twenty or more houses, and no play space for children: 'The prospect for the future of a city on these lines is dismal – though hygienically it is better than the architecturally noble tenements' (Abercrombie, 1922, p. 40). The plan included a highly detailed consideration of the park system in Dublin. Prior to its publication, the issue of parks and open spaces had not taxed the Corporation greatly. Marino (begun 1924) was the first suburban scheme developed by Dublin Corporation to include generous provision for gardens, playing fields and allotments from the outset, but it was not until the 1930s that Dublin Corporation began to pursue a serious policy of playground and park provision in the centre of the city.

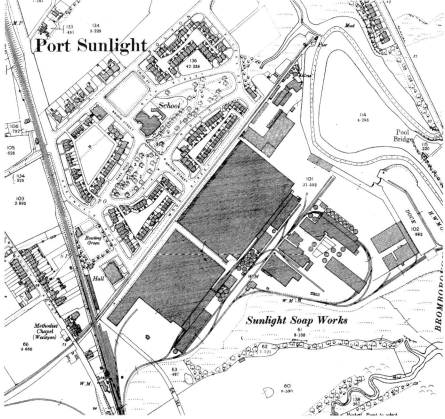

8 Example of housing and layout plan of village and factory at Port Sunlight near Liverpool. (Photograph by J. Brady.)

Town planning was considered essential to the successful completion of the new schemes:

> Without good town-planning 'many advantages are lost; wider streets for main routes, cheaper construction for non-traffic streets, direct communication, open spaces, the preservation of trees and the limitation of the number of houses to the acre all tend to a healthful and sanitary state of civilized life.
>
> (Abercrombie, 1922, p. 27)

In order to develop the three proposed Corporation estates 'on town-planning lines', new legislation, preferably a local Housing and Town Planning Act, promoted by the city authorities, would be required. A new town planning act should:

• amend and consolidate existing Housing Acts;
• give the Corporation the power to purchase land and to develop, lease or sell it;
• secure State aid for housing, so that grants for the erection of houses for the working classes could be advanced either to the municipality or to public utility societies on easy terms;
• to sell or deal with the derelict sites in the central area, the rentals/purchase money obtained to then be set off against expenditure in the new housing areas.

While some of these powers were acquired through the various Housing Acts of the 1920s and 1930s, Ireland's first Town Planning Act was not passed until 1934.

The plan also suggested the different lines on which development could occur. The Corporation, as owners of the land, could carry out the whole as a gigantic housing scheme. It could erect a few blocks in each area to alleviate the present 'house famine', and to commence the development. Alternatively, Dublin Corporation could sell or lease the land to public utility societies for the erection of houses for the re-housing of the dispossessed tenants as the central area was gradually dealt with. Finally, it suggested that the Corporation could sell or lease the land to private builders on the same conditions, that is, that preference would have to be given to the dispossessed tenants of the central area.

Indeed, Abercrombie's suggested form of development is very close to what actually happened in Dublin during the 1920s, where the Corporation began to lease serviced sites at the edges of its own developments to private builders and public utility societies, as well as building housing itself. However, the provision that preference should be given to dispossessed tenants from the city centre in housing allocation was not introduced, so that the 1920s schemes tended to cater for the better-off members of the working class. It was not until 1931 that legislation targeted the rehousing of those dislocated from slum clearance areas.

The practical consequences of Abercrombie's proposals were limited, particularly as the plan had no legal status. It was claimed that 'if Dublin were to embark upon a town plan of this magnitude it would find that it would turn out a commercial success as great as that of Paris, and it should even exceed the success of Paris in its provision for the real health and happiness of the people' (Abercrombie, 1922, p. 48). However, because it lacked its own development plan, Dublin Corporation seems to have followed some of the suggestions made in the competition plan, particularly in relation to road widening schemes and communications improvements. Many of the ideas relating to housing were also modified and applied to the Corporation schemes of the late 1920s. Drumcondra, Cabra and Crumlin were among the suburban sites to be chosen for local authority development, as had been suggested by Abercrombie, while Clontarf was developed privately as he had predicted. In selecting Abercrombie and Kelly as consultants in the late 1930s, the Dublin Corporation Town Planning Committee made reference to the 1914/22 proposals 'which have been found suggestive and helpful in subsequent development schemes in Dublin' (Report 12/1937, p. 108).

In more recent years, further suggestions made in the plan have resurfaced in modified form. Today the former Royal Barracks, now Collins Barracks, houses part of the collection of the National Museum, while the wedge of institutions near the Broadstone terminus has partially been replaced by new apartment developments, including the Richmond, and a business incubator centre.

Although the Corporation would borrow liberally from the plan, it appears that there was no attempt to develop an integrated approach to the development of the city. Abercrombie had stressed that planning was essential: 'The re-housing of over 60,000 persons is the immediate need, and unless this is undertaken in conjunction with radical town planning the latter state of Dublin will be worse than the present' (Abercrombie, 1922, p. 19). Early town planning had derived much of its persuasive force from the promise that it would provide a logical approach to the problems of urban life, by co-ordinating previously separate strands of improvement policy. As the evidence to the Housing Inquiry and the subsequent proposals by Geddes, Unwin and Abercrombie have shown, in the second decade of the twentieth century there was a recognition that housing was one element of a more complex picture.

Unfortunately, in attempting to tackle the problems of the city, Dublin Corporation remained essentially reactive and failed to accept the necessity for coherent solutions in a town planning context.

Dublin's traumas, 1914–22

Dublin Corporation has frequently been criticized for its lack of action following the Dublin Housing Inquiry. Certainly, it would seem that the dreadful conditions of the working classes which were highlighted by the Housing Inquiry demanded an immediate response, but it is equally clear that the Corporation was bound by political circumstance and could do little. With the outbreak of World War I, the British Government which ultimately controlled grants for housing activity in Ireland was distracted from the task in hand. There had also been a loss of interest in Home Rule. The political circumstances made it extremely difficult for local government to function effectively. In Ireland as a whole, something approaching anarchy existed from 1916 to 1922. Tom Garvin's excellent book, *The Birth of Irish Democracy* (1996), provides some of this political context. By 1922, much of Dublin's city centre was in ruins, many of her major public buildings had been damaged or destroyed, and unsettled political conditions persisted. Little wonder, then, that the housing issue had to wait. Indeed, it is almost more surprising that the Dublin Corporation succeeded in building any housing at all during this difficult period. Because the Dublin Town Plan which had won the competition was not published until 1922, its preface reflected the anguish of the citizens of Dublin in the intervening years. 'Few towns but have suffered a change, physical and psychological, during these intervening years of war, trade boom and subsequent depression – but Dublin has added the double tragedy of war and civil war' (Abercrombie, 1922, p. ix).

The association of the housing question with public order (or disorder) remained strong in the public mind with the outbreak of violence in 1916. A number of commentators, indeed, suggested that the Easter Rising could never have happened, were it not for the unhappy living conditions of such a large proportion of the population: 'The rebellion of 1916, with its terrible results in loss of life, vast material waste, the re-birth of dying antagonisms, the creation of new enmities, and the setting back of the clock in many most vital movements for the welfare of Ireland might possibly have been prevented if the people in Dublin had been better housed' (Cowan, 1918, p. 31).

The Rising resulted in considerable destruction at the heart of Dublin city, with most of the lower end of Sackville Street, from Bachelor's Walk to the

9 The ruins of the Custom House 1921. (Postcard.)

GPO, and from Eden Quay to Cathedral Street reduced to rubble. The Dublin Fire Brigade Chief estimated the extent of the damage at about £2.5 million, with considerable concern arising in relation to the hiatus in the city's commercial life, and the related question of compensation. After the initial shock, however, the *Irish Builder and Engineer* and professional bodies such as the RIAI began to stress the potential for civic improvement afforded by the fires: 'A wonderful and unlooked for opportunity has arisen in Dublin' (Butler, 1916, p. 570).

The reconstruction of O'Connell Street was perceived by some as a question of national importance. For example, R.M. Butler, editor of the *Irish Builder and Engineer* and principal of one of the busiest private architectural practices in Ireland, considered that the reconstruction might become the focus of a greater scheme, with the creation of magnificent riverside frontages on both sides of the Liffey from the Custom House to Kingsbridge (now Heuston Station). He called for State aid and statutory powers to allow for uniformity of height and co-ordination of material and design, as well as for the removal of Nelson's Pillar 'to a less obstructive and more suitable position'. Professor Scott of UCD also considered that the reconstruction of O'Connell Street presented 'an opportunity rare in the history of cities', calling for a 'unified plan of reconstruction' which would provide 'unity amid variety' (Scott, 1916, p. 165).

New legislation was required to promote planned reconstruction, and because the principles and powers involved were held to be novel and controversial, lively debate was provoked during the second reading of the bill on 7 August 1916 (Miller, 1985). In an attempt to break the deadlock surrounding the bill, the 'King's High Planner', Raymond Unwin, was brought to Dublin to obtain the co-operation of the various interests in support of the legislation. The outcome of intense negotiations, The Dublin Reconstruction (Emergency Provisions) Act, 1916 had three main objectives:

- Design control of rebuilding (the City Architect was empowered to examine, modify or if necessary reject redevelopment proposals);
- To enable the acquisition of land for street widening, and of derelict sites if rebuilding had not commenced within two years;
- To enable the making of loans by the Local Government Board towards rebuilding.

A compromise, the Act did nothing to bring about the comprehensive restructuring of the city centre which the 1914 Dublin competition had sought. A special Reconstruction Committee of Dublin Corporation was assisted by an advisory committee of Dublin architects including P. Caulfield Orpen (President of the Royal Institute of Architects of Ireland), W. Kaye-Parry of Messrs Kaye-Parry and Ross, George L. O'Connor (who was involved in preparing housing schemes for the Corporation at Mary's Lane and Boyne Street in 1919), Michael J. Buckley and City Architect, Charles MacCarthy, as well as Raymond Unwin himself. However, the evidence suggests that the advisors were limited by the caution of the Reconstruction Committee, which confined the remit considerably. Thus Dublin Corporation limited itself to the widening of part of North Earl Street, the laying out of what became Cathal Brugha Street, and the control of building design, particularly in O'Connell Street (see Miller, 1985 and Shaffrey, 1988 for further discussion).

The reconstruction of O'Connell Street was delayed by further unrest and damage, although composite designs for the new street frontages were published in *The Builder* in July 1918. Horace O'Rourke produced the designs, influenced by Unwin and Abercrombie, which have been described as promoting a 'commercial classicism' with relatively uniform cornice heights, avoiding the eccentricities of many of the destroyed buildings. An advertisement from Battersby and Co. in 1917 suggests that there was a lively interest in the rebuilding of the city, somewhat at odds with the foot-dragging behaviour of the authorities: 'In view of the exceptional interest in the rebuilding of

10 Upper Sackville (O'Connell) Street pre- and post-destruction. (Postcards.)

Sackville Street and beautifying the principal thoroughfare in our City, we have to announce that within the past few months we have sold sites in Sackville Street ALONE, the consideration money actually negotiated through us amounting to £36,100' (*Irish Times*, 19 May 1917).

Rebuilding the city centre was a slow process. It was not until May of 1922, some six years after the Easter Rising, that the *Irish Builder and Engineer* reported that the reconstruction of what was termed 'the Destroyed Area' of Dublin was almost finished. In the interim, one of Dublin's finest buildings, the Custom House, had been burnt to the ground on 25 May 1921 during the War of Independence. The rebuilding of Lower Sackville Street had not been quite complete when Civil War broke out, with the loss of another of Dublin's great civic buildings, the Four Courts (June 1922) and the destruction of much of Upper Sackville Street. The destruction of June 1922 left the north-eastern side of the street from Cathedral Street to Parnell Square in ruins, and most of Upper Sackville Street remained a desert after 18 months. One of the consequences was a shortage of hotel accommodation, as the Gresham and other adjacent hotels were still in ruins in 1924. The first temporary timber building to be erected in Upper Sackville Street was not completed until September 1922, three months after the destruction, by M. Jolley of Haddington Road for the Grogan firm. Some two years later, in October 1924, the *Irish Builder and Engineer* reported that building was about to begin on some of the sites in Lower Abbey Street which had remained vacant since the rebellion of 1916, while work on the rebuilding of a number of houses in Upper Sackville Street would be started shortly.

The delay in rebuilding after the destruction of 1922 was a cause of considerable concern. Eventually, on 15 September 1924, a lengthy meeting was held at Government Buildings between representatives of the Institute of Architects of Ireland, the Master Builders (represented by Messrs Crampton, White and Clifton) and Mr E.P. McCarron representing the Ministry for Local Government, with the express purpose of considering the deadlock in connection with the rebuilding of Upper Sackville Street. It appears that, rather than rebuild, most of the owners were trying to sell their interests and had failed to do so. The reluctance to rebuild was caused by the difference between compensation awards and the actual costs of rebuilding, but also by questions of irregular frontages and overlapping holdings. Indeed, by the time that the meeting was held, only one proposal to rebuild had been submitted to the City Architect. Possible designs and plans for rebuilding were discussed, with general agreement that a co-ordinated scheme should be adopted. There was also a consensus 'that it would be a disaster if every owner were allowed to follow his own devices in building, even to the extent permitted in Lower Sackville Street in 1916' (*Irish Builder and Engineer*, 20 September 1924, p. 801).

At the invitation of the City of Dublin Commissioners, the RIAI appointed a small committee to confer with the City Architect on the subject of the rebuilding of Upper Sackville Street in October 1924. The members were the President of the RIAI, Mr G.P. Sheridan, Mr J.J. Robinson, and Mr F. Hicks. The intention was that 'at least harmony of skyline, material and character should be secured'. By now, designs for rebuilding had been received for sites 19, 19a, 23, 43 and 44. Number 44, the premises of Messrs Adam Scott & Son, wine merchants, had been partially destroyed, while the former YMCA premises at number 43 had been acquired by Patrick Moylett, formerly of Ballina and Galway. Building operations began at the first of the vacant sites, number 43, in the last week of October 1924. At the same time, scaffolding was erected within the pillars of the 'old GPO' in Lower Sackville Street (a temporary GPO, also on Sackville Street, had also been destroyed in 1922). The rebuilding of the first section of the GPO had begun on the Henry Street side in September 1924, under the care of contractors H. & J. Martin and W. H. Clarke.

Legislation similar to the 1916 Emergency Provisions Act was promoted by Dublin Corporation, as seen in Report 185/1922 of the Reconstruction Committee 're obtaining statutory powers to deal with the reconstruction of the premises destroyed or damaged in the recent military operations', and finally became the Dublin Reconstruction (Emergency Provisions) Act, 1924. Horace T. O'Rourke was now City Architect, and the plans for the rebuilding of the street were carried out under his direction and control. This time the rebuilding was more successful, achieving unified façades, with a number of owners within united schemes. The Hammam Building is one example, occupied above by the Revenue Commissioners, and at ground level by two shops. By December 1924, the rebuilding of Upper Sackville Street was truly underway, although progress was very slow. One of the major undertakings was the rebuilding of the Gresham Hotel 'on the most modern lines' to designs by Mr Robert Atkinson, FRIBA, London. Meanwhile, Messrs W.H. Byrne and Son had prepared plans for a granite-fronted building for Sir James Mackey & Co., seed merchants, to be constructed by Messrs R. & J. Thompson of Fairview.

The Reconstruction Committee of Dublin Corporation remained active during the 1920s. Penal rents were imposed upon the tenants of City Estate property who had failed to comply with the rebuilding clauses in their leases, including Messrs Boyd & Dickson, with premises at 13 Wicklow Street

(Report 192/1922). In 1924, reference was made to a proposed new thoroughfare in continuation of Gloucester Street from Marlborough Street to O'Connell Street, which became Cathal Brugha Street (Report 6/1924). In December 1925, the Dublin (Destroyed Area, 1922) Reconstruction Section recommended application to the Ministry of Local Government for sanction to borrow £50,000 for the purpose of making advances to building owners, while as late as March 1932, advances were being made under the Dublin Reconstruction (Emergency Provisions) Acts for the rebuilding of premises in Upper O'Connell Street. In this case, Messrs Meagher, Hayes & Co. Ltd. were to be the recipients (Report 20/1932). The rate of interest and method of payment of loans made under the Reconstruction Act was on the same basis as the Small Dwellings Acquisition Acts (see later discussion), but because the buildings were of a more substantial character, it was decided that the period for repayment of the loans would be the unexpired term of the new 5 per cent stock, which was redeemable in 50 years from 1 January, 1926 (Report 87/1926).

It might be suggested that the need for reconstruction generated an increased interest in the necessity for town planning. In December 1924 Professor Abercrombie returned to Dublin, where he was reported to be engaged in the consideration, with the County Borough Commissioners, of the preliminaries of town planning for the capital, because 'the Commissioners have been … confronted with a succession of difficulties consequent on the absence of a definite town plan for the city', especially due to increased house building and the need for new roads (*Irish Builder and Engineer*, 13 December 1924, p. 1046).

Criticism of the rebuilding of Dublin was persistent, however. With the benefits of hindsight, E.A. Aston, writing in 1930, referred to the situation following World War I, when many European countries launched great reconstruction schemes and extended their town planning measures: 'Meanwhile Ireland, engaged in the throes of a political revolution, had no thought for her civic problems. Dublin, with its central areas laid in ashes, proceeded to rebuild without thought of architectural amenity or future civic convenience. So a rare opportunity was lost' (Artifex, 1930, p. 38). As we have seen, there had been a more thorough consideration of the rebuilding process than this quote would lead us to believe, but despite this many commentators were clearly unhappy with the end result.

The unsettled conditions during the period of the Civil War were considered a mixed blessing by the leader writer of the *Irish Builder and Engineer*. On the one hand:

the present disturbances in Dublin and throughout the country will, it is to be feared, have a very adverse effect upon the building industry, already suffering from serious depression. On the other hand, the destruction wrought affords the melancholy satisfaction that it will provide considerable work for architects and builders. The destruction in 1916 provided the building industry in Dublin with several millions worth of work, that not only tided it over the worst years of the war, but supplied almost a 'boom'.

(Irish Builder and Engineer, 15 July 1922, p. 480)

Providing for a new régime: the Irish Free State

The state of housing in Dublin is so intimately connected with the general life of the nation, and reacts so deeply and so widely outside the metropolis, that it assumes the importance of a national issue.

(McKenna, 1919, p. 280)

Although, as Professor Scott pointed out, the destruction of many public buildings and much of the area around O'Connell Street offered an unexpected opportunity to replan Dublin, it certainly posed additional problems for the new Free State Government requiring accommodation for its Parliament and offices. The desire to make Dublin a fitting capital for the new State, while maintaining priority for the housing problems of the urban working-class, ensured that Dublin once again became the primary focus of planning debate and activity in Ireland. The change of Government inevitably gave scope for considerable finger pointing. In its review of the year 1924, the *Irish Builder and Engineer* could quite safely comment that: 'Housing, or rather the lack of it, still remains the most urgent and pressing problem of the hour in the Free State, which unhappily came in for the evil heritage left by previous Governments and Corporations' (*Irish Builder and Engineer*, 27 December 1924, p. 1090).

One of the most lively debates of the time concerned the location of the Parliament. When, eventually, it was decided to 'evict' the Royal Dublin Society from Leinster House, the *Irish Builder and Engineer* was vocal in bemoaning this 'melancholy decision'. It suggested that 'the removal of the headquarters of the Society to the show ground in the suburbs must inevitably curtail its useful national activities, fetter its powers, and completely change, if not destroy, its social and literary side' (*Irish Builder and Engineer*, 18 October 1924). Clearly, then, suburbanization was not favoured for all!

Meanwhile, the Greater Dublin Reconstruction Movement, which included E.A. Aston, Lady Aberdeen, William Purcell O'Neill and Frank Mears (Geddes' assistant and son-in-law), published its proposals as *Greater Dublin: Reconstruction Scheme Described and Illustrated.* The Movement sought a comprehensive solution to the plight of the city, which by this time included the legacy of unfit housing, tenements and derelict sites, an accommodation problem for the new Irish Government given the destruction of virtually all major public buildings, and the aggravation of the traffic circulation problem caused by the destruction of Butt Bridge. It repeatedly called for municipal reform by the amalgamation of the various existing local councils. The report stressed the continued necessity of massive effort in the field of working-class housing. Various transport improvements were proposed, including the removal of the Loop Line bridge. The Custom House would become the new GPO, alongside which a new Central Station would be built. Legal functions would remain in Dublin Castle, while the restored Four Courts would become an art gallery and the former GPO would become the new City Hall. The Catholic Cathedral would be placed on a site adjoining Christ Church, which was favoured by Lady Aberdeen, although she had a more practical proposal for the Episcopalians to hand over Christ Church cathedral to the Catholics! (a proposal which still surfaces from time to time). The Oireachtas would be housed in the Royal Hospital, Kilmainham, rather than the popular choice of College Green, which would revive the west end of the city, as well as improving western access to the city. An enlargement of the port, and the removal of the cattle market to the port area was also proposed. Although few of these proposals were implemented, the Reconstruction Movement succeeded in rekindling in the public consciousness a recognition that development proposals should conform to a plan which was derived from a thorough civic survey.

While all of this political upheaval and debate continued, the plight of the ordinary citizens of Dublin continued to deteriorate. 'Irish folk have come, through long use, to regard Dublin slums as something normal, inevitable, something at which indignation would sound stale and unprofitable' (McKenna, 1919, p. 280). In a Dáil question of May 1923, Alfie Byrne TD asked the Minister for Local Government whether he was aware 'that many thousands of Dublin citizens are now sheltering in rat infested basements of slum property, and whether he is now in a position to state the Government's Housing Policy for the year 1923–24'. However, in reply, Ernest Blythe stated that 'when the estimates for the current year were being considered it was not found possible to provide further State aid for municipal schemes owing to the prevailing unsettled conditions, and the heavy financial deficit. There is the added difficulty that building costs in this country have remained at inflated figures' (Dáil Debates, 3, p. 469).

It is worth noting too that the wretched conditions experienced in Dublin City were not unknown in the rural districts surrounding the capital. In 1928, Seán Brady TD raised the question of houses in the Malahide district which had been condemned in 1914 but were still occupied, despite the fact that three of them had fallen in on the occupants in the previous three or four years. He described one house where the rafters had cracked and the roof was being held up by a board resting on the mantelpiece. 'Nothing has been done, the explanation being that nobody was killed' (Dáil Debates, 24, p. 772).

Given a by-now general shortage of housing, the expansion of the building industry was a top priority after 1921, and in the following year, on St Patrick's Day, the Provisional Government made £1 million available as a grant for urban housing schemes. This sum was to be divided among the municipal authorities in the ratio of £2 for every £1 provided by the local authority. However, supporting Blythe's assertions, building costs in Dublin in the early 1920s had certainly become prohibitive. In January 1922 the *Irish Builder and Engineer* reported that the cost of building was still from two to three times what it had been in 1914, so that only the most absolutely necessary building works were being undertaken. An ordinary labourers' cottage of a good type which would have been built in County Dublin for £150 or £160 before 1914, could not now be built for less than £400. The all-in cost, which comprised land, roads, sewers, legal and architectural fees in addition to the actual building cost, had been about £200 per house (inclusive), but was now close to £600 (*Irish Builder and Engineer*, 23 September 1922).

By August 1922 yet another building strike was feared. Wages for skilled trades in Dublin were over 2s. per hour at this time, whereas in London and the north of England the equivalent trades earned 1s. 8d. per hour and in the southern English towns the average wage was 1s. 4d. The cost of living in Dublin was high, while continuing profiteering some four years after the end of the Great War was a contributory factor driving up building costs. The master builders wanted to gradually reduce wages over a three month period, by 4½d. per hour for tradesmen and 3½d. per hour for labourers, but unsurprisingly the workers refused. Despite Government intervention, the strike came into effect in September, having been delayed for a week as a mark of respect to the memory of General Collins. By late September the Irish

Builder and Engineer reported that some 650 labourers were on strike, out of between three and four thousand men engaged in the city.

As an illustration of the very high cost of living in Dublin, in September 1922 the *Irish Builder and Engineer* compared the official Government prices, based on the average for a number of Irish towns, for a number of goods with the current Dublin prices.

Table 4 Prices in Dublin compared to average Irish prices, 1922.

Product	Official Government prices	Current Dublin prices
Butter (per lb)	1*s.* 6¾*d.*	2*s.* 2*d.*
Bacon (per lb)	1*s.* 7*d.*	2*s.* 3*d.*
Mutton (per lb)	1*s.* 3½*d.*	1*s.* 8*d.*
Eggs (per dozen)	1*s.* 5¼*d.*	2*s.* 6*d.*
Milk (per quart)	0*s.* 4¾*d.*	0*s.* 6*d.*

(*Irish Builder and Engineer*, 23 September 1922, p. 649.)

In October 1922, the building industry was still 'under a cloud, and no-one will build now who is not obliged. What is needed is a restoration of public confidence, and an inducement to the private building owner to once again hazard capital in building enterprise, without the certainty of dead loss. If this is to be accomplished, some reduction in building costs is essential' (*Irish Builder and Engineer*, 21 October 1922, p. 702). By this time, apart from the Corporation's housing schemes, there was very little work in prospect in Dublin for the coming winter or spring. Almost the only building activity which had been undertaken in the country was housing for ex-servicemen returning from World War I, and many new bank buildings, a fact which generated considerable comment about war-time profiteering! Tenders were also being advertised for the reconstruction of co-operatives and for the design of war memorials.

In reply to a Dáil question from Alfie Byrne, celebrated Lord Mayor of Dublin and TD, the Minister for External Affairs, Desmond Fitzgerald, stated that the Government was aware 'that large numbers of small new dwellings are required, and that the main cause why they cannot be provided is that building costs, particularly as regards labour and materials, are grossly excessive, resulting in the cost of construction of houses in Ireland being nearly twice the cost of similar houses in England' (Dáil Eireann, 2, p. 2400). By September of 1923 the housing shortage throughout the country was severe. It was reported that people of all classes, not just the working classes, were badly in need of houses. Some were paying rents of £150 to £200 a year for tiny flats which would have been worth £25 to £30 a year before the War. 'They are all wanting houses, if they could get them, and all are waiting for the hearty co-operation of capital and labour to solve the housing problem and to create prosperity for the building trade, as well as constant employment' (*Irish Builder and Engineer*, 8 September 1923, p. 678).

The 'excessive cost of building' decried by a leader in the *Irish Builder and Engineer*, meant that rents for local authority working-class housing were now being fixed at rates beyond the reach of those people who were much in need of accommodation. In the summer of 1923, for example, Rathmines UDC had fixed rents of 124 new houses at between 16 and 25 shillings per week, which was entirely beyond the capacity of the average worker, especially with wages falling. As the *Irish Builder and Engineer* noted, '25*s*. a week is £65 per annum – formerly the rent of quite a pretentious house in the suburbs of Dublin, or of a small mansion in the country … If progress is to be made, something new must be done' (*Irish Builder and Engineer*, 2 June 1923, p. 421).

Table 5 Increase in material costs in 1924 over 1914.

Timber	+105.2%
Cement	+60.6%
Bricks	+102.1%
Average Increase	+91.1%

(*Irish Builder and Engineer*, 19 April 1924, p. 350, based on calculations by Mr John Good, TD.)

The situation was not helped by a series of strikes, causing the *Irish Builder and Engineer* to remark in its leader: 'if industrial peace cannot be brought about, it is difficult to see what is to save the country from lapsing into a state of Bolshevism' (*Irish Builder and Engineer*, 6 October 1923, p. 769).

This background helps to explain why, in the period between 1922 and 1931, housing legislation was mainly concerned with financial assistance to promote house-building, rather than being directed specifically to slum clearance. The severity of the housing problem at this time can perhaps be judged by the communication between the Corporation's Housing Committee and the Surplus Property Disposals Board in late 1920, ascertaining whether any army huts were available for sale 'it having been suggested that these structures could be used as temporary habitations, and thus help to relieve the pressing demand for housing accommodation' (Report 56/1921). The general need for housing was very great, as was the need for State subsidy. As Richard Corish, the Wexford TD put it in September 1922 'if there is not State aid forth-coming … the economic rent of the house built entirely without State aid would be an impossible proposition altogether' (Dáil Debates, 1, p. 259). There is no doubt but that the housing problem was increasingly seen as a national issue. In 1924, when speaking to the Dublin Rotary Club, President Cosgrave stated that the housing question was probably the most important issue before the Free State. Clearly reflecting the concerns for public order, he suggested that 'it [the housing question] directly or indirectly affects every aspect of the national life, and until it is settled there will be no genuine peace or contentment in the land. For no populace housed as so many of the people of Dublin are, can be good citizens, or loyal and devoted subjects of the State, no matter what the State may be' (Cosgrave, quoted in the *Irish Builder and Engineer*, 8 March 1923, p. 169).

Meanwhile, there was concern that speculative development, which was slow to recover following the wartime cessation, would resume. Alfie Byrne, TD, frequently asked Dáil questions in late 1922 and early 1923 regarding the possibility of making Government grants available to private builders which would be sufficient to make the building of houses a paying proposition. He asked the Minister whether he was aware 'that many private builders are prepared to immediately start building if sufficient encouragement is offered, and that there is at present a demand for thirty thousand cottages containing three, four and five rooms' (Dáil Debates, 2, p. 2399). Eventually, in June 1923, Ernest Blythe stated that the Government was not in a position to assist private builders in easing the housing shortage in Dublin in that financial year, due to its heavy obligations arising from the destruction of property.

Legislation was introduced to encourage private development in the following year, however. The Housing (Building Facilities) Act, 1924 and the Housing Act, 1925, enabled the Government and local authorities to make grants to private individuals or groups wishing to build or reconstruct dwellings in urban areas. The 1925 Act also encouraged the activities of public utility societies and other forms of co-operative housing action. This legislation encouraged owner occupation, tending to favour the middle classes, rather than the working-classes for whom the housing problem was so severe. Similarly, the Corporation's model development at Marino marked a trend towards tenant purchase in its schemes, again excluding the poorest members of the working class. The financial provisions of the Housing (Building Facilities) Act were similar to those of the Housing (Additional Powers) Acts, 1919–21, but the grants were on a lower scale, partly due to the long-awaited reduction in building costs. Under the Act the size of the proposed houses was restricted to 1000 square feet (93 m^2) of floor area. Limits were prescribed with regard to sale price and rentals, and partial remission of rates by the local authority for 19 years was one of the many facilities offered. The positive reception afforded the Housing (Building Facilities) Act of 1924 is reflected in the fact that it generally escaped attack, other than 'friendly criticism'. Its measures are discussed briefly in Chapter five.

In 1924 another political decision was taken which was to have important ramifications for Dublin. Considerable controversy was generated when the new President of the Executive Council of the Irish Free State and a former Councillor of Dublin Corporation, W.T. Cosgrave (1880–1965) dismissed the Corporation unceremoniously. The Government was accused of taking the measure out of political fear, while Thomas Johnson TD, in referring to 'this very extraordinary and unprecedented action' suggested 'we are rapidly going towards oligarchy and dictatorship' (Dáil Debates, 7, p. 1870). In March 1924, Nicholas O'Dwyer, a Local Government Inspector had investigated the proceedings and conduct of the Dublin Corporation, but James A. Burke, Minister for Local Government, did not plan to publish O'Dwyer's report. He claimed that the Inspector had called to attention 'many glaring defects in their (Corporation's) administration which certainly justified their abolition', while 'the question of trying to bring down the rate to a normal figure, a rate which is at the present time paralyzing business in the city, is a proposition that I do not believe could be effectively handled by any body situated as the Corporation was' (Dáil Debates, 7, p. 1874). However, the political background to the controversy was evidently important in the decision taken. To an extent, Dublin Corporation had been a public platform for the Government's political rivals. Alfie Byrne suggested that 'very many resolutions emanated from that body – resolutions which, I think, did good work for the city recently, resolutions asking for the release of the prisoners, proper treatment of the prisoners, examination of the jails, inspection by our Medical Officer – all these probably the Government have taken into consideration, and not the Inspector's report' (Dáil Debates, 7, p. 1880). Certainly, in February 1923 the *Irish Builder and Engineer* had reported on the threatened stoppage of the Government grants for housing, amounting to £423,000, but noted that the Corporation had since rescinded the resolution that led to the threat, whatever that might have been (*Irish Builder and Engineer*, 24 February 1923, p. 117). Yet, many others applauded the dissolution of Dublin Corporation. In a leader in the *Irish Builder and Engineer*, 31 May 1924, it was suggested that 'it is doubtful whether any other step taken by the present Government has proved so generally endorsed as the appointment of Commissioners to administer the affairs of the city' (p. 483). Whatever the reasons behind the decision, for the next six years the city was administered by three Commissioners appointed by the Government. Among their achievements were civic improvements such as the transformation of some city streets from the old cobblestone surfaces to concrete and asphalt, and the financing of house purchase schemes for a growing population.

Under the Housing (Building Facilities) (Amendment) Act, 1924, which became law in December of that year, the State grants which were available to private persons under the Act were extended to local authorities operating under the Housing of the Working Classes (Ireland) Acts. In anticipation of this legislation, the Dublin Borough Commissioners had acquired Keogh (formerly Richmond) Barracks and had begun to reconstruct part of the barrack buildings into flats for over 200 families. A limited number of temporary houses were to be erected on the adjoining land, while schemes were being prepared for the erection of *c*.220 new houses on the lands attached to the barracks as well as the extension of operations on the Marino/Croydon Park area. In March 1925, the *Irish Times* reported that, under the Act, the Dublin Commissioners planned to advertise for contracts for the completion in one year of not fewer than 1000 houses (*Irish Times*, 5 March 1925).

The new housing developments which were being undertaken at this time increasingly conformed to the relatively low-density garden suburb ideal, while there was a growing recognition of the need for enlightened site planning and seeing each development in its wider urban context. Public housing developments increasingly adopted the planning standards in vogue in Britain. The Local Government Board's regulations issued under the Irish Housing Act of 1919 had accepted the new standard of housing densities of not more than 12 houses to the acre outside central urban areas. O'Rourke's 1919 plans for the 50-acre (*c*.20 hectare) suburb at Marino used small terraces of two storey houses at an overall density of 11 houses to the acre (*c*.28 houses per ha). There was ample open space, with an allocation of land for schools, shops and public buildings. The final scheme for the larger Marino site was at a density of 9.5 houses to the acre (*c*.25 houses per ha), while the Irish Sailors' and Soldiers' Land Trust homes at Killester (laid out by Frank Mears) had a density of just four houses to the acre (10 houses per ha) (Aalen, 1988). In addition to the adherence to garden-city norms, the overall layout of estates was increasingly seen in a wider metropolitan context. Thus Griffith Avenue, 'the 100 foot road', was seen as the first stage of a major metropolitan ring road, as well as a connector between two new housing areas.

Civic Survey, 1925

The oft-mooted Civic Survey was finally undertaken by the Civics Institute of Ireland in 1923, with H.T. O'Rourke as its driving force. Representatives from a large number of bodies were involved, including the RIAI, Institute of Civil Engineers of Ireland, Social and Statistical Inquiry Society of Ireland, RSAI, CII, Greater Dublin Reconstruction Movement, Dublin Citizens' Housing Association, Irishwomen's Association of Citizenship, Rotary Club, Dublin Corporation and the Urban District Councils of Pembroke, Rathmines, Dún Laoghaire, Blackrock and Howth. The Survey was seen as the necessary precursor of a town plan, 'as necessary to a town plan as a physician's diagnosis is to his prescription' (*Irish Times*, 1 March 1924, p. 9). The report once again called for a Dublin town plan. It adopted a fairly positive view of Dublin's potential, emphasizing the national importance of Dublin as a capital city, and reflecting the somewhat naive optimism in the potential of the new State which was current at the time. The results, based in part on questionnaire surveys, air photography and traffic counts, were presented under seven headings, including archaeology, education, industry and commerce, recreation, hygiene and traffic. The section dealing with housing emphasized the elimination of the tenement problem through the erection of suburban dwellings, and noted the increasing congestion in the city which was caused by in-migration from rural areas. The Survey warned that 'the elimination of the problem is nothing short of perpetual construction at the required rate'.

O'Rourke, chairman of the Civic Survey Committee was a firm believer, like Geddes, in the education of the public as to the merits of town planning. He gave many lectures about the Survey and its significance, including an address to the Dublin Rotary Club on the publication of the final report. In an *Irish Times* article (published on two successive Saturdays in March 1924) aiming to teach the importance of the Civic Survey, his ideas, the influential ideas of the City Architect, are revealed. He appealed for a broader vision than had been evident in the past, with the elimination of trivial differences, since

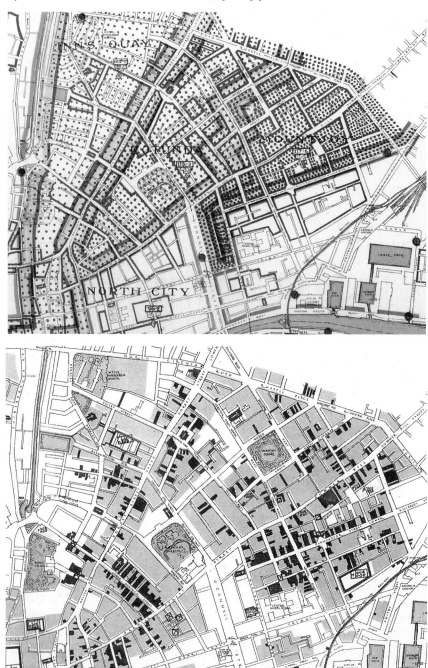

11 Extracts from two maps of the Civic Survey. The upper shows population density
and the lower shows housing quality, poor housing shaded in black.
(Civics Institute of Ireland, 1925.)

'the small things are not the things that matter when great schemes are being planned ... Dublin of today needs a great awakening, a freedom from politics and religious controversy, and a disregard of the individual standpoint'.

Clearly O'Rourke, while in accord as to the merits of the survey-analysis-plan advocated by Geddes, did not favour the latter's 'conservative surgery' approach: 'I would put Dublin on the operation table and drastically apply the surgeon's knife to its cancerous growths'. 'Demolition and demolition, and more demolition is the only remedy for a building or a city falling from decay. After that – reconstruction. As nation-planning is every citizen's concern today, so let us add capital-planning, and, in the words of Professor Reilly, think of the future' (*Irish Times*, 8 March 1924, p. 9).

Like Abercrombie's 1922 Plan, and unlike the Dublin Reconstruction Movement, the Civic Survey stated that the true centre of Dublin was located at the Four Courts, and that its present 'artificial' location in the Sackville (O'Connell) Street area was too far eastward and too near the dock district. Analogies were drawn yet again between the layout of Dublin and that of Paris, with the Phoenix Park in the north-west corresponding to the Bois de Boulogne, while the south-eastern location of the buildings of the legislature and seats of learning corresponded with the Chambre des Députés and the Quartier Latin. The Survey hoped that future plans would increase and enhance this resemblance, with a traffic centre like the Place de la Concorde, the national cathedral at the head of a principal thoroughfare, like the Madeleine, and the national theatre corresponding to the Opéra. Clearly, the authors of the Survey were at one with Abercrombie (1922) on such matters.

Housing was recognized by the Survey as a major cause for concern: 'Housing in Dublin today is more than a "question", and more than a "problem" – it is a tragedy!' (Civics Institute of Ireland, 1925, p. 58). Dublin's housing problem was seen as the result of the changing political, industrial and social conditions of the people over generations. Its solution, according to the Survey, lay in a combination of a limited amount of central housing together with suburban methods, the ultimate hope being to eliminate the former. New route connections in the tramway system could allow the adoption of a circular non-stop system, while the Survey foresaw the importance of motor bus services in the extensions to 'rising neighbourhoods'. An 'appropriate density' of 12 houses per acre (30 per ha) in the suburbs, with 20 per acre (50 per ha) in the city, was suggested. Not less than ten per cent of the gross housing area was to be reserved for open spaces and playgrounds. These were the standards promoted in Britain after World War I by Raymond Unwin and the Tudor Walters Report (1918), which had also been applied in the 1914 Dublin planning competition. The Survey drew attention to the report of the Medical Officer of Health for Hendon, Middlesex, who demonstrated that children aged six to eight years living in the Hampstead Garden Suburb were on average heavier and more than an inch taller than those living in other areas. The Survey thus called for the provision of open spaces to provide fresh air for the children, as well as to avoid the dangerous use of roads as play areas.

The Dublin Civic Survey suggested that no insanitary area which had been cleared should be built upon again, given the lack of open spaces in the city. However, it did discuss the possibility of tenement remodelling, which had been suggested by Geddes and Abercrombie, and recommended by the Dublin Corporation Housing Committee in 1917. It is noteworthy that a memorandum subjoined to the 1917 report by Councillor, by now President, Cosgrave, had set out a number of serious objections to remodelling. At the time of the Survey, a structurally sound house in Marlborough Street was being remodelled for the occupation of ten families with the approval of the Department of Local Government and Public Health at a cost of £800. It was argued that the minimum tenement provision should be not less than two rooms, with sufficient cooking and individual sanitary accommodation.

While the report echoed the oft-repeated refrain that the high cost of site acquisition was an impediment to housing development in central areas, it also argued against central housing for social reasons which relate to an idealized image of the nuclear family with clearly defined gender roles. It shunned 'the inevitable surroundings of the dwelling, the public-house and the street corner, and the paved thoroughfare as a playground for the children. Contrast these surroundings with those obtained in suburban areas, where the father has a little plot for gardening, the mother a space for drying clothes, and the children in the garden are immune from traffic dangers. The inexorable conclusion is that the first environment is a slum, the second a home' (Civics Institute of Ireland, 1925, p. 69). In addition, the Survey authors countered the familiar claim that workers should be housed close to their place of employment, by suggesting that factories would continue to be built in the suburbs where sites were cheap, so that in time the artisans would not necessarily be too far from their work.

In April 1926 a Census of Population was undertaken, the first in 15 years. Up-to-date and reasonably accurate figures relating to housing provision and population were now available. The census showed that population growth in Dublin had been slow since 1911, at less than four per cent, giving a total population in the County Borough (that is, Dublin Corporation) area of 316,693. However, it should be remembered that much of the development in Dublin took place beyond the city limits, including the remaining 'townships' of Rathmines and Pembroke (by now governed by UDCs) so that the figure was artificially low. The total area of the city as defined by the County Borough boundary was 8357 acres (c.3380 ha), with a total valuation of £1,178,800. By 1926, some 90 per cent of the City's population was Roman Catholic, compared to 83 per cent in 1911 and 82 per cent in 1901. Some 283,938 people were living in private households in 1926, and the following tables illustrate the type of accommodation available to them.

Table 6 Size of dwellings occupied by private families in Dublin, 1926.

Total persons living in dwellings of		% of total persons	Maximum Ward*	Minimum Ward
1 room	78,920	27.8	50.2	1.7
2 rooms	63,458	22.3	33.5	3.3
3 rooms	40,894	14.4	33.4	4.5
4 rooms	36,639	12.9	22.9	5.4
5 rooms	26,584	9.4	46.2	2.9
6 rooms	16,895	6.0	21.4	1.7
7+ rooms	20,548	7.2	39.1	2.0

*Per cent of total persons in the ward with the highest proportion in that classification.
(Census (1926), tables 9 and 10.)

Table 7 Housing density of private families in Dublin, 1926.

Persons in private families in dwellings having:	Persons	% Total	Max	Min
Less than 1 person per room	37,300	13.1	45.2	7.0
1 but less than 1½ persons per room	52,223	18.4	35.5	11.4
1½ but less than 2 persons per room	31,532	11.1	19.0	6.4
2 persons per room	31,352	11.1	15.3	4.0
More than 2 but less than 3 persons per room	25,860	9.1	17.4	3.4
3 but less than 4 persons per room	36,335	12.8	17.7	1.4
4 or more persons per room	66,454	23.4	38.2	1.1

In addition some 1 per cent (2,882) were not classified by housing density.
(Census (1926), tables 9 and 10.)

In Saorstát Éireann as a whole, the census showed that more of the population was living in three-roomed dwellings than in dwellings of any other size. The figures once again emphasized the problem of tenement dwellings in Dublin, and illustrated that one-room tenements remained all too common. Almost half of the population of Dublin was living in dwellings of only one or two rooms, while in some wards half the population lived in one-roomed dwellings. High housing densities continued to be prevalent. Over 23 per cent of the population lived at a density of four or more persons per room in 1926. Thus, despite slow population growth in the city, the housing problem had eased little. This was confirmed in 1927, when it was reported that there were 1826 third-class tenements in the city which had been condemned as unfit or unsafe and which would be demolished if alternative accommodation could be provided for the 9535 families occupying them.

Table 8 Number of families living in one-roomed
tenements in Dublin, 1927.

Total	18,932
Two person families	5,312
Three person families	4,224
Four or more persons	9,396

(Dáil Debates, 21, p. 365.)

By 1928, Alfie Byrne was asking for a larger number of smaller houses at reasonable rents to be built, along with the continuation of grants to private builders, utility societies and persons anxious to build their own houses. The Minister agreed that terms similar to the Housing Act 1925–6 would be arranged, but that special consideration would be given to the question of the smaller types of housing for letting at reasonable rents (Dáil Debates, 1928, 26, p. 16). In 1930 Robert Briscoe was asking what consideration was being made for families in single rooms who could neither purchase houses nor pay the rents demanded. The Minister responded by stating that the high costs of house production precluded the provision of houses on better terms. In November of that year, the Minister reported that proposals dealing with overcrowding and insanitary areas were under consideration. Reflecting the perceived Government procrastination on the issue, when it was finally announced that the new Housing Bill was to be introduced after Easter, Seán Lemass retorted 'Which Easter?' (Dáil Debates, 1930, 37, p. 425).

Meanwhile, throughout the 1920s, the case for town planning legislation was constantly being raised. The arguments made reference to the necessary rebuilding of devastated city areas, to the need for proper control of new housing developments, and the fact that such legislation was a necessary corollary of local government reorganization and municipal reform. Ireland's first comprehensive Town Planning Bill was introduced on 2 May 1929, but it was not until 1934 that the Town and Regional Planning Act finally came into force. Although the Act had considerable potential, the adoption of its measures by local authorities was slow (see Nowlan, 1989 for further discussion).

New municipal boundaries

By the 1920s, the rationalization and extension of the municipal boundary of Dublin Corporation had been under periodic discussion for 50 years or more (see Horner, 1985). The Municipal Boundaries Commission Report of 1881 had made far-sighted recommendations for the restructuring of local government in the interest of an expanding urban area, so that two authorities would have replaced the existing nine, allowing for the provision of centralized services and the co-ordination of future growth. However, the townships were fiercely independent, while local interests resisted any idea of comprehensive planning. From the mid-1920s, a growing preoccupation with the problems of expanding the built-up area was evident. The spoilation of the countryside by new housing, and the poor quality of many of the private suburbs, was a frequent cause of concern. The upsurge in building activity in Dublin had resulted in a rapid expansion of urban areas, and this haphazard growth was lamented in the influential *Irish Builder and Engineer* as well as by authorities such as J.F. McCabe (1925), Professor Butler (1927) and H.T. O'Rourke (1927). In 1924 the Government appointed a 12-member parliamentary committee, chaired by Professor William Magennis, to examine and report on local government reform in the Dublin area. The Report of the Greater Dublin Commission of Inquiry (1926) provided a badly needed official boost for the introduction of town planning. It recommended the creation of a 'Great Council' which would be responsible for a wide range of services throughout an enlarged city area, while under it two district councils would administer a limited range of local services including roads and refuse collection. As in the 1881 Report, one district council would have responsibility for an extended Corporation area including the remaining urban districts of Rathmines, Pembroke and Howth, while the second would cover the existing urban districts of Blackrock, Dún Laoghaire (formerly Kingstown), Dalkey, Killiney and adjacent rural areas. The Great Council area would cover 41,400 acres (c.16,700 ha), five times the area hitherto under the control of the Corporation.

Both Aston and Abercrombie had emphasized the need for a housing or planning authority with regional powers as the only means of avoiding piecemeal development. Only through such a co-ordinating body could the spirit of town planning resist the encroachments of mercenary interests. The 1924 Commission paid particular attention to the role of town planning in solving Dublin's problems, arguing that it 'does not aim at mere beautification; it aims at creating first a good city rather than an ornate city'. Like earlier advocates of town planning including Geddes and Abercrombie, it argued that the foresight involved would actually reduce the cost of civic development. Dr Oliver St John Gogarty also added a minority statement to the report which called for a grand town plan to impose order on the low-density housing extension which he desired.

However, the proposals were largely ignored under the Local Government (Dublin) Act, 1930. Although the Corporation area was extended so that, some 50 years after it was first proposed, Rathmines and Pembroke were finally incorporated into the City, the area enclosed by the city boundaries was much less than had been suggested, and did not include all of the contiguous built-up parts of County Dublin. Nor was there any reference to town planning in the legislation. Aston was among those to voice criticisms of the Greater Dublin Bill, suggesting that the failure to make provision for a Greater Dublin regional planning authority meant that 'Dublin is merely destined to change the character and the magnitude of the kind of irretrievable blunders which have marked the administration of recent years' (Artifex, 1930, pp 41–2).

We have seen that on the eve of its great suburban expansion, Dublin was a city of many contrasts. While there was considerable wealth evident among certain classes, the question of providing adequate accommodation for the poorer citizens was considered an urgent one, although those whose lives would be most dramatically affected by the new housing were rarely consulted for their views. Ideas about the nature and location of new housing provision were influenced by discussions of town planning, which was a notion which was now gaining greater acceptance. Other issues which helped to shape housing policy included the major political changes which were occurring in Ireland at this time. At the time of the foundation of the Irish Free State, Dublin Corporation was planning to embark on an ambitious project to provide quality housing for the masses. The means by which this goal was to be achieved will be discussed in the following chapters.

Building the City: the Corporation as developer

Introduction

In this chapter we will look at how Dublin Corporation undertook housing development during the years between 1913 and 1939. These dates provide a useful start- and end-point as each was marked by an inquiry in to the housing of the city's working classes. A key point that will emerge is that the line between public and private developments and public and private developers was more blurred than might be generally appreciated. Rather than the polar opposites of public developments and private developments, it is better to think of a continuum, a scale, between public and private along which individual developments lie; some more public than private, some more private than public. Not only was the line between types of development somewhat fuzzy but individual developers moved between public and private business as the opportunities presented themselves. This was the operation of 'public-private partnerships' long before the phrase was invented.

We will consider the whole development process, including the funding of local authority housing schemes, the sourcing of materials, labour used and ultimately the disposal of accommodation through either tenant purchase or rental schemes. Decisions as to the location and nature of accommodation to be provided are also discussed. We shall see that the city never quite made up its collective mind about the relative merits of providing suburban or city centre housing, though the prevailing view was that houses were innately superior to flats. While the bulk of Dublin Corporation's provision was newly built, there were some examples of refurbishment and conversion of existing buildings during this period. In addition, the local authority contributed to non-public housing provision in a number of ways. In particular, it was an important source of funding, under the Small Dwellings Acquisition Acts, for those wishing to purchase their own houses. This role sometimes conflicted with its responsibilities in direct provision of housing, due to the limited funding available to the Corporation.

The development continuum

The extent of City and State involvement in housing, aside from the obvious Corporation-erected flats and cottages, is generally uncelebrated. The tendency is to assume that 'public' housing is easily recognizable by its architectural style, location and upkeep. In fact, the notion of a clear distinction between the private market and public responsibility became increasingly blurred in the twentieth century, so that the concept of State intervention in housing cannot be seen as an entirely separate entity from private provision. Rather than considering a simple division between 'public' and 'private' housing, housing developments can be seen in terms of a broad continuum, from public housing in its 'purest' form, that designed and erected by the local authority, through various intermediate stages, to 'pure' speculative development, that is, the work of the private speculative builder with minimal outside interference.

As we have seen, it was increasingly recognized by the first decades of the twentieth century that, for a variety of reasons, the State had an obligation to provide adequate housing for its citizens:

> The provision of decent housing for the working classes is a public health obligation, and thus immediately concerns local authorities; it is a measure of social insurance against the consequences of subversive propaganda, and so immediately affects the State; it is a humanitarian duty, and so immediately concerns every citizen in the State.
>
> (Gerald J. Sherlock, City Manager and Town Clerk of
> Dublin, quoted in McGrath, 1932, p. 547)

Public intervention can take many forms, including direct provision of housing, financing of development through State housing banks, and the promotion of the private sector through financial subsidies or tax incentives (Pooley, 1992). In Dublin, while the Corporation erected a substantial number of dwellings in the 1920s and 1930s, public intervention in the private housing market had an even more significant impact on development. The Corporation acted as developer in many schemes which were then built either by public utility societies or by private speculative builders, while the State encouraged home ownership by providing subsidies for building and cheap loans for owner-occupiers.

The dual ideology of the single-family house (thought to promote stable family life) and home-ownership (believed to create responsible citizens and a stable society), was to the fore in the advancement of such policies, but did little to solve working-class housing problems, instead benefiting the skilled working class and middle classes. State provision of rented housing, an increasingly common feature in the 1930s, was generally seen as a transitional stage in the attainment of the 'goal' of home ownership. In all cases, the concept of State housing provision was clearly linked to the idea of social control, not only by easing the threat of revolution among the working-classes, but also by reassuring the 'moral majority' of middle-class voters who protested at the horrors of the slums.

The role of the Roman Catholic clergy in promoting this goal is difficult to pinpoint but was probably significant. The stated preference of Monsignor Michael Cronin was for the 'one house, one family' ideal. The clearance of tenements to be replaced by many small houses had resulted in extraordinary transformations with 'no more sickness and misery, physical or moral' (McGrath, 1932, p. 544). McGrath himself referred to the 'worker's little estate surrounding his castle … the more men you deprive of even the minimum of property represented by a garden and a really private entrance, the more you are weakening throughout the state that clinging to and respect for property that is the expression of man's desire for liberty' (McGrath, 1932, p. 271). The perceived importance of personal property was recognized by the Corporation, and even the consideration of the enclosure of that property was taken seriously. After consultation with the City Architect on the importance of front garden boundaries at the Drumcondra Scheme, the Housing Commissioner decided that a type of boundary, consisting of a spiked chain suspended from concrete posts, be given a trial in the houses on Walsh and Ferguson Roads. The remaining houses in Drumcondra were to be treated in the usual manner with 4-bar horizontal fencing, as originally provided for (Report 171/1928).

The Corporation influenced housing developments in the city in a number of ways. While we tend to think of the Corporation contribution in terms of its own purpose-built schemes of housing for the working classes, be they flats like Fatima Mansions or Oliver Bond House, or cottages like those at Marino, Cabra, Crumlin or Maryland, in fact there was much more to the Corporation's role than this. (The term 'cottage' was invariably used by the Corporation to refer to its two-storey houses.) Dublin Corporation was involved in different ways in the production of housing for various groups within the city. For example, it assisted the lower-middle classes who were seeking to purchase their own homes, through the mechanism of the Small Dwellings Acquisition Act. It assisted builders through a variety of means, including the provision of Corporation lands for private speculative building. Architects who worked on private developments were also involved in the preparation of Corporation schemes, as were master builders, thus increasing the level of cross-over between different types of building. Additionally, both Corporation and private speculator were generally calling on the same pool of labour.

The reasons for the broadening of the concept of local authority and State-aided housing provision in the 1920s are manifold, and may be related to social fears, political ambitions and financial considerations. Following political independence in 1922, the colonial State organization was replaced by a new conservatism, favouring the propertied, farming and middle classes. The 'conservative revolutionaries' forming the new government were almost exclusively drawn from the ranks of the middle class, and the housing policies of the 1920s are a reflection of their views, with an emphasis on the supply of good middle-class housing. The need to do better, and to be seen to do better, than their former British rulers spurred considerable intervention in the housing market. The Million Pound Grant announced in 1922 was made available to local authorities erecting housing under the Housing of the Working Classes Acts, but the Housing Acts of 1924 and 1925 focused on the provision of grants for owner-occupied, middle-class housing, rather than leaving the solution of the middle-class housing shortage, the result of years of political turmoil, in the hands of speculators. The 1924 Act made specific provision for housing grants for civil servants, such dwellings having a floor area between 1001 and 1500 square feet (*c.*93 to 140 m²), in addition to those for four- and five-roomed houses under 1000 square feet (*c.*93 m²). Thus Government policy in the 1920s promoted housing for the middle classes and it was not until the Housing (Miscellaneous Provisions) Act, 1931, that the emphasis changed back to that of slum clearance.

Of course, the provision of low-rental housing for the poorest members of the working class was an uneconomic, though virtuous, goal. In a city already burdened with considerable debt, facing a distinct lack of co-operation from the British authorities responsible for financing housing schemes, it is not surprising that Dublin Corporation began to provide more expensive suburban accommodation for better-off artizans after World War I. Even these schemes were not paying propositions, but they did accord with the belief that houses were superior to flats. Meanwhile, the housing continuum began to evolve as the Corporation became a developer in schemes which it did not itself build. The trend began at Marino, where sites along the main frontages of the scheme were leased to private interests for the erection of better class houses. Thus, the Corporation was to have a highly significant role along the continuum, becoming involved with other agencies concerned with housing provision, including the Irish Sailors' and Soldiers' Land Trust, public utility societies and some philanthropic bodies. It also developed closer links with private builders, who began to build houses on Corporation-developed land, while the joint-development of the Vernon Estate with private interests marked a completely new departure for the Corporation. Thus, while Dublin Corporation's output of housing seems relatively small, it must be recognized that, through its role as land-owner, developer, provider of grants and lending facilities, that body played a highly important and complex part in the evolution of Dublin's housing during the 1920s and 1930s.

The role of the State in influencing the number, type, style and location of housing was fundamentally important. Policies encouraged particular types of building or nature of tenure, as we shall see. In addition, there was a strong political element, especially in the early years of the Irish Free State. For example, in January 1924 it was announced that in the placing of Government contracts special regard would be had to the extent to which firms employed, or were prepared to employ, demobilized National Army soldiers. The State policies extended to types of building materials used, with priority being given to locally manufactured materials.

The need for State intervention in private building as well as in the direct provision of housing was recognized. In an article on the cost of housing in Dublin from March, 1923, the *Irish Builder and Engineer* stated 'we have little doubt that if the housing shortage is ever to be effectively met, the State will have to augment its own particular housing effort by helping the private builder by means of subsidies. The task of meeting the whole shortage by means of public schemes alone is too big' (24 March 1923, p. 218).

The cause for State intervention was of course something which arose frequently in Dáil debates, particularly given the fact that some builders were also politicians. A number of building contractors became members of the Oireachtas at various times. In December 1923, for example, the *Irish Builder and Engineer* paid tribute to Mr Thomas O'Mahony TD, a well-known building contract of Fermoy, who was considered to be 'a worthy and watchful representative in the Dáil … of all that pertains to the building trade' (15 December 1923, p. 971). Among the candidates in the 1923 General Election were Mr Batt O'Connor, Chairman of Pembroke UDC, a builder and Michael Collins' confidential constructor of secret hiding places in Dublin, Mr John Good, a well-known building contractor, and Mr W.J. Larkin who was a strong advocate of housing reform.

John Good is an interesting character in his own right. Born in Dublin in 1865 he had trained under Mr James Pile before going into business with his brother as Messrs J. & P. Good which, by 1922, ranked with the most influential contracting concerns in Ireland (according to the *Irish Builder and Engineer*). Good had constructed the aerodrome at Collinstown and demolished the dome of the destroyed Custom House. He was Honorary Secretary, Dublin Master Builders' Association from 1905–1911 and President of the Dublin Building Trades Employers' Association when that amalgamated with the former organization in 1918. He was a member and past chairman of Pembroke UDC, a council member of the RDS and had also acted as honorary secretary of the Dublin Chamber of Commerce. Finally, in 1922, Good became the Chairman of the National Federation of Building Trade Employers of Great Britain, the first Irishman to fill that role. Good's town residence, the Moorings, was designed by A.J.C. Millar, while he also had a residence in Greystones. From such a profile, one would expect the new TD, elected as representative of the Business Men's Party, to champion the interests of the builder in the Dáil. Yet, Good seems to have truly cared about the people he was elected to represent. He frequently argued in favour of housing for the poorest members of the working classes, rather than middle class and private housing subsidies.

Aside from political will, it is clear that decisions made by individuals, including individual speculative builders, could sometimes have a considerable impact on the nature of housing developments. A relatively small number of strong personalities were also highly influential through their writings, their work in the Civics Institute of Ireland and membership of other groups. Among these can be numbered E.A. Aston and the Reverend D.H. Hall. Yet, the people seeking accommodation seem to have had little or no influence on the type of housing which was provided for them. This holds true for the lower-middle classes as well as the working classes.

The changing strategies employed by the Dublin Corporation to deal with housing problems were greatly influenced by the State's attitudes and accompanying legislation. However, if we look further, we can see that the broad changes in policy were in line with general trends right across Europe. Across the continent, there was a movement towards regulation and State involvement in the housing market by the 1930s, illustrated in Pooley's 1992 text. This marked a radical change from the late-nineteenth century situation, when there was a relatively unregulated market of privately rented accommodation, with little effective intervention and a persisting assumption that housing demand from all sectors of society should be met by the private sector. Although the move towards increasing intervention was gradual, it has had a profound effect on both the spatial and social structure of cities across Western Europe.

How many dwellings?

As we have seen, by the time of the 1913 Housing Inquiry, Dublin Corporation had developed 1385 houses and flats, while there was still an estimated shortage of 14,000 dwellings in the city. Up to this time the Corporation had concentrated on small-scale housing schemes on cleared sites within the city, such as the popular cottages at St Joseph's Place, off Dorset Street, where housing densities were often more than 30 per acre (*c.*75 per ha) but which were nonetheless heavily in demand. However, despite considerable opposition from within the Corporation, it was gradually accepted that large-scale suburbanization of the working classes was the only means by which the housing problem could be adequately solved, and this policy was actively pursued from the 1920s.

As previously mentioned, the Housing (Ireland) Act of 1919 provided substantial subsidies for housing. However, unfavourable subsidy terms and strained relations between the British administration and local authorities impeded progress in house-building. By the time that the British government halted all housing work in Ireland in 1921, only 800 municipal houses had been built under the 1919 Act. The steady rise of prices resulted in the inability of slum-dwellers (who were the prospective tenants) to pay the level of rent necessary to avoid a heavy burden on the already high rates. Thus the period between the end of World War I and the foundation of the Free State was a time when housing schemes were planned, but could not be carried out.

Prior to April 1922, the Corporation had erected 2243 dwellings, just over half of which were cottages, and had acquired a further 1507 dwellings, 80 per cent of which were cottages. There was considerable delay before the Irish Free State confronted the problem of working-class housing seriously, with Government housing policy in the 1920s tending to favour the building of private middle-class houses. At this time, Dublin Corporation built schemes of over 400 cottages each for tenant purchase at Fairbrother's Fields, Marino, Drumcondra, Donnycarney and Cabra. No major slum clearance schemes were undertaken until after 1932, when there was a return to central flat building. In addition, large schemes of cottages for renting were developed, so that by 1939 the Corporation had developed 7420 cottages for rental, 4248 for tenant purchase, and over 3200 flats.

12 Layout plan of St Joseph's Place, off Dorset Street.
(Ordnance Survey 1:2500 plan, Sheet 18 VII, Dublin, 1939 revision.)

Between 1922 and the Housing Inquiry of 1939–43, 13,026 dwellings were completed by Dublin Corporation. Approximately five cottages had been built for every flat over this time period, although this average figure masks significant policy shifts over the years. Prior to March 1922, flats formed 36 per cent of the total dwellings erected by the Corporation and the township councils. From 1922 to 1932 flats formed only eight per cent of the dwellings erected by these bodies, a time when a large proportion of new development consisted of tenant-purchase cottages. Between March 1932 and March 1939,

22 per cent of the dwellings erected were flats. The rate of building had also increased. From 1887 to 1931, the Corporation had built 7246 dwellings, but within the next eight years, more than the same number of dwellings again had been erected. Thus, it was really only during the 1930s that suburban development was implemented on a large scale, with major projects at Crumlin to the south-west and Cabra to the north-west.

Table 9 Dwellings erected and acquired by Dublin Corporation to 31 March 1939.

Type	Numbers Erected	% Total Dwellings	Number of Rooms				
			1	2	3	4	5
Cottages for renting	8776	52.3	0	233	5389	3136	18
Cottages tenant purchase	4493	26.8	0	0.0	296	1941	2256
Cottages, Total	13269	79.1	0	233	5685	5077	2274
Flats for renting	3507	20.9	675	1414	1191	210	17
Total dwellings	16776	100	675	1647	6876	5287	2291
% of Total dwellings	100		4	9.8	41	31.5	13.7

(Housing Inquiry, 1939–43, Appendix 1, Table C, p. 232.)

Despite these efforts, it was clear that the housing need was not being met. In 1929 the Department of Local Government and Public Health carried out a survey which estimated that the total housing need for the country stood at 43,656 housing units (DLGPH, 1931). Of these, some 17,593 were required in the Dublin Corporation area, with a further requirement of 2124 from the neighbouring districts of Pembroke, Rathmines and Rathgar, Blackrock, Dun Laoghaire and Dalkey. Within the Dublin County Borough, the greatest need was for 7978 houses to replace unfit houses, while a further 5433 were needed to replace houses 'below a reasonable standard'. The remainder were required either to meet unsatisfied demand (3600) or to rehouse those displaced by slum clearance schemes (582).

The rate and scale of building was also a constant cause for concern. In 1936, Mr Norton TD asked for the number of houses completed by Dublin Corporation in each of the years 1930 to 1935 (see below). He commented that 'it might be well if the Parliamentary Secretary caused that reply to be circulated to some of the members of the Dublin Corporation, who avail of public functions in Dublin to declare that 2000 houses per annum are being built for the housing of the working classes. These figures might help to cure that unhealthy optimism' (Dáil Debates, 60, p. 1121).

Table 10 Dwellings completed by Dublin Corporation (including Pembroke and Rathmines Districts).

Year ended 31 March 1930	717
1931	223
1932	850
1933	251
1934	910
1935	1085

Thus both the number and rate of completions gave cause for concern. In order to understand the factors influencing both of these, it is necessary to consider the way in which Dublin Corporation undertook its building schemes.

Dublin Corporation's housing schemes: the builders

One of the important areas of overlap between public and private development was in the field of labour used on housing schemes. In the early 1920s, Dublin Corporation had a number of means at its disposal when it came to building housing schemes. Construction work was sometimes undertaken by the Municipal Workshops Department, whereby the local authority engaged its own staff as 'direct labour' on building programmes. Alternatively, private contractors could be invited to tender for the schemes, with the lowest tender generally being awarded the contract. Many of Dublin's important contractors were involved in both public and private house building, which was to prove significant in the building boom of the 1930s as we shall see. A third, less common method, was to involve building guilds in the tendering process.

The plans to which the builders worked became quite standardized over the time period in question. In the early 1920s a number of outside architects were employed, whereas the 1930s schemes were generally drawn up by the Corporation's own architects. Furthermore, in order to facilitate the preparation of schemes and promote certain minimum standards for houses eligible for Government grants, the Department of Local Government and Public Health provided outline specifications and detailed drawings which were made available to municipal authorities and their architects. This explains the references to 'B-type' cottages and various other plans (see chapter three).

Whatever the means used, it is clear that local authority housing schemes built around the country in the 1920s and 1930s had a twofold significance. Not only were they seen as measures to relieve appalling shortages of housing accommodation, but they had an added importance in terms of the employment which they provided both directly and indirectly. For example, the following outlines the number of workers to be employed on a hypothetical but arguably typical contract for 2000 dwellings in 1937:

Bricklayers	150
Carpenters	300
Plasterers	200
Plumbers	65
Slaters and Tilers	20
Labourers	1100
Total	1835

(Dáil Debates, 66, p. 7).

In addition to the labour which was involved directly on any housing scheme, there were numerous other parties indirectly employed. The sheer number of individuals involved in the development of any housing scheme was huge, particularly in a relatively unmechanized era. Very many specialists provided particular skills. For example, Messrs J. Gallagher and Son, the Liffey Ironworks, Liffey Street and Great Strand Street, supplied the iron entrance gates and railings for the 202 houses at Mount Brown in 1922. Irish materials had been used, as far as possible, in building these two-storey brick houses. The cut stone for the windows and door openings had been brought from the Dublin mountains in a rough state and worked on the job by Dublin stonecutters. Other suppliers to Fairbrother's Fields included the following: timber (W. & L. Crowe), rainwater and plumbing goods (C.P. Glorney), ridge tiles, hip tiles, Bangor slates, ranges (Brooks Thomas & Co.), stone (Mr E. Little), ironmongery (J.J. O'Hara), gates and railings (Messrs Smith & Pearson).

Although planned housing schemes were frequently praised for their employment provision prospects, labour shortages were a common cause for concern when attempts were made to increase the rate of housing output. One problem experienced during the 1920s was a general shortage of skilled building labour, a problem which was further exacerbated by the fact that working hours had been reduced from 50 hours per week in 1914 to 44 hours per week in 1924. Even in 1922, when very little building work was being undertaken in Dublin, it was extremely difficult to obtain enough labour, particularly in the plastering, bricklaying and carpentering trades. This persistent problem was linked to restricted entry to the trades, where the number of recruits was kept artificially low. While the larger firms of contractors were able to keep a staff of men constantly employed because they had a fairly constant run of big work, the smaller contractors found it almost impossible to get enough reliable workers to carry on and to develop. This meant that the small contractor was frequently debarred from tendering for large works, limiting the number of contractors who tendered for the Corporation schemes of the 1920s.

The lack of a steady supply of labour for Corporation schemes was a constant worry, especially in the 1930s. However, one problem which was never really tackled was that of conflict of interest. As advances under the SDAA increased, the shortage of skilled labour for Corporation schemes also increased. Clearly, the availability of cheap loans for house purchase under the SDAA provided a stimulus to speculative house building, by ensuring a ready market for those houses. Under this legislation, it was Dublin Corporation which was tasked with making these loans available. With a strong market in speculative housing, there was a greater demand on skilled labour to engage in the building of these houses. Inevitably, with more labourers tied up in the speculative arena, there would be fewer available to undertake work on behalf of Dublin Corporation. This point was made in the Citizens' Housing Council's Interim Report in 1937, while its 1938 Report provided the Trades Unions' estimate that 40 per cent of all available labour was currently engaged in speculative building which was State aided by means of housing subsidies. While the Corporation was encouraging middle-class speculative house production through the SDAA, it was also trying to undertake its own working-class housing schemes. All schemes, whether public, private or something in between, relied on the same pool of labour, however. Thus, ironically, legislation that intended to increase housing provision was counter-productive, since it ignored the reality of a finite supply of skilled labour.

Despite constant grumbles that a shortage of skilled tradesmen, especially plasterers, was restricting output, the reality was not necessarily that simple. In October 1937 a total of 3311 building workers were on the live register at the Dublin Employment Exchange, leading Mr Norton to comment 'So there is really no shortage of skilled operatives in the building trade' (Dáil Debates, 69, p. 2907). The issue of labour was an important one, since wages constituted approximately half of the building cost of any house. Therefore the relatively high rates of Dublin building industry wages were one of the factors which created a higher level of building costs than in Britain (Housing Inquiry, 1939–43).

Direct Labour and Building Guilds

From time to time during the 1920s and 1930s the shortage of building workers became a problem. This happened in the immediate aftermath of World War I, leading to proposals for alternative methods of building, experimental techniques and materials. At this time, the *Irish Builder and Engineer* carried a number of articles relating to experiments in Britain, such as the use of direct labour at Walsall in Stafford and building under the guild system. In 1921 Dublin Corporation decided to experiment with both of these methods rather than the more usual system of tendering for contractors to build housing schemes. It was Alderman Cosgrave TD who c.1920 initially suggested that the Dublin Building Operatives should be asked to build a limited number of houses at Fairbrother's Fields, in competition with a contractor (Report 24/1921). It was thought that the use of a guild of building workers might be a solution to the twin problems of wages and housing. Trades guilds had already been established in England and Scotland, where it was claimed that they could build better, cheaper, and more quickly than master builders. The Corporation's Housing Committee agreed to the experiment on the basis that it involved a comparatively small outlay, and that the system should at least be given a trial in Dublin. The onus would be on the workers to prove their capacity to undertake directly the carrying out of such schemes, and if successful it could be beneficially adopted on a much larger scale in future building operations. The conditions governing the carrying out of the work on the guild system were based on a modification of the Glasgow scheme. The Trades' Representatives were asked to submit terms for the erection of ten four-roomed houses and the construction of foundations for a further 11 four-roomed houses and four five-roomed houses. The actual cost of the completed work was ascertained by calculating the cost on a time and materials basis, plus five per cent on the same; and should the result show a saving on the agreed figure, the guild was to receive half of the saving. A clause was inserted in the agreement providing for the adjustment of the agreed estimate in the event of price fluctuations. Certainly, in March 1922 it was noted that a considerable saving was anticipated in respect of the 25 houses which the guild had at present in hands (Report 68/1922).

When additional houses were proposed for the Fairbrother's Fields Area in March 1922, it was decided to put the three methods of building employed by the Municipal Council to the test. Thus, 80 houses were to be erected by a private contractor, 58 by the Dublin Building Trade Guild, and 60 by the Municipal Workshops Department at a pro rata rate on the basis of the accepted tender for the 80 houses built by the contractor. This third option was described as 'direct labour', in that the workers were employed directly by the Corporation rather than a third party. Messrs H. & J. Martin were to erect the five-roomed houses in their area using brick construction, asbestos roof tiling, wood window sashes and frames, and Irish-made cast-iron rain-water goods. Construction was to begin as soon as possible, given the pressing need for housing coupled with the necessity for relieving unemployment.

However, not everyone was happy with the proposed experiment. In September 1922, a meeting of the Dublin Citizens' Association (Incorporated) expressed strong disapproval at the Corporation's eventual decision to give a contract for the building of 134 houses at Fairbrother's Fields to the Dublin Building Guild (70 houses) and the Municipal Workshops (64 houses) without specifically inviting tenders for this particular undertaking. This was in contravention of both Statute and bylaws which stipulated that such contracts had to be offered for public tender. Eventually, in February of 1923, 'because the Local Government Minister felt competitive tenders should be optioned for some of the houses', the original arrangement was changed. Some 54 of the houses (eight based on what was known as type B1, which had space for a bath in the scullery, and 46 of type D6 with space provided for future bathroom accommodation on the upper floor) were put out to tender, while the Guild was to build 46 houses and the Municipal Workshop, 34. The tender of J.L. Wild & Co. Ltd., at £34,669 18s. 9d. was accepted, despite some reservations that the company was unknown to the Dublin building trade.

The idea of the building guild seems to have met with opposition from other quarters too. In Cork, the Corporation failed to receive any tenders in June 1922 for housing on the Wycherley site, because the Cork Builders' Association felt that the Cork Building Guild was receiving preferential treatment.

Meanwhile, back in Dublin, by December 1923 a total of 58 houses had been completed by the Dublin Building Guild under contract in Fairbrother's Fields. It had been arranged that, should the cost of erection per house be less than the amount of the contract figure per house tendered by the contractors (Messrs H. & J. Martin Ltd.) for another section of dwellings in the same area, the saving effected should be divided equally between the Guild and the Corporation. The cost of the 58 houses in question was to be taken as the wages and cost of materials and a percentage on the sum of these two items, amounting to 7½ per cent, to cover overheads. The actual outlay, as certified by the City Architect, had amounted to £15,432 19s. 8d. for materials and £18,284 1s. 4d. for wages. Allowing the 7½ per cent for overhead charges (i.e. £2528 16s. 6d.) the total came to just over £36,245. The actual outlay on overhead charges (i.e. clerical services, stationery etc., deed of contract, fire insurance, employers' liability insurance, national health and unemployment insurance, depreciation of plant) was £1744 11s. 5d., so that the percentage charge was more than sufficient to cover these charges. Based on the other contract for a different section, the price of the 58 houses would be £36,483 13s. 6d., whereas the total cost calculated in agreement with the Guild had been £36,245 16s. 6d. The saving was divided equally between the Corporation and the Guild.

The Guild did not simply exist for the purpose of erecting houses. In December 1923 the Dublin Guild of Building Workers forwarded a 15-guinea cheque to the Dublin Technical Education Committee to be expended on prizes in connection with the Committee's building trades classes. However, following the completion of the Dublin Building Guild's contract for 58 houses (contract No. 3) on the Fairbrother's Fields area, no more references to the Building Guild were found in the Corporation Records. It seems surprising that such an apparently successful venture should have been abandoned, but the reasons may have been political rather than economic. Perhaps pressure was brought to bear by the ordinary contractors and master-builders, or even by the Roman Catholic Church, which evinced an almost paranoid fear of Communism at the time. One incident during Lent 1933, for example, illustrates contemporary feelings. Following Cardinal McRory's denunciation of Communists:

> On Monday, 27 March a mob of several hundred, singing 'God Bless Our Pope' and 'Hail Glorious St Patrick', attacked Connolly House (number 64 Strand Street) where a meeting was being held under the auspices of the Revolutionary Workers Group … In itself, the attack … was of no great significance, though it was indicative of a widespread obsession with the threat of communism. This was taboo, largely because it was atheistic …
>
> (Lincoln, 1992, p. 55)

Alternatively, the Dublin Building Guild may have metamorphosed into the Guild of Building Workers 1927 (Dublin and District) Ltd. when the Housing Acts of 1924 and particularly 1925 began to encourage co-operative societies. Certainly, in March 1924 President Cosgrave voiced his disapproval for building guild methods in an important speech to the Dublin Rotary Club: 'Building through Guilds, attractive at first, was not a practical proposition, said the President, and the facts and past experience, unfortunately, bear him out' (*Irish Builder and Engineer*, 8 March 1924, p. 169). Unfortunately, it has not been possible to discover to which facts and experience the President was referring in this speech.

In relation to the whole question of direct labour, the President's silence on the matter in the same 1924 speech was considered to be eloquent. In June 1923, Thomas Nagle, TD, had asked the Minister for Local Government whether his refusal to allow the town commissioners of Newcastle West to proceed with the building of houses by direct labour indicated a general objection to direct labour by local authorities for such work. The response from Ernest Blythe was in the affirmative, but no explanation was given as to this reluctance to proceed with direct labour. There had been a proposal early in 1923 to undertake a portion of the work at Marino by direct labour. This suggested that 75 per cent of the men required for the work would be Corporation employees, while the rest would be taken on by the Corporation and paid at the ordinary labourer's standard wages in the city. However, there is no evidence that this plan ever came to fruition, probably due to the wage costs which would have been incurred. In 1924, the *Irish Builder and Engineer* noted the negative experience of the Corporation of Dublin with direct labour, and the history of the Stanley Street Workshops. These Municipal Workshops had become notorious for the expense of their output, which seems to have been related to the extremely high wages being paid to Corporation employees in the early 1920s, which were well above the market rates. In 1923 the *Irish Builder and Engineer* outlined how the minimum wage for a labourer in the Corporation had gradually risen from 22s. per week in 1914, to meet the increased cost of living. Now, in April 1923, the casual labourer was earning 73s. per week, which was proving a heavy burden on the rates. Even after a reduction of 9s. per week was made, in 1924 the average minimum wage of unskilled labourers in Dublin Corporation was 64s. per week for 44 hours of work (*Irish Builder and Engineer*, 5 April 1924). By contrast, the average building labourer in the city at the time was earning 1s. 4d. per hour, that is, 58s. 8d. per week based on a 44-hour working week, which was still considered high in comparison with British cities.

The difficulty of uncompetitive wages in the Corporation extended to other items also. Of six tenders submitted to the Housing Committee for the electric wiring of 84 houses at Donnelly's Orchard, for example, the highest was that of Dublin Corporation's own Electricity Department. The reason given was that the Department's electricians were receiving 3½d. per hour over and above the current rate outside the Corporation (*Irish Builder and Engineer*, 29 December 1923). In this case the contract went to Messrs Roche & Magennis of Dublin. Ultimately in 1924 the Dublin City Commissioners decided to retain the Municipal Workshop at Stanley Street but to restrict the scope of its operations and to reduce the managerial staff.

The issue of building houses by direct labour was reconsidered during the 1939–43 Housing Inquiry, which suggested that the earlier experiments were hardly entitled to be called direct labour building, as the Corporation did not itself carry out the projects, instead employing a system whereby a contract was made between the Corporation and representatives of the trades. While a saving was secured in one of them, 'in the other the experience was such that the system was not again tried' (Housing Inquiry, 1939–43, p. 109, para. 307). It is not clear when or where this second experiment took place, or whether it refers to the second contract undertaken at Fairbrother's Fields. By contrast, a 1930s experiment at Ellenfield was operated directly through the Corporation through the medium of a works manager appointed by that body. Whereas the quality of the work was apparently equal to that of contract work, the time taken was longer, and in the final analysis the scheme was more costly than if it had been carried out by contract. The Inquiry concluded that another experiment under direct labour should be tried under improved conditions, 'now that cartels, syndicates and rings of various kinds are in many directions tending to bring the value of competitive tendering to an end, it would be unwise not to explore thoroughly the feasibility of an alternative method, if only to serve as a check and guide on the whole building system' (Housing Inquiry, 1939–43, p. 111, para. 316).

The role of private builders in public housing schemes
Private contractors were extremely significant in the building of Dublin's public housing schemes. The list of tenders for the erection of dwellings on the Boyne Street (First Section) area illustrates the large number of companies tendering for Corporation schemes in the early 1920s, representing as it does most of the major builders in Dublin at the time. The nineteen tenders received by 24 March 1922 included both large, well-known contractors

(Messrs H. & J. Martin, Messrs McLaughlin & Harvey, Messrs G. & T. Crampton) and fairly small-time operators including F. Manning and R. Gough. In 1925, Frank Manning was involved in the development of the Vernon Estate, building on Castle Avenue. In the 1930s he also built shops on Cabra Road, and on Garville Avenue. The latter location was close to his home at 70 Rathgar Road. Gough built houses on Botanic Avenue and Mannix Road in Drumcondra and was a member of the Dublin and District Housebuilders' Association. Other tenderers were Messrs Fitzgerald and Leonard, William Ferris, Messrs Alex Hull & Co., Mr L. Monks, Messrs Joseph Pemberton and Son, Messrs W. & A. Roberts, Messrs James Beckett Ltd., Messrs T. & R. Macken, Messrs J. & R. Thompson, Messrs W. & J. Bolger, Messrs J. & T. Pemberton, James Clarke, Messrs J. & W. Stewart, and Messrs S. H. Bolton & Sons. The architect was G. L. O'Connor. The first section of the scheme, containing three semi-detached, three-storey blocks, each with six dwellings was awarded to Messrs Fitzgerald and Leonard of Terenure Park, at a cost of £10,000.

Some contractors seem to have focused quite heavily on building for the local authorities. One such person was Mr Louis Monks, of Albert Road, Glenageary, who died suddenly in 1924 when he was still a comparatively young man. Monks had been the contractor at Mount Brown (McCaffrey Estate) which was completed in 1921. His obituary in the *Irish Builder and Engineer* noted that he had undertaken a very large amount of building work throughout the city and county, chiefly housing schemes for the various local authorities of the southern district of the county. Held in high esteem for his uprightness and probity in business, it was said of Monks that 'No contractor in the County of Dublin was better known and more genially liked than he' (15 November 1924, p. 985).

During the 1920s there seems to have been some debate about the awarding of contracts for various Corporation works. On occasion, the local authority invited tenders from specific companies, although as time went on it seems that open competition for tenders became the most common form of selection. Whereas the Municipal Workshops Department carried out much preparatory work in the early days (that is, road and sewer construction, foundations etc.), from 1923 a new policy was employed, whereby part of the road construction work in connection with the local authority's housing schemes was entrusted to contract. This was first applied at Donnelly's Orchard. In later Corporation schemes, contractors undertook all stages of the building work.

13 Two views of the Boyne Street development. (Photograph by R. McManus.)

14 Layout plan for Donnelly's Orchard, off Clonliffe Road.
(Ordnance Survey 1:2500 plan, Sheet 18 IV and VIII, Dublin, 1938 revision.)

It was not uncommon for tenders to be received from Britain for larger works. Six tenders received for the electric wiring of 84 houses in Donnelly's Orchard included two from the UK, from A. Burton of Liverpool and G. Morrison, Blackpool. In terms of the housing schemes themselves, Wild of London was involved in building at Fairbrother's Fields, while the Housing Corporation of Great Britain successfully tendered for the Donnycarney scheme (see chapter three). By and large, however, Irish contractors were favoured where practicable, in the same way that Irish materials were preferred.

During the 1930s the huge increase in Corporation housing construction placed that body in a weak position as regards tenders. By the time of the 1939–43 Housing Inquiry, there was a degree of unease about the use of contractors and the prices being charged to Dublin Corporation for work carried out. It was noted, for example, that the same type of house was costing the Corporation £50 more on one site than on another. When the Housing Architect, Mr Simms, was pressed to give an opinion as to the 16.7 per cent increase in costs between 1934 and 1938, which had initially been ascribed to 'sundry unenumerated factors', this item was explained by him as 'some other thing which we don't know' (Housing Inquiry 1939–43, p. 94, para. 258). The Housing Inquiry commented that, in view of the comprehensive nature of the other items listed, it was difficult to explain exactly what this item might cover. Simms, however, attributed the cause of the increase mainly to boom conditions and to the introduction of small contractors.

Although the Housing Inquiry was 'unable to find reliable evidence on which to base a statement that the contractors sought or secured exorbitant profits' (Housing Inquiry 1939–43, p. 94, para. 258), it seems that boom conditions enabled them to realize prices which would not have been secured in normal times or in an atmosphere of healthy competition. In the period from 1931 to 1938, just three contractors secured 82.7 per cent of the total number of dwellings given out to tender. Thus, effective competition for Corporation housing contracts was confined to three firms, at a time of boom conditions, resulting in an undue increase in the price of dwellings. Although these contractors are not named, it seems likely that Messrs Crampton, Messrs H. & J. Martin, and either Messrs Fearon or Messrs Kenny and Son were the top three builders.

One would imagine that the maintenance of such a large-scale housing programme between 1933 and 1938 would have allowed for new working techniques giving rise to economies of scale. However, the Corporation did not seem to benefit greatly from reduced costs during this period. Although allegations of a 'ring' to maintain prices to the Corporation were denied, and no evidence to the contrary was submitted to the Inquiry, the Housing Architect stated that in 1937 and at the start of 1938 in several cases only two tenders would be received for large contracts. In the same period, when the usual large contractors had obtained sufficient work to keep them going, smaller and newer contractors began to compete for contracts. 'As there were plenty of contracts on offer it only became a case of waiting long enough to obtain an acceptance of one of the various offers at a price suitable to themselves' (Housing Inquiry 1939–43, p. 94, para. 260). The Chief Quantity Surveyor stated that, following the 1937 building strike, the point of super-saturation had been reached, thus explaining the lack of tenders received as a function of the limit to what one contractor could undertake.

Building materials in Corporation schemes

The sourcing and availability of building materials was important to the success of Dublin Corporation's building activities. The Corporation relied on private enterprise for supplies of building materials, with some interesting consequences. Political considerations had a significant impact on both these factors, as Government protectionist policies forced up costs through monopoly conditions, while local interests 'encouraged' reliance on particular manufacturers.

After the 1913 Housing Inquiry, as we saw previously, building operations in Dublin were practically halted by a World War and national strife. Thus, between 1914 and 1920, house prices more than doubled (Meghen, 1963). The city's new housing programme, together with repair and improvement work of other kinds which had been postponed due to war conditions, and central reconstruction, caused an enormous demand for labour and materials. Prices inevitably rose for the key house-building materials (that is, timber, cement, steel and bricks). Meanwhile, in the June Quarter, 1921, the Dublin Corporation Housing Committee received a letter from the Department of Labour, Dáil Eireann, urging that no English materials be used in the building of any Corporation houses (Report 21/1922). This policy was a further complication, at a time when resources for housing were scarce.

It was not simply a Government decision that led to the use of Irish materials wherever possible, as there was strong pressure from other sources also. In August 1923, following complaints at the Irish Labour Party and Trades Union Congress concerning Government attitudes to housing, the Free State Government Publicity Department countered with a statement that 'no effort has been spared to secure the use of Irish materials where practicable in connection with the 71 current housing schemes' (*Irish Builder and Engineer*, 25 August 1923, p. 643).

However, the unnaturally high prices could not last, a fact which was recognized by the Minister for Local Government when the tenders for the two sections of the Marino Scheme were under consideration. The lowest tender was that of Mr John Kenny, Harcourt Road, at £645 per house for Section I, the first proposed tranche of housing, and £634 per house for Section II, or alternatively £640 per house for the entire scheme. The Minister proposed some alterations to reduce the cost per house (to under £589). More importantly, he 'expressed the opinion that it was not reasonably possible to provide more than 200 houses (approximately) within 1 year'. Therefore, it

15 Early layout plan for Fairbrother's Fields in the City Archive. The lower image shows the completed development. (Ordnance Survey 1:2500 plan, Sheet 18 IX and XV, Dublin, 1938 revision.)

16 Advertisement for building materials.

was inadvisable, in a falling market, to contract for a greater number of houses at the prices at present prevailing' (Report 267/1923, p. 438). The Minister's opinion was proven to be justified when Section II of the scheme was put out to tender a second time and Kenny's revised tender was accepted in June, 1924 at an average cost per house of just £565, as against £589 in the contract for the first section.

Where possible, the Corporation used local building materials, particularly bricks, the price of which was locally controlled. Thus, when Mr Alexander Strain (see chapter six) wrote to Dublin Corporation in October 1919, intimating that he had made arrangements for the manufacture of bricks at Inchicore and would probably be able to turn out from 80,000 to 120,000 per week, the move was welcomed by the City Architect (Report 110/1920). The latter stated that the cost of bricks was unnaturally high at the present time and some healthy competition would result in a price reduction. In addition, he noted that it would be of great advantage to have this source of supply when the work at Fairbrother's Fields began. In 1922 the Corporation accepted the Dublin Brick Company's tender for the supply of bricks at £5 per thousand, less a 3s. per thousand discount. By the June Quarter, 1923, the Dublin Brick Co. had further reduced the contract price of bricks from 90s. less 2½ per cent to 85s. less 2½ per cent per thousand. However, for bricks delivered to the Marino site an additional 2s. per thousand was charged to cover the extra cost of cartage (Report 149/1922).

Slates were also available in Ireland, and by mid-1923 it was reported that the Killaloe Slate Quarry (Nenagh) and Benduff Slate Quarry (Leap, Co. Cork) were busy day and night producing slate for various housing schemes, their produce having been specially approved by the Housing Department of the Ministry for Local Government. Heretofore, it was estimated that £100,000 left Ireland annually in payment for imports of such slates (*Irish Builder and Engineer*, 22 August 1923). Unusually, in October 1923 a deputation from Dublin Corporation, including the City Architect, O'Rourke, Senator Farren and Mr John J. Murphy, the Chair of the Housing Committee, visited the slate quarry at Killaloe.

The year 1923 saw a series of allegations about price-fixing among the builders and builders' suppliers of the city, leading to the publication of letters in the *Irish Builder and Engineer* on the 19 May, 1923, denying the existence of a timber ring (from the Irish Timber Importers' Association), a cement ring (from the Dublin Cement Importers' Association) and a general building ring (from the Dublin Building Trades Employers' Association). In its lead article, the journal noted that even before 1914, but especially since the declaration of peace in November 1918, there was a widespread belief that 'rings' or 'combines' existed to control prices and co-operated to keep them at a high level. The table below shows how building costs in Dublin remained above the London rates in mid-1924.

Table 11 Building costs in London and Dublin in 1924 compared.

Present Rates (1924)	*London*	*Dublin*
Tradesmen's wages (hourly rate)	1s. 7d. to 1s. 8d.	1s. 9½d. to 1s. 10½d.
Labourer's wages (hourly rate)	1s. 3d.	1s. 4d.
Stock bricks/thousand	£3 19s.	£4 5s.
Portland cement/ton	£2 19s.	£3 1s. 6d.

(*Irish Builder and Engineer*, 17 May 1924.)

In the emerging years of the new State, the importance of using native materials was psychological as well as economic. At Fairbrother's Fields, under construction in 1922, it was considered that although wooden sashes and frames would be more costly and less durable than steel alternatives, as would

Irish rain-water goods, 'the necessity for greater employment in the home trades at the present juncture outweighs the considerations mentioned, and justifies us in recommending the home manufactured articles, which will mean an expenditure of about £5,000 in Dublin in respect of these two articles alone' (Report 68/1922, p. 414). At Marino, too, Irish materials were to be used wherever obtainable at a reasonable price. However, the use of home produced goods could not always be justified, so that when the quality and delivery of Benduff (Co. Cork) slates proved unsatisfactory, Welsh (not English!) slates were used at the scheme. Problems also arose because the only two cement factories in Ireland in the early 1920s, at Magheramorne in the North and Drinagh Works, Co. Wexford, were owned by the Great British Cement Combine, which fixed prices in London. As concrete construction became more popular in the 1930s, the skilled craftspeople in stone and brick were often left unemployed, a matter which was raised in the Dáil in 1933 (Dáil Debates, 46, p. 1051). In 1935, Mr Seán T. O'Kelly, Minister for Local Government and Public Health and Vice-President of the Executive Council of the Free State, stated his preference for brick and stone construction rather than the concrete blocks and mass concrete which had largely been used in the house-building schemes financed by the Government in the previous decade. However, the preference for concrete was largely economic rather than aesthetic, a fact which O'Kelly himself recognized (Dáil Debates, 46, p. 1051).

Incidentally, the preference for Irish materials was not an exclusively post-Independence phenomenon. As early as 1905, the material used in the construction of the houses at the Corporation's Mooney's Lane scheme in Clontarf was 'Irish as far as possible' (*Irish Builder and Engineer*, 11 March 1905, p. 170). However, the bias became institutionalized from the mid-1920s. In a 1928 report, the Department of Local Government and Public Health noted that 'the use of Irish materials, where consistent with efficiency and economy, has been commended and encouraged as much as possible' (DLGPH, 1928, p. 96). Outline specifications issued by that Department for the guidance of those providing houses under the Housing Acts from 1929 onwards carried a proviso that all materials, where possible and practicable, were to be of Irish manufacture or origin. Government policy continued to favour the use of Irish manufactured products in the 1930s, when the payment of grants under the Housing Acts became conditional on the use of Free State materials as far as possible, while an annual 'Home Products Week' was promoted through the newspapers, encouraging the use of Irish goods and providing lists of appropriate suppliers. In 1936 it was reported that Irish

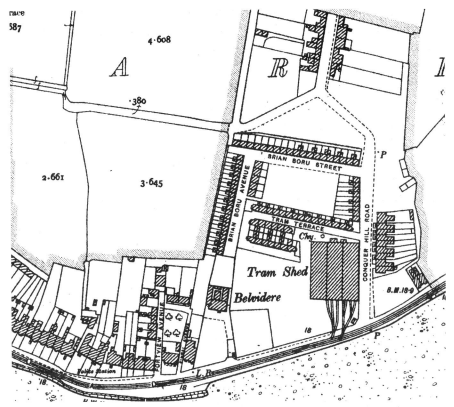

17 Plan of Mooney's Lane, Conquer Hill, Clontarf.
(Ordnance Survey 1:2500 plan, Sheet 19 V, Dublin, 1910 revision.)

housebuilders were now using 53 per cent Saorstát (Free State) materials (*Irish Times*, 14 March 1936). One side effect of this promotion was a difficulty in fulfilling orders, such that it became impossible to get supplies of Irish roofing materials. However, in response to a Dáil question on the subject, Minister O'Kelly stated that 'I am anxious to have every available article of Saorstát manufacture used up first before I give anybody facilities to use foreign manufactured articles' (Dáil Debates, 46, p. 1645).

As the rate of building increased in the 1930s, Dublin Corporation had difficulties maintaining its building programme due to a serious shortage of materials such as bricks, tiles, slates, concrete pipes, rain water goods and timber. The problems caused were so grave that 'unless a remedy be found, a perceptibly increased building programme will become a practical impossibility for the Corporation' (Report 16/1934, p. 127). The 1939–43 Housing Inquiry noted that the Glasgow Corporation had sought sanction to establish a factory for the manufacture of reinforced concrete floor, wall and roof slabs, with an annual output sufficient to build 2000 houses. Perhaps if the Corporation had been in a position to control supplies and costs of building materials, its housing programme could have been more productive.

The price of materials was affected by the existence of tariffs and quotas, in addition to restrictions in favour of home-produced materials. Although the tariffs were imposed for industrial protection, acting as import barriers and as part of the machinery of the 'Economic War' with Britain, in fact many of them were prohibitive. In some cases the price level of the native article was higher than that of the imported materials. Occasionally tariffs resulted in the substitution of a different material with no increased cost, or even a reduced cost. This was the case when a tariff on slates caused the use of concrete tiles, for example. However, the Citizens' Housing Council (1938, p. 46) found that 'in many cases costs in Dublin are considerably above world prices. The reason for this is to a large extent due to the effort that is being made to foster local industries'. Despite these drawbacks, however, Government economic policy was generally applauded. During 'Home Products Week' in 1935, the *Irish Times* published an article entitled 'Bright Prospects for the Building Industry' in which it stated that the Government, by its double-edged tariff and quota policies, ensured that home manufacturers would find a market for their output, and 'that the bulk of the capital employed in these new industries shall be Irish owned, and the employment, as far as is humanly possible, confined to Irish people' (*Irish Times*, 14 March 1935).

Certain materials such as timber and steel were imported and therefore the prices were beyond national control. In 1931, following global economic collapse, wholesale commodity prices touched their lowest point, but from then until 1937 a more or less steady improvement was experienced, with a consequent general rise in prices. From 1937, as programmes for re-armament began, the enormous consumption of construction materials preliminary to arms production coincided with a great expansion in house-building and ship-building, causing a rapid rise in materials prices (Jackson, 1973). These British price trends were reflected in Dublin, except with regard to cement, which, prior to 1937 was exceptionally cheap compared with Britain. On 15 April 1937, the 'Home Builders' page of the *Irish Times* referred to the rapid rise in the cost of all building materials that year, varying from 30 to 50 per cent. Builders were quick to cash in on the change, with advertisements warning potential purchasers 'Building costs are increasing, be wise, purchase now!' (*Irish Times*, 6 March 1937). The effects of 'The Emergency' (World War II) were felt relatively soon in the building trades, as in Crumlin North, for example, where Messrs Fearon were obliged to use steel window frames, due to the scarcity of red deal timber (Report 49/1939).

Funding housing schemes

The provision of proper housing accommodation in Dublin – the Capital City – is a national problem of first importance.

(Dublin Corporation Housing Committee in a call for increased State aid for housing, Report 28/1934, p. 173)

In the first chapter we saw that the Local Government Board oversaw the funding of Corporation schemes until the 1920s, and that the difficult relationship between the two bodies had retarded housing development. With the foundation of the new State came new funding mechanisms, which had a further impact on the nature and scale of housing development in Dublin. The legislation under which local authorities such as the Dublin Corporation operated had survived, with amendments, from the 1890s, as the Housing of the Working Classes (Ireland) Acts.

When the new Free State Government came to power in 1922, it was faced with an overwhelming housing problem. The housing programme was thus begun with an unusual scheme, commonly known as the 'Million Pound Grant', whereby the State made a capital grant of £1,000,000 available to local authorities towards the provision of houses under existing legislation, the Housing of the Working Classes Acts. The local authorities were required to raise a capital sum by striking a special housing rate of 1s. in the £ for one year, and to raise loans equal to three times the produce of the special rate. Under this scheme Dublin, including the townships of Pembroke and Rathmines, provided 1168 dwellings and received £561,910 of the Government grant, an average contribution of £483 per house.

In order to understand how the Million Pound Grant affected specific schemes at the time, two 1923 reports discussing the proposed funding of housing schemes at Marino and Drumcondra can be examined (Report 14/1923, Report 106/1923). In both cases, monies were raised using the same proportions of grant/loan/rate. Two-thirds of the funding for the Marino scheme was to come from a Government grant, with the remaining third divided in the proportions of three parts loan and one part rates. Following the same proportions, the all-in cost of £900,000 for the Drumcondra scheme was raised as follows: £600,000 grant; £225,000 loan; and £75,000 rates. Thus, in addition to availing of State grants for each scheme, the Corporation had to raise its own funding by means of a loan and an increase in the rate payable by all property owners in the city.

With the regularization of conditions in the Free State, attention was turned to new Irish legislation to deal with the housing crisis. Thus in 1924 the first of a series of Housing Acts was passed which aimed to ease the housing situation using both public and private means. Provision of financial aid for local authority housing was provided under the Housing (Building Facilities) (Amendment) Act, 1924, where the State grants available to private persons under the 1924 Housing Act were extended to local authorities operating under the Housing of the Working Classes (Ireland) Acts. In effect, private builders and the local authority were operating under similar financial regimes and according to the same standard specifications.

In 1929, the Government requested a survey of all urban areas providing details of the housing need. The returns showed a serious problem, and the need for a renewed attack on the slums, which resulted in a change of policy under the Housing Acts of 1931 and 1932. The 1931 Housing Act was intended to facilitate procedure and provide improved terms of financial assistance for slum clearance schemes. The 1931 Act made important changes allowing for the speedier clearance of unhealthy areas, with the use of a Compulsory Purchase Order system and changes to the basis on which compensation was paid (now compensation for property in an unhealthy area was calculated as the site value less the cost of clearing and levelling the site). Although directed primarily at slum clearance, the Act also amended the Small Dwellings Acquisition Act (SDAA) so as to revive private building.

Most of the dwellings built by Dublin Corporation under the 1920s housing grants had been allotted to tenant purchasers, so that it was not until the introduction of the 1931 Housing Act that a direct effort was made to provide for the housing of the poorer classes on a scale commensurate with their needs. The local authorities were no longer assisted through a single capital grant for each house, but by way of contributions towards the annual loan charges incurred in connection with the provision of houses under the Housing of the Working Classes Acts. The State contribution under the 1932 Act was of two kinds. The 'major subsidy', a sum not exceeding two-thirds of the annual loan charges, applied to slum clearance/rehousing schemes, while a minor subsidy, applying to 'normal' housing schemes (that is, houses provided other than for rehousing persons displaced by local authority operations) consisted of a sum not exceeding one-third of the annual loan charges. By 31 March 1939, the Corporation had provided 7611 dwellings in respect of which annual contributions under the 1932 Act were available. The proportion of the capital repayment for which the State assumed responsibility amounted to £1,410,462 (Housing Inquiry, 1939–43, p. 207).

It is important to note that limits were made to the all-in cost of houses on which contributions would be paid (under the Housing (Loan Charges Contributions) Regulations, 1932), so as to secure strict economy on the part of local authorities. The all-in cost per dwelling was not to exceed £500 per dwelling in a block of flats, while £400 per house (all-in) was allowed for the rehousing of persons displaced by slum clearance, and £450 for any other houses provided by Dublin Corporation. The regulations also provided that the dwellings were to be let at rents approved by the Minister. Unfortunately, such well-intentioned guidelines led to the provision of much poorer dwellings than had been erected in the 1920s, with a general trend towards fewer, and smaller, rooms. Thus, Government legislation was instrumental in the changing housing policy of the Corporation in the early 1930s.

The raising of large capital sums became a persistent problem in the 1930s. The debt of the City of Dublin in 1934 was over £6 million, while the 1934 Housing Programme, combined with ongoing commitments including the Small Dwellings Acquisition Acts, required the raising of almost £2.8 million over the next two years (Report 16/1934). By the end of March, 1937, the total capital indebtedness of Dublin city had reached £8.9 million, of which £5.6 million represented the housing debt (Report 6/1938). The increasing debt was partly due to the turn towards slum clearance and central flat building in the 1930s. Whereas the majority of schemes in the 1920s had been for tenant purchase, and tended to favour the better-off artizans, the new rental schemes aimed to help the poorest members of the community. Since it was not feasible to require these tenants to pay full economic rents, the Corporation was shouldering an increasing pro-portion of the housing cost. Until early 1937, when there was an increase in housing costs, the economic rent of a three-room flat had been 16s. 5d. per week, of which the Corporation tenant paid just 6s. The economic rent of a three-room cottage was 13s. 3d., while the tenant paid a rent of 7s. 6d. Under the altered cost conditions, the economic rents were now 23s. for flats and 17s. 9d. for cottages, but it was not practicable to charge higher rents, nor was it possible for local rates, already among the highest in Britain and Ireland, to bear the deficits.

Thus, during the 1930s, Dublin Corporation came to bear an increasing proportion of the burden of the housing debt. Up to 31 March 1939, the

Corporation's total capital expenditure on housing schemes was £8,776,979 (excluding expenditure on repairs, maintenance and advances or expenses in connection with the SDAA, discussed below). The money was acquired by mortgage loans, stock issues (*c*.68 per cent of the capital), Government contributions and revenue transfers. However, the Corporation could not continue in this fashion indefinitely, and the Housing Inquiry of 1939–43 suggested that drastic policy changes would be necessary to ensure satisfactory financial, social, and economic results of future housing schemes. New policies would have to cope with the housing problem without further impoverishing Dublin.

The Small Dwellings Acquisition Act (SDAA)

The Small Dwellings Acquisition Act has been mentioned above and the time has come to look at it in more detail. It was an important piece of legislation, designed to help people obtain cheap mortgages, but which came to be an albatross around the neck of the Corporation. Together with the need to find money to pay for its own housing schemes, during this period Dublin Corporation also provided funding for people buying their homes on the private market; yet another link between the local authority and private building operations. The Small Dwellings Acquisition Act (SDAA) was a piece of British legislation which remained in operation throughout the first half of the twentieth century. The original Act was passed in 1899, but was updated in 1919. The SDAA empowered local authorities to provide cheap mortgages to people purchasing houses below a certain market value, which was periodically changed. The idea was that the authority could advance up to 90 per cent of the value of a house, enabling people to acquire the ownership of small houses in which they either lived already or in which they intended to reside. For this purpose, the local authority could borrow money from the Board of Public Works, or in the open market, with the sanction of the Ministry of Local Government and Public Health. Loans were to be granted in various periods of years not exceeding 50 at a rate of interest fixed by Order made from time to time by the Minister for Local Government, with the approval of the Minister for Finance. The original purpose of the 1899 Act had been to extend the type of house purchase facilities already available in rural areas under the Land Acts to urban areas (Aalen, 1992d). However, it seems that these facilities were 'availed of by the middle classes to a considerable extent in Dublin, at a time when the operations of the speculative builder were widespread, and the cost of building low' (Civics

Institute of Ireland, 1925, p. 63). In effect, the SDAA was one of the means by which the Government promoted the goal of home-ownership. This was made clear by the amendment to the Act in 1932 which enabled the local authorities to advance loans to people intending to build houses, as well as for the purchase of existing houses, which had been its main use prior to that date. In any case, the operation of the SDAA in Dublin resulted in a significant drain on the Corporation's finances.

As an increasing number of applications were made under the Small Dwellings Acquisition Acts in the late 1920s and 1930s, the strain on Dublin Corporation's finances increased. During the period from September 1932 to 31 March 1934, for example, 632 advances were made by the Corporation, amounting to £366,633 (Report 21/1934). The Corporation had to borrow the money which it would lend under the Acts, and in June 1932, application was made to the Minister for Local Government and Public Health for sanction to the borrowing of a sum of £250,000 for the purposes of making advances to borrowers under the provisions of the SDAA. A further half a million pounds was required in two separate requests during 1933, but such was the demand that by September 1933, practically the entire £250,000 borrowed in the previous month had been applied for by persons wishing to obtain loans under the SDAA. 'It will be necessary for the City Council to authorize further borrowing if the operations of the Corporation under the Acts are to be continued, as applications on a large scale for house-purchasers continue to be received in the Finance and General Purposes Section' (Report 51/1933, p. 286). Between September 1932 and mid-1937, funds amounting in aggregate to £1,145,384 had been provided for financing operations under the SDAA, enabling the purchase of houses of not greater than £700 in market value (Report 33/1937). The requirement for the Corporation to cater for middle-class home owners under this legislation interfered with its ability to provide for the working classes, as borrowing for the Small Dwellings Acquisition Act (SDAA) became a persistent tax on the local authority's resources.

The location debate: city vs. suburbs

The establishment of small colonies like Mooney's Lane is the best method of combating our high death rate and arresting the ravages of consumption and other diseases, in the engendering and spread of which the squalid tenements of Dublin are a potent factor.

(*Irish Builder and Engineer*, 11 March 1905, p. 170)

The very earliest housing schemes completed by Dublin Corporation were located in the heart of the city, at Benburb Street and Bow Lane. Both were built on land which was part of the city estate, that is, land which belonged to Dublin Corporation. In other cases, the Corporation acquired building land in central areas in the slum clearance process. There was strong and persistent opposition to the suburbanization of the working-class population of Irish cities in the early-twentieth century. This was partly due to the recognition that many low-income workers needed to live near their workplace, especially given the absence of cheap working-men's tram fares. Suburban housing schemes also involved an unprecedented scale of development, sometimes requiring land acquisitions outside the municipal boundary. Many of the workers themselves resisted moving from their homes and communities. In spite of this, as early 1903, a strategy of suburban housing related to the tramway system was proposed, and this view was promoted by the *Irish Builder and Engineer*, which emphasized the importance of healthy air in avoiding the spread of disease.

As we have seen, much of the evidence to the 1913 Housing Inquiry strongly favoured suburbanization of the working-classes, and the final report included a map indicating the large tracts of land available for development in Drumcondra, Glasnevin, Clontarf, Cabra, Inchicore, Dolphin's Barn and Ballyfermot. The expert opinion of Geddes and Unwin, presented in their 1914 joint report, reinforced this line of reasoning, although the response of many senior Corporation officials to planned suburbanization remained negative.

Despite the critical attitude adopted by many officials, the tide gradually turned in favour of suburbanization. Professional and propagandist bodies including the Royal Institute of the Architects of Ireland (RIAI) and the Civics Institute of Ireland called for a new response to housing problems, while the Dublin Town Planning Competition and the Civic Survey placed a great deal of emphasis on the planned suburbanization of city centre residents. The Corporation put many of the ideals of Unwin's garden suburb into practice, initially by a token redesign of the Fairbrother's Fields Scheme, and more fully at Marino, and generally followed the standards which he had promoted in the Report of the Tudor Walters Committee (we will turn to this report later). The Chief Engineer of the Local Government Board, P.C. Cowan, recommended in 1918 that 12,000 of the 16,500 new houses required should be built in Clontarf, Drumcondra, Cabra and Crumlin, all greenfield suburban sites.

However, the official view was not constant at this time, since in the same year, the 1918 North City Survey (Report 13/1918) saw tenement refurbishment as the first line of attack in the 'housing war', followed by central housing at 25 houses to the acre (c.62 houses per ha). Suburban building came a poor third, as it was somewhat grudgingly accepted that the remaining 8100 dwellings needed by north-side residents would have to be built on virgin sites, at a density of 20 houses to the acre (c.50 houses per ha), due to lack of available central sites. Many Councillors continued to prefer an infill approach to the housing problem. W.T. Cosgrave argued the importance of providing dwellings near people's workplace, and pointed out that most applicants preferred cottages in city areas to houses in a suburban location. Ironically, it was under his Government that planned suburbanization was to become the dominant housing approach in Dublin. Among the common arguments against suburban developments were the claims that people would not be willing to move out to them, and that they could not afford the transport costs involved. The proposed location of the suburban sites was questioned, and it was wondered what would be done with the slum sites. It was also argued that a policy of suburbanization neglected the poorest and worst-housed classes.

However, one strong argument against rebuilding in central areas was the high cost of land acquisition. Between 1886 and 1912, for example, a total of 18 acres (c.7 ha) of slums had been acquired by the Corporation at an average cost of £6160 per acre (c.£15,400 per ha). By contrast, open land at Inchicore had cost £320 per acre (c.£800 per ha) in 1903, while the 22 acre (c.9 ha) Fairbrother's Fields site had cost £717 per acre (c.£1790 per ha) in 1914. Within a radius of three miles (c. five kms) from the centre of Dublin, there were 18,000 acres (c.7300 ha) of open land which could be used for building purposes (Housing Inquiry, 1914).

Despite continued debate, the standard Corporation terraced house, often on a cleared site, was to remain the acceptable norm with most politicians until around 1920. From this time on, the lack of availability of land in the central area forced the issue of suburbanization to be addressed, often somewhat reluctantly. In the case of Marino, for example, the site was under discussion for nearly ten years before the first Corporation plans for its development were prepared. However, once the Corporation's Housing Committee accepted the inevitability of suburbanization as the major approach to the housing question, solutions by means of infill development were not seriously considered again until the 1930s. By 1922 the Committee was suggesting 'that the best policy would be to undertake schemes on the north and south sides of the City in preference to small schemes here and there throughout the City' (Report 162/1922, p. 95). Later that year the preference for a suburban approach was further emphasized in the recommendation that any housing scheme under-taken (within the next four or five years) should be carried out on virgin soil (Report 309/1922).

As a result, throughout the 1920s the erection of five-roomed tenant purchase suburban cottages was the most common form of Corporation housing provision. The schemes developed at this time include Donnelly's Orchard (figure 14), Fairbrother's Fields (figure 15), Marino/Croydon Park, Emmet Road, and Drumcondra. Flat schemes were rare, the only examples being Ormond Market, Boyne Street and Kehoe Square, which also included some houses for rental. The erection of houses in the suburbs, where land costs were lower, encouraged the development of lower density layouts on the lines advocated by the British Tudor Walters Report as discussed in chapter three. High densities were associated with the slums, and one of the most potent arguments of the pro-suburban lobby was that, by erecting new houses in central areas the old slums were merely being replaced by new ones (see McKenna, 1919).

As late as 1928, when the Commissioner responsible for the Housing Section reported that all the building land in the possession of the Corporation for housing purposes would soon have been utilized, he recommended the compulsory acquisition of three areas, two of which were suburban, with a view to the formulation of a housing programme for 1929 (Report 189/1928). The proposed sites for compulsory acquisition were at Marrowbone Lane (11 acres; c.4.5 ha), Cabra (46 acres; c.19 ha) and Donnycarney (31 acres; c.13 ha). Clearly, then, towards the end of the 1920s, the Corporation continued to favour a policy of suburban cottage rather than central flat building. The fact that just three large sites were to be acquired also signalled the increasing scale of estates to be built in the 1930s.

However, the suburban schemes of the 1920s had one major disadvantage. Because the houses were built for tenant purchase, only the well-off members of the working classes could afford to live in them. Even so, many of those who were allocated such houses had to struggle to make ends meet, and would in all likelihood have preferred the option of a rented cottage. By focusing so heavily on this 'better class of dwelling', the Corporation was, in effect, turning its back on the most needy members of society. In a Dáil question in November 1928, Peadar Doyle voiced the concerns of many by asking whether the Minister would consider 'the necessity of accommodating more people in central areas, and so save cost of transport and extra cost of food away from home' (Dáil Debates, 27, p. 586). The North City Survey had suggested that

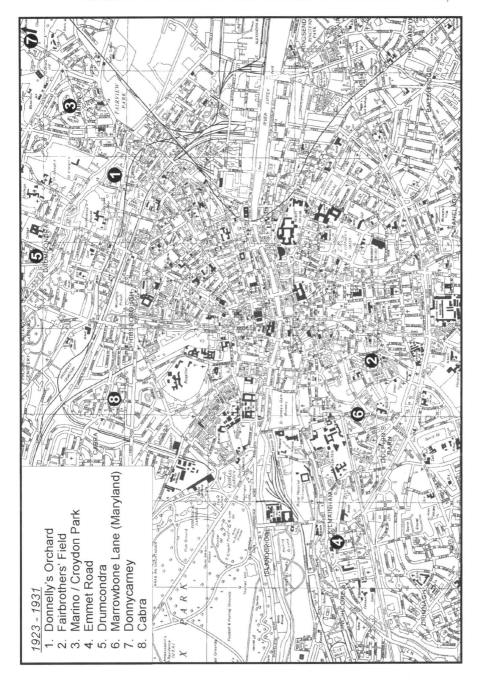

1923 - 1931
1. Donnelly's Orchard
2. Fairbrothers' Field
3. Marino / Croydon Park
4. Emmet Road
5. Drumcondra
6. Marrowbone Lane (Maryland)
7. Donnycarney
8. Cabra

18 Location of Corporation schemes during the 1920s.

those moved from condemned areas were to be rehoused as near as possible to their sources of employment, while the more remote sites would be reserved for the better-paid artisans who could afford to pay the expenses of transit. Thus, the Corporation policy would inevitably reinforce social segregation in the city, as those who could afford to would move from the decaying core. However, this aspect of the housing strategy was not consciously referred to, and apparently did not prompt any debate at the time.

The problem of the 1920s policy was, of course, that even extensive suburban building would not enable any single slum area to be actually cleared, as the majority of the inhabitants were unable to afford the cost of living in the outer areas. However, the suburban ideal had taken strong hold by the early 1930s, and it was difficult to return to a central slum clearance and flat building policy. Even the special Committee formed in 1930 to consider the methods to be adopted for the speedy and effective dealing with the City's housing needs was beguiled by the idea of suburban dwellings. 'While ... the Committee recognized that their labours should be primarily directed to the clearance of the slums they agreed ... that consideration should likewise be given to the provision of schemes on virgin sites in the outer districts of the City' (Report 16/1934, p. 122).

During the 1930s, the focus of Corporation housing policy changed again. Suburban cottage schemes were still being erected, but these were now for rental rather than tenant purchase. The Marrowbone Lane houses (1930) mark the transitional stage, since some were for rental, others for tenant purchase. The 641 cottages at Cabra (Fassaugh Lane, 1931) were the last tenant purchase cottages to be erected in the 1930s. In addition to the huge Crumlin scheme, other cottage schemes of the 1930s included Donnelly's Orchard, Friend's Fields, North Lotts, Terenure, Harold's Cross and Ellenfield.

The Housing (Miscellaneous Provisions) Act of 1931 made important changes by providing a more speedy method for the clearance of unhealthy areas and the repair or demolition of houses considered unfit for human habitation, including the use of Compulsory Purchase Orders. The types of grants available to local authorities such as Dublin Corporation also changed. A 1932 Circular Letter to all of the local authorities in Ireland from the Department of Local Government and Public Health reminded them that 'special assistance' was now available under the Act to local authorities undertaking the rehousing of people living in slum areas. It also asked that efforts should be confined to providing small three- or four-roomed houses, with specifications which eliminated all non-essentials.

By August of the following year, the State's policy had become more firmly focused on slum clearance, as was seen by the introduction of yet another Housing (Financial and Miscellaneous Provisions) Act, 1932. This Act increased State subsidies available to local authorities for housing for the working classes, particularly for people living in slums or unfit houses. The State would contribute up to two-thirds of the loan charges for houses built to rehouse people displaced by slum clearance schemes, and up to one-third of the loan charges for houses built by local authorities for the better paid worker who was unable to pay a full economic rent.

A greater number of flat schemes was now being erected, generally under the 1931 legislation. By 1934, when the new assault on the slums began, the City Manager, Gerald J. Sherlock, called for a balanced housing programme, suggesting that one suburban cottage should be built for every two central dwellings. Assuming that families with a minimum weekly income of 45s. (making allowances for discontinuities in employment and for very large families) would afford the rent of 7s. 6d. per week for a suburban cottage and 2s. 6d. per week for transport, about one third of the families to be housed by the Corporation (or 6000 families) could afford to live in cottages in the outer areas, while the remaining 12,000 families should be housed in central areas (Report 16/1934). The Housing Committee was in general agreement, suggesting that some 33 to 40 per cent of the 18,000 dwellings required should be suburban cottages. It was still felt that suburban dwellings were desirable, but the extremely small means of the people for whom accommodation was to be provided would preclude the successful carrying out of a general housing programme for such classes in suburban areas (Report 28/1934).

The preferences of the tenement dwellers were largely overlooked in all of the discussion which took place at the time. To them, the closely-knit fabric of their communities would be unravelled as the people were dispersed to various outlying estates.

Housing type: flats vs. cottages

The flat has one fatal defect. It is not a proper home for human beings.

(McGrath, 1932, p. 271)

If a Communist organizer wished to lay plans for the development of Communist cells throughout Dublin for the building of 'red forts' for revolutionary purposes, could he do better than dot the city over with large barracks of propertyless men.

(McGrath, 1932, p. 272)

The question of suburbanization became closely associated with the decision on whether to build flats or cottages. Prior to about 1920, high-density central area cottage schemes had been built, but after that time, cottages became almost exclusively associated with greenfield suburban sites. Opponents of flat building therefore tended to side with those lobbying in favour of suburbanization, despite the recognized fact that the slum dwellers wished to remain in the city centre, preferably in houses. In a letter to the *Irish Builder and Engineer* from Mr W.J. Larkin, President of the Dublin Tenants' Association in May 1921, he argued that 'the Corporation must build on "virgin" sites cottages, not cages or "warehouses" – they have been forced into recognizing this as the true method of housing' (Larkin, quoted in the *Irish Builder and Engineer*, 7 May 1921, p. 317). It is noteworthy that in more recent times many public housing schemes built for the less-well-off have been described as 'warehousing' the poor.

The belief that flat life was somehow 'unnatural' was a frequently used argument against this form of habitation. McGrath's 1932 article warned of 'the moral dangers of the common staircase', echoing the sentiments of many Victorian commentators, and claimed furthermore that the building of large numbers of flats was a 'positive menace', as it was in line with the philosophy of Communism. Whatever about the wilder allegations concerning tenement life, one fact alone helped to secure the opposition of many to the erection of flats. This was the persisting negative example of the tenements with their slum living conditions. It was useless to argue that modern block dwellings could produce comfortable and sanitary homes when the negative experience of multiple-family occupancy was so close at hand. The argument in favour of flats was not advanced by the Corporation's initial forays into public housing provision, which had been decried as creating new slums in place of the old ones. For example, R.M. Butler wrote in the *Irish Builder and Engineer* that 'the practice was to buy up slum areas at enormous cost, and to build thereon what will, in time, become other slums to vex future generations' (*Irish Builder and Engineer*, 2 February 1921, p. 118).

Very few flat schemes were built, therefore, in the years following the 1913 Housing Inquiry, and as early as 1914 a Housing Committee report stated that 'the policy of the Corporation for years past in connection with the question of housing the workers has been in the direction of erecting self-contained dwellings' (Report 82/1914, p. 814). As a result, when it was decided that flats would be built as part of the Trinity Ward scheme, a rather spatially diffuse scheme, the Committee felt required to justify itself. In this case, the Trinity

19 Two examples of housing in the Trinity ward scheme. (Photographs by R. McManus.)

Ward Improvements Association had advocated the erection of flats to be let to the dock workers at cheaper rents than those charged for self-contained dwellings. Only having been fully satisfied that it was in the best interests of the workers that flats be built, did the Housing Committee decide to depart from the general principle of building self-contained cottages (Report 51/1912, Report 82/1914). A 1919 proposal to erect 90 flats at Crabbe Lane was greeted with hostility by the Local Government Board, particularly due to the proposed use of three-storeyed blocks of flats: 'Such buildings are in many ways most unsatisfactory and are more costly and less convenient than self-contained houses, or even two-storeyed blocks of flats' (Report 110/1920, p. 400). The plans were dropped.

Even though the Corporation more or less stopped building flats in the 1920s, the early schemes were still being used to house the less fortunate. When Lily O'Connor's family moved into one of the flats on Benburb Street in the 1930s, she described the block as a 'high, grey, dismal concrete building', with women wearing black shawls standing around the main hall door. 'The hall itself was cold, drab and stank of urine – there was a pub at the corner … Climbing the stairs of our block of flats, I'd hear children screaming behind one of the doors and the sound of delph breaking against the wall as their parents fought' (O'Connor, 2000, pp 163–5). Eventually the family managed to get a house in Cabra West, but only after staying in Benburb Street for six months, after which time the Corporation would consider them for another transfer. The ageing flats also led to increasing maintenance costs for the Housing Committee, as in the case of the Bow Lane property which, according to the Committee itself, 'was badly designed, constructed with poor materials, and had bad drainage' (*Irish Builder and Engineer*, 31 May 1924, p. 482).

However, the Corporation architects and engineers continued to develop new ideas for flat schemes. For example, the Boyne Street Housing Scheme (1922–3) was a new departure in Corporation construction. At the front of each three-storey block were two hall doors to the ground floor lettings, while at the back four hall doors leading to self-contained 'cottages' were approached by wrought iron stairs. The ground and first storeys were faced with Irish manufactured red brick from Courtown, while the top storey was built of Co. Dublin brickwork, cement pebble-dashed. Each dwelling contained a living room, two bedrooms, kitchen, scullery and w.c. These were the first in Ireland to be built on this principle.

However, the Boyne Street scheme was loudly condemned. In a harsh editorial, the *Irish Builder and Engineer* warned of the dangers of reverting to the 'bad old flat system', stating that the true solution for Dublin remained 'the small, self-contained detached or semi-detached house on virgin sites' (*Irish Builder and Engineer*, 12 August 1922, p. 549). A letter from J. Vincent Brady, the honorary secretary of the Civics Institute of Ireland, called for 'the assistance of authoritative public opinion in condemnation of such extravagant facilities as this last scheme of the Dublin Corporation for "rehousing" the people in inhuman packing-cases, regardless of protest' (letter dated 16/8/22, published *Irish Builder and Engineer* 26 August 1922, p. 578). He went on to describe the tenement system as a 'filthy abomination', and specifically referred to the new Boyne Street dwellings as 'tenement flats' in order to hammer home the point. Thus, as the *Irish Builder and Engineer* stated 'the action of the Corporation, in reverting, even to a small extent, to the block system, has occasioned, and rightly so, much hostile criticism' (24 March 1923, p. 211).

The progress of similar schemes abroad, particularly in Britain, was closely monitored by the Housing Section. When the Crabbe Lane Scheme was again contemplated in 1926, Mr Simms of the City Architect's Department was authorized to visit London, Liverpool and Manchester to inspect the latest type of building on the flat system in those municipalities, while Commissioner W.C. Dwyer and the City Architect inspected the latest flat schemes undertaken by the London County Council (Report 137/1926; *Irish Times*, 11 March 1926).

Apart from a few small schemes, however, Corporation housing policy in the 1920s strongly favoured the erection of cottage estates which were, rather optimistically, termed 'garden suburbs'. Not everyone was happy with suburban schemes, least of all inhabitants of the central areas who were uprooted from their communities. For them, cottages were preferable to flats, but they wished to remain in the centre of the city. However, accepted practice, by then, was to maintain low housing densities in cottage estates, and to restrict higher density housing to flat schemes.

Slum clearance areas

Unfortunately slum clearance and central area building are in the nature of the case vastly slower than suburban housing, so that the tragedy of the situation is that relief for the most necessitous and most numerous class must in present circumstances lag painfully behind provision of accommodation for the better-off working class.

(Report 16/1934, p. 128)

As we saw above, the 1930s saw a new attack on the real housing problem, that of the poorest members of the population. Following new legislation in 1931 and 1932, a series of slum clearances was undertaken, and in this context the importance of the flat dwelling came to be more fully recognized. The largest schemes at Hanover Street and Cook Street provided *c*.350 dwellings each, while more modest developments were undertaken at Marshalsea and Beggarsbush Barracks. Other new flat blocks were erected in areas including Mary's Lane and Chancery Street, Watling Street, Townsend Street, Poplar Row, Railway Street and Henrietta Street.

However, the procedures involved in declaring Clearance Areas were time-consuming and unwieldy, since the legal system's respect for property rights generally required a public inquiry before development could take place. The average time lapse from the inauguration of a Slum Housing Scheme until the contractor could proceed with the work was 14 to 18 months. The lengthy process required in order to create a Clearance Area is seen in the case of Hanover Street, the plans for which were first submitted in 1931, while building was still on-going in 1937. Mary's Lane and Cook Street were among the first of the Clearance Areas, with the inhabitants of the former area being rehoused in the immediate locality, while the 484 people living in the Cook Street (Section I) Clearance Area were to be relocated out in the new Beggsboro' Scheme in Cabra.

In addition to such legal delays, the absence of sufficient vacant sites in central areas impeded the speed and extent of slum rehousing, because the 1931 Act required that persons to be displaced by slum clearance schemes would first be rehoused, a stipulation based on past experience where 'improvement schemes' had actually caused a deterioration in conditions for the inhabitants (Report 16/1934). This obligation caused considerable difficulties for Dublin Corporation, since before any extensive area could be cleared a substantial number of dwellings had to first be erected. These new dwellings were generally flats, which took longer to construct than cottages, while the cleared site when rebuilt on with flats would still not house the total number of families displaced from that site, such was the degree of over-crowding in the slums. The regulations resulted in piecemeal site clearances, which delayed the building process. Early in 1937, the City Manager urged the necessity for comprehensive en bloc clearances, together with the provision of temporary accommodation for the displaced families at nominal rents, but the scheme was never implemented. The Housing Inquiry of 1939–43 also proposed the use of clearing-stations as an alternative to piecemeal site clearances.

In addition to the time-consuming nature of slum clearance schemes, cost was a major problem for redevelopment. For example, in 1914, when the Trinity Ward flats were built, it was decided that they would be reserved for those earning less than 25s. per week. At the request of the Trinity Ward Improvements Association, the flats were to be let at cheaper rents than those charged for self-contained cottages. However, the figures presented in the Housing Committee report showed that, based on the cost per room at this site, cottages were 25 per cent cheaper to build (Report 82/1914). The North City Survey of 1918 had estimated that the average cost per dwelling on a central site was £553, compared with just £450 on a virgin site. The block schemes were generally intended to house those who simply could not afford to move to more distant suburbs where the rents were relatively high, and additional transport costs had to be met. Unfortunately, flat construction was more expensive than cottage construction, while the cost of acquiring central sites was also much higher than that for suburban sites, so that, in order to house the poorest classes, whose rent-paying capacity was very small, greater cost had to be incurred in both respects. The 1939–43 Housing Inquiry found that flat building was uneconomic, with an all-in cost twice that of suburban cottages. It was also found to be more expensive than the earlier high-density, low-rise, inner-city cottages which had been more popular with tenants. The problem was exacerbated by the fact that the Corporation flat dwellers were paying lower rents than those living in the cottage schemes.

There was also a general belief that, despite generous playground provision, block dwellings were not really suited to family life. In his 1934 Report, the City Manager's position was made clear. He considered cottage dwellings to be preferable to flats, but considered that limitations of space and increasing population precluded the cottage system from being adopted in central areas. However, he stressed that modern flats such as those in Mercer Street or Greek Street provided 'to the utmost that this system of construction will permit', a self-contained home for each family in addition to children's playgrounds. While the average density of the slum housing was c.65 families per acre (c.160 families per ha), modern flat rehousing would approximate to 50 families per acre (c.125 families per ha) (Report 16/1934).

When the Housing Inquiry of 1939–43 considered the relative suitability of flats and cottages, it urged a policy of minimum building of flats mainly due to 'their general inferiority as compared with cottages for family dwellings for the working classes of Dublin', but also because of costs of provision as against the subsidized rent payable (Housing Inquiry, 1939–43, p. 120, para. 338). The

City Housing Architect, Herbert Simms, stated that 'Dublin is the only city I know that lets its flats at a lesser rent than that of cottages' (Housing Inquiry 1939–43, p. 122, para. 338).

The three main arguments generally used in favour of a flat-building policy were addressed by this Inquiry, only to be overturned, and it is particularly interesting to note that town planning was seen as having a key role in future developments. Generally, it was argued that some workers needed to live near the city centre, but the Inquiry considered that this was a well-established custom rather than a necessity, while improved, cheaper transport facilities combined with the decentralization of industry would remove this particular reason for building flats. The need to fill unsightly gaps left by demolition, and the need to avail of existing public services and utilities, were not considered to be persuasive arguments in favour of flat building. The Inquiry remarked that town planning would suggest other suitable uses for sites, and other ways of fully exploiting these services.

Thus, by the time of this second Housing Inquiry of 1939–43, Dublin Corporation had moved through two phases of flat building, separated by an era of almost exclusive cottage development. After World War II, large-scale public housing development took the form of further suburban cottage estates, such as those at Artane and Ballyfermot. Some of the Clearance Areas were developed as planned, but the bulk of construction was in the suburbs. A dual policy of building inner-city flats such as O'Rahilly House, Thorncastle Street and McDonagh House, Whitefriar Street, and low-density suburban housing, contributing to urban sprawl, persisted in the 1950s and 1960s.

Alternative solutions to the housing problem

Barracks turned into Houses: 2000 people provided for in Dublin.
(Headline, *Irish Times*, 9 April 1925)

While the main thrust of housing policy in Dublin was the erection of new dwellings, some attempts were made to find alternative solutions to the housing problem. Refurbishment of the 'first class' tenement houses had been suggested by Sir Charles Cameron, the Medical Officer of Health, even before it was recommended by the Committee of Inquiry of 1913. In a letter to the Corporation dated 18 July 1913, Cameron warned that Gardiner Street, 'one of the finest streets in the City' was rapidly becoming a street of tenement houses. 'In some of them the tenements consist of a single room. The hall-doors are open, the windows and fanlights broken, and the usual dismal appearance of the tenement is presented to the passer by'. However, he recognized the architectural quality of these buildings, suggesting that if they were acquired and converted into flats for letting at between 5s. and 7s. 6d. per week they would be popular with families 'who would prefer to pay, say, 6s. per week for a flat with large, healthy rooms, and exclusive use of a water-closet, than to pay the same sum for a small house with small rooms' (Cameron, letter printed in Report 236/1913, p. 286). In making this recommendation, Cameron stressed that for some of the Corporation's existing working-class housing schemes, the sites had cost as much as the houses.

During the Housing Inquiry a few months later, Geddes voiced his approval for quality refurbishment, but there was strong opposition to the idea from the City Architect, Charles MacCarthy, and from members of the Committee of Inquiry. The issue, so closely related to that of the general suitability of houses rather than flats, was to remain a difficult one for the Housing Committee during the 1920s, although, as we saw, the 1918 North City Survey saw renovation of first-class tenements as the first line of attack in the housing problem. Even before 1922, some experiments in refurbishment were undertaken at Darby Square, Bride Street, but it was generally an unpopular concept.

As well as refurbishing existing dwellings, some consideration was given to the possibility of converting some of Dublin's many disused army barracks into working-class housing. In his competition plan, Abercrombie (1922) had suggested that open space near the Royal Barracks should be used as a model infilling project, while the Dublin barracks themselves (which were State property) should be handed over to the Municipality at nominal prices for use as linked-up playgrounds. 'It would be a great mistake if, acquired thus advantageously, they were used for housing. It is recreation that it is so difficult to get money for' (Abercrombie, 1922, p. 43). Thus 'neighbourhood parks' would be created at Beggar's Bush, Portobello, Richmond and Royal Barracks. However, Abercrombie's advice went unheeded, as in June 1924, the President of the Executive Council of the Irish Free State, W.T. Cosgrave, announced the decision to hand over Keogh Barracks for the purpose of a housing scheme.

Keogh (formerly Richmond) Barracks was leased to the Corporation from October 1924 for 98 years and converted into 202 flats and 24 temporary three-roomed dwellings. In addition to the conversion of the existing buildings, the unbuilt land on the site was to be used for the erection of c.220 Corporation houses by contractors Messrs Kenny and Sons. Later that year buildings were leased to a Mr James Finerty of Castleblakeney, Co. Galway for

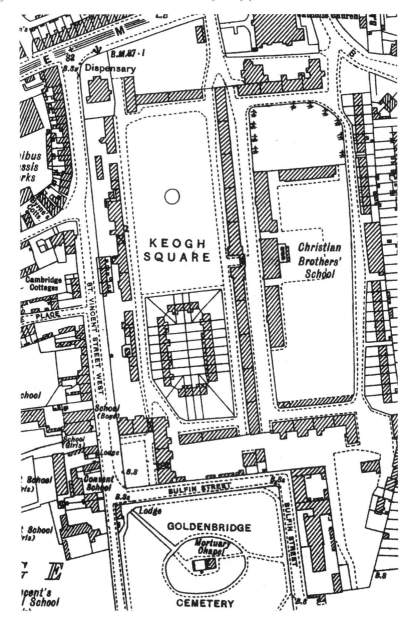

20 The development of the Keogh Barracks site.
(Ordnance Survey 1:2500 plan, Sheet 18 X, Dublin, 1943 revision.)

alteration into shops, while the 'Officers Mess' was let to the City of Dublin Child Welfare Committee for use as a milk depot. A further 36 acre (c.14.5 ha) market garden site adjoining the Kenny-built houses was soon acquired for building purposes, so that the idea of a park became a distant memory in a sea of housing. Throughout the 1920s, the Corporation Housing Committee continued to acquire barracks for housing purposes on reasonably long leases. For example, in September 1925, a 99-year lease of the 2¼ acre (c.1 ha) Linenhall Barracks site was secured for the erection of 70 temporary dwellings 'for the poorer class of workers' (Report 224/1925).

The use of barracks for housing purposes continued to be a Corporation policy into the 1930s. In 1932, the Corporation corresponded with the Minister of Defence with a view to the release of Collins Barracks for housing purposes, in view of the shortage of housing accommodation in the City. In the same year, the stores at Marshalsea Barracks were taken over from the Board of Works to provide nine one- and two-roomed flats, while 44 flats were supplied at Beggarsbush Barracks in 1933.

Although changes in Government policy in the early 1930s, with a return to slum clearance, suggest that there would have been a renewed interest in refurbishment, attempts at reconditioning under the 1931 and 1932 Housing Acts were largely unsuccessful. This lack of success was largely due to the difficulty of obtaining houses of a suitable quality, since the remaining tenement houses had deteriorated still further by this time, and it was now recognized that reconditioned tenements could only form a small part of the solution to the housing question. About 25 dwellings were reconditioned by philanthropic housing organizations such as the Old Belvedere Housing Society and the Family Housing Association.

With World War II and the scarcity of building materials, several streets received a new lease of life, including Gloucester Street, York Street, sections of Lower Gardiner Street, Sean MacDermott Street and Summerhill (since demolished). By 1948, about 500 flats with modern amenities had been provided out of 'decrepit and insanitary' tenements, and the need for prolonging the usefulness of old buildings was officially recognized.

Trends in the size of Corporation dwellings

It is highly probable that future generations will stigmatize, and not praise, the results of our best endeavours to house the workers.

(Citizens' Housing Council, 1938, p. 42)

> The standard of accommodation provided in Corporation dwellings
> has been unfavourably criticized, but it should be pointed out that the
> policy of affording the greatest good for the greatest number with the
> financial resources available, has influenced the Corporation.
>
> (Report 6/1938, p. 43)

In the early Corporation schemes, the majority of dwellings had three-rooms,
while the ill-regarded Foley Street scheme comprised mostly one-roomed flats.
Indeed, none of the dwellings built prior to 1923 had more than four rooms.
However, in 1922 the Housing Committee recommended that the number of
dwellings with four or fewer rooms ought not to be increased, and that,
instead, the Council should turn its attention to the provision of a 'better
class' of dwelling, with the five-roomed house becoming the minimum
standard (Report 68/1922). This recommendation was based on the reasoning
that three bedrooms were 'essential' for the average family (a room for the
parents and a room each for the boys and girls). The 'parlour' was considered
by the average householder to be an essential adjunct to the house, so that the
family might enjoy the ordinary comforts of home life. These criteria were
based on the current wisdom of the day. Similar reasoning had been used in
Britain's 1918 Tudor Walters report which argued for five-roomed houses as a
minimum standard.

Consequent on the Million Pound Grant, the Dublin Corporation's Housing
Committee again argued that 'for at least the next four or five years the most
suitable type of house to be constructed is a five-roomed house' (Report
309/1922, p. 722). The idea was not unreasonable, since it was anticipated that
a large number of existing Corporation tenants would desire a transfer to the
new houses, thus leaving a number of houses with smaller accommodation at
cheaper rents available for disposal to those with lower incomes or smaller
families. Indeed the cottage estates completed between 1923 and 1928 largely
fulfilled this promise although both Fairbrother's Fields and Emmet Road also
included some four-roomed houses. With the completion of the Drumcondra
scheme in 1928 there was a change, as 211 three-roomed houses were included,
the smallest dwellings yet built by the Corporation in a garden suburb setting.

Of the 5043 Corporation dwellings completed between 1923 and 1931, over
45 per cent were five-roomed tenant purchase cottages. The concentration on
five-roomed dwellings is even more apparent when it is recognized that all
were built in a concentrated five-year period between 1923, the year of
completion for Donnelly's Orchard and Fairbrother's Fields, and 1928, when

the Drumcondra Scheme was finished. A further 19 per cent of housing provision took the form of four-roomed dwellings, while just over 5 per cent of dwellings built had only one or two rooms. These smallest dwellings all formed part of flat schemes erected after 1927, at Kehoe Square, Mercer House, Marshalsea Barracks and Mountpleasant/Hollyfield.

The size of dwellings had already begun to alter after 1928, with a return to four-roomed and smaller buildings. Three-quarters of completions between 1928 and 1931 had four rooms, but this was to change when the serious attack on the slums commenced. Between 1932 and 1937 the majority of dwellings built or planned were three-roomed. Two-thirds of dwellings supplied during this period were three-roomed, while just over a quarter had four rooms. No further five-roomed dwellings were completed until 1938.

The erection of smaller dwellings was largely a response to Government pressures, as previously discussed, since 1932 legislation limited the all-in cost of dwellings on which contributions would be paid. This was intended to ensure strict economy in the housing drive, but actually had a negative effect, as smaller dwellings of meaner proportions were erected in order to secure Government assistance. However, the trend towards smaller dwellings was not purely a response to Government pressures. There had been a gradual recognition within Dublin Corporation that 'some cheap type of dwelling should be made available for a number of families inhabiting premises condemned as structurally dangerous or otherwise unfit for habitation, and who, as a rule, are not in a position to pay for the larger type of flat now being provided on clearance areas' (Report 7/1934, p. 31). The 1934 Report suggested that some one-room and two-room self-contained flats be provided on ground between Charles Street and Chancery Place, but the experimental proposal was rejected by the Minister, on the grounds that a policy of one-room flat provision was 'inadvisable', fearing the unintentional creation of future slums. Instead, the Chancery House flat scheme (1935) would ultimately contain 16 two-room and 11 three-room flats. Despite this negative response, the City Manager's 1934 Report called for an alteration of the Corporation's policy by erecting more one- and two-roomed flats to assist poorer small families, whose conditions had remained substantially unchanged due to the policy of housing the larger families. Opposition to flat developments was not confined to the operations of Dublin Corporation, as illustrated by the fact that the Iveagh Trust received protests from the Dublin Trade Union Council when it planned to build one and two-roomed flats in 1935. Incidentally, John Good TD noted that such two-roomed flats were a great boon to old people (Dáil Debates, 56, p. 168).

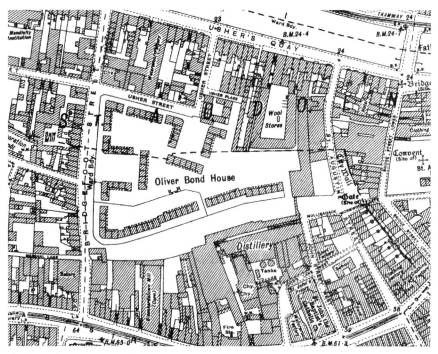

21 The Oliver Bond development.
(Ordnance Survey 1:2500 plan, Sheet 18 XI, Dublin, 1939 revision.
Photograph by R. McManus.)

The year 1934 therefore marked a return to the erection of smaller dwellings, as the City Manager aimed to provide approximately 18,000 'one, two- and three-roomed new dwellings and abolish the slums, by a balanced programme of building in suburban and central areas respectively' (Report 16/1934, p. 125). The Housing Committee agreed to the provision of flats in the proportions 3:2:1, three-room flats: two-room flats: one-room flats (Report 28/1934). However, this ratio was never adhered to, with fewer one- and two-roomed flats being completed than anticipated.

The problem which arose regarding flat dwellings of this period had less to do the actual number of rooms provided, and more with the size of those rooms. Even Oliver Bond House (the Anchor Brewery site), considered by Dublin Corporation to be the showpiece of its 1930s flat schemes, was severely criticized. When Mr Dillon, a Donegal TD, visited the scheme in 1937, he found that the exterior was attractive, but was 'appalled' to find that internally the flats consisted of 'three or four miserable cubby-hole rooms' which were described in the *Irish Times* (8 April 1937) as 'deplorably small and dark'.

In Ireland, the provision of flats was almost exclusively confined to Dublin at this time. In a Dáil Debate in November 1937, Dillon commented 'that the vital necessity for a working-class family in this city is one decent living room rather than a whole rabbit warren of dark small cubby-holes such as are at present being provided in some of the flat buildings in Dublin' (Dáil Debates, 69, p. 761). Despite the protestations from the Minister, O'Kelly, that 'they are as good as any buildings I have seen in different cities in Europe that are regarded as setting a headline', unfavourable public opinion led to a change in policy. As the wisdom of erecting small flats continued to be questioned, at the instance of the Minister for Local Government and Public Health, the Corporation altered its approach, agreeing that at least 70 per cent of its dwellings would have four rooms (Housing Inquiry, 1939–43, p. 128). In fact, the proportion of four-room dwellings completed in 1938 and 1939 was closer to 50 per cent, while about 18 per cent of all dwellings completed still had only one- or two-rooms (actually a higher proportion than before Ministerial intervention in 1937).

Perhaps Cameron was not too far wrong when, in 1913, he had argued for the reconditioning of the better tenements which, despite their squalor, would provide high, airy and bright rooms when refurbished. The Citizens' Housing Council echoed Dillon's views in its 1938 Report. While recognizing that the blocks of flats were substantially built and of excellent appearance, doubts were raised as to the wisdom of spending large capital sums on flats or houses with rooms which were 'obviously smaller than they should be'. It continued by suggesting that 'with a rising demand for comfort and floor space occasioned by increased standards of living, such buildings will be out of date long before they are worn out' (1938, p. 42).

Table 12 Size of Corporation dwellings, 1926–39, and recommendations of the 1939–43 Housing Inquiry.

	Per cent				
	1-room	*2-room*	*3-room*	*4-room*	*5-room*
Dwellings built 1926–32	0.1	2.4	11.4	44.0	42.1
Built or in progress 1932–37	1.2	9.3	73.0	16.5	Nil
Entire housing estate, 1939*	4.0	9.8	41.0	31.5	13.7
Recommendation of Inquiry	Nil	10.0	28.0	44.0	18.0

*All housing controlled by the Corporation on that date, including any housing built by other authorities and subsequently acquired by Dublin Corporation.
(Housing Inquiry, 1939–43, p. 127, para. 350.)

One of the important recommendations of the Housing Inquiry of 1939–43 was that the floor area of local authority dwellings should be increased. While flat schemes might contain a higher proportion of two-room dwellings than the cottage schemes, the Housing Inquiry warned against the pitfall of building large proportions of small flats. It recommended that the embargo on one-room flats should continue, the proportion of two-room flats should not exceed 15 per cent, while the numbers of three- and four-room flats might be increased at the expense of the five-room, to be balanced by an increased number of five-roomed cottages. The Committee of Inquiry considered that the absolute minimum for a normal family dwelling was three bedrooms, the approach which had been adopted in the 1920s and later dropped.

Sales vs. rental

The earliest schemes of housing provided by Dublin Corporation, whether cottages or flats, were let to their tenants at weekly rents. However, that was to change in the early 1920s. In January 1922, the Dublin Corporation considered what the *Irish Builder and Engineer* described as an 'interesting experiment', namely, the sale to the occupiers of some 1172 self-contained cottages built by the Corporation. The total rental income from these cottages was £20,694 per annum, but the outgoings came to £14,435, so the profit rents were small. This was an early step towards the trend of owner occupation which became so prevalent by the latter half of the twentieth century. In applauding this move, the *Irish Builder and Engineer* (14 January 1922, p. 5) suggested that 'there is probably no country in the world where so many of the people live in hired houses'. It continued by saying that 'it is the ambition of most men in these countries to own their own dwellings. That principle should be encouraged and facilitated. It tends to the stability of the State, and to a sense of good citizenship'. In approving the sale of the cottages to tenants, Mr J.J. Murphy stated that this would add to the number of ratepayers in the city as well as creating a keener sense of civic spirit among the purchasing tenants. Thus, once again the idea of private ownership was seen to enhance civic spirit.

The tenants were able to purchase their house at an annuity which was only a slight increase on the weekly rent which they were currently paying. They could also invest £5 or any multiple of £5 in the house, so as to pay it off quickly. The purchase terms were based on annuities which practically corresponded to twice the Poor Law Valuation (PLV), reserving a ground rent which was approximately a quarter of the PLV.

The policy of selling houses to occupants on a 'tenant purchase' basis was first adopted by the City Council in 1921, and first applied at Donnelly's Orchard and Fairbrother's Fields, both schemes of five-roomed dwellings. In fact, the sale scheme operated until the 1930s 'in all cases of what may be described as comparatively "luxury" houses, the object being to encroach to the minimum extent on the Corporation's resources' (Report 38/1931, p. 252). Although the report reasoned that those resources were required to tackle the problem of housing the 'less fortunate sections of the working classes', there is little evidence that any serious attempt was made to do so during the 1920s when, with the exception of Kehoe Square and the Boyne Street flat development, no dwellings were made available for rent by the Corporation. Dublin Corporation's house building centered around the provision of 'superior' dwellings in tenant purchase schemes, which were beyond the means of the most poverty-stricken slum dwellers. Prices for new local authority houses in 1927 ranged from £330 (for centre of terrace houses at Fairbrother's Fields) to £460 (for semi-detached houses at Emmet Road) (Report 97/1927). Further schemes of sale are included in the sections dealing with specific schemes.

How did it work? Formerly, all houses had been let to tenants at weekly rents but over the five years from 1924 to 1929, some 2436 houses were sold on

lease for a term of 99 years. Over the year to March 1930, 412 houses had been
sold at from £230 to £460, with ground rents ranging from £2 to £5 per house.
Where the purchaser was unable to pay the entire or any portion of the purchase
money in cash, the amount was advanced by the City Commissioners for a term
not exceeding 40 years at 5¾ per cent. The building cost of these houses was
£392 for three-roomed, £416 for four-roomed, and £492 for five-roomed
(DLGPH, 1931).

One major explanation for the Corporation's preference for purchase rather
than rental schemes was financial. A discussion of the disposal of the 88 houses
at Marrowbone Lane in 1931 showed that their sale by tenant purchase would
incur an annual loss of £361, whereas the annual loss incurred by letting on
weekly tenancies (at 2s. 6d. per room) would be £1176. 'Seeing that the
Housing Programme decided upon is chiefly concerned with the provision of
healthy dwellings for workers who cannot afford to pay anything approaching
economic rents, it is clear that wherever it is possible to reduce the inevitable
burden which must be shouldered by the ratepayers in meeting the needs of
this latter class, opportunities like the present should be availed of to this end,
especially when no hardship is involved' (Report 38/1931, p. 252).

Interestingly, on occasion, the Corporation also advertised some of its
'tenant purchase' houses for sale, perhaps following default of payment by the
original tenants. The following notice appeared in the *Irish Times* housing
advertisements for 14 March 1931:

> For Sale – 16 Houses: **Drumcondra Scheme:** Three-room houses at 15 O
> Neachtain Road, 42 Fleming Road, 21 Joyce Road and a four-room house
> at 47 Joyce Road; **Marino Scheme:** Two five-roomed houses at 23 St
> Aidan's Park Road and 88 Shelmartin Ave; **Emmet Road Scheme:** Ten
> four-roomed houses at Anner Road (2, 55, 56), Devoy Road (3), Kickham
> Road (48, 55, 57, 83), Goldenbridge Avenue (47) and Stephen's Road (12).
> Proposal forms and particulars obtainable in the Housing Department,
> Exchange Buildings, Lord Edward Street. Offers must be lodged in the
> Housing Department not later than 12 noon on 25th March 1931.

The promotion of owner occupation by Dublin Corporation was a
reflection of more general trends away from renting in the private as well as
the public sector. At the time, it was suggested that this move to supply
housing for tenant purchase was demand driven and there is certainly some
evidence that people were interested in buying out their houses. For example,

in November 1923, the Rathfarnham Improvement Society discussed a suggestion that powers should be sought to enable the Rural District Council to sell its houses to the 600 tenants in the area. This is backed up by the Department of Local Government, which noted that: 'During recent years, urban local authorities have found an increasing desire amongst tenants to purchase their houses either outright or by installments payable over a fixed number of years' (DLGPH 3rd Report, 1929, p. 76). It was also noted that the houses which had been sold were being well maintained by the purchasing tenants.

Thus until about 1931, Dublin Corporation was essentially in the private market, providing houses for sale, albeit with sale prices set at rates below the actual building costs. However, the new sales policy was not uncontroversial, even at the outset. In August 1923 a resolution adopted at a meeting of the Irish Labour Party and Trades Union Congress (reported in *Irish Builder and Engineer*, 25 August 1923, p. 643) states that 'as the workers are being compelled to purchase these houses, and be saddled with the cost of maintenance, they at least ought to have a voice in the form of construction'. The report of the Housing Inquiry of 1939–43 was even more critical:

> We are of opinion that many tenants did not want to buy a house, but used the only means at their disposal of getting a house. If similar accommodation could have been got on renting terms most of them would have preferred it. Large numbers had to borrow the initial deposit (or a large portion of it) privately from friends and from other sources.
>
> (Housing Inquiry, 1939–43, p. 183, para. 539)

By the 1930s, serious concern was being expressed in the Dáil that the Government's housing policies to date had not succeeded in tackling the worst cases of deprivation. Robert Briscoe, TD, asked whether the people living in single room tenements would be given consideration when the new Corporation houses were being allocated, or 'are these houses to be built and sold to people at prices ranging from £300 to £400, or set at uneconomic rents?' (Dáil Debates, 33, p. 1652). In the same debate, Mr Cooney asked whether or not it was a fact 'that the people who are in real need of houses are not in a position to pay rent'. In March 1930, the Dublin Medical Officer of Health had said that the city now contained more insanitary rooms and dwellings than before, notwithstanding all of the houses built.

A move towards rental schemes in the 1930s followed the recognition that the tenant purchase policy had done little to solve the slum problem. In 1929,

Table 13 Rental housing (cottages) erected by Dublin Corporation 1914–39.

Scheme	Completion Date (approx.)	Total	Rooms			
			2	*3*	*4*	*5*
Cook Street	1914	45	0	45	0	0
Lurgan Street	1914	48	0	48	0	0
Trinity Ward	1917	28	0	28	0	0
Church Street	1917	146	28	94	24	0
Ormond Market	1917.1921	61	0	61	0	0
Ceannt Fort	1917	202	0	0	202	0
Colbert Fort	1917	60	20	40	0	0
Spitalfields	1918	75	0	75	0	0
Spitalfields	1928	6	0	6	0	0
Kehoe Square	1927	57	3	54	0	0
Marrowbone Lane	1930	166	17	138	11	0
Ormond Market	1932.1935	9	0	9	0	0
Malone Gardens	1933	65	0	59	6	0
Beggsboro	1933.1934	684	0	596	88	0
Donnelly's Orchard	1934	148	0	137	11	0
Friends Fields	1934	144	0	140	4	0
Annamoe Road	1934	311	0	297	14	0
Crumlin South	1934.1939	2903	0	1799	1104	0
North Lotts	1935	582	0	486	96	0
Cook Street	1936	3	0	0	3	0
South Lotts Rd	1937	16	0	14	2	0
Terenure	1938	313	0	66	247	0
Ellenfield	1938.1939	327	0	0	326	1
Crumlin North	1939.1939	353	0	92	261	0
Harold's Cross	1938.1939	161	0	83	78	0
Total		6913	68	4367	2477	1
Per cent of Total		100	0.98	63.2	35.8	0.01

a survey of urban housing in the Free State (see above) revealed a serious problem, and led to the introduction of the Housing Acts of 1931 and 1932. The new legislation, combined with a renewed concern for the welfare of the poor in the early 1930s, resulted in a change in Corporation housing schemes. Tenant purchase was abandoned in favour of rental schemes, more flats were built, and in general the dwellings were smaller with an increased emphasis on cost-cutting measures. Under the 1932 Housing (Financial and Miscellaneous

Provisions) Act, subsidies were granted on condition that the houses were let at rents approved by the Minister. The main activities of local authorities were now devoted to slum clearance and the rehousing of families displaced by the demolition of houses condemned as unfit for habitation. The Act marked the initiation of a plan under which it was hoped to meet the entire housing needs of the Free State within a ten-year period.

The standard rental for these 1930s schemes was fixed at the initiation of each scheme after loan charges, maintenance costs and other outgoings, as well as State contribution, were taken into account. Basic Corporation rent was 2s. per room for flats, 2s. 6d. per room for cottages. It was not an economic rent, in that it did not at all meet the costs incurred by the Corporation, and it was far below the rents payable by the working classes for inferior housing accommodation in private ownership. One example of the typical loss incurred was the Mountpleasant and Hollyfields flat scheme, initiated by Rathmines UDC but completed by Dublin Corporation in June 1931. The all-in cost of these flats worked out at £346 per flat, and the loss at a rent of 2s. 6d. per room was £770 p.a. (Report 38/1931). The City Manager's calculations of family incomes in three 'fairly typical' city housing areas showed that over one-quarter of families had a weekly income of 5s. to 20s., so that even these low rents presented a heavy burden on the family budget. For the Corporation, even at these low costs, revenue from rents was not steady (Report 28/1934). In 1934, the City Manager claimed that organized agitations for the payment of no rent in some instances, and for large reductions in many others, had been hampering the Housing Committee and the staff for a considerable time past, sometimes culminating in rent strikes (Report 16/1934).

Thus standard (uneconomic) rents were the Corporation's answer to accommodating the poorest members of the working classes. The idea of charging differential rents, that is, varied rents for the same class of accommodation, based on ability to pay, was rejected. It was believed that a system involving the reduction of rents on a graded scale corresponding with income would prove difficult to operate. Firstly, people in casual employment experienced continual variations in wages, while there would be a temptation to misrepresent income. The Corporation would also be open to complaints regarding discrimination. In 1934, the possibility was ruled out on a number of grounds, most tellingly because of 'the numerous cases where family means indicate practically no rent could be paid' and 'the additional enormous burthen cast on the citizens by the wholesale reductions involved' (Report 16/1934, p. 131). Thus, the Corporation placed greater importance on revenue and ability to pay than on solving the true housing problem. It did not address the question of how such families were being provided for under the existing system.

Unfortunately the system of standard rents created economic difficulties for many tenants. Although subsidized, rents on the new estates tended to be higher than the accommodation from which the residents came, thus discouraging some from accepting tenancies and creating hardship for those who did. Referring to the Crumlin-Kimmage-Drimnagh developments, 'it is evident … that the Municipality have concentrated on families in the higher income brackets for the new settlements' (Dillon, 1945, p. 16). In a 1944 article entitled *Two Dublin Slums*, the author explained why this 'death-trap' had not been completely evacuated.

> The more affluent tenants have moved to Crumlin or Kimmage. Those who remain are unemployed with large families and simply cannot pay the rent of a Crumlin house. One family has been offered a house for 10*s.* 8*d.* per week, minus bath, heat, and light. But the family consists of an unemployed man, his wife and nine children. Their income is 23*s.* from the Labour Exchange, plus 13*s.* a week in food vouchers. They would have to cope with bus fares and the wife would miss the cheap stew she gets from a nearby food kitchen; these factors, combined with bigger rent, would make it impossible for the family to exist at all. They must wait for cheaper accommodation; and in the meantime the children must remain in wet, verminous, stinking surroundings.
>
> (May, 1944, p. 356)

When a 'zoning system' was finally introduced in Corporation housing in 1938, it was intended as a means of increasing income from rents. Certain new housing areas were scheduled as zones for the accommodation of the better-off families being rehoused, and the rents of houses in these zoned areas were fixed at levels substantially in excess of the normal Corporation standards. It was not until the 1939–43 Housing Inquiry that a proper system of differential rents was recommended, under which tenants would pay the maximum rent which they were able to pay, up to a maximum rent based on the full economic rent. This would enable the local authority to use subsidies where they were really needed, giving rent rebates to those of low rent-paying capacity according to their needs. Referring to the former City Manager's 1934 Report which had rejected the idea of differential rents as impracticable, the 1939–43 Report quashed his objections, citing the example of experiments undertaken in Cork and in British cities including Leeds.

Over time the Corporation altered considerably. By pursuing a sales policy during the 1920s, Dublin Corporation had targeted the upper end of the working-class market, and was, in effect, operating like a private developer. A similar class was being housed by private speculative builders at this time. Indeed, until the late 1920s the housing provided by private speculative developers was quite likely to be rented, so that the tenant purchasers of Corporation schemes were little different from their 'private' counterparts, and were, in ways, better off, because they would eventually own their homes.

However, owner occupation had become increasingly common, if not quite the norm, in the private sector by the 1930s, when the Corporation moved away from tenant purchase and into rental schemes. Now there was a significant difference between those availing of local authority rather than private accommodation, as the social gap between tenancy and owner-occupation became more pronounced. Ironically, the private builders of the 1930s found that, as the market became saturated, they had to offer 'hire purchase' schemes on their houses, with a very small down-payment, a very similar concept to the tenant purchase schemes offered by the Corporation during the 1920s. As well as the differences in tenure, there was an increasing physical distinction between the type of accommodation offered by public and private developers in the 1930s, as the Corporation cottages were now smaller and less elaborate than the average speculatively-built houses, while flat provision was almost exclusively associated with the Local Authority. Thus, changing Corporation policy in the 1930s resulted in a significant physical difference between the local authority and private schemes of the period, and led to an increased social differentiation between those in local authority housing and those living in private housing.

Other public housing providers – Urban District Councils

It should be noted that from 1930 the Dublin Corporation area was expanded to include the former townships of Pembroke and Rathmines. These had previously been governed by Urban District Councils and operated their own housing schemes separately from the Dublin Corporation. In many ways these schemes were similar in their nature, though inevitably they were on a smaller scale than those undertaken by the Corporation.

One of the biggest schemes undertaken by an Urban District Council in the Dublin area was the planned 120 houses in Pembroke discussed in December 1922. In order to provide the houses, an additional rate of 1s. in the pound would have to be levied, supplementing a grant of £55,482 from the local government board. The attitude of the local councillors to the proposed scheme was summed up by Mr Forsyth, the Chair of Pembroke's Housing Committee, who said that 'it was a Christian duty to adopt the scheme' (*Irish Builder and Engineer*, 2 December 1922, p. 816). In May 1923 the Pembroke UDC accepted the tender of local builders, G. & T. Crampton, Ballsbridge, for the erection of 62 houses for £36,020. The houses were to be in two locations, with 34 at Ringsend Park and the remaining 28 at Bath Avenue.

In the same year, Dalkey UDC took a different approach. Rather than undertaking house building on its own account, it aimed to encourage speculative builders to provide housing for poorer families by resolving 'that the rates be remitted for a period of 20 years on all houses built in Dalkey within the next two years and let at any rent under 12s. 6d. per week' (*Irish Builder and Engineer*, 20 October 1923).

Rathmines and Rathgar UDC, like Pembroke UDC, was involved in direct provision of housing. In the winter of 1922, the first sod on the Kimmage Road area (south side) was cut. The UDC made particular note of 'the sympathetic and helpful action of the Government'. The site was opposite Mount Argus 'and on pleasant open country to the west and south'. The scheme of 124 houses came to an all-in cost of about £731 per house, as outlined below:

Table 14 Cost of different house types on Kimmage Road.

Type	Number	Rooms	Cost per house
A	6	Living, 2 bedrooms	£509
B	6	Living, parlour, 2 bedrooms	£600
C	96	Living, 3 bedrooms	£555
D	16	Living, parlour, 3 bedrooms	£680

(*Irish Builder and Engineer*, 2 December 1922, p. 816.)

Designed by Mr Edwin Bradbury, FRIAI, each house had a large scullery, pantry, coalhouse and w.c. In every case either a space or a room had been made available to accommodate a bath. The contractors for the houses were Messrs James Beckett, while Messrs Fleming Brothers were contractors for the roads, sewers and water mains. However, the scheme ran into difficulties, for in August 1924 the *Irish Builder and Engineer* reported that 'innumerable defects' were arising in the houses at Kimmage which had cost £750 each to build.

Bradbury was also the architect for 16 houses at Church Place, for which tenders were sought in the summer of 1924. Competition was keen, as no less than 12 contractors competed for the project: J. & R. Thompson, Geo. Squire & Co., W. Goulding, T. & R. Macken, Jas. Beckett Ltd., L. Monks, F. Manning, H. & R. Martin Ltd., W. & A. Roberts, Jos. Pemberton & Son, T. McMillen, J. Murphy, J. & F. Pemberton.

Interestingly, the Rathmines UDC recognized the value of public utility societies (discussed in detail in chapter four) in housing provision in the mid-1920s. When, in 1927, the council found itself unable to borrow further money for housing, it was decided to call a residents' meeting with the intention of forming a utility society to further a housing scheme. Not only did this local authority build its own schemes, but it also developed ground at Kimmage which it leased to private builders and utility societies in the late 1920s.

With the extension of the city boundaries in 1930, the schemes developed by the former UDCs were absorbed into the Dublin Corporation totals and are thus included in the Corporation totals from the 1939–43 Housing Inquiry. This tends to mask the variations in supply and nature of building in the formerly independent areas.

Housing allocation and associated problems

The Committee has no housing policy, demands no definite qualifications of intending purchasing tenants, and has prepared no formula denoting order of preference to guide members in selecting tenants.

(Findings of Sworn Inquiry into allegations of mis-allocation of Corporation Dwellings, Report 161/1922, p. 91)

Despite the frequent public condemnation of Dublin Corporation housing for various reasons, there was always a strong demand for its cottages during the 1920s. For example, in 1920 it was noted that over 2000 applications had been received for houses at McCaffrey Estate (later Ceannt Fort) and St James' Walk (Colbert's Fort) (Report 22/1921). However, in 1922, scandal erupted over the allocation of houses in the Fairbrother's Fields area, when Councillor John Lawlor alleged 'that the members of the Housing Committee gave, or attempted to give, possession to their friends of houses which cost £1025 3s. 9d. each, at prices ranging from £246 to £379 each. Further, that some of the persons to whom houses were given did not live within the City' (Report 93/1922, p. 616). The demand for the houses was huge, with 2755 applications received for the first 25 houses to be completed. The Superintendent had been instructed to select a preliminary list of 100 applicants for consideration by the Housing Committee, the main criteria being that the maximum earnings in each case should not be more than £7 a week, while there should be at least five in the family. Following a Sworn Enquiry into Councillor Lawlor's statements, the Inspector (Nicholas O'Dwyer of the Local Government Department of Dáil Eireann) was:

> satisfied that the most deserving persons did not and could not, in the absence of a systematic method of selection, secure the support of the Committee in every case. If we may take it that Councillor Lawlor's statement is meant to convey that the personal element was not eliminated, then I am of the opinion that his statement is justified.
>
> (Report, 161/1922, p. 90)

Later that year, following the announcement of the Million Pound Government Housing Grant, a Report outlining the Corporation's general housing policy recommended that houses should be allocated in two ways. In the case of the transfer of existing Corporation tenants, they should apply to the Housing Committee, with all applications to be reported upon by the Superintendent. The rest of the places were to be filled by a ballot of the applicants recommended by the Superintendent (Report 309/1922). It seems that this scheme operated until the Slum Clearance Policy of the early 1930s superseded it.

In July 1924, the issue of housing allocation was brought before the Dáil. The case concerned a Mrs Tierney, wife of a railway worker at Amiens Street (now Connolly) Station, who had been refused a house at the Donnelly's Orchard scheme. The Tierney family was living in a house which had one lavatory for the 42 people residing in that dwelling. They had been deemed eligible for one of the houses, and had secured it as a result of a public draw of eligible persons held in the Mansion House. The Government response was that the letting of houses provided by local authorities under the Housing of the Working Classes Act, 1890 to 1919, was entirely within their discretion, so that the Minister had no power to control such lettings. In the same year, the Minister for Local Government and Public Health was asked whether preference for accommodation at the Keogh Barracks housing scheme would be given to 'ex-National soldiers' (that is, Free State forces). While the Minister stated that the fixing of rents and selection of tenants were matters for the Dublin Commissioners, it is interesting to note that such a bias was considered possible.

By 1927 it seems that, when allocating houses, the Dublin Commissioners were giving first consideration to families occupying houses which were considered to be structurally dangerous. 'They have ordered that no vacancy in any of their cheaper dwellings is to be filled except from dangerous houses. It is part of the Commissioner's policy also to induce persons living in low-rented Corporation houses to transfer to better types so that vacancies so arising may be made available for persons from dangerous houses' (Minister for Local Government, Dáil Debates, 21, p. 602).

In March 1930, Richard Mulcahy, Minister for Local Government and Public Health, stated that it was the policy of the city to take families with the largest number of young children, and in so far as they could pay the rents necessary to be paid for these houses, to house the greatest number of such families who were in the greatest need for houses.

Lily O'Connor (2000, p. 137) describes the feelings of the tenement dwellers regarding housing allocation.

> It was the dream of most tenement mothers to be given a small Corporation house out of the city. These little pebble-dash houses were being built on the north and south side of Dublin to relocate the large families living in tenement rooms. The demand was great, and unless someone put a good word in for you, you could be waiting for years. Mothers with babies in their arms persecuted the men behind the counter in the Corporation offices in Lord Edward Street, although some wouldn't take the house that was allotted to them; they'd be wanting a house of their own choice. Mammy and I could be there for hours, upstairs in the narrow, stuffy offices behind crowds. Most were like Mammy and Mrs Murphy – they just wanted a house.

Under the 1931 slum clearance legislation, the local authority was required to provide replacement accommodation for all those displaced by its clearance schemes. This was a laudable objective, since it ensured that slum clearance would not result in further hardship for the poorest of the poor. However, the procedure was slow and unwieldy, while those being rehoused had little say in where they were moved. For those rehoused to St Joseph's Mansions on Killarney Street this was not a problem, as many came from nearby Sherriff Street and Summerhill. However, the people displaced in the Railway Street and Glorney's Buildings Clearance were less fortunate, being uprooted and sent out to a completely new environment in the suburbs of Crumlin and Kimmage.

Under the 1932 Housing Act, priorities for housing allocation were required to be operated by the Corporation wherever practicable, so that all families living in one-roomed dwellings which contained TB cases, adult children, or where the dwelling was condemned as unfit for human habitation, were given precedence. The return to a slum clearance policy and an increase in the rate of building increased the amount of work involved in housing allocation. In September 1933, a special sub-committee appointed to deal with applications for houses on Beggsboro, Friends' Fields and Donnelly's Orchard Areas recommended 'that the representatives for each area submit a list of deserving cases under the headings of tuberculosis, condemned and overcrowded dwellings in proportion to the number of houses available for each area' as per the analysis prepared in the Housing Department (Report 47/1933, p. 270).

By 1934, an extraordinary growth in the number of direct applications for housing had been experienced, with the number now standing at c.11,000. As a result, the Housing Department was radically reorganized, with enlarged offices and a considerable addition to the staff. A Housing Director was appointed to take control of the Department and the housing plan of campaign, co-ordinating the activities of the Engineer, Law Agent, Medical Officer of Health and Housing Architect to ensure the maximum possible progress.

Despite the huge increase in house building by the Corporation in the 1930s, the pace of development did not keep up with demand. In 1937 the Corporation Allocation of Tenancies Branch wrote to one enquirer that it would be some considerable time before cases of six persons in one room were dealt with, adding that 'apart from tuberculosis, dangerous buildings and slum clearance cases, we have not finished dealing with the over-crowding cases of nine and upwards in one room' (quoted in Horner, 1992, p. 332).

Further controversy erupted in 1938, when, following a statement reported in the public press on 30 January regarding housing allocation, the Lord Mayor called a special meeting to investigate the alleged existence of 'hampering methods'. At that time, some 6006 urgent cases were under consideration according to Mr Bourke, Head of the Tenancies Branch. Of these, 4670 cases involved families (including tuberculosis and basement cases) of between 6 and 11 people living in a single room, while the remaining 1336 cases concerned families of 6 to 11 persons occupying two rooms. Following this meeting, an agreement was reached with Housing Committee members whereby they were to end their custom of attending personally with applicants at the Housing Department. The bringing up of applicants for personal interviews had created discontent among other applicants who were unable to obtain these interview facilities. Mr Bourke, head of the Tenancies Branch, expressed the view that if this habit ceased 'much time could be saved both to the Members themselves and the officials, and the work of allocation of houses would proceed more expeditiously' (Report 31/1938, p. 222). Reading between the diplomatic lines, it would seem that Corporation members were attempting to exert undue influence on housing allocation.

Repayment difficulties

The 1939–43 Inquiry found that the ability of the tenant to pay the rent formed the basis of the Corporation's allocation system, cutting across the operation of the statutory priorities under the 1932 Housing Act. Thus ability to pay remained the foundation of the allocation system throughout the period under consideration.

That tenants had difficulties paying even the most basic rent was undeniable. The situation led to considerable difficulties for the local authority. How could housing be provided for people who could not afford to pay anything approaching an 'economic' rent, without imposing a severe burden on the ratepayers? This difficulty was experienced by Dublin Corporation but also by the neighbouring townships, now governed by Urban District Councils. In a meeting at Pembroke UDC, Mr John Good, who was a masterbuilder and later a TD who championed the cause of the tenement-dweller, argued that:

> what was wanted was a house for the unskilled worker, not as had been once described there as for a labourer aristocrat. They should have a house for the poor man at a rent he could pay, not as in the case of previous schemes where tenants had to break their agreements with the Council by sub-letting, as they could not otherwise pay the rent.
>
> (*Irish Builder and Engineer*, 2 December 1922, p. 816)

On the tenant-purchase estates the difficulty of making ends meet, not just in terms of finding the repayments for the house itself, but also for furniture and other requirements, was even more pronounced. Lily O'Connor describes how the neighbours had pride in their new homes in Cabra: 'They kept their windows sparkling and tried to outdo each other with fancy lace curtains and shiny brass letter boxes. Our windows had bright flowered cotton curtains.

Mammy had made these by hand and hung them up with a wire. Then Mammy saw a fender she wanted. She scrimped and scraped to save the five shillings to pay for it' (O'Connor, 2000, p. 140). The costs of running one of the new Corporation dwellings were inevitably higher than those of the tenement flats from which most of the occupants came. For example, in the wintertime, the new houses were icy cold. The coalman would come once a week with fuel. There was a meter for the gas and people often feared to leave their houses when the meters were due to be emptied, for on many occasions people arrived home to discover their scullery window broken and the meter robbed.

Proposals following the Housing Inquiry of 1939–43

The Report of the Housing Inquiry 1939–43 showed that discrimination occurred in housing allocation, with the families with the lower incomes receiving the least attention, and those with the higher incomes receiving the most.

> We find that the great and all powerful cause was that the Corporation, under its existing regulations and system, could not freely give houses to families under the £2 to £3 income category, without facing the fact that a few weeks or months later they would have to bring Court proceedings to evict many of them for non-payment of rent, thus leaving them eventually in a worse position than that in which they found them.
>
> (Housing Inquiry, 1939–43, p. 56, para 142)

The Inquiry proposed a new approach, including differential rents, reduced building costs, improved transport facilities, reconditioning of existing dwellings, a new system of allocation of tenancies, special provision for aged couples or single persons, State responsibility for raising capital and assistance/

Table 15 Private families in Dublin City, 1926 and 1936.

	1926	1936	Increase	Percentage Increase
Persons in Private Families	364,300	424,988	60,688	16.7
One person families	8125	9905	1780	21.9
Two person families	14,393	17,639	3246	22.6
More than Two Persons	62,618	71,789	9171	14.6
Totals	85,136	99,333	14,197	16.6

(Census 1926 and 1936.)

encouragement for non-municipal housing activities. The 1936 Census of Population had shown that, while there was an increase of almost 17 per cent in the number of private families in Dublin City between 1926 and 1936, the proportion of one and two person families had increased ahead of the overall growth. However, there was an almost complete lack of Corporation provision for these smaller families in its housing schemes.

Demographic imbalance in the new schemes

As previously indicated, the 1932 Housing Act required that priorities for housing allocation be operated by the Corporation. Allocation policy was heavily biased in favour of large families, creating a demographic imbalance in Crumlin and other housing areas. Analysis of a sample population in a new suburban area by the Citizens' Housing Council (1938) showed the abnormally high proportions of large families with young children, and concluded that the only remedy was to change the allocation policy to one which would also cater for families of newly-married and elderly couples. Young couples and children under the age of 16 were over-represented at the start of the life of the estate, and, while this pattern would change over time as the population aged, it would remain skewed in respect to the general population unless specific action was taken.

Demographic imbalance would bring social problems to the new housing area. Dillon (1945) warned of the unbalanced composition of the population in Crumlin, especially since preference was given to large families. As the Citizen's Housing Council Report stated, in 10–15 years time these children would have grown up, with no factories, no technical or secondary schools, no football grounds for them. 'The only possible result must be a great increase in street gangs and juvenile crime. This harvest is now in process of reaping. A fine police barracks has been provided …' (Dillon, 1945, p. 19). Such population imbalances and lack of provision of services were to be repeated again when Tallaght was developed in the 1970s.

By this time, the social problems of many of the new housing schemes were becoming evident. The Citizens' Housing Council considered that the layout of every new housing area should 'supply opportunities of developing a community as well as a civic spirit and in time allow of a traditional culture being built up' (1938, p. 30). This would only happen if the population included a range of family sizes and ages. To cater for a mixed population, it was necessary to provide a range of accommodation, rather than the rows of standard, mainly four-roomed, houses at present being erected. While the Housing Committee had considered erecting houses of varying sizes at Marino, in fact all the houses had the same number of rooms, and most subsequent schemes had a similar lack of variety in house size.

The Housing Inquiry of 1939–43 recognized that insufficient attention had been paid to the need for 'after-treatment' among the rehoused working classes.

> There is need for a service specially directed towards the solution of difficulties encountered by families suddenly removed from surroundings which, however defective in many essential respects, had some compensatory advantages the loss of which often causes serious upset in the tenant's way of life. In addition there are difficulties arising immediately from the nature of the new surroundings.

> (Housing Inquiry, 1939–43, p. 138, para. 387)

Not everyone was happy to move to new houses in the suburbs, and in many cases families returned to the city centre, giving up their Corporation houses. Others tried to exchange their homes for other Corporation dwellings. This was a common procedure in Dublin, with people advertising in the evening paper asking for someone willing to transfer with them. Columns of such notices would appear, but the exchange had to be approved by the Corporation. Despite the obvious flaws, however, the provision of housing for those who would otherwise have been destined to remain in the slums was a noble cause and one to which many individuals, both within the local authority and acting independently, dedicated themselves unstintingly.

Conclusion

Housing policy evolved in fits and starts during these years and not always in a positive direction. One could not argue that there was a linear and straightforward development of ideas that were initially given shape in the 1910s. Many reasons conspired to ensure this less than steady progress. Finance was one of the most important influences on Dublin Corporation housing policies to 1940. Its dependence on Government subsidy meant that the city's response to the housing need was not always the most appropriate one. Delays in funding left the problem unsolved for much longer than was necessary, while the actual form of that funding influenced the type of schemes being undertaken. In the 1920s, tenant purchase cottage schemes appeared to be the most attractive option, while the 1930s slum clearance schemes, encouraged by new legislation in 1931 and 1932, were restricted by a Government limit placed on total expenditure.

Politics and ideology were also important factors in the 1920s and 1930s. Improved building methods were not used due to the mistrust of anything which smacked of Communism, while quality building materials were replaced by inferior or more expensive products because of anti-British sentiments and a misplaced confidence in 'native' produce, inspired by patriotic zeal. The erection of expensive, high-quality, five-roomed cottages for tenant purchase in the 1920s reflected a new era of optimism as Ireland enjoyed self-government. However, it was also a reflection of middle-class rule with a middle-class ideology which favoured home ownership. That same ideology was behind the promotion of semi-private schemes and the operation of the SDAA, which drained the Corporation's resources. The erection of flat dwellings was avoided at this time, as single family dwellings were considered to be ideologically superior.

In the 1930s, a worsening international economic situation resulted in a greater pragmatism in the approach to the housing problem. It was recognized that the high quality suburban schemes of the 1920s, while idealistic, had not succeeded in tackling a worsening working-class housing crisis. Government legislation encouraged a new approach based on slum clearance. There was a return to flat building, perceived as a necessary evil, while larger scale suburban rented cottage schemes were erected. In general, dwellings had fewer, smaller, rooms, as financial constraints limited the quality of housing. Because of the increased output of housing in the 1930s, the Corporation experienced difficulties in operating a fair tendering system, while political pull (or sheer good business) may have been behind the dominance of just three firms in securing local authority housing contracts. At the other end of the building process, the allocation of those houses was also subject to the whims of politicians, and it was not until the very end of the 1930s that fairer rental and allocation systems were initiated.

Throughout the period, debates concerning the relative merits of houses versus flats, and of suburban versus central locations, continued. The young town planning movement was to have a say in both of these questions. Its impact, and the physical and social results of Dublin Corporation's housing policies, are considered next.

Dublin Corporation housing schemes to 1940

Building houses in Dublin in the years before 1940 was a complex affair and we have seen that there were many controls and influences on the operation of the Corporation. We now turn to look at what was built and here the focus is on the built environment. The operation of housing policy can be conveniently divided into a number of phases, linked to prevailing planning and architectural guidelines but most importantly to particular social goals which were considered in the previous chapter. To begin with, we will look at where the inspiration for the housing schemes came from, starting with the role of architects and planners, the changes in British policy from World War I, specific influences on flat dwellings and their design and the general debate concerning town planning in Dublin.

We will concentrate on the development of some of Dublin's key schemes, in terms of vision, design, planning, style and of course, what it was like to live there. This begins with three housing schemes of the 1920s, at Marino, designed and planned as an ideal 'garden suburb', Drumcondra and Donnycarney. The schemes built in the 1930s are of a different character, associated with a change in Government policy and an increasing emphasis on slum clearance. Both flat schemes and cottages built for rental are considered. In particular, we will focus on the development of Crumlin during the 1930s, the largest scheme completed prior to 1940 and one which has been heavily criticized. We end by considering some of the issues raised by the nature of development at Crumlin and the impact of housing policy on communities.

Changing housing styles in Corporation schemes

The past schemes of the Corporation show little evidence of conforming with modern ideas. They have looked to a part and not to the whole of the city. The maximum number of houses has been put on each site, and the resulting density of population perpetuates slum conditions.

(Memorandum by J.F. MacCabe, Housing Inquiry, 1914, p. 30)

As we have seen, the initial efforts of the Dublin Corporation to provide housing for the working classes arose out of nineteenth-century concern for public health, and more generally from a somewhat paternalistic belief that the poor, or more specifically, the 'deserving poor', should be adequately housed. However, in attempting to achieve these goals, there was a tendency towards functionality. Thus, working-class housing schemes built by Dublin Corporation before 1914 were generally built of the most inexpensive, plain materials to minimum space standards and using simple technology. The background to these developments is discussed by Daly (1985) and Aalen (1985). Dublin Corporation's early flat schemes (described as block dwellings in contemporary reports) were relatively small, of two or three storeys, and consisted of apartments off common halls. By the time of the housing inquiry report, 967 flats had been completed in six schemes (Benburb Street, Bow Lane, Bride's Alley, Blackhall Place, Foley Street and Townsend Street). The earliest of these, at Benburb Street and Bow Lane West, aimed to house the most needy, but gave rise to fears that new slums were being created. Within ten years of completion, the death rate in the Benburb Street flats was higher than the city average, leading critics to claim that Dublin Corporation was demolishing slums only to recreate them. Of course, the reality was more complex than suggested by the scheme's decriers. The fact was that the link between mortality and low socio-economic status persisted even in improved dwellings, but this correlation was not commonly recognized. The Bow Lane scheme of 1889 did little to alter public opinion regarding the schemes, but was important in establishing the precedent by which rents were purposely restricted to sums within the reach of the least well-paid of the 'labouring classes'. Thus, in 1889 for the first time the Corporation accepted the principle of a small annual loss on its housing schemes, in order to provide for the needy. Despite this important step, from the erection of the Blackhall Place scheme in 1894/5, higher rents became the norm, reflecting both an increase in building costs and the Corporation's desperate need to make the schemes pay. One exception was the 1905 Foley Street scheme, a brave, but failed, experiment in housing for the very poor, the success of which was jeopardized from the start by its proximity to Dublin's red-light district, 'Monto'. Even the poorest of the poor preferred 'respectable' slums to 'immoral' quality housing. The experience of these early flat schemes contributed to the belief that by building block dwellings the Corporation was creating slums for the future, while their lack of financial viability gave critics further scope for censure.

22 Early Dublin Corporation cottages at Inchicore (*c.*1911). (Photograph by J. Brady.) Notice the width of the road relative to the size of the houses.

In this early period of housing development, prior to 1914, Dublin Corporation built a mixture of houses and flats. More successful and popular than the block dwellings, but also more expensive and less availed of by those in real need, were the individual two-up two-down plain red-brick terraced cottages laid out in streets and squares. The cottage schemes built prior to the Housing Inquiry provided 552 dwellings in a generally unimaginative layout. Even at the eight-acre (*c.*3ha) virgin site at Inchicore, which afforded possibilities for a more interesting and lower density layout, the rigid plan of terraces was used with little public open space. Front doorways opened directly on to the street, while there were yards at the rear of the houses. The 1914 plans for Fairbrother's Fields and Ormond Market show the typical use of space at the time, with small houses in rigid grids at high densities, and the only public open space taking the form of a very large central playground. These layouts were very similar to the layouts used in the pre-World War I housing schemes built by the London County Council (LCC), such as the Totterdown Fields scheme. As in Dublin, there was a sharp contrast between the early suburban estates and those erected post-1919, where the influence of town planning ideals largely through the Tudor Walters report (discussed below) was to become apparent in greater openness, variety and lower density housing. Indeed, when looking at the early layouts, two of the most influential town planners of the day, Geddes and Unwin, considered the layouts to be unsuccessful, with too-high densities and rigid grid-like plans, far removed from the 'garden suburb' layout promoted by the modern town planning movement.

Table 16 Dublin Corporation housing schemes pre-1914.

Scheme	Completion Date (approx)	Total	Rooms			
			1	*2*	*3*	*4*
Benburb Street	1887	144	63	67	10	4
Bow Lane	1889	86	0	76	10	0
Bride's Alley	1895	173	0	94	79	0
Blackhall Place	1896	86	0	81	5	0
St Joseph's Place	1896	80	0	0	80	0
Elizabeth Street	1904	14	0	0	14	0
Clontarf	1905	57	0	24	24	9
Foley Street	1905	458	378	64	16	0
Townsend Street	1907	20	0	15	5	0
Inchicore	1912	333	0	0	279	54
Total		1451	441	421	522	67

Table 17 Dublin Corporation schemes completed 1914–21.

Scheme	Completion Date (approx.)	Total	Rooms			
			1	*2*	*3*	*4*
Cook Street	1914	45	0	45	0	0
Lurgan Street	1914	48	0	48	0	0
Trinity Ward	1917	48	48	0	0	0
Trinity Ward	1917	28	0	28	0	0
Church Street	1917	146	28	94	24	0
Ormond Market	1917/1921	56	56	0	0	0
Ormond Market	1917/1921	61	0	61	0	0
Ceannt Fort	1917	202	0	0	202	0
Colbert Fort	1917	60	20	40	0	0
Spitalfields	1918	75	0	75	0	0
Total		769	152	391	226	0

Although the start had been slow, by 1914 Dublin Corporation had 35 housing schemes in hand, under the auspices of a newly formed Housing Committee, suggesting that a determined effort was about to be made to address Dublin's working-class housing problems. However, the outbreak of war and the growing uncertainty about the political future of Ireland as a whole, meant that only a handful of these schemes was initiated.

A number of these delayed schemes benefited from official town planning guidance in 1914, as discussed previously. There were some innovations, such as the inclusion of electric lighting at Cook Street. At Ceannt Fort, façades were enlivened with gables, while parts of the site which were unsuitable for housing were given over to playgrounds and gardens. In the schemes at Ormond Market and in the Trinity Ward area, a mixture of flats and cottages was provided. This combination of different dwelling types in one scheme was to be extremely unusual when the Corporation's suburban policies got underway in the 1920s. Of the dwellings completed between 1914 and 1921, the majority were three-roomed cottages, with only 104 two-roomed flats being completed. In total, just 769 units were completed in these small-scale schemes.

Suburban cottage estates in the 1920s

During World War I, in anticipation of the end of hostilities, a new housing programme was planned by the Dublin Corporation Housing Committee. The suburban 'cottage estates' which were the major fruits of the programme showed the advances in thinking which had taken place during the war years. Although many of the sites chosen for the schemes had been identified long before, given the unstable political situation and the financial difficulties of the city, it is not surprising that the first cottage estates to include suggestions of 'garden city' planning were not undertaken until 1923. These two schemes, at Donnelly's Orchard and Fairbrother's Fields, were also the first tenant purchase houses to be built by Dublin Corporation, which was to complete more than 4200 such houses over an eight-year period. The Donnelly's Orchard cottages were the first five-roomed dwellings to be erected by the Corporation since its housing programme had begun, and this larger house size was to become the norm for the model 'garden suburb' at Marino. All but a handful of the five-roomed dwellings (2256 in total) erected by the Corporation to 1939 were on its tenant purchase estates. However, the high ideals of these new schemes gradually gave way to a more pragmatic approach. The Drumcondra Scheme (c.1928) included three-roomed dwellings, while the final purchase schemes, completed in 1930 and 1931, omitted five-roomed houses in favour of smaller four-roomed dwellings.

The 1920s tenant purchase schemes also marked a trend towards larger scale cottage schemes as, with the exception of Donnelly's Orchard and Marrowbone Lane, each of the new suburban estates provided more than four hundred dwellings. The Marino/Croydon Park scheme was the largest of all, with *c*.1300 Corporation-built cottages. With this general trend towards the erection of large schemes, the Corporation had to rely more heavily on tenders from private construction firms, rather than building the dwellings itself through the Municipal Workshops Department, thus generating further linkages between public and private enterprise.

Table 18 Tenant purchase schemes, 1914–39.

Scheme	Completion date (approx.)	Total Cottages	Rooms 3	4	5
Donnelly's Orchard	1923	84	0	0	84
Fairbrother's Fields	1923/1927	416	0	82	334
Marino	1926	431	0	0	431
Croydon Park/					
Philipsburgh Ave.	1927	931	0	2	929
Emmet Road	1927–1929	702	0	421	281
Drumcondra	1928	535	211	145	179
Marrowbone Lane	1930	87	0	87	0
Donnycarney	1930	421	0	421	0
Cabra	1931	641	0	641	0
Total		**4248**	**211**	**1799**	**2238**
% Tenant purchase houses		100	5	42.3	52.7

Of the 14,884 dwellings provided by Dublin Corporation to 1939, 4248 (28.5 per cent) formed part of the tenant purchase policy of the 1920s. Meanwhile, outside the Corporation area, the Pembroke Urban District Council followed this lead, swapping the cottage rental schemes of 1912 and 1914 for a tenant purchase approach in its 1925 and 1929 schemes, which included larger three-, four- and five-roomed dwellings. By contrast, the four schemes undertaken by Rathmines UDC prior to its absorption by Dublin Corporation in 1930 were all rental cottage and flat schemes (Housing Inquiry, 1939–43, p. 232).

The tenant purchase policy meant that local authority houses were beyond the means of all but the most highly paid workers, despite the fact that the Corporation was failing to recoup full costs. Often those who managed to get a house because they were regarded as being capable of meeting the relatively high rents found it a hard struggle to make ends meet, particularly since they now had to find money to pay extra fares to their work in central areas. At Marino, the money-lenders who came to collect their interest each Monday were often greeted with flying pots and pans!

Influences on the new schemes – Architects and Planners

A number of influences combined in the new schemes built in the 1920s and 1930s. In particular, Dublin Corporation was influenced by town planning ideas and debate, in terms not just of individual architects and planners, or the work of municipal authorities elsewhere, but also by new housing guide-lines drawn-up after World War I. Of course, the political situation has already been mentioned, and was undoubtedly significant in terms of various housing policy shifts over the period in question.

One of the major difficulties experienced by the Housing Section of Dublin Corporation in the housing drive of the 1920s was the lack of skilled architects and draughtsmen at the design stage. Therefore, at the time of the 1918 Housing Policy Report, it was decided to secure the services of six architects practising in Dublin and recommended by Charles MacCarthy, the City Architect, to prepare the plans and supervise the works in connection with the eight proposed schemes (Report 18/1919).

The decision caused controversy, as it was felt that the architects should have been chosen by open competition. In particular, Assistant City Architect Horace T. O'Rourke was disappointed by the decision, and requested that he be allowed to take complete charge of the proposed schemes, in light of his considerable experience in housing design, and the much reduced costs to the Committee if his department were to undertake the work. He further suggested that he should act either as Architect to the Housing Committee in addition to his present position, or that he should be appointed Director of Housing on the same lines as English municipalities. Nothing came of these suggestions, and the Corporation therefore employed outside architects for a number of the schemes to be built in the 1920s. Later schemes were to rely solely on the services of the Housing Department's own team, encouraging conformity in design and layout plans.

Table 19 Proposed architects for Corporation schemes, December 1918.

Scheme	Architects
Millbourne Avenue	Messrs McDonnell & Dixon
Friends' Fields	Messrs Orpen and Dickinson
Crabbe Lane and Spitalfields	Mr T. F. MacNamara
North Lotts	Messrs O'Callaghan & Webb
Mary's Lane and Boyne Street	Mr George L. O'Connor
Newfoundland Street	Messrs Batchelor and Hicks

(Report 18/1919.)

MacCarthy, who was the son of well-known architect J.J. MacCarthy, resigned due to ill-health in 1921. He had been appointed City Architect in 1893, succeeding D.J. Freeman. According to the *Irish Builder and Engineer* (4 June 1921, p. 381), MacCarthy was a very popular municipal official and ever-receptive to new ideas. It noted that he was 'tolerant' to modern suggestions, indicating that there was a certain reluctance to go further, but that he at least listened to colleagues with whom he disagreed. In February 1922, H.T. O'Rourke, who had been Acting City Architect, was appointed to succeed MacCarthy as City Architect, at a salary of £800 rising to £1000 by £25 increments. The position had not been advertised and there was some dispute as to the appointment on this basis. By April, the position of Assistant City Architect was advertised at £500 per annum, rising to £750, again by £25 increments. The age limit was 35 years and it was stated that the candidates should be Irishmen. In May 1922 the position of Temporary Draftsman in the City Architect's Department was advertised, at £6 6s. per week, the same rate as applied to Clerks of Works on the Corporation housing schemes at the time. In November a temporary Quantity Surveyor position was advertised at £500 p.a. The request was for an Irishman between 30 and 40 years of age.

Although it favoured the employment of Irishmen, Dublin Corporation's Housing Committee was more broad-minded when it came to seeking appropriate solutions to the housing question, and contacts with both British and Continental European cities were promoted. On a 1921 visit to several English cities, for example, the Town Clerk was particularly impressed by the five-roomed semi-detached suburban houses being constructed by the local authority in Liverpool. In 1926 when a new Dublin flat scheme was contemplated, inspection visits to London, Liverpool and Manchester were undertaken. Also in the 1920s, interest in the new Dutch housing was reflected in a series of study trips to Amsterdam and Rotterdam. In the early 1930s, with the return to inner-city flat-building schemes, this Dutch architecture was to have renewed relevance. Similarly, the Housing Committee was well aware of developments in Vienna during this period, although it was to look more to the Netherlands for architectural inspiration in its flat developments. Rothery's book (1991) *Ireland and the New Architecture* gives an interesting account of these 'modern' influences.

Influences on the new schemes – post-World War I Britain
Despite the political change which occurred during this period, and the antipathy towards Britain in many quarters, both local authority and private developers largely looked there for their ideas, and for Dublin Corporation the influence of the garden city model was strong. The report of a committee, chaired by Sir John Tudor Walters, MP, which had inquired into working-class housing provision in Britain in anticipation of a post-war shortage, gave an important boost to town planning, and also had an important influence on public housing in Ireland. The Tudor Walters report (1918) involved a study of construction and design standards, and set out minimum standards which it hoped would profoundly affect the general standard of housing. The Report was followed by a *Housing Manual* (1919), revised and updated regularly, which provided a very practical body of advice about housing development and which was relied on heavily by local authorities for their post-war schemes. From the 1920s, Britain's local authorities actually built much of suburbia, and following the Tudor Walters-inspired housing manual, set very high minimum standards which private developers were forced to copy. Dublin Corporation generally adopted similar standards for its suburban housing schemes. For example, the Local Government Board specified that the number of houses on a site should not exceed 12 to the acre (*c.*30 per ha) in urban areas and eight to the acre (*c.*20 per ha) in rural areas. The housing manual also stated that 'the self-contained two-storey cottage type should generally be adopted'. Appendix IV noted that there did not appear to be any justification for the claim of economy in the construction of tenements or two-storey flats as compared with two-storey cottages, although 'exceptional circumstances' might justify one or other of these alternative methods or one-storey bungalows.

The housing manual included designs of the Royal Institute of British Architects and plans recommended by Sir J. Tudor Walters' Committee. Similarly, the rather smaller 1919 Housing of the Working Classes in Ireland report, published by HMSO in Dublin, provided 'plans for the layout of typical sites and for various types of houses', including a selection from plans submitted to an architectural competition. That competition had arisen 'in

23 Model housing designs from the UK. (Housing Manual on the design, construction and repair of dwellings, 1927, p. 19. HMSO.) Variants exist in many Dublin schemes.

view of the proposals of the Government to assist local authorities in the provision of houses for the working classes', when the Royal Institute of the Architects of Ireland (RIAI) suggested to the Local Government Board for Ireland that an architectural competition should be arranged. Recognizing the importance of professional know-how, the Board agreed to this suggestion and obtained authority to provide 'premiums' to a total value of £500. The intention was 'to secure designs for suitable and economical types of houses grouped in the most advantageous manner on typical sites'. There were two parts to the competition. The first looked for plans for four types of houses and the layout of a housing scheme on each of three typical sites. Notably, the competition conditions specified a density of not more than ten houses to the acre (*c*.25 per ha). However, the tenement dwellers were not forgotten. The second part of the competition sought plans showing how 'existing four-storeyed houses, originally built for the occupation of one family, might be suitably and economically adapted to provide flats of moderate size for a number of families'. The three assessors were Mr Kaye-Parry (president of the RIAI), Mr Henry Seaver (president of the Ulster Society of Architects, 1912–13) and Mr T.J. Byrne (Chief Architect of the Office of Public Works in 1925).

Although R.M. Butler praised the designs obtained in the Irish Local Government competition as 'a great advance on what was previously considered good enough', he cautioned 'I venture to think that some of them have been too closely influenced by English precedents' (*Irish Builder and Engineer*, 2 February 1921, p. 119). However, modified versions of these designs were to be used in Dublin and elsewhere for the next number of years. Although the lack of a truly Irish style of architecture was sometimes bemoaned, the advantages of the adoption of new standards in construction quality, site design and layout far outweighed any perceived national disappointment at this state of affairs.

The Tudor Walters report which influenced both the British housing manual and the Irish designs discussed above was itself largely inspired by the garden city movement. In particular, it codified many of the ideas applied by Unwin and Parker (see Appendix) at Letchworth and Hampstead and was to create a new form of suburbia. One of the most fundamental changes which it influenced was the adoption of a maximum housing density of 12 houses to the acre (*c*.30 per ha) in suburban locations. This advice resulted in low-density layout using culs-de-sac for full site development as at Hampstead, rather than a rigid grid, and this was to become the norm for speculative builders and local authorities alike. Both aesthetic and practical considerations were to be taken into account in the layout of estates, with a stress on the

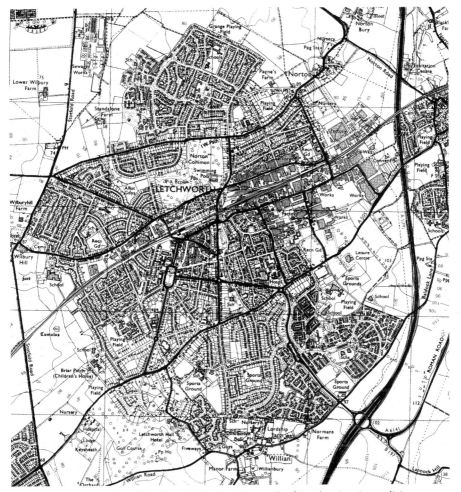

24 Layout plan of Letchworth Garden City north of London (see Appendix).

preservation of existing trees and shrubs, and the creation of pleasant vistas. It was for aesthetic reasons that the semi-detached house was rejected in favour of short terraces of four to six houses, with tunnels to give rear access to back gardens of a good size. House frontages were wider and avoided 'tunnel back' rear projections so that most rooms received natural sunlight. Terraces were generally adopted on Corporation schemes, although some semi-detached houses were also built. The report warned against the creation of monotonous uniformity, a cry which was echoed by O'Rourke and Simms in calls for variety of design on various estates including Crumlin. In Marino, for example, the houses were to be built in blocks of eight, six, five, and three, and in pairs, using

a variety of materials and different methods of construction, with the explicit
intention of avoiding a monotonous appearance.

The normal house was to have two living rooms and three bedrooms, all
with stated minimum sizes. Privacy was considered important, so there were
no shared facilities. Fixed baths were considered essential although they were
often covered by a 'work-top lid' in the scullery, an idea practised in Dublin
Corporation housing at Mount Drummond. In relation to bath and toilet
facilities, there was some attempt to roll back on provision of these facilities
as the 1920s wore on, both in Britain and Ireland. A leader in the *Irish Builder
and Engineer* in March 1923 noted some suggestions that the standard of
housing enforced by the late Local Government Board for Ireland and
continued by the Ministry for Local Government was too high. In the same
year, the British House of Commons decided that baths in State-aided
working-class houses were luxuries rather than necessities, leading to a
scathing article in the *Irish Builder and Engineer* suggesting that the MPs
might like to do without such a 'luxury' for themselves! In response, Page L.
Dickinson, a noted columnist, argued that at least 70 per cent of the baths in
working-class houses were regularly used, while he had found no case of
failure to use a w.c. when provided (*Irish Builder and Engineer*, 21 April 1923).

One of the most obvious influences of the Tudor Walters report and subsequent housing manuals in Dublin was in the adoption of the five-roomed house
as standard during the 1920s. The red-brick terraced Corporation houses typical
of the Clontarf and Inchicore schemes were replaced by larger houses which
used more varied designs at Marino. However, apart from the Marino scheme,
the suggested importance of open space, allotments and existing shrubbery
was largely ignored in Dublin Corporation schemes.

More specifically, looking at the city of London we can see how the two
capital cities pursued similar paths in the post-World War I period. London, like
Dublin, had focused on high-density central housing schemes before the First
World War, with a few tentative suburban cottage schemes undertaken at
Totterdown Fields, White Hart Lane, Norbury and Old Oak. The scarcity of
labour and materials, and the high interest rates in the period immediately after
the war resulted in a severe housing shortage. From 1919, legislation placed the
responsibility for supplying low-rent housing on the local authorities. Rents were
to be fixed according to capacity to pay, and all plans were to be approved by the
Ministry of Health with obligatory Tudor Walters' standards. With this Act in
place, London County Council concentrated on the erection of large cottage
estates in the suburbs, much as Dublin Corporation was doing here. The estates,

built at a 12 house per acre (*c.*30 per ha) density, generally included both parlour and non-parlour type two-storey houses (with five-, four- and three-rooms) and some three-storey flat blocks. The LCC built eight new cottage estates between 1919 and 1939, most of them of considerable size, and started a further seven estates in the late 1930s. In total, about 61,000 cottages and flats were provided, of which 26,000 were at Becontree alone. Despite the clear difference in scale, a comparison of layout plans and house designs clearly illustrates close parallels between the housing estates built by local authorities in Dublin and London.

In 1925 the Irish Free State's Ministry of Local Government provided further model plans for housing when it issued a five-volume series of *House Designs prescribed by the Minister for Local Government under the Housing Act, 1924*. The volumes covered three-roomed, four-roomed (parlour and non-parlour) and five-roomed cottages, including a special volume of designs for four-roomed dwellings for areas where sewers and water mains were unavailable. The model house types were numbered and were often used as a sort of shorthand when discussing new schemes. For example, type C7 was noteworthy as the design used for the first houses to be built under the Million Pound Grant of 1922. The dwellings at Marino, Donnelly's Orchard and Fairbrother's Fields were based on types D8 and D9, both designs for five-roomed 'parlour houses'. The importance of providing a 'parlour' in working-class houses was often debated, as it was felt that the costs would be better spent in offering a further bedroom. However, the little-used parlour was very important psychologically. Hugh Leonard, who grew up in a tiny cottage in Dalkey in the 1930s, describes the nature of this room:

> The back room of our house was the kitchen; it held a dresser, a table, wooden chairs, a gas stove and a double bed where my parents slept. The front room was always referred to with fitting deference as 'the room' and contained a black wardrobe, a sideboard, two balding furry armchairs and a matching divan which was my bed. It held our treasures – two coloured photographs of Blackpool, God knows how come by, china dogs, fancy egg cups that had once held Easter eggs, brass fire irons, the good – the only – tea service and a silver flower holder containing honesty. Apart from serving as my bedroom, it was used only at Christmas and on the solemnest of social occasions. In our town, as elsewhere, even the smallest cottage was and still is divided in two – one part for living in, the other as an ideal, a regret and an aspiration, all in one.
>
> (Leonard, 1979, p. 81)

25 Dublin Corporation's flat developments at Pearse House, Hanover Street (*above*) and Markievicz House, Townsend Street (*below*). (Photographs by R. McManus.)

26 Dublin Corporation's flat developments at Mercer House *(above)* and
Chancery Street *(below)*. (Photographs by R. McManus.)

Flat Dwellings

Although only one flat scheme was built during the 1920s (Boyne Street), the architects working in Dublin Corporation were continually seeking new ideas and inspiration. The buildings designed for the Amsterdam Housing Authority from *c.*1913 to the mid-1920s provoked great interest throughout Europe because of the innovations in their architecture and the massive scale of the building developments. Official interest in the new Dutch housing was reflected, in the 1920s, in a series of study trips to the Netherlands by Irish Government architects and Dublin Corporation officials. In 1925 the most important such trip took place when the City Architect, Horace T. O'Rourke, the Chief Architect of the Office of Public Works, T.J. Byrne, and the Commissioner of the County Borough of Dublin, W.C. Dwyer, travelled to Rotterdam and Amsterdam to inspect systems of house construction.

While the early Free State schemes such as Marino were of suburban cottages in garden city-type layouts, when the Dublin Corporation architects began to design flat blocks again in the 1930s the influence of the Amsterdam dwellings was evident. Two strands of Dutch architecture seem to have been combined in the Dublin flat schemes. The first influence was of the Amsterdam School, the Expressionist style of which is exemplified in de Klerk's flats in Amsterdam South, especially on the Amstelkade and Rynstraat (1921–3). In Dublin, the style is evident in the Townsend Street scheme designed by Herbert Simms (1934–6), where an arched entrance is treated in an Expressionist manner with a flat reinforced concrete canopy over roof level to emphasize the entrance feature. The idea of an arched entrance with apartments taken across at first-floor level was common in the Amsterdam housing schemes and was adopted in the Hanover Street scheme in 1935 (Report 57/1935). Projecting balconies with rounded corners echo those of many schemes in Amsterdam South. Indeed, the most important features of the Amsterdam housing, the brick buildings aligned along and forming the street façades, and the definition of the corners, entrances and balcony features, were all faithfully followed in the Dublin schemes, although perhaps the greater social concerns behind the style of housing selected in Amsterdam were not taken up.

The second strand of Dutch architecture which can be seen in Dublin is the De Stijl movement (Rothery, 1991; Taverne, 1994). The characteristics of this style include a strongly horizontal quality, rounded ends and use of reinforced concrete cantilevers for roofs and canopies. Such qualities also appear in Dublin schemes such as Townsend Street. The use of a plaster finish rather than brick was also copied in Dublin at the Hanover/Sandwith Street and Greek Street schemes.

While Rothery (1991) has discussed the influence of Dutch architecture on Dublin Corporation's flat blocks of the 1930s, mention should also be made of British developments, particularly those of the London County Council, which appear to have provided a further influence for the Dublin Corporation architects. Mercer House (figure 26) near Cuffe Street is the Corporation development which suggests the closest influence from the London flats. Indeed, in March 1926 the *Irish Builder and Engineer* reported that City Commissioner Dr Dwyer and the City Architect had recently inspected the latest flat schemes undertaken by the London County Council and were now discussing the question of erecting similar dwellings on the Crabbe Lane site (adjacent to Cuffe Street and Mercer Street). Mr R.S. Lawrie, ARIBA had been appointed at eight guineas per week, to enable the City Architect to have the requisite plans prepared (*Irish Builder and Engineer*, 6 March 1926). The four-storey blocks which make up the scheme were built from 1930. They have yellow brick facades to the lower three storeys, the fourth being occupied by a Mansard-style roof. The flats are reached by external balcony access from the rear of the buildings. The classical treatment of the facade bears similarities to some London County Council flat schemes of the late 1920s, such as the Tabard Garden (Bermondsey), China Walk (Lambeth) and Comber Estates (Camberwell).

The town planning debate in Dublin

> You cannot afford to delay in chasing ideals; steady, progressive development is shown in the record of your past schemes. The last is a long way in advance of the first, and even if perfection has not yet been obtained, you have provided decent dwellings in substitution for kennels not fit to house a dog, whilst others were discussing questions of town planning and garden cities on the basis of wealthy English towns and well-paid English workmen.
>
> (Letter to the Housing Committee from its Joint
> Secretaries, quoted in Report 18/1919, p. 124)

While the ideas of town planning were becoming more widely known and attracted considerable attention as possible tools in the struggle to provide suitable accommodation for the working classes, many officials within Dublin Corporation were dubious as to the feasibility of the new concept. The point was repeatedly made that town planning was too idealistic for the job in hand, that in some way these new-fangled ideas would distract from the reality of the housing problem. An unfortunate early rift between the Corporation and the Housing and Town Planning Association of Ireland, which became apparent in 1914, shortly after the publication of the report of the housing inquiry, resulted in the Housing Committee cutting itself off from a potentially important source of ideas and encouragement.

However, in the 1920s the ideas of town planning gradually came to earn some respect among Corporation members. After about 1910, professional planners had become quite involved in promoting the town planning movement in Dublin, with lectures and exhibitions organized by Geddes, and his joint report with Unwin. The city authorities maintained contact throughout the 1920s with Abercrombie and Kelly, winners of the Dublin International Town Planning Competition, and it appears that there were several abortive attempts to prepare a new town plan. Although no representatives attended the Housing and Town Planning Congress in London in June 1920, in the following year it was considered worthwhile for the Town Clerk to visit several English cities, where he was particularly impressed by local authority housing in Liverpool. During the 1930s, Corporation officials were to attend conferences organized by the Garden City and Town Planning Association, while delegations were also sent to study town planning schemes in Britain's principal cities.

Despite the greater degree of acceptance given to planning ideas, the amount of development control available to the Corporation (outside of its own housing schemes) was strictly limited in the 1920s. Generally, only objections based on the bylaws could prevent building, and even then the bylaws were frequently suspended. For example, the Corporation did not see anything wrong with the plan of a house to be erected across the angle of Seafield Road and a new road intended to be constructed at right angles to Seafield Road, since it would be some time before the district was developed (Report 252/1920). When the Ryan Manufacturing and Construction Company defied the City Architect and proceeded with buildings which he had disapproved under the bylaws, appealing to the Housing Department of the Local Government Board, there was nothing that could be done to prevent the construction. As a further blow, the company ultimately received full grants under the 1919 Housing Act (Reports 36 and 56/1921). In at least one case where plans infringed the bylaws, the Corporation was so keen to encourage development that the City Architect actually drew up the new plans (Report 23/1924). Thus, the tendency in the 1920s was to invite and bolster building activity, with bylaws only invoked in extreme cases.

In the 1930s controls over development were tightened as the rate of house building increased, heightening concerns regarding ribbon development. Leading up to the introduction of the 1934 Planning Act, there had been a gradual recognition of the need for planning, and thus the applications for 'planning permission', although not described as such, were more carefully screened, with a greater number of provisos being added to any approval. An assessment of the Corporation printed reports from 1910 to 1939 shows an increasing tendency towards the regulation of building and development within the City, through bylaws and restrictive clauses in leases of the City Estate. By 1935, every plan submitted by private owners for estate development and for building was carefully examined from the town planning aspect, so that (the City Manager claimed) substantial improvements had been made in hundreds of cases by way of better layout of new roads, by road widening, by setting back the building frontage line and by splaying corners. The significance of the policy was in no doubt, given that, in the previous 18 months alone plans for 128 private development and building schemes had been sanctioned by the City Manager only following amendments 'in the interests of sound town planning principles' (Report 50/1935, p. 257).

In addition to a recognition of the need for control of private schemes, the concern for more careful planning of the Corporation's own housing schemes led to the appointment of a Housing Architect, Mr H.G. Simms, in January 1932. A Housing Director was finally appointed in 1934, almost 16 years after H.T. O'Rourke had appealed for such a role, while a Town Planning Committee was appointed to the Corporation late in 1935 (Report 50/1935). It was this new Committee which recommended that the Town and Regional Planning Act 1934 be brought into operation in Dublin County Borough, and in 1936, Abercrombie and Kelly were engaged to give a preliminary report on the organization which would be required for its implementation (Report 65/1936). In the interim, the City Manager and Town Clerk was authorized to carry out the requirements of the Town Planning Committee regarding control of building development. In 1937, Abercrombie and Kelly were appointed as Joint Consultants for the Dublin Town Planning Scheme, with offices on Dame Street. The Town Planning Consultants did not confine themselves to the preparation of the Dublin Plan, but were consulted on a regular basis regarding day-to-day planning issues. For example, the leasing of ground in Fleet Street at the rere of the GSR Omnibus Department's offices to a private proposer was deferred, pending discussions with the Town Planning Consultants, 'as it was considered that the leasing of this ground might interfere with a proposal for an internal omnibus station contemplated on Aston's Quay site' (Report 6/1939, p. 35). Proposals made by two private owners for building schemes adjacent to Ballymun Road, Finglas in the County Council area were rejected by the Acting Planning Officer, since this development would prevent a westward continuation of the Collins Avenue extension to form an outer ring road and would also interfere with a proposed new radial thoroughfare, Griffith Avenue Extension (Report 24/1939). At last the importance of good long-term planning was recognized, and the Corporation was no longer slave to the will of the private speculative builder. This general acceptance of the necessity of planning, and zoning, was a belated one, such ideas having been argued by witnesses to the 1913 Inquiry, the first Dublin Town Plan (1914/22) and the Civic Survey (1925).

Marino: the Corporation's first garden suburb

A building scheme at Marino had first been mooted in 1910, when a public meeting at Clontarf Town Hall called for a 'Garden City' at Marino, following which James Walter, lessor of the land, wrote to the Corporation, informing them that he was willing to sell his interest in the Marino farm for a 'Miniature Garden City'. Three years later, a Corporation report noted that Walker held about 50 acres (*c.*20ha) with space for 1250 dwellings on a sub-lease with an unexpired term of eight years (Report 23/1913). As part of their consultancy work in 1914, Unwin and Geddes prepared a plan for a garden suburb at Marino. The preliminary layout plan involved 96 acres, including the Marino House grounds and additional land from the Christian Brothers Seminary. Eleven hundred houses at a density of 11½ per acre (*c.*29 per ha) were planned, with 12½ acres (*c.*5ha) of allotments. The ideal of 12 houses to the acre (*c.*30 per ha) was the classic garden suburb density, advocated in Unwin's famous document *Nothing Gained by Overcrowding* and later taken up in the Tudor Walters report and 1919 Housing Act. Existing trees and woodlands were to be incorporated into the layout where possible. The roads varied in width depending on anticipated loading, while 'green paths', analogous to the Radburn traffic-free pedestrian network first employed in 1928 in Fairlawn, New Jersey, were also proposed. The Radburn idea involves the complete separation of traffic and pedestrians. Housing areas known as superblocks are ringed by roads from which culs-de-sac service roads lead into

27 General plan of Radburn, New Jersey, USA showing the superblocks.

the interior of the housing area. Thus traffic is filtered to ensure that only local traffic enters each housing area. Pedestrians travel via a network of footpaths, separate to the road system. Where footpaths and roads intersect, they are kept segregated by the use of bridges and overpasses. Cumbernauld new town in Scotland is a good example of the use of different circulation systems.

Finally, in 1915 the Corporation obtained control of the land, which was then used as allotments by the Land Cultivation Committee for a number of years. In 1918 the Housing Committee 're-entered on the consideration of the scheme in connection with the post-war housing programme', and received a report from Charles MacCarthy, City Architect, giving an outline of the proposed housing scheme (Report 301/1918). He proposed that 600 houses should be built on the 50 acre (*c.*20ha) site – 12 houses per acre (*c.*30 per ha). The previous mention in December 1913 had suggested more than double that density, illustrating the influence of garden city norms, and probably more specifically the Unwin-Geddes plan, in the intervening years. MacCarthy suggested that the houses should be larger than those hitherto provided by the Corporation, the majority having at least three bedrooms, although a limited number of two-bedroom houses should be provided for tenants with small families. The approximate cost of the 600 houses would be £659 per house, or £395,400. Following on Geddes' advice at the Housing Inquiry, he called for the provision of baths with a hot and cold water supply in every house, despite the costs. MacCarthy's proposals also indicate that the scheme was being thought of in a broader town planning context, rather than with sole regard for housing provision. He suggested that provision be made for two future roads, one leading to Philipsburgh Avenue and the other through Whitehall to Glasnevin.

In October 1919, the Municipal Council approved MacCarthy's Marino scheme, adopting the types of construction known as A, F and K (instead of H) and reinforced concrete roadways as recommended by the City Engineer, P.E. Matthews, giving rise to a total additional estimated cost of £5328, or £36 per house. These house types were related to the standard plans that we met above. Application was made to the Local Government Board for its approval to the amended scheme and its sanction to the loan of £503,673. The usual Local Inquiry into the application was held on 2 January 1920, despite the absence of a key witness, the Chairman of the Housing Committee, Alderman Thomas Kelly, MP, who was detained without charge in Wormwood Scrubs Prison at the time, a reminder of the difficult political climate in which the Corporation was forced to operate. The LGB generally approved of the scheme, but introduced certain modifications to the house plans and layout which reduced the number of houses to be built (Report 110/1920). Later the City Architect revised the plan to 530 houses, extending a portion of the layout on the western boundary outside the line of the Corporation boundary (Report 56/1921).

In comparing the detailed layout of the City Architect's plan for Marino with that prepared by Geddes and Unwin, Miller (1985) notes that this later plan as a whole appears much more rigid and formal, although MacCarthy's use of certain 'garden suburb' norms should be acknowledged. In fact, by the time that the Marino scheme was finally implemented in the mid-1920s, further land in Croydon Park had been acquired by the Corporation, so that the rationale for both earlier plans had disappeared. The final Marino layout is a grandiose geometrical composition, similar to the large British council

28 A cul-de-sac at Becontree, North London. Note the similarity with the
later Drumcondra image.
(Photograph by R. McManus.)

estates of the 1920s and 1930s such as Becontree. A similar but less elaborate
approach to symmetry was applied to Dublin Corporation's Crumlin scheme.
The beauty of the composition is best appreciated from the air or on a map,
whereas on the ground the layout can appear confusing. Indeed, such layouts
have received criticism on a more general basis. Jackson (1973, p. 126) points
out that: 'In the thirties, some planners favoured highly symmetrical patterns of
roads which looked satisfying on the drawing board but frustrated easy
communication on the ground, both within the estate and exits and entrances.
And these very formal plans, coupled with the regular building lines almost
universally adopted, served only to underline the tedious similarity of the houses.'

In 1922, a Housing Committee report noted that the Marino scheme, in
common with many other housing proposals, had not been proceeded with
owing to the political situation. It was advisable that the whole scheme be
reconstructed and that it would include additional land, so that the original
50 acres (c.20ha) would be added to with a further 76 (c.31ha), all of which
was to be developed at 12 houses to the acre (c.30 houses per ha), giving a total
of 1500 houses (that is, 600 + 900) (Report 68/1922). By the following year,
negotiations were in progress for the purchase of the additional acreage,
extending westwards from the 50-acre section towards Philipsburgh Avenue.

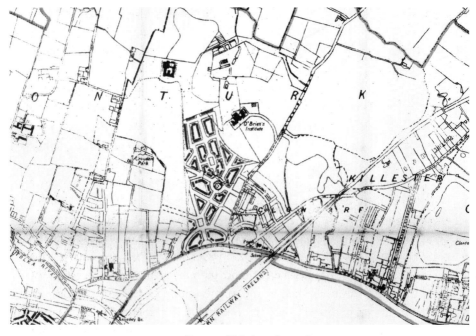

29 Suggested Marino plan 1918.
(Report of the Housing Committee, Dublin Corporation.)

Meanwhile, the Housing Committee proposed plans for the 50-acre section of the Marino Housing Scheme already in possession of the Corporation (Report 14/1923).

The Committee was keeping in mind 'the desirability of making the scheme a model one', especially due to the many exceptional advantages of the site with regard to situation and healthy surroundings. Initially, it was hoped to have a superior class of dwelling erected, but the Committee found itself somewhat handicapped by the Local Government Minister's decision that the Government grant would not exceed £500 per house, so that to rank for full subsidy a house could not exceed an all-in cost of £750.

The architect for the 431-house section at Marino was Mr F.G. Hicks, whose layout providing for 618 houses on the 50-acre (c.30ha) site had been approved by the Minister. Building on the proposed new thoroughfare on the northern boundary (Griffith Avenue) was deferred until some future date when building costs would permit the erection of a superior class of dwelling within the prescribed limit. In the meantime, the Council would consider letting these main frontages for residential or business purposes to private builders, whose plans would be subject to Corporation approval. This was the start of what might be termed the 'reserved areas' policy, discussed in more detail in the following chapter. After leaving the main frontages at Marino Mart, Philipsburgh Avenue, Griffith Avenue and Malahide Road vacant, 428 houses would be erected. All of the houses would be of the 'parlour type', including a living room, parlour and three-bedrooms, with scullery, larder, bathroom, w.c. and coal cellar. As previously mentioned, Tudor Walters ideals were applied at Marino. The houses were to be built in blocks of eight, six, five, and three, and in pairs. A variety of materials and different methods of construction were included in the various types and blocks of houses, so as to prevent a monotonous appearance, and Irish materials would be used where possible.

The appearance of the houses in the scheme varied considerably, despite the fact that all included the same basic accommodation and number of rooms. Some pebble-dashed houses with slate roofs and a prominent string course between the two storeys are characteristic of other Corporation houses of the same period elsewhere. However, others have yellow brick facades, large rectangular windows on the upper storey, or more prominent chimneys. The variety of building style is complemented by the variation in layout. Houses are built in groups of varying numbers. Some are set back further from the roadways than others, increasing the variation in the scheme. The grouping of houses around open green areas or in culs-de-sac also increases the sense of variety at Marino.

The Minister wanted development works to be executed by contract, and the estimated inclusive cost of the 428 houses was £319,808. This was based on two-thirds Government grant to one-third dividend in proportions of three parts loan, one part rates (Report 14/1923). Ten tenders were received for the first section of the Marino scheme, comprising 231 houses, including alternatives

Table 20 Cost of development at Marino.

	£	Per House		
		£	s.	d.
Land	4974	11	12	5
Development	23,000	53	15	0
Building	278,200	650	0	0
Electric Wiring	6741	15	15	0
Architect	4697	10	19	0
Quantity Surveyor	1512	3	10	8
Clerk of Works	684	1	10	3
Total	319808	747	2	4

(Report 14/1923, p. 48.)

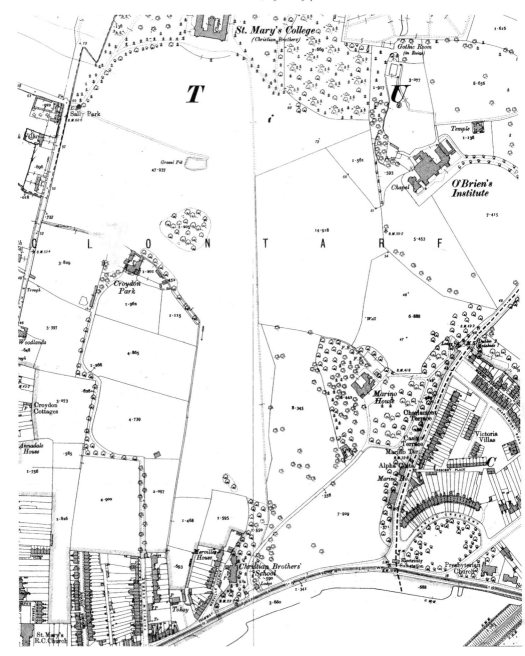

30 The Marino site in 1911.
(Ordnance Survey 1:2500 plan, Sheet 18 IV, Dublin, 1911 revision.)

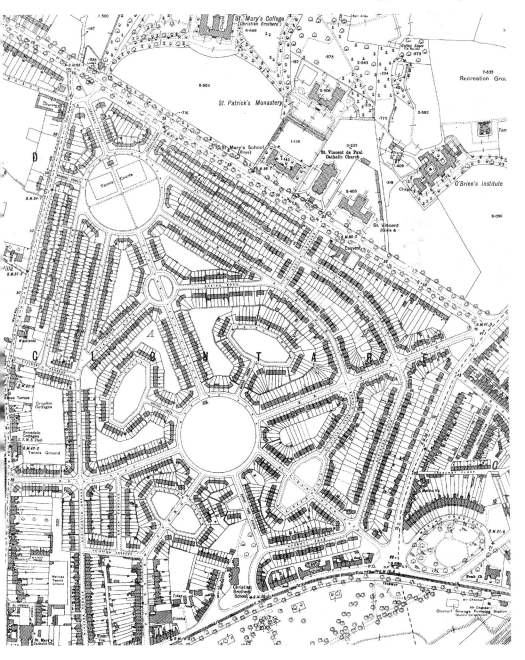

31 The completed Marino scheme.
(Ordnance Survey 1:2500 plan, Sheet 18 IV, Dublin, 1938 revision.)

should it be decided to use different materials, specifically 'Silcon' flooring in halls, 'Endurol' roof slates, and Portland Stone (*in lieu* of County Dublin granites) for door and window sills. The lowest tender was from Mr John Kenny, Harcourt Road, at £645 0s. 7d. per house for Section I (231 houses) and £634 9s. 0d. for per house for Section II (197 houses), or alternatively £640 3s. 6d. per house for the entire scheme of 428 houses.

However, the Minister for Local Government and Public Health suggested certain alterations in the specification with a view to reducing the cost per house, resulting in an average cost per house of £589 19s. 5d., or a total of £136,282 12s. 10d. Mr Kenny was to complete the 231 houses in Section I within 12 months from signing the contract. The award of the contract for Section II was delayed, at the suggestion of the Minister, until June 1924, by which time costs had fallen considerably. Again Kenny submitted the lowest tender, at £565 per house for the 197 houses, as against £589 per house in the contract for the first section. Other tenders were received from Messrs H. & J. Martin, Messrs Meagher & Hayes, Cork, and Messrs H. & C. McNally & Co.. The electric power and lighting installations in connection with the Marino building scheme were carried out by Mr R.H. Farmar of Nottingham Street. In December 1923, Mr Robert J. Payne of 12 Avoca Road, Dublin, was selected as the Clerk of Works, from 32 applicants, of whom 12 were from Britain. His wage was £6 6s. per week.

The development at Marino did not proceed entirely without incident. In the summer of 1924 the Dáil noted an 'unfortunate dispute between workers at Marino'. The strike was finally settled in early September through the efforts of the Priests' Social Guild. All of the men who were engaged on the date of the stoppage were allowed to resume work, and the contractor was free to engage additional men when necessary, as long as they belonged to either of the two unions concerned in the dispute. According to the *Irish Builder and Engineer*, 'the only result of the strike, so far as the workers are concerned, has been the loss of £40,000 in wages and a forced idleness of three months' (6 September 1924). The strike was not associated with pay or employment conditions, and the people who suffered most were 'the workers themselves, and the other workers for whom the houses were intended' (6 September 1924, p. 801).

By 1926, several of the tenant-purchasers on the first section of the scheme had applied to have baths and hot water services installed in their houses. These facilities had been recommended by Charles MacCarthy and provided for in the original plans, but had been eliminated at the request of the

Minister in order to reduce costs. The houses built slightly later on the adjoining Croydon Park scheme contained these services, and it was decided to take a contract with Messrs Baird to provide such services for the 431 original Marino houses (Report 105/1926). It is worth noting that the supply of baths in the tenant purchase schemes was a moot point. A Dáil question in April 1928 referred to representations made by the tenant purchasers of houses in Donnelly's Orchard to have baths installed in their homes, and stated that they were in dispute with the Dublin City Commissioners over the conditions under which the work would be done (Dáil Debates, 30, p. 770).

Soon after work began on the first phase of the Marino scheme, the Corporation compulsorily acquired 90 acres (c.36ha) of land running westwards from the original 428-house scheme (Marino, Sections I & II) to Philipsburgh Avenue. For this area, known as the Croydon Park extension, the City Architect drew up plans for 918 five-roomed houses of various types of elevation:

A Stock brick facing with slated roof.
B Concrete block facing with Du Nord/other approved clay tiles.
C Stock brick facings on ground floor, rough cast above, slated roof.
D All rough cast facing with red asbestos tiled roof.

Although a late-1924 report noted that part of the site was to be set aside for 50 four-bed houses according to plans and specifications furnished by the Ministry, these houses were never built, and the entire scheme consisted of five-roomed houses. In total, 852 houses were eventually completed. The contractors for the Croydon Park Extension included Messrs H. & J. Martin, Messrs G. & T. Crampton, and a German firm, Messrs Kossel which built over three hundred houses, at a rate of six to eight per week, in the Marino Park area. The final tender for 104 houses was allocated in May 1926, thus completing the Croydon Park extension of the scheme, which (including the original Marino Scheme) would then comprise 1283 five-roomed houses.

In 1925, the scheme for sale of the Marino houses to tenant purchasers was agreed. The houses were to be sold for between £400 and £440 each, with minimum weekly payments of 16s. 1d. for house type A, 15s. 6d. for type B, and 15 shillings for type C. Later the same year, the Streets Section noted the naming of some of the new roads in the Marino Housing Area – Marino Park, Marino Park Avenue; Haverty Road; Carleton Road; St Declan Avenue; St Aiden Park, St Aiden Park Avenue; Brian Road and Brian Terrace (Report 163/1925). When the arrangements made for the sale of houses to the purchasing tenants at Croydon Park were outlined in 1926, the houses, divided into three classes, were marginally more expensive. The annuity, ground rent, insurance premium and rates would be collected half-yearly, quarterly, monthly or weekly as desired by the purchaser.

Sale scheme for houses at Croydon Park –

A	all semi-detached houses, end houses of blocks of three built in a straight line	Poor Law Valuation £13	£460
B	all blocks of three built on an angle, centre houses of blocks of three in a straight line, and end houses of blocks built in terraces	Poor Law Valuation £12 10s	£440
C	Intermediate houses of all blocks built in terraces	Poor Law Valuation £12	£420

Incidentally, the scheme of sale at Marino caused difficulties because the original leases had been drawn up so that the houses should be let and not purchased. The question had created a great deal of anxiety and ill-feeling among the occupiers of the houses, who had entered into provisional agreements terminating on 31 March 1926, and led to the raising of a Dáil Question. By the end of July 1926, the 431 houses on the first (50 acre; 30ha) section of the scheme were occupied, while 284 houses were occupied in Croydon Park. The remaining 568 houses were in the hands of the contractor.

One impression of life in the early days of Marino was provided by Christina Hughes (Mrs Tobin), who moved from a Capel Street tenement house with her parents and four siblings to the newly completed number 36 St Aidan's Park Road in 1924/5. A minimum of four children was required before a Marino house could be allocated, but in the Hughes' case this was not a problem. Following the move, a further six children were born. Large families were common on the estate. Her uncle's family, living around the corner, had 12 children, as did the Gallagher's down the road.

The allotments at the back of the houses have long since been taken into gardens, but Mr Hughes grew vegetables in their back garden, including cabbage, carrots, lettuce, scallions, rhubarb and strawberries, while at one time they kept about 12 chickens. In addition to home-grown food, there was the opportunity to buy potatoes and cabbage from local farmers. Milk was delivered twice a day (8 pints, *c.*4.5 litres, morning and evening) by a local dairy-man on his bicycle, while the breadman called each morning. Twice a week, on Wednesday and Friday, a fishmonger called to the estate. There was no fridge, but there was a marble slab in the pantry which stayed cold, and the jug and basin of milk would be kept there. The family would consume a stone (over 6 kgs) of potatoes, three or four cabbages and cauliflowers, and a large joint (leg of lamb, roast beef, ham or corned beef) for the main meal of the day. Looking after the family was a full-time job which took its toll, and Mrs Hughes died while she was still in her fifties.

In 1926 it was decided to erect 28 houses on the Philipsburgh Avenue frontage of the Croydon Park Area. Efforts to induce building by private enterprise had been unsuccessful, and due to the desirability of having the frontage covered without delay, the Housing Section intended to erect houses to the same plan as those in the housing scheme, but of increased dimensions and improved elevations. The houses built had an area of 966 square feet (*c.*90 m²) as opposed to the 844 square feet (*c.*78 m²) which was the size of the rest of the Croydon Park houses. Desirable extras including bay windows were to be included 'so that the buildings will be of a character conforming to the importance of this main thoroughfare, and which can be readily disposed of on economic terms' (Report 191/1926, p. 555). The houses, built by Crampton & Co., had a purchase price of £650, with a minimum deposit of £200. The repayment of the balance was to be by equal annual instalments over 40 years at 5¾ per cent interest. Thus the cost and repayment terms, as well as physical appearance, distinguished these houses from their near neighbours in the main area of the scheme.

In addition to the Corporation-built houses on the Philipsburgh Avenue frontage, some private development also took place there. For example, a lease of a building site at Philipsburgh Avenue was granted to Mr W. Green in 1926. He was to build a shop with residence consisting of three bedrooms, living room, kitchen, bathroom and lavatory, with a separate entrance for shop and dwelling, and would pay £7 p.a. ground rent. A further private lease for a shop and residence was granted to Mr M. Sheehan of 38 Edenvale Road, Ranelagh for 150 years at £10 p.a.

At the end of 1925 it was decided to convert the open spaces at the rere of the houses in the Marino Area into allotments, which were to be let at 6*d.* per week to tenant purchasers. Meanwhile, the large circus in the centre of the Croydon Park extension was to be reserved for public buildings (which were never built), and as a result the layout plan of the original 428 house section was altered, adding three houses to John Kenny's building contracts. In fact, a church and schools were built on a separate site selected by the Catholic archbishop of Dublin. As early as February 1924, the parish priest of Fairview, the Very Revd Canon Pettit, had written to Dublin Corporation, pointing out the need to provide a church and schools for the large population of the Marino Housing Area. It was decided that a suitable site would be a triangular plot of land forming part of the City Estate on the north side of the new 100 foot (*c*.30 m) roadway, later known as Griffith Avenue, and the fee simple of 8¾ acres (*c*.3.5ha) was sold to the trustees at £325 per statute acre in 1925. By late 1926 plans were drawn up for two schools, one to accommodate 1300 girls and infants, the other to cater for 1000 boys. The circus adjoining Philipsburgh Avenue was earmarked for a playground.

In September 1927 tenders for fencing Marino Park, the large circle situated in the centre of the housing scheme, were considered, with a view to its use as a sports ground. In addition, £9500 was to be made available for the completion of the open spaces, laying of footpaths, planting of trees and shrubs, and general clearing up of the area. In the following year, sanction was given to the erection at Marino Park Avenue of a direction post and an oak signboard, framed and glazed, showing a detailed map of the entire Marino and Croydon Park scheme. This marked the completion of what was probably the most successful housing scheme ever undertaken by Dublin Corporation. Unlike the layout of Inchicore (*c*.1911) where the roadways were disproportionately wide relative to the height of the houses, the Marino scheme employs narrow roads. There are two large 'circuses', open green areas and four smaller, irregularly shaped green areas, two of which are bisected by roads. All of the houses are two-storeys in height, but there is a range of treatment thereafter. Every house has its own garden both front and rear, although the plots vary in shape and size depending on the relationship between house and roadway.

The plainer terraces include pebble-dashed exteriors with a characteristic white string course often separating the two storeys. These have two windows at first floor level, with front door and living room window below. More attractive are the yellow-brick terraces with low-sloping roofs containing dormer windows and a more picturesque appearance with white multiple-paned windows. Here tunnel access to the rear is provided via round-arched gated tunnels. Another house type has a reddish brick façade with bright orange roofing. The end houses on these terraces project beyond the building line of the others, giving the whole terrace the appearance of a unit. A further

32 Housing on Philipsburgh Avenue and Croydon Park. (Photographs by R. McManus.)

house style in Marino has a façade with the appearance of large concrete blocks, with large chimneys, dark tiled roofs and projecting porches. These presumably equate to Type B applied at Croydon Park extension (see p. 191).

The narrow roads, coupled with the absence of garages or other provision for car parking, have led to modern-day traffic problems. In some cases, residents have sacrificed their front garden to provide for a parking space, while others living in larger corner sites have added a garage to the side of the house.

Drumcondra housing scheme

New Dublin Housing Scheme – The Dublin Commissioners today invite tender for the erection of 266 houses on the Drumcondra and Glasnevin housing area, which is situated on the ground rising from the River Tolka at Botanic Ave, through the fields between Marlborough Hall and St Patrick's Training College. The feature of this new building scheme is that it provides for the erection of 128 three-roomed houses, 77 four-roomed houses, 61 five-roomed houses. This is the first occasion when small houses of the capacity of three rooms have been included in a Corporation scheme in a garden suburb.

(*Irish Times*, 10 March 1927)

Like Marino, the Drumcondra Scheme was in gestation for a considerable period of time before it was brought to fruition. Even before 'the Troubles', and the break with the British Local Government Department, the acquisition of a large area of land at Millbourne Avenue had been contemplated. In 1923, when the political situation had eased, negotiations for the acquisition of the land were reopened, but as the owners were not amenable to its sale, powers were sought for the compulsory acquisition of as much of the 100 acres (c.40ha) as was required to develop adequately the district and carry out the housing scheme. Like Marino, this area was felt to be an ideal situation, and a very desirable building site. In all there would be space for c.1200 houses (clearly a density of 12 houses to the acre, c.30 per ha, was planned) at an all-in cost of £900,000. The Corporation was thinking along town planning lines, with the intention 'that the layout for the scheme now proposed should provide for the continuation of the main thoroughfare initiated in connection with the Marino scheme, so as to link up the Glasnevin and Clontarf districts' (Report 106/1923, p. 486). In April 1927 this road running from Howth Road to Ballymun Road, previously referred to simply as the '100 foot road', was

33 Different housing styles and layouts in Marino. (Photographs by R. McManus.)

34 Different housing styles and layouts in Marino.
(Photographs by J. Brady and R. McManus.)

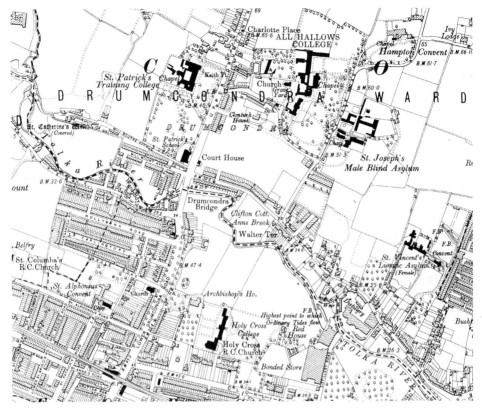

35 Drumcondra in the early twentieth century.
(Ordnance Survey 1:10,560 plan, Sheet 18, Dublin, 1912 revision.)

named Griffith Avenue/Ascal Ó Gríofa (Report 73/1927). The money would
be raised in the same proportions as Marino – £600,000 grant; £225,000 loan;
and £75,000 rates. The *Irish Builder and Engineer* reported on the proposed
scheme in September 1924, suggesting that 1500 new houses would be built at
a cost of more than £1 million, employing about 3000 men for three to four
years. Although the claim was exaggerated, there was no doubt but that an
extensive scheme of this nature would give much-needed employment.

Despite the high regard in which the site was held, it was not until June
1926 that tenders for road and sewer construction through a portion of the
'Drumcondra Housing Area', and the supervision of the contract works, were
considered. The delay was due to the necessity for a Public Inquiry held by the
Local Government Inspector following the request to the Minister for Local
Government and Public Health for the power to compulsorily acquire the
land. Although a provisional order was then made, a Court appeal was

launched by some of the parties interested in a portion of the lands who opposed the scheme. Meanwhile, the owners of part of the area known as the Butterly Estate consented to the Commissioners (Dublin Corporation had been dissolved by Ministerial order in 1924 for unspecified reasons and the city was now in the hands of three Commissioners) taking possession of their land (approximately 32 acres; c.13ha) lying south of the proposed line of extension of Home Farm Road, pending the issue of the Arbitrator's award as to the amount of compensation to be paid. The Commissioner decided to have the roads and sewers constructed through these 32 acres (13ha), in accordance with the layout plan approved by the Minister for Local Government, 'with a view to facilitating building operations at a later stage, and incidentally relieving unemployment' (Report 127/1926, p. 356). The lowest of the seven tenders was received from the Pioneer Construction Co., East Wall, which was awarded the contract. This portion of the site was intended to provide space for 534 houses – 176 five-room; 143 four-room; 215 three-room houses. The total estimated cost of this section of the scheme, including land acquisition, development, buildings, electric lighting and supervision was in the region of £300,000. The Scheme for the remaining portion of the area (containing c.100 acres; 40ha) was to form the subject of a later report, after the objections had been disposed of. Space was provided in this section for ecclesiastical and school buildings. In March 1928, the Commissioners agreed with his Grace, Most Revd Dr Byrne, Archbishop of Dublin, to rearrange the boundaries of the site of Corpus Christi Church, situated on the Home Farm Road. The Church Authorities handed over to the Commissioners a section of their original site in exchange for a plot to the north of the existing temporary church, thus enabling the church authorities to have an entrance fronting Griffith Avenue, as well as another from Home Farm Road (Report 79/1928).

In June 1927, the eight tenders received for this first 266-house section of the Drumcondra scheme were considered. The public advertisement had invited contractors to tender for the form of construction specified by the City Architect, and, alternatively, for wall construction and finishings other than those specified. O'Rourke, as City Architect, had examined the tenders for the second section, finding that the two lowest were from Messrs H. & J. Martin and Messrs G. & T. Crampton. Since Messrs Martin had failed to submit an alternative tender specially requested in the Form of Tender, whereas Messrs Crampton did so, the City Architect felt that Crampton was entitled to the Contract for Section 2, while Messrs Martin should get the contract for Section 1 (now 269 houses) on the same schedule of rates. This arrangement

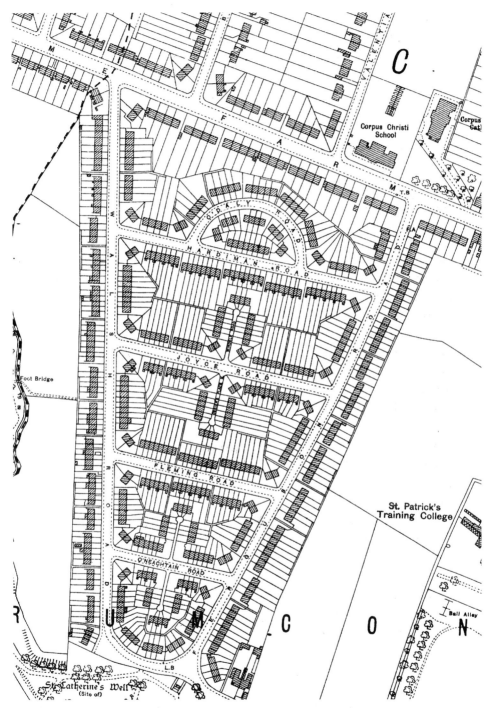

36 Layout plan of the Drumcondra scheme
(Ordnance Survey 1:2500 plan, Sheet 18 III, Dublin, 1938 revision.)

37 Ferguson Road, Drumcondra soon after completion. (Postcard.)

would obtain for the Corporation 'the greatest number of houses in the quickest time at the lowest cost, and securing for these purposes the two most satisfactory building firms of which the Corporation has yet had experience' (Report 146/1927, p. 403). The Clerk of Works appointed for the scheme was a local man, Mr John Hand of 42 Clonliffe Gardens.

By the end of November 1927, only five months after the receipt of the tenders, the houses in the Drumcondra area were nearing completion, and a number of the roads were fully constructed. At the request of the Housing Department, the Commissioner (Séamus O Murchadha) had selected names for 11 of these roads, as follows – Barron Place, Comyn Place, Ferguson Road, Fleming Road, Hardiman Road, Joyce Road, O'Brien Place, O'Daly Road, O'Neachtain Road, Walsh Road, Windele Road. Walsh Road is in commemoration of the late archbishop of Dublin, and the other names are those of former leading Irish writers whose memories it is desired to perpetuate' (Commissioner Séamus Ó Murchadha, Report 235/1927, p. 691).

As at Marino, the layout of Drumcondra was of considerable interest, although in general the house type is similar throughout the area. Culs-de-sac are used to give a sense of enclosure, while again houses are set back from the roads to varying degrees and are grouped variously in pairs, threes, fours and fives.

38 Hardiman Road, Drumcondra (*upper*) and Windele Road, a cul-de-sac in Drumcondra.
Notice the similarity of the cul-de-sac to that in Becontree (figure 28).
(Photographs by J. Brady and R. McManus.)

The overall effect is to give a sense of unity while at the same time avoiding monotony. Built on ground which slopes down towards the Tolka River at Griffith Park, the Drumcondra scheme includes two long straight roads (Walsh and Ferguson) where an attempt is made at diversity by mixing the lengths of the terraces, with houses generally in groups of four or three to the terrace, and by varying the length of the front gardens so that some houses are closer to the roadway than others. There are four shorter roads running across the area of the scheme, linking Walsh and Ferguson Roads, where the majority of the houses are arranged in groups of four to a terrace. At the junctions where these roads meet, a pair of larger semi-detached houses is placed across the angle of the road. The appearance of these houses is also varied. In some cases, the front door is located in the longer 'front' of the house, with a window to one side and two above. However, in a number of cases the main entrance is to the shorter side of the house, while the upper storey contains three narrower windows rather than two of a more regular size.

One of the more attractive features of the Drumcondra scheme is the layout of four small culs-de-sac off O'Neachtain and Joyce Roads. The arrangement of the houses in these cases is strikingly similar to that employed in the London County Council schemes such as Becontree. The majority of houses are pebble-dashed and carry the 'signature' white string course demarcating the upper storey. The original casement windows survive in some cases, consisting of six panes in the larger front windows and four panes in the 'box room' window. Along Ferguson and Walsh Roads, the houses have yellow-brick facades. Although they are arranged in long terraces, these terraces are stepped because of the sloping ground, giving the houses more of a paired, semi-detached appearance. In a small number of cases, a timber detail is used in the upper storey of the house, giving a suggestion of a timber frame. As in Marino, the roads are relatively narrow and no allowance was made in the original scheme for motor vehicles.

The sale scheme of the Drumcondra houses was based on the standards fixed for Croydon Park's five-roomed houses and the recently completed four-roomed houses at Fairbrother's Fields, 'with a reasonable differentiation as between the latter and the proposed new three-roomed houses', the first of this type provided under the sale scheme. The calculations, which provided only for the portion of the acquisition cost relating to the 32 acres (c.13ha) actually occupied by new houses, show an annual deficit of £2500 for the scheme. Number 1 Ferguson Road was converted to become the Estate Office. In 1931 permission was granted to the Drumcondra (Corporation) Tenants'

Association to use the Estate Office for one hour on one evening each month to facilitate the Association in carrying out its arrangements for keeping houses on the area properly maintained in accordance with the obligations imposed upon the tenant-purchasers by the leases.

Table 21 Upper Drumcondra area sale scheme.

Type	PLV	Sale Price	Annuity 40 yrs	Ground Rent	Rates*
		5-roomed Houses			
24 semi-detached	£13	£460	£29 12s. 4d.	£3	£10 1s. 6d.
58 end of terrace	£12 10s	£440	£28 6s. 7d.	£3	£9 13s. 9d.
98 intermediate	£12	£420	£27 0s. 9d.	£2 10s.	£9 6s.
		4-roomed Houses			
18 semi-detached	£10 10s	£350	£22 10s. 8d.	£4	£8 2s. 9d.
44 end of terrace	£9 10s	£340	£21 17s. 10d.	£3	£7 7s. 3d.
82 intermediate	£9	£330	£21 4s. 11d.	£2	£6 19s. 6d.
		3-roomed Houses			
8 semi-detached	£9	£250	£16 1s. 11d.	£4	£6 19s. 6d.
70 end of terrace	£8	£240	£15 9s. 1d.	£3	£5 1s. 8d.
133 intermediate	£7	£230	£14 16s. 2d.	£2	£4 9s.

Type	Fire Insurance	Service Charge	Total p.a. Charge	Weekly
		5-roomed Houses		
24 semi-detached	9s.	£2 8s.	£45 10s. 10d.	17s. 7d.
58 end of terrace	9s.	£2 8s.	£43 17s. 4d.	16s. 11d.
98 intermediate	9s.	£2 8s.	£41 13s. 9d.	16s. 1d.
		4-roomed Houses		
18 semi-detached	7s. 6d.	£2 8s.	£37 8s. 11d.	14s. 5d.
44 end of terrace	7s. 6d.	£2 8s	£35 0s. 7d.	13s. 6d.
82 intermediate	7s. 6d.	£2 8s	£32 19s. 11d.	12s. 9d.
		3-roomed Houses		
8 semi-detached	7s. 6d.	£2 8s	£29 16s. 11d.	11s. 6d.
70 end of terrace	7s. 6d.	£2 8s	£26 6s. 3d.	10s. 2d.
133 intermediate	7s. 6d.	£2 8s	£24 0s. 8d.	9s. 3d.

Notes: *(based on 1927–28 assessment). The period of the lease was for 99 years from 1 April 1929 and the rate of interest was 5¾ per cent per annum. The service charge was a booking keeping and collection charge.
(Report 26/1928, p. 81.)

Table 22 Average retail price for principal food items in
Irish towns in mid-July 1928.

Beef – sirloin (per lb)	1s. 2¾d.
Bacon – Irish streaky (lb)	1s. 5¾d.
Eggs – dozen	1s. 5d.
Irish creamery butter (lb)	1s. 9¼d.
Fresh milk (quart)	0s. 4¾d.
2lb loaf bread	0s. 5¼d.
Potatoes (14 lbs)	1s. 3¾d.
Tea – cheapest (lb)	2s. 2½d.
Sugar (lb)	0s. 3½d.

(*Irish Trade Journal*, IV, November 1928, p. 34).

Compared to the cost of common household foodstuffs, the weekly charge
on the Drumcondra houses seems reasonable. The most expensive of the five-
roomed semi-detached style houses cost 17s. 7d. per week in rental, while the
cheapest of the three-roomed houses cost 9s. 3d. At this time, a dozen eggs
cost 1s. 5d.

39 Advertisement for Cosgrave and Co.

In addition to the housing provided in the
Corporation's 32 acre (*c.*13ha) site, it was
decided to make the further land available to
builders for the erection of higher quality
houses, much as had been done at the main
frontages of Marino. In this case the area
under consideration was more extensive,
being more than double the size of the local
authority scheme. The Drumcondra Scheme,
including the 'semi-private' section (see
following chapter) had an enormous impact
on the area. Home Farm Road had been
built as far as houses 47 and 49 by 1911, but
until 1925 the road ended just past the last
house with a simple wire fence. Beyond were
the fields of Dr Eustace and Mr Butterly,
with a rhubarb field on the site of Home
Farm Park. Similarly Clare Road ended
beside the first two houses on each side for

many years. A large gate in the fence across the road allowed access by manure carts and wheelbarrows to the plots behind the fence up to what is now the south side of Griffith Avenue. The area was plunged from a rural landscape to a suburban one, the transformation occurring far more rapidly than would have been the case where speculative development was acting in isolation (Corpus Christi Parish, 1991).

Donnycarney area housing scheme, 1929–31

The site at Donnycarney was particularly suitable for a housing scheme, since much of the land constituted part of the City Estate and was therefore relatively easy to acquire. A report of 28 August 1928, recommended that lands at Donnycarney, in addition to lands at Cabra and Marrowbone Lane, be acquired compulsorily for the purpose of house building. In the case of Donnycarney, the land involved amounted to just over 31 acres (c.12.5ha), providing space for 547 four-roomed houses, with an estimated cost of £256,673. Things moved quickly, and by December notices to quit had been served on tenants of the City Estate premises on the Malahide Road which were required in connection with the scheme.

On 17 July 1929, the building tenders for the Donnycarney Housing Scheme were discussed. Nine tenders had been received for the 434 houses to be built on the site. Section I, consisting of 255 houses, was to be built by Messrs J. Kenny and Sons within 45 weeks at a cost of £96,000, while Section II, consisting of 179 houses, would be erected by Messrs Housing Corporation of Great Britain in 52 weeks, at a cost of £67,086 12s. 2½d. It was later decided to retain the tennis courts on part of the site comprising Section I, so that 242 houses were now to be built, at £92,102 17s. 11d. (less 13 houses) with concrete wall construction (Report 157/1929). In February 1931, it was reported that 100 houses remained to be completed by Messrs Kenny in the Donnycarney Area, and it was improbable that they would be ready for occupation before the first of April (Report 17/1931).

At the time that building began, Donnycarney was still a rural area, considered to be well outside the city. This is reflected in the report, which appeared in the *Irish Builder and Engineer* of 18 January 1931, describing the 'daring outrage' which had been perpetrated on Mr John Kenny, the contractor. Accompanied by his nephew, Mr Sheehan, Kenny was travelling in his motorcar to Donnycarney with over £1600 for the week's wages. The money was stolen by three armed men, one in the uniform of the civic guard.

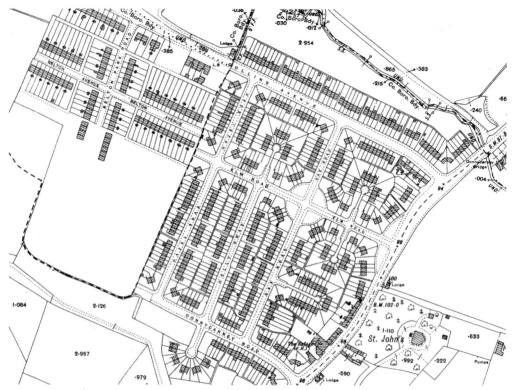

40 Layout plan of the Donnycarney development. Note the discontinuity between Belton Avenue and Elm Road. (Ordnance Survey 1:2500 plan, Sheet 18 IV, Dublin, 1936 revision.)

The editorial deplored recent attacks of this nature on builders who, by nature of their work, often had to travel to relatively remote, out-lying districts with the wages for their workers!

The Streets Section had approved the street names for the new roads in the Donnycarney area in 1929 – Puckstown Road, Elm Road, Donnycarney Road, Hazel Road, Holly Road, Oak Road, and a scheme of sale, based on that devised for the Emmet Road (Extension) Area, was planned in July 1929 (see Report 130/1929). House Number 1, Donnycarney Road, was fitted up for the purposes of an Estate Office, following the success of the similar office in Drumcondra.

A number of issues of interest are illustrated by the case of Donnycarney. The area covered by the same was roughly equivalent to that of the Drumcondra (Corporation) Scheme. As in Drumcondra, initially over 540 houses were to be built, suggesting a density of more than 17 houses per acre (*c.*43 per ha). However, the final total of 421 houses was closer to the new 'ideal' of 12 houses to the acre (*c.*30 per ha). As a tenant purchase scheme, this

Table 23 Scheme of sale of 421 4-room houses, Donnycarney.

	215 Intermediate			24 Intermediate (projecting)			126 End houses			50 Semi-detached			6 Semi-detached (Angular)		
	£	s.	d.	£	s.	d.	£	s.	d.	£	s.	d.	£	s.	d.
PLV	9	0	0	9	10	0	9	10	0	10	10	0	11	11	0
Sale Price	300	0	0	320	0	0	320	0	0	340	0	0	380	0	0
40-year Annuity	19	6	3	20	12	1	20	12	1	21	17	9	24	9	3
Rates	6	12	0	6	19	4	16	19	4	7	14	0	8	8	8
Ground Rent	2	0	0	2	0	0	3	0	0	4	0	0	5	0	0
Fire Insurance	0	6	0	0	6	0	0	6	0	0	6	0	0	6	0
Repair Reserve	2	12	0	2	12	0	2	12	0	2	12	0	2	12	0
Book-keeping	2	8	0	2	8	0	2	8	0	2	8	0	2	8	0
Annual Total	33	4	3	34	17	5	35	17	5	38	17	9	43	3	11
Min. Weekly Charge	0	12	10	0	13	5	0	3	10	0	15	0	0	16	8

(Report 221/1929.)

was one of the first to consist solely of four-roomed houses. In layout terms, it was less stylized than its predecessors at Marino and Drumcondra. Here, although culs-de-sac were used, and there is a circus at the junctions of Elm and Oak Roads, the layout was more grid-like. However, attention does seem to have been paid to infrastructure, with the permission granted, in January 1931, for a bus stop on the Malahide Road at the Scheme, indicating that, at least in this instance, public transport was keeping up with the growth of the city. The Donnycarney housing layout includes both a circus (bisected by Oak Road and Elm Road) and several culs-de-sac, off Donnycarney Road, Oak Road and Elm Road. Once again, houses at the intersections of roads received special treatment, being placed at angles to the roadway. While many of the houses employ the usual plain pebble-dashed exteriors, those located at important junctions are differentiated from the others. The houses at the junction of the Malahide Road and Collins Avenue, for example, incorporate

41 Semi-detached houses at Donnycarney at the junction of Malahide Road
and Collins Avenue. (Photograph by R. McManus.)

a timber-frame effect in the upper storey and utilise red roof tiles rather than
the black slate which is employed throughout the main body of the scheme.
This semi-detached house is designed to look more like one large residence,
with a central chimney. The central portion of the house is framed by two
wings which project at a 45 degrees, with the hall doors (originally) facing
inwards towards the centre.

A noteworthy feature of the Donnycarney layout is the lack of road connections between this public housing scheme and the neighbouring Belton Park
scheme built by a private speculative builder. For example, Belton Avenue and
Elm Road do not intersect. The scheme at Donnycarney also illustrates that the
new housing schemes were not necessarily greeted with enthusiasm. Local landowners (the Christian Brothers and Mr Belton) made representations to the
Corporation relative to the damage to their lands and consequent loss incurred
by them since the advent of the scheme on the Donnycarney Area, and in 1931
arrangements were made for a wall to be built (Report 49/1931).

The 1930s schemes: standardization and slum clearance

We urge an imitation of nature in its sameness and in its variety, and a blending of both is not only desirable but possible.

(Housing Inquiry, 1939–43, p. 104, para. 291)

There is a sameness, amounting in large schemes to dullness, if not actual dreariness.

(Citizens' Housing Council, 1938, p. 45)

Although the big push towards slum clearance only got fully underway following new legislation in 1931/32, from the late 1920s changes were already evident in Corporation housing policy. Among these were the return to rental cottage schemes and a renewed emphasis on central flats. One of the major changes in the 1930s was the greatly increased scale of building projects, and the speed at which they were undertaken. This necessitated a new approach to the whole design process, so that by 1934, the value of using standard designs for both cottages and flats was recognized. Standardization saved time with regard to plans and bills of quantities, and standard designs were now taken advantage of wherever possible.

The Citizens' Housing Council's report (1938, p. 41) praised the Housing Architect and his technical staff, whose designs for flats and houses were 'soundly and solidly built in a manner that ensures durability and low maintenance, and there is ample evidence that great care and technical skill have been exercised'. However, in general, the Council suggested that houses sufficiently durable to last for 50 years or so should be built, so as to house the rising generation comfortably and decently, while allowing for changing future circumstances with regard to the problem itself, and to materials and methods of construction. Planning of suburban schemes required further thought, since, although the layout of the houses themselves, and their gardens, was above criticism, 'the imagination of the authorities seems to have been exhausted at this stage and many grave omissions have been made' (Citizens' Housing Council, 1938, p. 33). These omissions included a need for improvements in the provision of open spaces, playing fields, recreation areas in connection with schools and the provision of community centres.

During the 1939–43 Housing Inquiry, standardization was both encouraged and defended. It was suggested that cottage design could be restricted to a small number of selected designs, producing the economic advantage of repetition, but with plenty of variation in the grouping of the designs in a particular scheme. Similarly with flats, the Inquiry recommended a restricted number of designs for the individual flat and a restricted number of flat-groupings or block designs based on the individual flat-designs, but a variety of block-designs as between different schemes, or between the parts of a large scheme. Whereas monotony could easily result from over-standardization, the report argued that this was not inevitable. The city Housing Department and its Architect had operated a large amount of standardization, and the report sought only to extend this fully and rapidly.

Flat schemes in central areas

Only three block dwelling schemes were erected by the Corporation between 1914 and the slum clearances of the 1930s. These were at Trinity Ward (1917), Ormond Market (1921), and Boyne Street (1924), and between them provided just 182 dwellings. The Trinity Ward Scheme, which provided flats on Luke Street, Moss Street, South Gloucester Street, and Townsend Street, had been in preparation for some time, and also included cottages. Its two-roomed dwellings were provided in pleasant-looking, but old-fashioned, four-storey blocks, faced with red brick but built of yellow brick. Access was provided by an internal staircase, reached through an arched doorway, with two flat dwellings on each floor. Similarly, the Ormond Market scheme was a combined cottage and flat scheme, with low-rise flat dwellings at first glance having the appearance of individual houses.

The Boyne Street-South Cumberland Street scheme, designed by George L. O'Connor, was most unusual in its use of the 'maisonette' style, with a ground floor flat and two upper storeys forming what was, in effect, a small two-storey house. The lower storey flat opened directly on to the street, while staircases with wrought iron balustrades provided access from the rear courtyards to the upper storey flat. The façades combined pebble-dash and red brick, with sash windows.

Flat schemes in the 1930s

In 1931 a return to flat schemes was envisaged on a much greater scale. The City Architect was instructed to construct a three-room model flat, 'the expenditure not to exceed £30, so that a clear idea may be gained of the class and extent of the accommodation which a dwelling of this type will contain' (Report 49/1931, p. 328). In the flat schemes undertaken at this time, a local

Table 24 Dublin Corporation flat schemes, post-1914 to 1939.

Scheme	Completion Date (approx.)	Total	1	2	3	4	5
Trinity Ward	1917	48	0	48	0	0	0
Ormond Market	1917/21	56	0	56	0	0	0
Boyne Street	1924	78	0	0	0	78	0
Kehoe Square	1927	208	5	63	77	49	14
Bulfin House	1929	8	0	0	0	8	0
Mercer House	1929–34	104	0	40	56	8	0
Mountpleasant	1931	57	0	57	0	0	0
Hollyfield	1931	18	0	18	0	0	0
Marshalsea Barracks	1931	53	40	13	0	0	0
Beggarsbush Barracks	1933	44	0	31	12	1	0
Mary's Lane	1933–34	120	0	10	109	1	0
Hanover Street	1934–39	345	14	125	181	25	0
Chancery House	1935	27	0	16	11	0	0
North Cumberland St	1936	66	0	30	36	0	0
Cook Street	1936–37	367	3	125	237	2	0
Watling Street	1938	72	8	20	36	8	0
Townsend Street	1938	40	0	12	24	4	0
Aldboro' House	1938	135	0	48	81	6	0
Poplar Row	1939	110	8	54	47	0	1
Thorncastle Street	1939	64	0	32	31	1	0
Railway Street	1939	181	36	92	44	7	2
Henrietta Street	1939	48	0	16	24	8	0
Total		2249	114	906	1006	206	17
Per cent of total dwellings		100	5.0	40.3	44.7	9.2	0.8

interpretation of European Modernism was the norm, with stylized detailing and methods of access arranged off open balconies facing internal courtyards. These developments attempt to achieve a sense of their location in the context of the city, reinforcing the streetlines while at the same time maintaining their own integrity as architectural units. Because the blocks were larger, with denser occupancy, there was greater opportunity to make them architecturally distinctive.

In addition to the large blocks such as Mercer House or Pearse House (see figure 25 and 26), some smaller schemes were also undertaken by the Corporation. One of these was the 1935 Chancery Place/Mountrath Street scheme, providing just 27 flats, with a small public garden. Barracks conversions

42 Chancery Place. (Photograph by R. McManus.)

continued, with developments at Marshalsea and Beggarsbush Barracks. Following the extension of the city boundaries in 1930, the Corporation took over schemes which had been initiated by the UDCs in the former Pembroke and Rathmines Townships, including the Mountpleasant and Hollyfield flat scheme.

The bulk of the 1930s flat schemes had four-storeys with access provided by shared staircases to external balconies. This had the advantage that every flat had its own front door. Open space generally took the form of concreted courtyards, which also provided washing lines and, in the case of Poplar Row, pram sheds. Almost all of the schemes had attractive brick facades, while there is a contrast between the 'neo-Classical' style of the Mercer House scheme and the more common 'modern' flat-roofed blocks such as Pearse House.

Like the Mercer House flats described previously, the Townsend Street flats are also four-storeyed, and again they are mostly yellow, with red brick detail. There is external stair and balcony access from the rear courtyard, which is concrete paved and also houses the washing lines for the block. However, the scheme differs from that at Mercer House in the treatment of the facade. The blocks and balconies have rounded corners, while a flat roof projects outwards

43 Flat development at Poplar Row, Ballybough (Photograph by R. McManus.)

beyond the edge of the building. These new features combine to create a very different, more 'Modern' impression than the traditionalism of Mercer House.

Pearse House, Sandwith Street Lower, is also a four-storey block, but it goes one step further in its Modern style. Here the appearance of the block is more massive and forbidding, partly due to the cement rendered facade. The block is set back from the street, with some trees. Its curved corners and flat roof suggest European architectural influences.

There was no great publicity for the work of the Corporation's Housing Architects in the 1930s. Many writers criticized the social aspects of multi-storey housing, but there were no observations on the urban quality or appropriateness of the architecture. One exception is the 1938 report of the Citizens' Housing Council, which praised the Housing Architect and his staff. The report particularly noted the high quality and excellent appearance of the flat blocks, while criticizing the 'sameness' of the houses. Thus, while the garden suburb idea was successful in the 1920s, when expensive, relatively large houses were built, it was less suited to the low cost, mass production of the 1930s cottage schemes. As cost precluded the use of devices to avoid monotony, the houses became depressing in their uniformity. By contrast, the

HANOVER STREET FLATS AND SITE WORKS
(Reinforced throughout with ' Twisteel')

44 Pearse House, Hanover Street flat development. (*Lord Mayor's Handbook*, 1944, fp.19.)

1930s block dwellings made a more positive architectural statement, contributing significantly to Dublin's streetscapes, although the impact on their inhabitants might be seen as less definitely affirmative.

Whereas the relative merits of flats and houses were hotly debated throughout this period in Dublin, there is no such ambivalence evident in the London County Council's attitude to block dwellings. Generally, the erection of block dwellings in a clearance area allowed for the rehousing of all those displaced by the slum clearance, while the building of cottages resulted in a surplus population requiring rehousing elsewhere. This fact had been grudgingly accepted in Dublin in the 1930s, but flats were still resisted. Importantly, the inter-mixing of housing and industrial uses in central areas meant that, were cottages to be erected rather than taller block dwellings, these would inevitably be over-shadowed by higher industrial buildings, an argument which would appear to have been overlooked in Dublin.

Cottage schemes for rental: late 1920s onwards

Almost two thirds of all tenant purchase cottages built by Dublin Corporation between 1928 and 1939 had just three rooms, and therefore fell below the minimum requirement for average families, as discussed previously. The programme covered 17 schemes, but was dominated by the vast Crumlin housing scheme. Including earlier schemes, the Local Authority housing stock included 7420 cottages for rental by 1939, just under half of the total Corporation housing stock.

The Cabra Scheme, undertaken in three sections from 1929 onwards, is particularly important because it straddles the old and new housing eras. The first section at Fassaugh Lane was begun in 1929, when Messrs John Kenny and Sons were awarded the contract for the construction of roads and sewers. By the following year it was decided that the two sections comprising in total' 641 four-roomed houses were to be erected by H. & J. Martin and G. & T. Crampton respectively. In the June Quarter, 1930, names were assigned to the newly-constructed roads, and shortly after it was decided to advertise for applicants for the Cabra houses at purchase prices similar to the Donnycarney Scheme. Applications from persons having fewer than four children under the age of 21 were not considered (Report 216/1930). By October 1931, it was reported that the 641 houses on the first section of the Cabra Area were practically complete, and that 442 were already occupied.

While work on the first section of the Cabra Scheme continued, some 610 four-room cottages were proposed on the Cabra Extension Area, also known as Beggsboro. In March 1931, the City Manager and Town Clerk approved of the erection houses on the Cabra Extension Area of a similar type to the first section houses – two-storeyed, four-roomed, with bath, hot and cold water circulating system. By the following August, 29 acres 1 rood 12 perches (c.12ha) had been purchased from Mr Gerald Begg, hence the land being known as 'Beggsboro', while negotiations for an additional eight acres (c.3ha) were underway with other owners. In fact, Report 34/1932 noted the approval by the Minister for Local Government and Public Health for plans and specifications for the erection of 678 houses on the Beggsboro Extension of the Cabra Housing Area, comprising 84 four-room and 594 three-room cottages. It was these smaller houses, rather than those advocated by the City Manager, which were eventually built. Thus, the larger, generally four-roomed tenant purchase houses of the Fassaugh Lane section were dropped in favour of smaller, mostly three-roomed rented houses.

The Beggsboro Scheme got underway in April 1932, when tenders were invited for the first section. In June of that year, G. & T. Crampton was granted the tender for 358 houses at the Beggsboro Extension, while in August, H. & J. Martin submitted the lowest of three tenders for the Second Section, comprising 320 houses. In February/March 1933, four of the streets in the Beggsboro Area were named St Jarlath, St Fintan, St Canice and St

Table 25 Cottage rental schemes, 1927–1939.

Scheme	Completion Date (approx.)	Total	Rooms			
			2	3	4	5
Spitalfields	1928	6	0	6	0	0
Kehoe Square	1927	57	3	54	0	0
Marrowbone Lane	1930	166	17	138	11	0
Ormond Market	1932/1935	9	0	9	0	0
Malone Gardens	1933	65	0	59	6	0
Beggsboro	1933/1934	684	0	596	88	0
Donnelly's Orchard	1934	148	0	137	11	0
Friends Fields	1934	144	0	140	4	0
Annamoe Road	1934	311	0	297	14	0
Crumlin South	1934/1939	2903	0	1799	1104	0
North Lotts	1935	582	0	486	96	0
Cook Street	1936	3	0	0	3	0
South Lotts Road	1937	16	0	14	2	0
Terenure	1938	313	0	66	247	0
Ellenfield	1938.1939	327	0	0	326	1
Crumlin North	1939.1939	353	0	92	261	0
Harold's Cross	1938.1939	161	0	83	78	0
Total		6248	20	3976	2251	1
Per cent of Total		100	0.32	63.6	36.0	0.02

Attracta. Subsequently St Eithne Road was substituted for St Canice Road (Report 47/1933). The contract for the third section of the Cabra development, at Annamoe Road, was undertaken by G. & T. Crampton, and the new roads were taken in charge in August 1934.

Lily O'Brien's family moved from the front room of a tenement house in Fitzgibbon Street to St Eithne Road in Cabra. She describes their amazement when they arrived at the new corner house:

> We ran through the empty house, deeply inhaling the smell of newly painted windows and walls … Johnny flicked a switch and a light went on. It was magic. We all had a go. A room with a small fireplace looked out into the front garden and street. Though it was the main room, it was called the kitchen. A tiny scullery, with a black iron stove, led off this room. A deep stone sink hung under a window … A lavatory was just outside the back door. "This is our lavatory," Sylvia said, staring in at it. "No one else can use it. Isn't that right, Mammy?".

(O'Connor, 2000, p. 138)

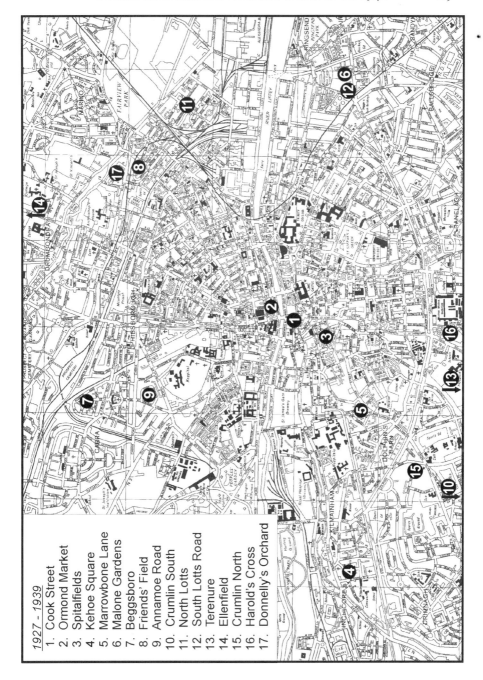

1927 - 1939

1. Cook Street
2. Ormond Market
3. Spitalfields
4. Kehoe Square
5. Marrowbone Lane
6. Malone Gardens
7. Beggsboro
8. Friends' Field
9. Annamoe Road
10. Crumlin South
11. North Lotts
12. South Lotts Road
13. Terenure
14. Ellenfield
15. Crumlin North
16. Harold's Cross
17. Donnelly's Orchard

45 Location of Corporation cottage rental schemes, 1927–1939.

The O'Briens found that their back garden was so big that they couldn't manage it, while the two girls took turns cutting the grass in the front garden with a big scissors. However, despite the difficulties, 'people settled in well and had pride in their new homes. They kept their windows sparkling and tried to outdo each other with fancy lace curtains and shiny brass letter boxes' (p. 140).

Crumlin: the great 1930s scheme

Between 1887 and 1931, Dublin Corporation had built 7246 dwellings, 78 per cent of which were houses. Within the next eight years, it was to more than double its housing stock as a result of a new, two-pronged attack on the slums (involving both flats and rental cottage schemes). Very large housing schemes were now being built, and of the 6019 houses built during this period, more than half were built at Crumlin. While this large scheme was to have an enormous impact on this largely rural area, it should be noted that Crumlin had already begun to experience a degree of private speculative development during the 1920s. The Iveagh Trust had also erected 136 houses here on a 30 acre (c.12ha) site from 1926. The Trust's site on Crumlin Road was developed as a suburban cottage scheme of two-storey family houses with small gardens to designs by the architectural firm of O'Callaghan & Webb. There was a mixture of four- and five-roomed houses in the scheme, which was built at a total cost of £134,000. The rents, at 19 to 21 shillings per week, were higher than those of the Trust's tenement schemes, and more expensive than Dublin Corporation's standard rental of 2s. 6d. per room. Aalen (1990) notes that the Iveagh Trust was aware that the new houses would be located in a rapidly developing part of Dublin.

Preparations for the new Corporation cottage estate in the Crumlin area had begun in the 1920s, when the sewerage scheme was laid down (Craft, 1971). In 1934 almost 250 acres (c.100ha) were bought, under a Compulsory Purchase Order, for £55,158 (£223 per acre, c.£557 per ha), and in the same year building at Crumlin South began. Almost 3000 houses were to be built in the scheme; 1803 were three-roomed, while 1172 of the cottages had four rooms. This phase of the scheme, centering on the 'circular' housing development east of the old village, was completed in 1940. In 1938, work began on the first of the 2416 houses to be built in Crumlin North, the area north of Kildare Road, which was completed in 1944/5. The peak of building occurred in 1936/7, when over a thousand houses were completed. A building trade strike in 1937/8 reduced the total to 200, while the outbreak of World War II

46 Crumlin before development.
(Ordnance Survey 1:10,560 plan, Sheet 18, Dublin, 1912 revision.)

resulted in a decline in building as the price of raw materials rose. Thus, in terms of scale alone, the Crumlin scheme marked a huge breakthrough for the Corporation, while the rate of building exceeded that of any previous housing project.

Perhaps because of its unprecedented scale, the Department of Local Government and Public Health was heavily involved in the Crumlin scheme's

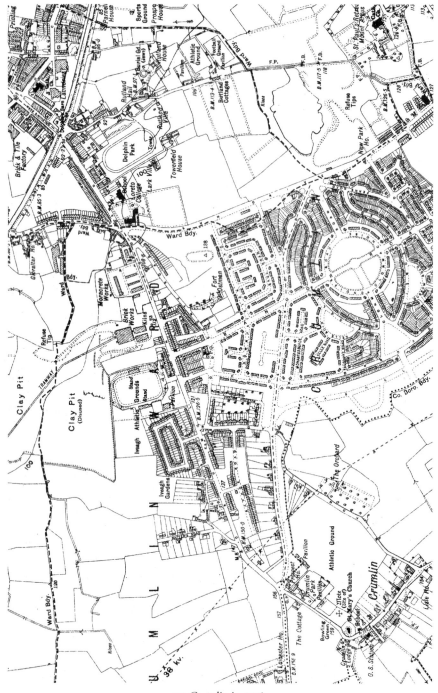

47 Crumlin in 1936.
(Ordnance Survey 1:10,560 plan, Sheet 18, Dublin, 1938 revision.)

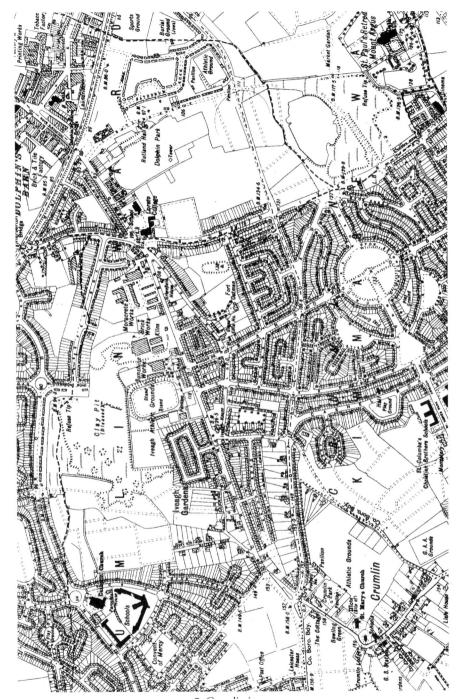

48 Crumlin in 1943
(Ordnance Survey 1:10,560 plan, Sheet 18, Dublin, 1943 revision.)

development. The layout plan of the scheme was discussed by representatives of the Local Government Ministry and the Corporation, and approved in late September 1933, subject to the sanction of the Minister. A total of 2915 houses was mentioned, including 2378 Corporation 'cottages' and 537 larger privately erected houses. This number was altered over time as more space became available, so that Report 71/1936 notes revised plans to erect 2507 houses rather than 2445. It was proposed to erect 1847 three-roomed and 531 four-roomed houses on the portion of the site which the Corporation itself intended to build on, while allowance was made for 537 five-roomed houses to be built by private enterprise or public utility societies on certain frontages on the outskirts of the scheme which would be reserved for leasing, as was done in Croydon Park, Marino and Drumcondra (see following chapter). The question of providing a proportion of two-roomed houses was left open for consideration at a later stage. The Housing Architect's proposal to include a small number of brick houses at important parts of the scheme, so as to give variety of treatment, was also approved (Report 62/1933). The building work (on the Corporation section) was undertaken by several large contractors, including H. & J. Martin, P.F. Fearon & Co. and G. & T. Crampton, all of whom were involved in other Corporation schemes in the 1930s.

Although the cul-de-sac, strongly advocated by Unwin in the Tudor Walters report, had already been successfully used in many of the Corporation housing schemes, where it was used on economic as well as aesthetic and social grounds, the idea was still viewed with suspicion by many official bodies. One 1933 communication from the Department of Local Government and Public Health considered that 'the amended layout still provides for too much cul-de-sac treatment'. In addition, the plan did not follow the lines agreed upon at the conference between representatives of the Dublin Corporation and of that Department in the following respects: 'a) the centre road running North and South is not carried through the circle; and b) an easy curve connection of Dark Lane (later renamed Sundrive Road) and the new main road crossing East and West the northern end of the area has not been provided' (quoted in Report 56/1933, p. 336). However, the Department finally agreed to a compromise whereby it would approve the scheme provided points a) and b) were amended, without raising further objection on the grounds of excessive cul-de-sac treatment.

By mid-summer 1934, 1100 houses were in course of construction. A numbering scheme was adopted, while names for the new roads were also approved. The Housing Architect again suggested that in a scheme of such magnitude as the Crumlin Scheme, it was desirable to introduce some variety of elevational treatment, and provided plans for the partial introduction of brick construction for this purpose. Some 125 dwellings were to be embellished in this way, at an estimated extra cost of £1800, but this would not apply in the case of contracts in progress. This meant that none of the initial 1000 or so houses would be differentiated in any special way (Report 41/1934).

The 1939–43 Housing Inquiry illustrated that the erection of relatively small houses had been the Corporation policy during the 1930s, at a time when, ironically, housing allocation was restricted to the largest families. Almost 70 per cent of the families who were allocated Corporation housing from 1934 to 1939 had more than six members, yet only 39 per cent of the houses built at Crumlin South had four rooms. We have already seen that three bedrooms was considered to be the minimum standard, with one room each for parents, boys and girls. Yet at Crumlin South (1934–40), the majority of cottages had only three rooms in total. When tentative layout plans for the Crumlin North scheme were approved by the Department of Local Government and Public Health in 1937, the Minister suggested that 80 per cent of the houses should be four-roomed, out of a total of more than 2400 houses to be erected at an estimated cost of £1,080,000 (Report 6/1937). In the event, some 96 per cent of all the Crumlin North houses erected between 1939 and 1945 were four-roomed.

Brendan Behan once said of his home in Crumlin: 'We had electricity, a bathroom, a toilet, and air … I detested all that' (quoted in Mikhail, 1982, p. 126). Craft (1971) has considered whether the people who went to Crumlin were a more adventuresome and aspiring group than those who remained in the city centre. There was certainly an element of self-selection, but it is unclear whether the poorest and most deprived families remained in the city tenements out of preference for a familiar environment and hostility towards the housing authority or because the nature of their employment and the higher rents and fares to work required them to stay there. Social selection would have affected the quality of life in new estates. The Corporation's policy was to rehouse families of the lowest rent-paying capacity in central flats, thereby increasing the social segregation of the city, and the perceived undesirability of multi-family dwellings.

For those who moved out, there was criticism that:

> the new settlements in Crumlin and Drimnagh are without any of the essential social amenities. There are no parks, no playing fields, no

town halls. No schools were provided at first ... The same mistake and for the same reason has been made in Drimnagh only last year. Experience does not teach our Municipality anything'.

(Dillon, 1945, p. 19)

In fact, much of the criticism was unjustified. Even before the scheme was begun, discussions began with the Dublin Board of Assistance regarding the need to rearrange the dispensary districts given the increasing number of houses in the Crumlin Area. As early as 1934, the church authorities and the Minister for Education had been informed of the sites reserved by the Corporation for church and school buildings 'in order that the said authorities might consider the provision of such facilities for the inhabitants' (Report 29/1934, p. 179). However, the primary schools at Crumlin had not been completed by 1938, and the large child population had to be transported to and from city schools daily. The delay was largely due to the unsuitability of the original site offered by the Corporation, both as to extent and cost per acre. Despite the critics, the 1939–43 Housing Inquiry found that basic services (with the exception of fuel distribution) were adequate in the new communities. However, it was felt that the provision of facilities such as youth clubs, nurseries, playgrounds and evening play-centres, community centres and sports grounds for adults were 'beyond the resources of the Corporation'.

When the schools were finally completed, they had to cope with one of the largest concentrations of children in Europe at the time. The Irish Times of 17 October 1944, described one aspect of life in Crumlin in an article entitled 'Exodus':

> Every day, at 12.30, nearly seven thousand children, between the ages of six and fourteen, emerge from St Agnes's Convent School, and from the Christian Brothers' School across the road. The schools attend to the swarming juvenile life of the Crumlin housing estate. The Reverend Mother of St Agnes's believes this to be the largest concentration of children in Europe. Yesterday morning we watched the exodus, from the roof. It begins slowly. A line of little girls forms in the playground below, in charge of a nun. They are obedient. The nun unlocks the gate of the playground. The little girls file out into the road. Suddenly, they start to run. They spread out in every direction. They are joined by a mob of little boys from the other school across the road. More children come pouring out. Now the road and the pavement vanish beneath

49 Crumlin – the developing landscape. (*Dublin by day and by night*, 1939, p. 33.)

hundreds and hundreds of bare feet, feet in gym shoes, feet in boots, feet in felt slippers. A noise arises that cannot be described- a high-pitched, undulating noise, rising and falling like the sound of a giant dynamo. Now the road is quite gone. It is covered with a moving carpet of black coats, red coats, green coats and grey coats. Away in the distance, no bigger than specks, are the little girls who came out first, leaping and running down the long, straight road.

The problems of adjusting to a new environment were generally considered by the authorities (and their critics) in terms of physical and material well-being, and the more subtle psychological and social aspects of rehousing were generally not considered. Such aspects included the impact of moving from an elaborate network of friends and relations to an area with a lower population density and no corner shops to facilitate the formation of new relationships. Despite its general focus on physical improvements, the Citizens' Housing Council (1937, p. 14) observed that people who had moved to the new suburban estates 'lack means of contact, and often miss the social life of the overcrowded tenements from which they have been moved'. The new environment was completely different, without industry, entertainment or heavy traffic, a quiet semi-rural setting. Many of those who moved out to the new estates had difficulties in adjusting. 'The Corporation was offering houses to some of the large families in the tenements and a few of them left and went off to live in North Crumlin, but the high rents and the lack of amenities had them back in a couple of months looking for rooms again' (Johnston, 1985, p. 123). In 1939 approval was given to layout plans for a 'shopping centre' at Galteemore Road (Crumlin North) with nine residential shops, a paltry number given the overall size of the development.

Brendan Behan (1923–64) and his family were relocated to Crumlin in 1937. According to Brendan himself: 'Our street (Russell Street) was a tough street, and the last outpost of toughness you'd meet as you left North Dublin for the red brick respectability of Jones's Road, Fitzroy Avenue, Clonliffe Road, and Drumcondra generally' (Behan, 1963, p. 149). In *My Brother Brendan* (Behan, 1965), Dominic Behan describes the move from 14 Russell Street to 70 Kildare Road, Crumlin. Dominic recounts how his big brother told him that 'the chisellers in Kimmage don't have time to play games, they have to go huntin' with their fathers. Take it from me, sondown, we're on our way to the wild west.'

Referring to the new housing area as a 'reservation', their arrival in the unlit, unfinished scheme did little to impress. 'We were in the middle of skeletoned houses, untiled roofs, unplastered walls, unglazed windows' (Behan, 1965, p. 21). Asking the way to Kildare Road from a terrified night watchman, they learned that ' "In the summer it was as hard to find where yeh lived as it is now. No names on the roads. Houses with no numbers. I hope yeh find wherever it is yer goin' but," he lowered his voice to a whisper, "if I was youse I'd turn back before it's too late" ' (Behan, 1965, p. 22).

In 1937, London County Council noted that:

> The health of the community depends on the health of the individual who is, in turn, dependent on his environment. There is nothing in the nature of things to prevent that environment being adjusted within limits in accordance with the wishes of mankind.
>
> (LCC, 1937, p. 25)

The housing erected by Dublin Corporation in the 1920s and 1930s reflected several key elements of planning. The first of these was the belief that physical, moral and social welfare might be improved by upgrading the physical environment. This conclusion grew from nineteenth century public health concerns, and persisted in the strong 1930s belief that slum clearance would solve many ills:

> Mental health and physical health go hand in hand, and the psychological effect of living in mean surroundings, in houses which are dark, damp and dilapidated, and where privacy and cleanliness are obtained with difficulty if at all, cannot be neglected in any attempt to assess the effect of faulty environment on the mental, moral and physical fibre of the occupants.

(LCC, 1937, p. 13)

The aesthetic element of planning was particularly important in the Corporation schemes of the 1920s and 1930s, because so many of those involved in planning were actually trained as architects. Town planning's concern for visual order, harmony, scale and townscape was rooted in its architectural and civic design heritage. Dublin Corporation's cottage estates reflected the strong links between Dublin and the early British town planners, with both architecture and layout illustrating the legacy of Hampstead and the influence of the London County Council.

Planning is spurred on by a vision for the future, and this generally assumes that a middle-class lifestyle is aspired to and is attainable by all. Certainly, these aspirations explained the development of suburban housing for the various strata within the middle classes (see later discussion), but it was also assumed that the working class would aspire to live in suburbs, which was a fallacy. In Dublin, as elsewhere, there was and remains a contrast between what the largely middle-class administrators and planners believe is desirable, and what is actually required by the largely working-class population they intend to house. The issues of central rather than peripheral housing, and of houses and flats, are at the heart of this dichotomy. The social structure of new communities developed in the 1920s and 1930s by large-scale Corporation-sponsored development reflects these contrasts.

The Corporation was criticized regarding the level of facilities provided on its new estates. However, the 1939–43 Housing Inquiry found that provision of basic services such as water, lighting and sewerage was adequate. In addition, it corroborated the Housing Sub-Committee's belief that every possible facility was provided for inhabitants of new housing areas, in the form of schools, churches and other public accommodation. 'Industrial areas are also provided for on new schemes, as well as shopping centres, sites for banks and other necessary public institutions, so that building on suburban areas will, to a large extent, ultimately evolve self-contained colonies' (Report 6/1938, p. 41). Indeed, the estates have generally matured well, and the Corporation's foresight in providing for suburban industrial employment was ahead of its time.

However, the 1938 report on slum clearance pointed out that, while of excellent quality, the dwellings being erected by the Corporation had very small rooms and that 'with a rising demand for comfort and floor space occasioned by increased standards of living, such buildings will be out of date long before they are worn out'. In fact, the Council considered it 'highly probable that future generations will stigmatize, and not praise, the results of our best endeavours to house the workers' (Citizens' Housing Council, 1938, p. 42). For a time this prophecy seemed to be coming true. However, nowadays many of the Corporation's housing schemes erected in the 1920s and 1930s are enjoying an increasing popularity, with houses at Marino in particular attracting very high prices.

One of the problems of the Corporation's approach, which does not appear to have been fully realized by that body, is that it never tackled the housing problem in a fully co-ordinated way. For example, even the 1939–43 Inquiry, with its wealth of statistics, did not have a complete analysis of the population of Corporation schemes in terms of economic status and rent-paying ability, and had to rely on a sample survey. The Citizens' Housing Council (1938) proposed that a statistics section of the Corporation should be established so as to provide a complete set of social statistics, enabling the distribution of residents in new settlements so as to avoid the existing population imbalances. Given the huge expenditure on housing at this time, when housing accounted for more than half of the municipal debt, it seems ludicrous that the problem was not tackled in a more scientific manner. Instead, however enthusiastic and hard-working, the untrained aldermen and councillors comprised an unwieldy Housing Committee, while the Housing Department officials were over-burdened with day-to-day work, and unable to undertake the arduous task of large-scale planning and co-ordinating policy and finance in a comprehensive, structured way.

There was a belief that a careful layout of residential areas would lead to the development of 'community' and social interaction by stimulating feelings of security and stability. This implies the belief in a co-operative model of society, the existence of a society comprising shared beliefs, values and aspirations. However, the existence of such a society is belied by a special report on the wanton destruction of civic property in Dublin which was prepared in 1933 (Report 44/1933). Gerald J. Sherlock, City Manager, complained strongly of the 'almost complete absence of any sign of civic spirit in Dublin' (Report 44/1933, p. 258). At the end of 1934 it was reported that the malicious damage to public property in Fairview Park was continuing unabated. 'There is apparently not only gross apathy on the part of ordinary citizens in preserving the amenities provided for their enjoyment, but a deliberate and continuous programme of organized wrecking' (Report 61/1934, p. 348). The lack of civic pride must have been particularly distressing to those members of the Corporation who were so actively engaged in trying to provide for the people of the city. No improvement was experienced despite an awareness programme involving the co-operation of schools, priests and gardaí. Throughout the 1930s, reports of wanton destruction in various housing areas continued to be listed in Corporation reports, including damage or theft of trees/shrubs in Fairview Park, Fairbrother's Fields, Bulfin Road, Cabra, and in the central schemes and parks. 'The wanton destruction of civic property continues – the latest case being that of seven trees which were planted during the past month in various Housing areas and have been destroyed' (Report 8/1936, p. 29). Within one week in February 1936, five trees valued at £5 were broken on the New Cabra Road, while in March, 16 trees were broken at Fairbrother's Fields and 12 at Bulfin Road (Report 18/1936). Also in 1936, eight shrubs worth 16s. were stolen from Fairview Park and the Gardaí were notified (Report 31/1936). 'Out of forty-five trees planted within the last month in housing areas at North Cumberland Street, Erne Street and Oliver Bond Street, 18 trees have been broken and one stolen. In Erne Street, out of 13 trees planted, ten were broken. As a result of this wanton damage, it has been decided that no further tree planting in this area will be done' (Report 2/1937, p. 22). Damage to ornamental trees at Stillorgan Road and Fairview Park, was reported in March, 1939. In addition, further wanton damage was reported at Griffith Park, Fairview, St. Patrick's Park and Mountjoy Square (Report 19/1939). However, none of the reports attempted to explain why the problem should have arisen. No link seems to have been made between the vandalism and the provision of large, single-class estates whose inhabitants had been torn from their roots and social network to the suburbs. Even those relocated within the city centre to new flat schemes experienced new difficulties. They now found themselves stigmatized, since it was generally only the poorest of the poor who were allocated flat dwellings.

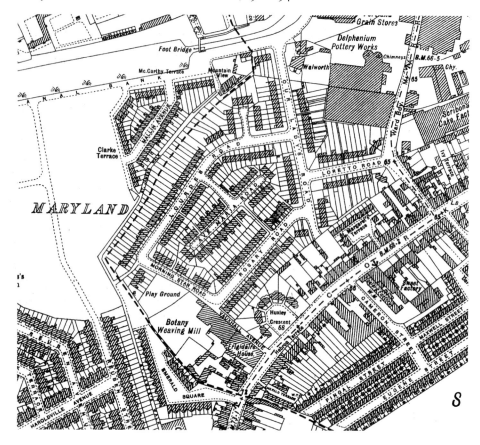

50 Layout plan of the Maryland development.
(Ordnance Survey 1:2500 plan, Sheet 18 x, Dublin, 1943 revision.)

Meanwhile, the naming of street names in the Corporation housing schemes suggests something of the political and religious affiliations of the majority of Dublin Corporation members. The euphoria of the International Eucharistic Congress of 1932 probably moved the Corporation to choose pious street names for 'Maryland' (1932) and Beggsboro (1933). The streets in Beggsboro were named after saints, while the six roads in the Maryland (Marrowbone Lane) housing area were initially named The Virgin's Road, Our Lady's Road, Annunciation Road, Morning Star Road, Rosary Road and Ave Maria Road (Report 4/1932). Loreto and Lourdes Road were later substituted for Virgin's Road and Annunciation Road. Not surprisingly, the area was popularly known as 'Maryland', and was referred to as such in several of the Corporation's own reports and on the Ordnance Survey maps.

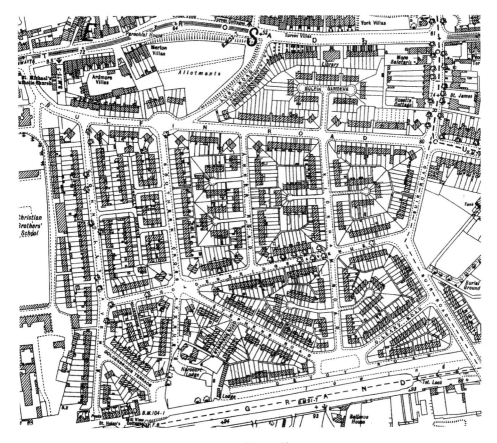

51 Layout plan of the Bulfin estate.
(Ordnance Survey 1:2500 plan, Sheet 18 X, Dublin, 1943 revision.)

The political element appears to have been present in earlier schemes including the naming of Ceannt Fort (1917, originally St James' Walk (Colbert's Fort)). In the Dolphin's Barn area, the Bulfin Estate (1920s) names are those of Fenians including Kickham and O'Leary. The streets at Fairbrother's Fields were allocated the names of writers and poets by 1922, while in 1929, Glasnevin streets were to be named Dean Swift Avenue, Lilliput and Stella Avenue, although only the last mentioned came into permanent use. The Clogher Road area (1944) was named after dioceses in Ireland, including Clogher, Clonmacnoise, Kilfenora and Monasterboice. In the Drimnagh area, roads were named after Irish mountains and hills, including Mourne, Galtymore and Keeper. Thus it would appear that the Corporation officials saw themselves building a Catholic and Nationalist Ireland. The people had little say in the policies of the city's government, but were shunted to new housing areas by their 'benefactors'. While in many ways laudable, the activities of the Corporation in this period neglected one fundamental particular. By basing their assumptions on their own lifestyles and experiences, the officials of Dublin Corporation ignored the possibility that their 'parishioners' may not have aspired to or accepted the same values. Thus the words of Patrick Geddes at the 1913 Housing Inquiry were forgotten – the poor were all too often treated 'as if they were mere passive creatures to be housed like cattle' (Housing Inquiry, 1914, p. 211).

Not so private!
Public Utility Societies and
semi-private developers

We now move to the middle ground which existed in Dublin's development continuum. Rather than a sharp distinction between public and private builders, it has been suggested that there was a range of development types which had links to both public and private sectors. In effect, many public and private agencies were dependent on each other. Public Utility Societies (PUS), semi-private co-operative type housing organizations, were at the heart of this interdependent relationship, and this section considers their role in the Corporation's 'reserved areas' policy, including a detailed examination of the development process in Marino and Drumcondra. The role of the public utility societies was particularly significant in the 1920s and 1930s, adding another level to the development hierarchy, between land-owner and builder. One particularly interesting feature of the public utility societies in Ireland is the extent to which a small number of individuals were influential in the spread of the movement across the country. While this chapter focuses on the role of public utility societies, our exploration of this middle ground will also consider the relationship between Dublin Corporation and the privately-owned Vernon Estate as well as Blackrock UDC's Temple Hill scheme.

Public Utility Societies in Dublin

Although the term 'public utility society' is unfamiliar today, the self-help, self-build groups which were active from the 1920s in Ireland were extremely important in tackling housing shortages across the country. The actual designation 'public utility society' came into use in Britain with the 1909 Housing and Town Planning Act, which did not apply in Ireland. Even before then, however, housing societies which were often described as 'co-partnership tenant societies' had provided housing for their members on a co-operative basis. Aldridge (1915) claimed that 'the movement for the establishment of Societies of Public Utility took its rise in the establishment of the Ealing Tenants Society by Mr Henry Vivian and a group of sympathizers ...' (p. 417).

As we have seen earlier, the issue of using such public utility societies as a means of treating the Dublin housing question had been raised by both Abercrombie in 1914 and by P.C. Cowan in 1918. Abercrombie had suggested that providing financial assistance for public utility societies who built houses for the working classes was a highly desirable element in solving the 'housing problem'. The sale or lease of land by the local authority to public utility societies for rehousing dispossessed tenants of cleared properties was also proposed. However, it was not until the 1919 Housing Act that legislation was introduced which dealt with public utility societies in an Irish context.

The public utility society has been described as 'a specialist form of combined limited dividend company and Friendly Society' (Skilleter, 1993, p. 125). This suggests a kinship with the 'five per cent philanthropy' of the nineteenth century whereby the wealthy invested in schemes aimed at helping the working classes, with dividends limited to a maximum of 5 per cent. Thus one could 'do good' and still make a respectable profit, although in the 1920s and 1930s the Irish public utility societies appear to have catered for the middle classes, and generally sold their houses much as the private speculative developers would have done, to 'all-comers'.

The Housing (Ireland) Act of 1919 provided an opportunity for both local authorities and voluntary associations, who would be offered substantial assistance to build houses. The first piece of legislation to directly deal with public utility societies, it allowed for a percentage contribution to be made towards the loan charges on loans incurred by the societies for the erection of houses. However, the measure was largely ineffectual given the high costs of development in the immediate post-war period, as well as an unstable political situation. Therefore, while the provisions of the Act were liberal, they were not availed of to any great degree. Only two public utility societies in Dublin, the St Barnabas and Killester, took action under the 1919 provisions, building a total of 44 houses. Although the initial output was small, these first public utility societies were extremely important in providing an example which others were to follow as the conditions for building improved. The work of the St Barnabas Public Utility Society, though interesting in its own right, stood out in a particular way (see McManus, 1999).

A Church of Ireland clergyman, Revd David Henry Hall was instrumental in the foundation of the St Barnabas society, which was registered as a Friendly Society on 9 January 1920 and based in the Church of Ireland parish of St Barnabas, East Wall. Assigned to St Barnabas parish in July 1918, Hall had encountered some of the worst conditions in the city, as reflected in a

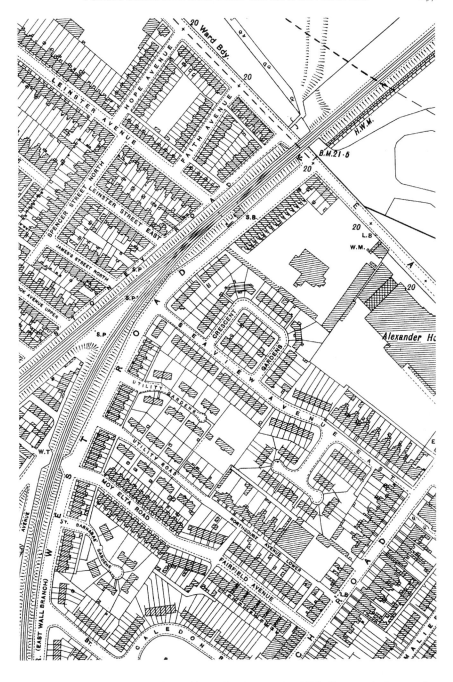

52 Activities of the St Barnabas Public Utility Society, East Wall. Contrast the layout of
the utility society houses in Utility Gardens with the houses on Moy Elta Road.
(Ordnance Survey 1:2500 plan, Sheet 18 VIII, Dublin, 1938 revision.)

53 Housing at St Barnabas Gardens. (Photograph by R. McManus.)

54 Housing at Utility Gardens, now Strangford Gardens. (Photograph by R. McManus.)

death rate of 46 per 1000 within the parish, compared with the city average of 18 per 1000. The parish was located close to Dublin port, surrounded by canals, railways and docks. Overcrowding was severe – in one case, Hall found 84 children living in a single house on Commons Street, in another, a family of five living in a room just nine feet by six (*c.*2.7 metres by 1.8 m), yet there were also large tracts of derelict ground in the area. Faced with extreme poverty and appalling housing conditions, Revd Hall actively began to search for some way of aiding his parishioners in a practical way. The introduction of the new legislation seems to have encouraged Hall in his efforts to make a meaningful contribution to the housing situation in Dublin. In August 1919, he attended a meeting organized by members of the Dublin Watch Committee at which the speakers urged the necessity of forming utility societies to deal with the pressing need to build working people's cottages. From then on, he never ceased researching the issue and working to get land upon which to build, eventually acquiring a site of about three and a half acres (*c.*1.4 ha) in his parish at a cost of £700 freehold. Hall saw a role for the Church of Ireland in focusing its members to meet the housing need through voluntary assistance, with the formation of public utility societies as a vehicle. In December 1919 he arranged a parish meeting at which a Local Government architect explained the construction of houses 'suitable for working people', while Hall himself explained what he had learned from Mr Hugh Law of the Local Government Board about the working of a public utility society.

Following the parish meeting on 23 December 1919, it was decided to form the St Barnabas Public Utility Society, which was registered on the 9 January 1920 as a Friendly Society (Reg. No. 1520) with Hall as the honorary secretary. The business of the society was listed as the building of houses, and the organization was affiliated to the Garden Cities and Town Planning Association (GCPTA) in London. The link with the garden city movement is notable, as the initial aim was 'to build a garden suburb of 40 houses, semi-detached, with a portion of ground to each house' (Hall, 1920, p. 196). In Britain, 'co-partnership' public utility societies had been involved in the provision of artizan houses at Hampstead Garden Suburb, as well as Bournville, Letchworth and Welwyn. The rules of the St Barnabas society were based on a model provided by the GCTPA which included 120 regulations. An eight-member management committee was established, of whom five were later to become residents of the new scheme.

Hall believed that the Society could improve the conditions in the area so as 'to render happy the lives of many who were existing under conditions too awful to be described' (*Irish Builder and Engineer*, 17 April 1920, p. 273).

Financial gain was never a motivation to the St Barnabas society. Instead, 'the whole scheme was initiated and carried on as a piece of pure citizenship' (*Church of Ireland Gazette* (CIG), 8 July 1921, p. 423). It was meant to be a Christian endeavour to meet and correct some of the appalling housing conditions of Dublin (CIG, 8 February 1924, p. 87).

The first ten houses built at St Barnabas Gardens (figures 52 and 53) had features characteristic of the early 'garden suburbs', including a low-density layout (10 houses to the acre/25 per ha) utilizing culs-de-sac. In addition to three bedrooms, the houses had a bath and 'other necessary conveniences'. Each house had a garden, while a recreation ground for children was also planned.

By raising loan stock and issuing shares, Hall raised 25 per cent of the cost of the first scheme, with the remainder to be loaned by the Government. Raising the money was not an easy task at such a difficult time, but Hall was a determined individual and went canvassing, preaching charity sermons and appealing through the press in order to raise the first £1000 necessary before Messrs J. & R. Thompson would start to build. The details of Hall's efforts have been described elsewhere by the author (McManus, 1999). The Society aimed to enable members of the working class to purchase a comfortable home of their own over a 20-year period, through a combination of tenant purchase and shares in the Society. The initial ten houses at St Barnabas Gardens included six houses with five rooms, at a rental of £65 per annum each, and 4 four-roomed houses, for which the annual rental amounted to £58 10s. 0d. The weekly rent included a portion which was placed to the purchase of the house and these monies being invested in gilt-edged securities, yielded a return which was also placed to the benefit of the purchasers after deductions for rates and ground rents. While the houses would be owned by the Society, the tenants elected a Tenants Committee to manage the houses and approve tenants. This followed the British co-partnership ideal where tenants were given real control over their own society by means of a management committee dominated by tenants (Skilleter, 1993). For a period of unemployment the tenant could use the holding of shares as offset to rent. Over the period of purchase the exteriors of the houses were painted and kept in good repair. Hall believed in making every person pay for their house, because 'deep in man's nature there is ingrained a contempt for that which can be secured without labour. That which a man gains by the strength of his own right hand is more prized by him than all the philanthropic sops that a generous public has in its gift' (CIG, 6 June 1924 p. 344). However, he succeeded in devising a means of making it possible for the artizan to pay gradually, eventually becoming the full owner of the house.

When the opening ceremony for the first ten houses took place on 24 June 1921, it received considerable publicity, particularly because it was one of the few 'good news' stories at that dark time in Irish life. The Lord Mayor, Laurence O'Neill, noted that it was particularly pleasant 'to find ladies and gentlemen of different degrees and forms of thought and religion gathered together with the one common object of benefiting their fellow citizens', expressing the hope that this scheme would be 'a beacon of light, the influence of which would spread throughout their beloved land' (*Church of Ireland Gazette*, 8 July 1921, p. 423). The attendance included the local Roman Catholic Parish Priest, Very Revd Canon Brady, Dr P. C. Cowan and staff of the Housing Department of the Local Government Board, the City Architect and members of the Dublin Corporation's Housing Committee, as well as representatives of local employers such as the secretary of the Port and Docks Board, the manager of the London and North Western Railway, representatives of the Great Northern Railway, the Dublin Harbour Master, and various other dignitaries.

A second phase of 26 houses (Utility Gardens, Utility Road) was planned for a two and a half acre (*c*.1 ha) site but was again dependent on raising investment through six per cent loan stock. With this money, with many donations and with support from Dublin Corporation, which installed the necessary water mains free of charge and made a grant equivalent to the rates on the houses for a ten-year period, these houses were built from March 1922 to April 1923 at a cost of £20,421. Rents for the houses started at 25 shillings per week, so only skilled artisans were really in a position to pay them. However, the building scheme also provided local employment at a time of considerable hardship. Although the St Barnabas PUS was associated with the Church of Ireland parish of that name, the new tenants were both Roman Catholic and Protestant, and included refugees from the Belfast pogroms.

The housing scheme was innovative in many ways. The houses themselves were built experimentally, using the new Colway method of walling which did not require the same level of specialized labour as more traditional methods. Messrs Batchelor and Hicks produced the plans for the first ten houses which were 'selected by the women'. Hall described how each house had been 'so economically planned, under the supervision of the wives, that the women can work the house conveniently' (Hall, 1920, p. 196). While the expectation of female domesticity was characteristic of the period, the inclusion of women in the planning process itself was quite a radical step. A recreation ground was provided with a hard tennis court, open space and sandpit. Later, Lady Ardilaun was to present further gifts of tennis courts, a 'pavilion' and a piano for the enjoyment of the tenants. Shrubs, thorn hedging and fruit trees were donated for the gardens.

In 1924, St Barnabas Gardens, West Road, was taken into Corporation control, while in the same year Hall submitted a scheme for naming the new roads and numbering the houses at what was termed 'St Barnabas Utility Gardens', comprising Utility Road, Utility Gardens, and the continuation of Seaview Avenue. The Society also built houses on Faith, Hope and Stoney Roads (north of the railway line), and on East Road in 1926.

By 1924 Hall's method in house-building had gained some popularity. The Church of Ireland Archbishop of Dublin recognized the significance of 'his works of public utility, which … had extended outside the parish, and which it had seemed he had been especially raised up for' (*Church of Ireland Gazette*, 1929, p. 181). In a special issue in 1934, the *Irish Builder and Engineer* referred to Hall as 'the pioneer of public utility societies in Ireland, who, not content with extending sympathy and writing on the subject of the sad housing conditions of Dublin, translated his sympathy into deeds by inaugurating and founding the first public utility society in Ireland … Happily not only did Canon Hall accomplish so much himself, but he set a headline that many others have followed to the public weal' (*Irish Builder and Engineer*, 21 April 1934, p. 329).

As the news of Hall's success spread, other societies were gradually formed in different parts of the country. While the Civics Institute soon took in hand all of the materials relating to the formation of public utility societies, it was to Hall that people tended to turn for practical guidance. He was involved in a direct and advisory capacity with the establishment of many of the early societies, including the Linenhall PUS and Dublin Commercial PUS. Through his encouragement, the Church Representative Body took loan stock in a number of societies, including the Rathmines PUS R1788 (1927–45) where Reverend Bluett was involved. When a public utility society was formed in Dundalk, Co. Louth in the 1930s, Hall wrote to congratulate the organization on its achievement and later took out some loan stock in the society as a gesture of support (McManus, 1998). In 1932 Hall joined with the Roman Catholic parish priest of Finglas in the formation of St Canice's PUS.

Hall does not just stand out because he was involved in the St Barnabas PUS, or indeed because he was an influence on others interested in the housing struggle. In time he became Director of the Association for Housing the Very Poor, and was also a member of the Citizens' Housing Council, with other activists including Dr Kathleen Lynn and Dr Robert Collis. His drive and energy served his parishioners, but also extended to the needy in society right across the city of Dublin. 'His work in the field of housing has gone unnoticed and unhonoured by a city he served so well, but a monument remains to his memory in the St Barnabas Housing Scheme' (Garrett, 1970, p. 137). In 1940, the Annual Report of the Linenhall PUS mentioned that 'in common with many in Dublin the members learned with much regret of the sudden death of Canon D.H. Hall BD, their president. It was due to Canon Hall's suggestion and initiative that the Society was started, and his advice and guidance was invaluable at the first. The reform of housing in Dublin owes much to his zeal and driving power.' Indeed, an obituary in the *Church of Ireland Gazette* stressed that Hall's motives were those of a true churchman and that, although it brought him to prominence, his housing scheme was not the main business of his life. 'The building of houses was due to the need for creating conditions more conducive to mental, moral and spiritual health, and in their building there were more prayers than bricks' (*Church of Ireland Gazette*, 1 March 1940, p. 101). His contribution to the field of housing in Dublin, and indeed in Ireland as a whole, was huge.

However, Hall could not have succeeded in popularizing the concept of public utility societies alone. The Civics Institute of Ireland became instrumental in promoting such societies and arranging for their registration. Meanwhile, a number of influential thinkers took up the idea. For example, the Killester PUS was another of the early public utility societies to operate in the Dublin area, being the second society to receive grants under the 1919 Act. Perhaps it is not surprising, therefore, to note that its Chairman was a man who was also driven with an almost missionary zeal in his concern for housing and planning reform – Mr E.A. Aston. Aston was Honorary Secretary of the Greater Dublin Reconstruction Movement and the Dublin Citizens' Association, as well as a founder member of the HTPAI. We saw in chapter one that at the 1913 Housing Inquiry he had called for the development of plantations for city workers in convenient rural areas. Not content with talk, he was involved in the registration of the Killester PUS Ltd in June 1921, which aimed 'to carry out co-operative building and management of suburban housing upon modern "garden suburb" principles' (RFS, R1694, letter). Initially, it seems that there were plans for a large number of houses in the district. The *Irish Builder and Engineer* of October 1921 noted, in relation to the Ryan system of construction, that Messrs H. & C. MacNally & Co. were erecting a large number of houses for a PUS at Killester, similar to those built at Victoria Road for ex-servicemen (*Irish Builder and Engineer*, 22 October 1921, p. 680). Presumably these houses were the first to be built by the Killester PUS at Vernon Avenue and Castle Avenue.

Like most building projects in the early 1920s, the Killester PUS scheme was not without its difficulties. In December 1922, Aston informed the North Dublin Rural District Council that owing to the withholding of Government grants they were unable to connect the drainage of their houses. Less than a dozen houses were completed before work ceased completely.

In a letter dated 28 January 1924, the Killester society informed the Registry of Friendly Societies that its work had been suspended for almost two years 'owing to the transfer of Government and difficulties in getting subsidy' (RFS, R1694, letter). However, these difficulties had now been overcome, and tenancies were being fixed by Mr J. Vincent Brady, the Society's solicitor. It is also noteworthy that Brady was a staunch supported of housing reform who wrote on themes such as *The Future of Dublin-Practical Slum Reform* (1917) and was one of the witnesses at the Housing Inquiry in 1913. All of the investors in the society were tenant members, and also members of the Committee.

However, even while building was disrupted, the society continued to function. In July 1923 the North Dublin District Council received a letter from the Killester PUS asking that the former would use its influence with the Great Northern Railway to have a halting place for trains at Killester, where a large number of cottages had recently been erected. Shortly afterwards, the GNR directors indicated that a station would be provided for passenger traffic at Killester.

Increasing interest in public utility societies, 1924 onwards

Although the Housing (Ireland) Act of 1919 dealt with public utility societies, they became prominent only after the introduction of new legislation in the mid-1920s. Thus it can be argued that Government housing policy stimulated the development of public utility societies. In particular, the 1925 Housing Act was a milestone in that it enabled the provision of State grants to public utility societies at the same rate as grants to local authorities. In other words, for every house built by a public utility society, that organization would receive the same level of grant aid as a local authority, which was a higher rate than that received by individual private builders. This stimulated the creation of a large number of societies, often comprising private individuals who decided to club together to avail of the higher grants. This was the intention of the Government, which hoped that public utility societies could prove of great assistance in house production. However, by forming such public utility societies, speculative builders were also able to avail of a higher grant than that to which they would have otherwise been entitled. As well as providing fixed-sum grants on houses of a certain size, the Housing Act of 1925 provided for rates remissions, and also brought the local authority into closer co-operation with the public utility societies, by giving it a role in land provision and site preparation.

The grants available to public utility societies under the 1925 Housing Act were £60, £80 and £100 respectively for three-, four- and five-roomed houses. No restrictions were imposed on the sale or letting of subsidized houses. The Registrar of Co-Operative and Friendly Societies noted in 1928 that the promotion of housing schemes was a relatively new co-operative activity, which had been stimulated by the subventions provided by the State and public bodies under the various Housing Acts. Thus, in 1925 there were only four such societies, whereas at the end of 1927 there were 16 societies and during 1928, 13 further societies were registered for the purpose of building houses for their members (RFS, Registrar's Report for 1928).

The Department of Local Government and Public Health similarly noted that the extension of the grants to include public utility societies had resulted in the submission of proposals for 190 houses across the country (DLGPH, 1928). The majority of these were built in the Dublin region. In March 1929, of the 961 houses completed by public utility societies in the Irish Free State to date, some 631 were in Dublin County Borough, a further 73 in the County of Dublin, 57 in Blackrock UD, 34 in Rathmines and Rathgar UD, 13 in Howth UD, ten in Dún Laoghaire UD, six in Pembroke UD. Thus, almost 86 per cent of the houses were built in the Dublin area. However, the public utility society concept gradually spread across the country and such organizations were founded in both rural and urban areas. Examples include the Dundalk Premier PUS (see McManus, 1998), Mid Cork PUS, West Connemara PUS and many others.

'Assisted private enterprise'

The favourable terms afforded to public utility societies by the legislation suggest that the Government was anxious to encourage the activities of such bodies. Apparently there were two reasons why public utility societies were favoured. It would seem that the intention was to help individuals who wanted to build their own homes, as well as to aid groups with a philanthropic intention of catering for the great working-class housing need. Certainly, the need for something to be done to assist those wishing to build their own homes was evident in the early 1920s. In 1923, for example, the *Irish Builder and Engineer* argued that 'it is probable that never before were there so many men with a little capital, ready to invest it in building a house for themselves, but the costs have been prohibitive, and so they contrived to rent a house or a flat' (*Irish Builder and Engineer*, 3 November 1923, p. 833).

The third Report of the Department of Local Government and Public Health, 1927–1928 (1929), discussed what it termed 'assisted private enterprise'. It was noted that grants for public utility societies in respect of both new and reconstructed houses were at the same rates as those payable to local authorities, explaining that the distinction had been made 'to induce persons to enter such societies which should normally prove of great assistance in house production' (DLGPH, 1929, p. 79). In the period to the end of March 1928, some 282 houses in Dublin County Borough (that is, the Dublin Corporation area) had been approved, amounting to almost £26,000 in grants.

During the late 1920s, many public utility societies seem to have been established for a brief time to take advantage of incentives under the recent legislation. Whereas the St Barnabas Society operated over a number of years, few of these seem to have completed more than one scheme. Their limitations suggest that, once they had completed a small scheme of houses for the founding members, their work was seen to be complete and the society was dissolved. One example of such a short-lived society is the Linenhall Public Utility Society which applied in 1926 for permission to erect 63 four- and five-roomed houses at the Linenhall Barracks. These houses, in miniature garden suburb layout complete with cul-de-sac, were built as Linenhall Terrace and Parade, with some further houses fronting onto Coleraine Street, and contrast sharply with the neighbouring 'bylaw style' Corporation-built housing. This particularly society had much in common with Hall's St Barnabas PUS. It was founded, as was the case with the St Barnabas organization, following a meeting of parishioners in January 1926. The former site of the Linenhall Barracks had been acquired from Dublin Corporation at an annual rent of £126 and Messrs Collen Bros had been awarded the building contract at a cost of £30,500. Two local firms, Messrs Jameson & Sons and Messrs Maguire & Patterson, because they were anxious to see their employees properly housed, provided substantial support to the society, while the Church of Ireland Representative Body invested £6000 in loan stock.

The formation of a public utility society was not a guarantee of success. Many societies were registered but never functioned, including the Wolfhill PUS (R1546), Irish Homes Building Guild (Dublin) Ltd (R1679), City Co-operative Builders Ltd (R1713), St Brigid's Housing Society (R2179), to name but a few.

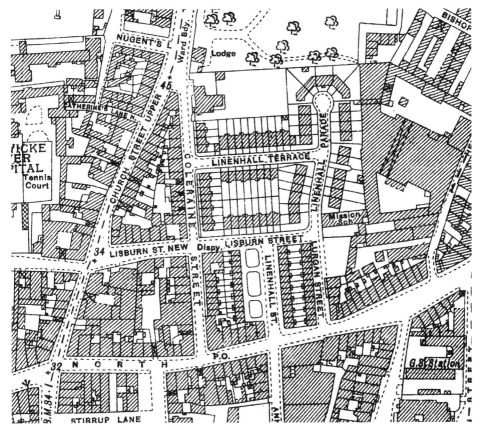

55 Linenhall Parade, North King Street.
(Photograph by R. McManus, plan from Ordnance Survey 1:2500 plan,
Sheet 18 III, Dublin, 1938 revision.)

Although the focus of housing policy was to change in the 1930s, the Government continued to legislate for the support of public utility societies. The Housing (Miscellaneous Provisions) Act which became law on Christmas Eve, 1931, provided for financial assistance for both public utility and philanthropic societies. A circular letter from the Department issued in March 1932 outlined the reasons for this provision— 'it is felt that it is only by the co-operation of all sections of the community that the conditions under which so many of the inhabitants of our cities and towns live can be effectively remedied' (DLGPH, 1933, Appendix XXVIII). The new legislation clearly influenced developments, with a huge increase in the number of registered public utility societies. A total of 52 public utility societies was approved during the year from March 1932 to 1933 (DLGPH, 1934).

Dublin Corporation and the Public Utility Societies: reserved areas

One of the most significant features of the public utility societies in Dublin is their close relationship with the Corporation. Most of them built on land leased from Dublin Corporation, as will be seen below. One practical example of the special treatment afforded to public utility societies was in the consideration of house plans. In late 1926, the City Architect proposed that the St Barnabas Public Utility Society be charged the reduced fee of five guineas in connection with the examination of plans for 73 houses erected under the Housing Act 1925, 'in consideration of the circumstances under which the Society operated'. The maximum fee chargeable under the Housing (New Houses) Order, 1925, was £1 1s. per house, so that this concession afforded the society a considerable saving. Official approval for such schemes was reflected in the 1932 ceremony whereby the Lord Mayor of Dublin 'who takes such a deep interest in the housing question', laid the first stone of a new block of houses to be built by the Civil Service Housing Association at Whitehall, on ground leased to it by Dublin Corporation (*Irish Builder and Engineer*, 16 March 1932).

The official preference for private or semi-private development (over local authority construction) where possible at this time is evident in the 1932 recommendations made by the inspector, Mr D.J. Hickie, in association with the Cabra (Annamoe Road) Compulsory Purchase Order. He suggested 'that the Corporation consider the feasibility of developing the site and leasing it to private persons and Public Utility Societies for the erection of a better type of house than the Corporation would themselves build' (Report 70/1932). The inspector made it clear that he would not object if the Corporation decided to develop the lands and then lease them to private persons and public utility societies, provided alternative arrangements were made for the acquisition of adequate lands on which to build Corporation housing.

The policy of reserving serviced sites on Corporation schemes for development by others was mentioned previously. The role of Dublin Corporation as development agent was shown to be important, since much housing not actually provided by the local authority was built following the layout plans devised by that body. In particular, public utility societies were to benefit from the town planning ideas of the Corporation, with the Dublin Commercial Public Utility Society estate at Drimnagh using the typical repertoire of contemporary Dublin Corporation planners, a circle and culs-de-sac. The reserved sites policy had particular advantages for public utility societies, since they could avoid the costs of site preparation and road building. Indeed, many of those who took on the 'reserved sites' were public utility societies operating under the provisions of the 1924 and 1925 Housing Acts, and their houses were generally for sale. However, while the use of serviced sites by public utility societies was common, it was not invariable, and some non-Corporation sites were also developed. In 1934, for example, the Dublin Commercial Public Utility Society invited tenders for the construction of concrete roadways and sewers on a site in Inchicore (*Irish Times*, 15 March 1934).

The next sections consider the development of the reserved areas at several Corporation schemes. While the lessees were not exclusively public utility societies, given their high proportion in these developments, it is easiest to consider the reserved areas development process in this chapter.

Leases for private development of the main frontages at Marino

As we have seen, in 1925 it was decided to reserve the main frontages of the Marino scheme for better-class residences and business premises, as the Corporation was not in a financial position to erect the quality of accommodation which it desired (McManus, 1996). From March onwards, leases of frontages were granted for residential shops which were to be built facing Fairview Strand. The sites were to be developed by the owner in accordance with the City Architect Horace T. O'Rourke's designs, and the ground rent of £10 per annum would be remitted in the first year provided the premises were built in that year (Report 64/1925). Within three years almost all the sites had been let, apart from the VEC College site let in 1932 and one corner site leased in 1933.

In the same year, 1925, the Dublin Commercial Public Utility Society of 9 Cavendish Row became the first body to lease sites at Marino for private

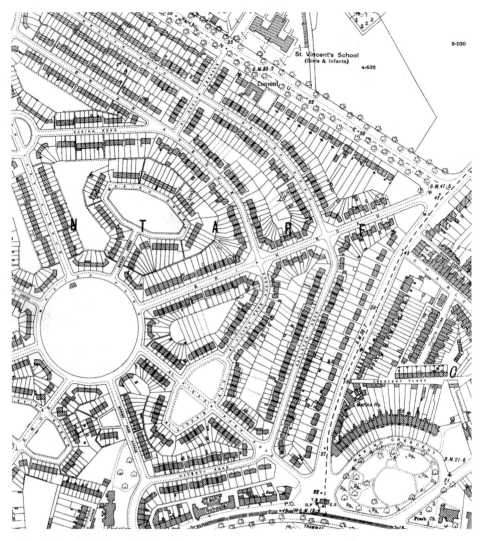

56 The frontage of the Marino scheme on Griffith Avenue and Malahide Road.
(Ordnance Survey 1:2500 plan, Sheet 18 IV, Dublin, 1938 revision.)

house-building. Twelve houses were to be built on ground fronting to Malahide Road, at an average cost of £750 each, for sale to the members of the society. Each house was to have a frontage of 35 feet (*c.*10 m), with an average depth of 100 feet (*c.*30 m), and the ground rent was to be £6 p.a. for each plot, over and above rates and taxes. The 150-year leases stipulated that the houses were to be used as residences and for no other purposes whatever. As these houses were to be built in accordance with the provisions of the Housing (Building Facilities)

57 The upper image shows 'Warden' housing on Griffith Avenue while the lower image shows DCPUS housing on Malahide Road. (Photographs by R.McManus.)

Acts, the Society would receive a Government grant of £100 per house, with a further £100 from Dublin Corporation. The first year's rent payable under these leases was remitted, as the buildings were completed within the stipulated time, and the Society acquired further sites on the Malahide Road over the next two years, with similar costs and stipulations.

The houses on the Malahide Road were the first to be built by the Dublin Commercial Public Utility Society (DCPUS) which had been registered in August 1925. The initial scheme was not ready for occupation until February 1927, due to a coal strike in 1926. The valuable help and assistance of Senator Farren, Reverend Hall, the town clerk, the Dublin Commissioners, the Corporation Housing Department, the LGB Housing Department and the central Housing Council of the Civics Institute was acknowledged in the society's annual report for 1926.

The north-eastern boundary of the Marino scheme was formed by the so-called '100-foot road' and leases for private houses on this road, which became known as Griffith Avenue, were first granted in 1927, when two house sites were leased to the Guild of Building Workers (Dublin and District) Ltd, 32 East Essex Street. Again the first year's rent was remitted, in accordance with the lease. It is notable that the Guild had been registered urgently at the behest of the same Senator Farren who had assisted the DCPUS. The Guild also won the contract for building 12 additional houses for the DCPUS, which were to be entirely of brick and 'of a superior type' (RFS, R1739). A private individual, Mr Daniel Caulfield, 32 Grove Park, Rathmines was granted the lease of two sites for houses at Griffith Avenue, Marino, in January 1928 (Report 10/1928). The 150-year lease was subject to the condition that the houses would be semi-detached and 'of a nature suitable to the roadway'. The annual rent was £7 10s. and £7 5s. respectively, with no ground rent for the first year.

Not all of the development on Griffith Avenue was by private concerns or public utility societies. The City Commissioners were responsible for the erection of some 32 houses between St Declan Terrace and Torlogh Parade. An award of £25,000 had been made to C.W. Warden under the Damage to Property (Compensation) Act, 1923 which was brought out by the city for £19,000 in order to erect these houses. H. & J. Martin's tender of £22,875 was accepted and the remainder of the award was used to pay costs. The houses, although terraced, are considered to be among the best yet designed by the Corporation, and were completed in 1930 at an average cost of £715. Four years later, the Dublin Board of Assistance acquired the lease of a triangular plot on

Griffith Avenue and Brian Road, for the purpose of building a dispensary, subject to several conditions, including one that the building was to be 'of suburban character', though there is no indication of what this implied (Report 32/1934).

Although many of the builders who took interests in the reserved areas were locals, this was not always the case. Mr Frederick Philip Smith of 264-5 Broad Street, Birmingham, acquired two plots of ground between Torlogh Parade and Croydon Terrace on which he was to erect at least 16 private dwelling houses (although this information may be incorrect, since there does not appear to be enough space for that number of houses). Again the lease was for 150 years, and was conditional on the houses built having a sale price of between £650 and £850. Smith also offered to take adjoining plots at the corner of Griffith Avenue and the Malahide Road to erect shops, but consideration of the offer was postponed (Report 14/1932).

At the same time as Smith was granted his lease, an application on behalf of the Sisters of Charity of St Vincent de Paul for a lease of ground on the south side of the Avenue, which had been advertised for some years, was considered. A plot comprising four of the proposed building sites was let on a 150-year lease at £24 p.a., on condition that a two-storey building costing $c.£5,000$ would be erected within 12 months for use as a Community residence. The lease specified that the front of the proposed building should not be forward of the established building line as indicated by houses already built, there should be no high boundary walls, and the materials of the elevations were to correspond with the new houses adjoining (Report 19/1932).

Thus, the Griffith Avenue frontage of the Marino site was built up gradually by a number of different interests. The main difference between this and purely private piecemeal developments was that, through the leasehold system, the Corporation was in a position to control the size and quality of houses being built. Its role was thus very similar to that of the Pembroke Township in the late nineteenth century.

Leasing of land included in the Drumcondra Housing Scheme
Given the success of the 'reserved areas' idea at Marino, a similar process was initiated for the Drumcondra housing area (figure 58), and in 1928 the first leases of land in the section of the area reserved for private building enterprise were granted (McManus, 1996). Two rectangular plots having main frontages to Griffith Avenue were each leased for 150 years, one to the Civil Service Housing Association Ltd., the other to Mr Louis Kinlen. In both cases the lessees intended that the houses provided by them would come within the

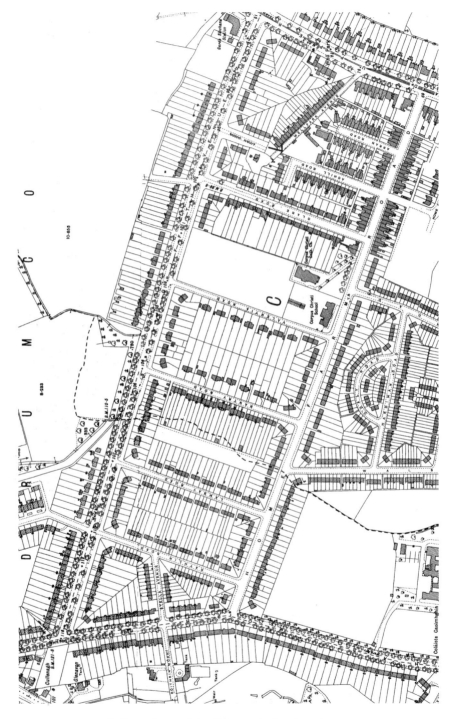

58 General map of the Drumcondra housing scheme.
(Ordnance Survey 1:2500 plan, Sheet 14 XV (1939) and 18 III, Dublin, 1938 revision.)

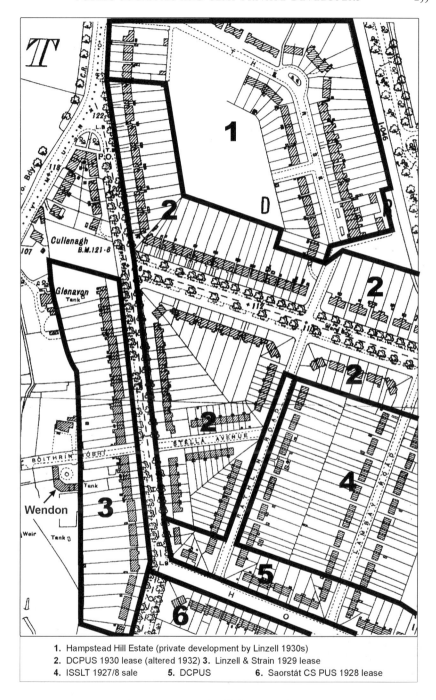

1. Hampstead Hill Estate (private development by Linzell 1930s)
2. DCPUS 1930 lease (altered 1932) 3. Linzell & Strain 1929 lease
4. ISSLT 1927/8 sale   5. DCPUS   6. Saorstát CS PUS 1928 lease

59 Home Farm Road and The Rise, Glasnevin.
(Ordnance Survey 1:2500 plan, Sheet 14 XV (1939) and 18 III, Dublin, 1938 revision.)

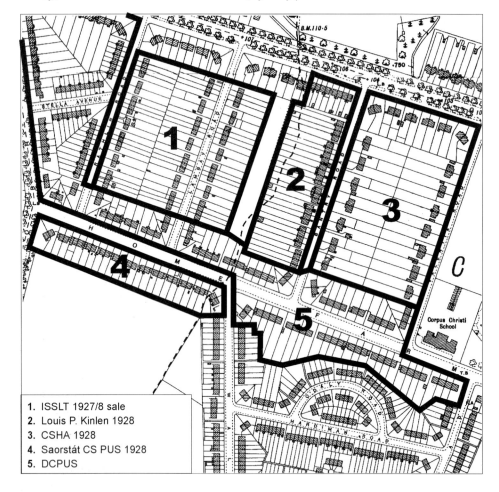

1. ISSLT 1927/8 sale
2. Louis P. Kinlen 1928
3. CSHA 1928
4. Saorstát CS PUS 1928
5. DCPUS

60 The activities of the Irish Sailors' and Soldiers' Land Trust, Saorstát Civil Service
Public Utility Society, Civil Service Housing Association, Dublin Commercial
Public Utility Society and Louis P. Kinlen. (Ordnance Survey 1:2500 plan,
Sheet 14 XV (1939) and 18 III, Dublin, 1938 revision.)

terms of the Housing Acts, 1925–26, so that they would qualify for State and
Municipal grants. All roads and underground services were to be constructed
by the Corporation free of expense to the lessees, and the latter would pay the
cost of all connections of light, water and sewerage of houses to said services.
Later it was decided that the cost of making crossroads adjoining the plots
leased to the Civil Service Housing Association and Mr Kinlen would be
charged against the housing account (Report 171/1928). Thus the Corporation,
rather than the builder, was bearing all development costs.

The leases in the Drumcondra reserved area were calculated on the basis of a fixed price per foot frontage, with higher costs for frontage on the main thoroughfares. The charge was 5s. per foot for frontage to Griffith Avenue (irrespective of depth of the plot) and 3s. 6d. for frontage to side roads. The cost of frontage along Home Farm Road varied from 2s. 6d. to 3s. 6d. Thus the rental for each plot would be calculated on the basis of the amount of road frontage at specific prices. The depth of the plot was less important, simply affecting garden space, since the layout ensured that all houses faced the roads.

The Civil Service Housing Association received a plot immediately to the west of the site of the proposed church, including frontage to Griffith Avenue and a new road which became Valentia Road, at a total annual rent of £273 3s. 9d. Kinlen's plot lay immediately to the west of that taken by the CSHA, including frontage to Griffith Avenue and to a new road which became Bantry Road, with a total rent of £222 9s. 3d. p.a. Further leases were granted later that same year to the Dublin Commercial Public Utility Society, including various portions of Home Farm Road and the south side of Griffith Avenue, and to the Saorstát Civil Service Public Utility Society, on the south side of Home Farm Road (Report 86/1928).

The rents were to commence from 25 March of the year following the date of the completion of each house, as certified by the City Architect. The houses were all to be built within the terms of the Housing Acts, 1925–26, in order to qualify for State and Municipal grants. A loan equivalent of 75 per cent of the amount of the accepted tender would be advanced by the Commissioners under the Small Dwellings Acquisition Act in respect of each house. This would ensure that the houses could be easily sold, as purchasers would avail of these mortgage facilities. Several alterations were made to the initial report, including the reduction of the total rent payable. In addition, in order to facilitate the Societies to provide houses for people with small capital, it was decided to make the maximum advances prescribed by the Acts (Report 144/1928). By the end of 1928, four new roads connecting Home Farm Road and Griffith Avenue had been completed and were named Bantry, Lambay, Rathlin and Valentia Roads.

The Dublin Commercial Public Utility Society (DCPUS) initially intended to build 50 houses at Griffith Avenue, with 34 to be semi-detached and the remainder in blocks of four. Significantly, garage accommodation was planned for each house. In Ireland in the 1920s, motor cars were still relatively uncommon. In 1927, there were just 22,415 cars licensed for private use in Saorstát Eireann. Thus, the market at which these houses were targeted was somewhat privileged. However, a management committee report for 1928 noted with

61 The upper image shows houses built by Louis P. Kinlen on the west side of
Bantry Road. The lower image shows houses built by the Civil Service
Housing Association on the east side of the same street.
(Photographs by J. Brady and R. McManus.)

some satisfaction that there were a large number of applications for the Society's houses, because 'the Society is appealing in a remarkable way to many hundreds of people who desire to take the initial step towards home ownership' (RFS, R1739, unpublished report). The DCPUS No. 3 contract for 50 houses at Griffith Avenue was followed quickly by a No. 4 contract for 134 houses at Home Farm Road, Griffith Avenue (western section) and Malahide Road, Clontarf. Work on these two contracts provided employment for more than 800 men for more than 12 months during a period when increased employment in the building trade was badly needed. These 184 houses were completed under the terms of the Housing Act, 1928 and over a hundred surplus applications were received for the houses.

The Saorstát Civil Service Public Utility Society was active in house-building on Clare Road, for which it had received both State and Municipal Grants, and in May 1928 it requested that the road be extended so as to provide the necessary building frontage for eight additional houses. If the Commissioners were to extend the road, the Society would cede the necessary ground to the Corporation free of charge. In considering the application, it was noted that 'the layout of the Drumcondra area contemplates that Clare Road will ultimately be one of the connecting roads between Home Farm Road and Griffith Avenue, so that from a town planning point of view the extension now proposed would ultimately rank as a public service' (Report 122/1928, p. 439). Plans were approved in early 1929, subject to the elimination of two houses to be erected on the site of a future road connecting Achill and Clare Roads. However, it will be noted from the present-day map (figure 62) of the area that this qualification was not upheld. Achill Road makes a right-angled turn, as if to join Clare Road, but is prevented from doing so by the existence of a pair of houses fronting onto the latter street which block its projected path.

Like the Dublin Commercial PUS, the Saorstát Civil Service PUS provided, at least in some cases, for the better-off worker. Its first scheme, at Cabra Road, undertaken in 1926 to designs by Messrs Hargreave & Horner, MRIAI, of Grosvenor Square, Rathmines, was for two-storey, semi-detached houses with space for a garage. Hargreaves also designed the houses at Clare Road. This time the 19 houses were built with a garage and the specifications were high. Each house had both drawing and dining rooms, hall (with verandah), kitchen, three bedrooms, water closet and bath. Such specifications were a world away from even the best of the Corporation's 'parlour' houses.

The Saorstát Civil Service PUS included among its members Victor W. Scales of 162 Rathgar Road. He built houses in his own right at Griffith

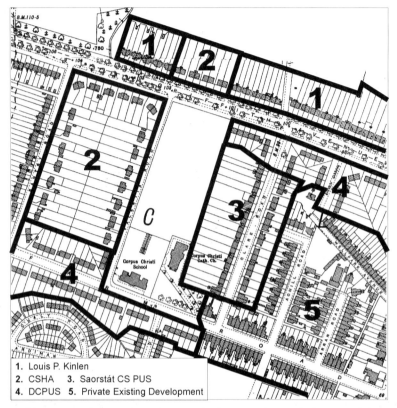

1. Louis P. Kinlen
2. CSHA   3. Saorstát CS PUS
4. DCPUS   5. Private Existing Development

62 Clare Road and Achill Road. The lower image shows housing by J.J. Flanagan on
Achill Road. (Ordnance Survey 1:2500 plan, Sheet 18 III, Dublin, 1938 revision.
Photograph by R. McManus.)

Avenue and in the Clontarf area, and it is quite likely that he was the contractor for the society's houses also. By 1932 the Society had 97 tenants by 1932 and had undertaken building schemes at Beaumont and Milltown, as well as an abandoned scheme at Rathmines.

Development of plots in the Drumcondra area continued well into the 1930s. In 1930, further sites on Clare Road were leased to the Saorstát Civil Service Public Utility Society, while a proposed shop premises and house was approved on Home Farm Road in 1933, subject to gates opening inwards and combined drain agreement, and in the following year two further houses were sanctioned.

Thus, the Corporation had clearly gained confidence following the success of its initial experiment at Marino, where a small amount of private development had been allowed at the edges of the site, in order to reduce costs. At Drumcondra, in addition to the housing provided by the Corporation on its 32 acre (c.13 ha) site, almost three times that acreage was specifically developed for disposal to private builders. The reserved area was more extensive than that at Marino, and was also more distinctive, due to the spatial layout of the development, with the line of Home Farm Road dividing the privately developed part of the scheme from the 'pure' local authority development.

In the privately developed section of the Drumcondra Scheme, builders could take advantage of State and Municipal Grants, while all roads and underground services were constructed by the Corporation free of expense to the lessees. Thus builders got a good deal, with considerable incentives to build on these sites, and easy sale practically guaranteed thanks to the availability of cheap mortgages under the Small Dwellings Acquisition Acts. In addition, the attitude of the Corporation towards the 'private' builders seems to have been relatively indulgent. In layout terms, the grid-like plan of the area north of Home Farm Road is far more traditional than the 'garden suburb' culs-de-sac of the public section of the scheme. Despite the original intention of developing a connecting road between Achill and Clare Roads, the Saorstát Civil Service Public Utility Society was allowed to build houses on the site of the proposed new road. The roads of the 'private' section were not laid out concurrently, prior to development, as can be seen in the unusual shape of Clare Road, which suddenly widens at its junction with Griffith Avenue. The fact that the whole area was not laid out in advance suggests a more lenient approach to planning on the private section of the Drumcondra development.

The Irish Sailors' and Soldiers' Land Trust

While most of the plots in the Drumcondra Reserved Area were leased either to private individuals or public utility societies, there was one exception. In the case of the Irish Sailors' and Soldiers' Land Trust, the land in question was sold outright (for more information on the work of the ISSLT, see Aalen, 1988). The terms of acquisition were favourable to the Trust, which acquired the fee-simple interest of approximately four acres (*c*.1.7 ha), free of all encumbrances, at a cost based upon the average price per acre awarded by the Arbitrator, plus a proportion of the costs of arbitration. The private builders and public utility societies were granted leases but the Trust became the owner of the land on which it built. The ISSLT finally paid £2395 8*s*. 10*d*. to the Corporation for the Drumcondra land in 1938. It is not clear why the Trust was treated differently to other applicants, but it seems to have received special treatment at other locations also. For example, the Rathmines Urban District Council sold a plot of developed ground at Kimmage to the ISSLT in 1929, whereas other builders were granted leases rather than outright sales.

In addition to acquiring the land at a good price, the ISSLT avoided much of the site development costs. Home Farm Road was extended by the City Commissioners, who also made two new side roads on either side of the plot, connecting the extension with the new main road. Sewers were extended, and water and public lighting services were supplied, all free of cost to the Trust. Some 40 houses were erected, in accordance with plans approved by the City Architect, and in early 1928 the Trust applied for an additional plot of approximately 2 acres (*c*.0.8 ha) on the east of the plot already conveyed, on which they built a further 20 houses. Many of the houses on Lambay and Rathlin Roads were completed by the ISSLT at this time.

In the late 1920s and early 1930s, the ISSLT continued to build on Corporation-developed land. It completed two new roads in the Kimmage Housing Area (Larkfield Park and Grove) in 1931, while work began in the Cabra area in 1932, an area which attracted much development from public utility societies throughout the decade in association with the Corporation Schemes there.

Public utility society development on Griffith Avenue from 1927

Land left over from road-making was sometimes developed and leased by Dublin Corporation to either private speculative builders or public utility societies. Among the public utility societies to benefit from this policy were the Dublin Commercial Public Utility Society, which acquired frontages along

Griffith Avenue in 1928, and at Griffith Avenue and Bóthar Moibhi in 1930, at rents varying from 3s. per foot to 4s. 6d. per foot frontage. The Civil Service Housing Association also acquired land on the north side of Griffith Avenue in May 1930, while the Saorstát Civil Service Public Utility Society built on the opposite side of the same avenue, east of Upper Drumcondra Road. While this discussion has illustrated the complexity of the development of the Corporation's lands at Drumcondra in association with the Drumcondra Housing Scheme, in the case of 'the By-Pass Road' (Moibhi Road) and Griffith Avenue, it is clear that only a relatively small number of developers, principally public utility societies, was involved (see next chapter). In particular, the Dublin Commercial Public Utility Society, later to become Associated Properties Ltd., played a highly active role in the development of the area.

Collins Avenue

Following the completion of Griffith Avenue, a further major road development was undertaken on the north side of Dublin in the 1930s at Collins Avenue. Some house building had already taken place on Collins Avenue as part of the Corporation's Donnycarney Estate erected by John Kenny from 1929 to 1931, discussed in the previous chapter. Immediately adjoining this development, the Belton Park Estate was being built by John Belton from c.1931 until at least the late 1930s. Belton seems to have been associated with Irish Developments Ltd, 3 Molesworth Street. Meanwhile, Mr Patrick Belton of Belton Park, Drumcondra, was described as a 'farmer and builder' as well as a TD who was first elected in 1927 (Flynn, 1939).

In mid-1932, it was decided to extend Collins Avenue by 73 yards (c.67 m) at an estimated cost of £560. An exchange of leases was undertaken with the Community of High Park Convent as part of the extension plans, while compensation totalling £2265 was granted in 1934 with regard to the Collins Avenue Widening Scheme. As at Griffith Avenue, lands left over from road building were made available for house-building. By 1936, the Corporation-assisted development of Collins Avenue proper was underway, with the first leases being granted in February 1936. The building ground acquired comprised nearly 4000 feet (1219 m) of frontage along the section of Collins Avenue between Donnycarney and Grace Park Road, consisting of six lots with varying frontage measurements. By now, Dublin Corporation had refined its 'reserved areas' policy. As at Marino and Drumcondra, the leases were granted for 150 years, and conditions included the erection of a specific number of two-storeyed houses valued at £800 each within 12 months. In addition, the adjoining property was to be protected from trespass through the holding, while a concrete wall five feet (*c*.1.7 m) high was to be erected along the rere boundary of the holding. This insistence on the lessee's responsibility for boundaries and trespass shows that the Corporation had learned from earlier schemes, following complaints regarding trespass at the Donnycarney scheme (see figure 40), and the high cost of boundary walls erected at Marino.

As in the final lettings at Griffith Avenue, the leases were granted to those parties making the highest offers following advertisements, and most of the builders involved were local: Thomas Patrick Wharton and Timothy Joseph Wharton, the partners in the firm T. & T. Wharton, 16 Bóthar Mobhi; Mr Edward Doherty, 13a East Road; and Messrs Patrick J. Campbell of 97 Shandon Drive and John Cooney, 8 Munster Street, with an office at 9 Clonturk Park. Certainly, the majority of those building on the reserved sites at Drumcondra, Griffith Avenue or Collins Avenue had addresses within a radius of two miles of the developments. Others, like Mr Michael Murphy of St Molin's, Swords, were involved in building on several other areas of Corporation land, including Gaeltacht Park and Griffith Avenue. In fact, Murphy died in 1938, at which time he was erecting 17 houses on Collins Avenue, five of which were still in course of construction. As a concession, the completion period allowed by the terms of the lease was extended for the executors (Report 58A/1938).

Shops were also erected along Collins Avenue, including one mentioned in October 1936, the frontage of which was required to harmonize with existing shop fronts. Building continued throughout 1937 and 1938, in which year the drainage of the Church of St Peter's and St Paul's was agreed. In this case, the provision of amenities was clearly of some concern to the authorities. Contrary to the popular perception of under-supply in newly developed areas, the Corporation seemed wary of over-estimating demand. Thus, in November 1938 a cinema was finally allowed on Collins Avenue, in the Ellenfield Area, with a limited number of shops 'as the demand for same develops' (Report 58A/1938). In August of the following year, L.E. Ging acquired the lease of a cinema site at Collins Avenue, having 90 feet (*c*.27 metres) frontage, at £2 5*s*. 6*d*. per foot. Ging was also involved in development at Grattan Crescent, Inchicore, another 'reserved area' and his name was also mentioned in connection with activities in Clontarf.

The Corporation seems to have begun to pay greater heed to housing design towards the end of the period, as in the case of approval being granted for four further houses on Collins Avenue in June 1939 'subject to elevational

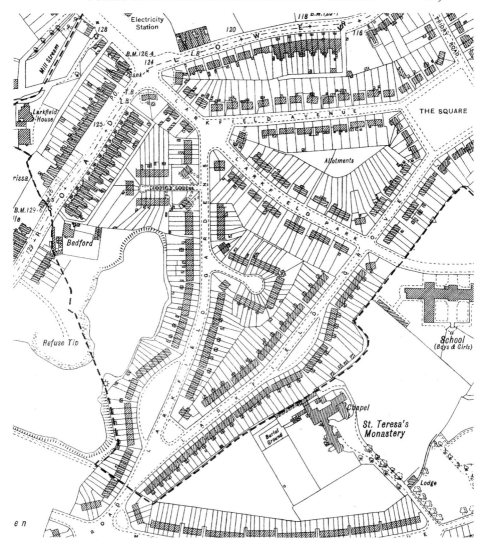

63 The Larkfield development, Kimmage. (Ordnance Survey 1:2500 plan, Sheet 22 II, Dublin, 1943 revision.)

design differing from the standard type being submitted for the houses designed in pairs and to a layout plan indicating a general scheme of wall and roof colouring for the differing blocks also being submitted' (Report 30/1939).

Reserved Sites in the 1930s Housing Areas: Kimmage, Crumlin, Cabra

As the city boundary was extended, particularly after 1930, Dublin Corporation availed of new suburban lands for building purposes. In both Kimmage and Drimnagh, for example, the Corporation prepared sites for

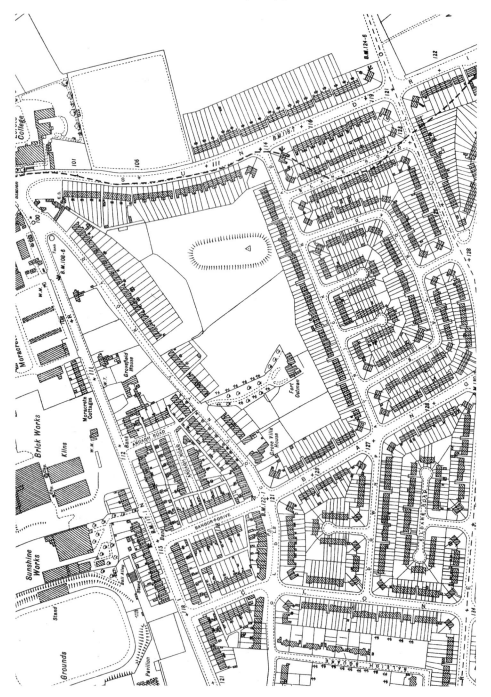

64 Sundrive Road / Old County Road, Crumlin. (Ordnance Survey 1:2500 plan,
Sheet 18 XIV, Dublin, 1943 revision.)

65 Croaghpatrick Road / Screen Road, off Navan Road, (*upper image*) and Annamoe Road, Cabra, (*lower image*). (Ordnance Survey 1:2500 plan, Sheet 18 II and VI, Dublin, 1943 revision.)

development by public utility societies as part of the 'reserved areas' policy. Among the societies to build houses on 'reserved areas' at the Kimmage Housing Area were the Saorstát Civil Service Society, which purchased a small amount of land in March 1931, and the Dublin Building Operatives Public Utility Society, which was granted a lease for the erection of eight houses under the provisions of the 1932 Housing Act. As noted previously, the ISSLT also built at Larkfield Park and Grove c.1931.

More importantly, some 11 acres (*c*.4.5 ha) of the Corporation land at Kimmage, which had originally been acquired by the Rathmines UDC for housing but had remained unbuilt in 1930 when Rathmines was absorbed in the city, was developed under a relief grant in the early 1930s. It was recognized that considerable financial savings could be achieved by Dublin Corporation if it accepted offers from public utility societies to develop the land, rather than undertaking house building itself. Therefore, offers were specifically invited from public utility societies for the erection of houses for sale on the area. The tenders accepted were from the Building Operatives Public Utility Society (Lots 1 & 2 at £152 and £160), the Post Office Public Utility Society (Lot 3 at £140) and the Dublin Commercial Public Utility Society (Lot 4 at £250 p.a. and 50 per cent of cost of a boundary wall with Mount Tallant Convent) (Report 38/1933). The area centres on Larkfield Avenue (figure 63). Thus the Larkfield area of Kimmage moved from being a prospective local authority housing area to a private, or at least 'semi-private' development.

In Crumlin, sites on Sundrive Road and Old County Road (figure 64) were reserved for leasing at between 4*s*. 6*d*. and 6*s*. 6*d*. per foot frontage. As in the case of Drumcondra, many of the lessees were local builders, such as Messrs Kevin McCann & Co., 45 Crumlin Road or Laurence Redmond, 80 Raphoe Road, although Patrick Farrell, from further afield at 149 Pearse Street, was also involved. The Dublin Building Operatives Public Utility Society built at least 20 houses on the Old County Road, while the largest utility society of all, the Dublin Commercial PUS/Associated Properties Ltd., also operated in Crumlin. In 1936 names were adopted for the roads which were being constructed by the DCPUS: Errigal, Comeragh, Mourne, Donard, Brandon, Slieve Bloom and Mangerton (Report 12/1936, Report 19/1939). There was no distinction between the names selected by the Corporation for these roads and those on which it had completed local authority housing in the same area, which were also named after Irish mountains.

The Corporation's Cabra (Annamoe Road) Extension also included reserved sites, although it is worth noting that public utility societies had already developed housing in the Cabra Road area from the 1920s. On 26 February 1936, approval was granted for the lease of 12 building sites to Mr John J. Moore of 2 Seafield Avenue, Clontarf, at 6s. 1d. per foot frontage, this being the highest of seven offers received in response to public advertisements. Building land in this area seems to have been in demand, since in 1939 a private builder made an inquiry as to whether the Corporation intended to extend the Cabra Housing Scheme across lands between the main Navan Road and the Great Southern Railway Company's line. Following the approval of the Town Planning Committee for the use of the whole or part of this site for the housing of the working classes, a layout by the Acting Planning Officer for the development of the lands was sanctioned.

Another significant development was undertaken by the National Housing Society in the 1930s, involving approximately 114 houses on the Croaghpatrick Road/Skreen Road site. The eight acre site ran from the north side of Blackhorse Road to the south side of Croaghpatrick Road, Skreen Road and Navan Road (*Irish Builder and Engineer*, 15 May 1937, p. 450). The plans for the layout, including plans for the maintenance of tennis courts, were reviewed in Report 13/1937.

Operations of public utility societies after 1932

The circumstances under which public utility societies operated were changed by the 1932 Housing Act. The definition of a public utility society under the Act, as:

> a society registered under the Industrial and Provident Societies Acts 1893 to 1913, or a friendly society registered under the Friendly Societies Acts 1896 and 1908, or a trade union registered under the Trade Union Acts 1871 to 1913, whose objects include the erection of houses for the working classes, or a company which satisfies the Minister that its objects are wholly philanthropic and include the provision of houses for the working classes

was fairly wide-ranging. Under Section 5 (I, i) of the new legislation, a special grant was made available for public utility societies providing housing for letting in an urban area. At the same time, as we have seen, Dublin Corporation returned to a policy of rental rather than tenant purchase.

The Dublin Commercial Public Utility Society was the first society to produce houses for rent under the 1932 Act, with a foundation stone laid on

20 June 1932 by Seán T. O'Kelly at its seventh scheme. In March 1932, the Dublin Commercial Public Utility Society was granted a 150-year lease for a plot in the Drumcondra area which was divided into two sections. The arrangements for the leases had been made some years before, forming portion of the recommendations contained in Report 214/1930. However, due to circumstances beyond their control, the lessees had been prevented from carrying out the arrangements contemplated in that report (Report 64/1932). Now 6 two-storey dwelling houses were to be erected on the Bóthar Mobhi frontage, for which an annual rent of £29 11s. was payable. The lease for the second section on Stella Avenue and Rathlin Road, at a rent of £84 9s. p.a., required the erection of 20 two-storey dwelling houses to be let for rent on monthly or lesser tenancies in compliance with the Housing (Finance and Miscellaneous Provisions) Act, 1932.

A further plot of ground was leased to the Dublin Commercial Public Utility Society from the end of September 1932, subject to similar conditions. In this case, the plot of ground was bounded by Griffith Avenue, Bóthar Mobhi, Stella Avenue and Rathlin Road, and the lettings were subject to a rent of £154 p.a. and £65 p.a. respectively. Again it was noted that the arrangements for the leases had been made some years ago and were now revised. On one section (Griffith Avenue and Bóthar Mobhi), the lessees were required to build 22 private houses, while on the other (Rathlin Road and Stella Avenue) they were to erect 18 two-storey dwelling houses to be let for rent on monthly or lesser tenancies in compliance with the 1932 Act. All 40 houses were to be completed within 14 months. The contrast between the two house types is noticeable, with the houses built for rental being considerably smaller and less attractive than the purchase houses built by the same organization on Mobhi Road.

The committee of the society considered the rents to be 'very low' at 17s. 6d., 16s. 6d. and 16s. per week. Each house had five rooms and a kitchenette, gardens front and rear, and 'every modern convenience' (RFS, R1739, unpublished report). More than 500 applications were received for the houses, showing that there was a significant demand for quality rented accommodation in the city.

Development process for public utility societies

While the public utility societies apparently catered for a similar clientele to the private developers, their role in the building process was somewhat different. Most of the public utility societies acted as intermediaries between the land developer (often Dublin Corporation) and the house builders. Generally they did not build the houses themselves, but contracted builders

66 Contrasting housing on Stella Avenue and Mobhi Road. Both housing developments were built by the Dublin Commercial PUS. (Photographs by R. McManus.)

to erect houses which were then sold through the society. One notable exception is the Guild of Building Workers 1927 (Dublin and District) Limited which had ten members, all of whom were delegates from trade unions. An average of 58 people were employed by the Guild, which was established to undertake 'building and construction other than for the society's own requirements' (RFS, R1781, annual return form). Some of the projects undertaken by the Guild involved the construction of housing for other utility societies.

Although the records of Dublin Corporation do not detail the mechanism of development employed by the public utility societies, it seems that the societies first acquired a site and then tendered for the erection of houses. For example, in 1926 a contract was made between the St Barnabas Public Utility Society and Messrs J.& R. Thompson Ltd. for the erection of 73 four-roomed houses with a hot and cold water supply on East Wall Road. The houses were to be completed within eight months from the signing of the contract, at a cost of £449 each. The *Irish Times* of 3 March 1932 noted that the Dublin Commercial Public Utility Society had tendered for the erection of 12 houses at Rathlin Road and Stella Avenue, with offers to be received within two weeks. Similarly, in developing the Gaeltacht Park area (see below), both the St Mobhi Public Utility Society and the Civil Service Housing Association Ltd. advertised for tenders (*Irish Times*, 11 May 1933). The builders of public utility society schemes were often well-respected companies such as Crampton and Co., one of Dublin's top building companies, which built houses on Beaumont Road in Whitehall for the Saorstát Civil Service PUS in the early 1930s.

Under legislation, public utility societies were entitled to the same grants as local authorities. This was based on the presumption that both public utility societies and local authorities were in a similar business, that of acting as developer and builder of houses, especially working-class housing. For this reason, grants for the public utility societies were higher than those for private individuals who were building houses for their own use or to sell on the speculative market. However, as we shall see, not all of the public utility societies were in the business of erecting houses for the working classes, nor indeed building houses for their members. While there were some societies which operated on philanthropic lines, others were basically in the business of collecting grants for individuals or were fronts for small building contractors who were operating in the speculative arena.

The public utility societies employed some of the best-known architectural firms in Dublin to design their houses. The houses for the Dublin Commercial Public Utility Society at St Moibhi Road were built to plans prepared by Messrs McDonnell, Dixon and Downes of Ely Place. This same company had previously been involved with Corporation developments, having been invited to work on plans for the Millbourne Avenue (Drumcondra) housing scheme in 1918. In the 1930s, Mr W. Goulding of Cabra erected 25 houses at Clonturk for the Civil Service Housing Association Ltd., to plans by Mr J. Gannon. Goulding also built houses on his own behalf in the area. In the case of the Christian Brothers Past Pupil's Union PUS, it was the architect, James V. McGrane, rather than the society itself, who advertised for tenders for the erection of 16 houses at Griffith Avenue. Of course, sometimes architects interested in housing reform were involved in the establishment of the public utility societies, as was the case with G.F. Beckett, who was secretary of the Bray PUS, while F.G. Hicks was closely associated with the St Barnabas PUS.

While many people became members of public utility societies and bought shares in the hope of acquiring a house, not all houses built for the public utility societies were necessarily sold to existing members, as newspaper advertisements reveal. For example, in March 1930 the *Irish Times* carried advertisements for the Blackrock and District Public Utility Society which was selling houses for £765. In March 1932, a dwelling at Beaumont Road, Whitehall, described as being an attractive Crampton-built house with five rooms and kitchenette, was advertised for sale. Additional features which were noted in the advertisement included the availability of a rates remission on the house, and the possibility that part cash would be accepted in payment. Applications were to be made to the Secretary of the Saorstát Civil Service Public Utility Society, Mrs Monaghan, who resided at 206 Griffith Avenue.

'Gaedhealtacht Park', 1924 to 1934

The scheme at Gaeltacht Park (the spelling varies) further illustrates the relationship between Dublin Corporation acting as land-owner and developer, and the public utility societies. This development is particularly interesting because initially there was no close involvement between the Corporation and the PUS which began building, so that basically the scheme was akin to a private development. However, following financial difficulties, the Corporation came in to 'bail out' the PUS. Because this scheme was not related to a public housing area, the Local Authority had gone a step beyond the 'reserved areas'-type development, adopting the role of a 'private' developer.

The development of the area known as Gaeltacht Park is a remarkable example of the relationship between Dublin Corporation and public utility

NEW DUBLIN SUBURB FROM THE AIR

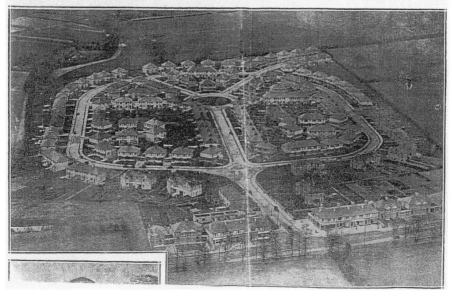

67 Gaeltacht Park in construction. (*Irish Independent*, 20 February 1932.)

societies in the late 1920s (see McManus, 1996). The story began in July of 1924, when a letter was received from Messrs James O'Connor & Co., Solicitors, enquiring on what terms lands held by the Corporation in the townland of Clonturk, adjoining Albert Villa, would be let to their clients, 'An Ghaedhealtacht', who were forming a Public Utility Society and would require two acres (*c.*0.8 ha) for building purposes. Their intention was to build ten houses, allowing five per acre (*c.*12 per ha), for the accommodation of their members. Long negotiations ensued, and eventually, a 150-year lease of two acres (*c.*0.8 ha) of land was arranged for Nua Ghaedhealtacht Atha Cliath Teo., at a rent of £25 per statute acre p.a. from 29 September 1927. By the June Quarter of the following year, houses were approved for the society (Report 233/1928). The rules of the society set out its objects 'to establish and maintain a community of Irish speakers at places to be selected by the society', while eligibility for membership was based on being a native speaker of the Irish language or having passed the first exam for the Fáinne.

However, difficulties arose in carrying out the scheme, the Society finding that it was not in a position to construct the necessary roads, as required in accordance with the terms of the lease. By January 1929, it had appealed for assistance to the Corporation, which accepted the surrender of the original lease, in place of which ten individual leases were granted to the individuals who had built houses in the area (Report 48/1929). In view of the position which had arisen, and bearing in mind the fact that the ground immediately adjoining and to the west of the plots in question was considered to be very suitable for a housing scheme, it was decided that the balance of the 29 acres (*c.*12 ha) owned by the Corporation in the area should be taken over by the Housing Section and developed for housing purposes, including the necessary road work.

By mid-1929, reference was made to the laying out of the Nua Gaelteacht Housing Area adjoining the grounds of the Albert Agricultural College, involving the extinguishing of certain rights of way. In May 1930 the developed sites, which adjoined the plots let to members of the Nua Ghaedhealtacht, Atha Cliath, Teo., were advertised for letting, but no offers were received for some time. The Corporation spurred development by drawing the attention of the Civil Service Housing Association to this land, when it applied for a developed building site in late 1931. In January 1932 a 150-year lease was granted to that body at an annual rent representing 3*s.* 6*d.* per foot frontage, over and above rates and taxes. The plot in question had frontages on all sides to the new roads constructed some years previously in connection with a Dublin Union Relief Scheme, with provision for the development of the inner portion by a cul-de-sac avenue. The lease specified that the Association would build 56 dwellings costing £600 to £650 each, the work to be completed within 12 months. It was noted that the rent of 3*s.* 6*d.* per foot frontage was the equivalent of that obtained for the building grounds fronting the less important roads lying between Home Farm Road and Griffith Avenue, Drumcondra. However, in March of the same year, following representations from the Civil Service Housing Association, it was agreed that due to the shape of the plot a deduction would be made in arriving at the rent payable, while the average ground rent of the houses would otherwise be excessive. A rent of £280, with taxes of £5 p.a. for each house, was agreed, rather than the initial total rent of £311 17*s.* p.a.. The period of building was extended to two years, with at least half of the houses to be erected within the first year (Report 16/1932).

Meanwhile, in the summer of 1932, a letter was received from Mr Seán O Cuill formally objecting to the proposed lease of ground to the Civil Service Housing Association, in view of an assurance stated to have been given to him that the land would be utilized solely for the erection by the Nua Ghaedhealtacht Society of houses for occupation by Irish speakers (Report 36/1932). It seems, however, that the protest fell on deaf ears, since the development of the area continued apace.

The Saorstát Civil Service Public Utility Society was also granted a large tract of land in the area, and by July 1932 its houses adjoining the Nua Ghaedhealtacht were ordered to be numbered and the name 'Pairc na Gaeltachta' given to the area. In the following month a temporary numbering scheme was adopted for the Civil Service Housing Association's houses in 'Pairc na Gaeltachta'.

Further leases of building ground at Pairc na Gaeltachta were granted in late September, 1932. The rents were based on a standard of 4s. per foot frontage to roads, with reasonable allowance made for double frontage at corners, or for awkwardly shaped sites. All leases were for 150 years, with houses to be completed within 12 months. Lessees were required to construct buildings in accordance with the design, plans and specifications approved of by the City Architect, with each house being at least equal in value to those erected by the Civil Service Housing Association Ltd. on the initial 56-house plot, and roofed with natural Irish slates (a reflection of the concern for use of native materials). Following a number of further applications for the grant of leases of sites at Pairc na Gaeltachta, a special Sub-Committee was set up to handle them. Lessees included Mr W.H. Goulding, 37 Old Cabra Road; the Post Office Public Utility Society Ltd, 52 Parnell Square; St Mobhi Public Utility Society Ltd., 9 Bachelor's Walk; and the State Servants' Public Utility Society Ltd, 122a St Stephen's Green. Due to the nature of the leases, requiring rapid completion of building, the lessees lost no time in submitting plans for approval by the Corporation, and there was a series of approvals granted in 1933.

The Sub-Committee also recommended the reservation of sites for six shops on the Swords Road frontage, despite opposition from the City Architect who 'deprecated the building of shops on the frontage of a residential area' (Report 19/1933, p. 119). This objection raises the whole issue of zoning and provision of amenities in new developments. Throughout the 1930s, the Corporation seemed reluctant to grant permission to new 'shopping centres', perhaps reflecting the City Architect's views. We have already seen that in the case of Collins Avenue, the Corporation was wary of granting permission for shop developments until the demand was clearly present. In this case, the shops at Gaeltacht Park were built, with three each to be located on either side of the junction of the Swords Road and the Gaeltacht Road. The 150-year lease of the corner site south of the Gaeltacht Road was granted to Mr John Slevin, Oakley, Vernon Avenue, from 25 March 1933 at £15 12s. p.a., and the letting of shop sites continued throughout 1933. All sites had a frontage of 26 feet (c.8 m) to the Swords Road, with varying depth, but it was agreed in all cases that a two-

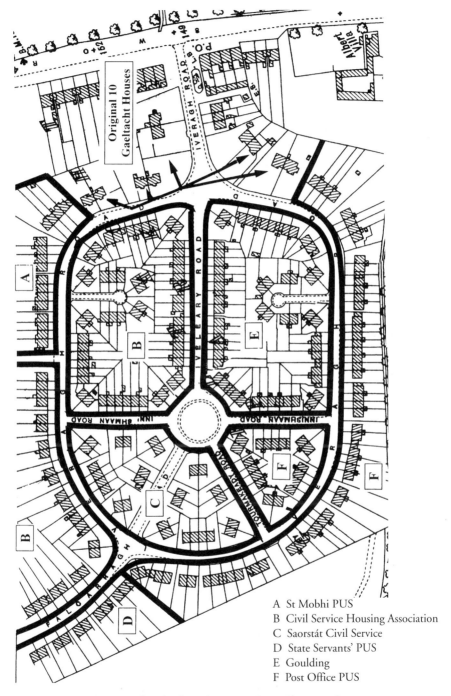

A St Mobhi PUS
B Civil Service Housing Association
C Saorstát Civil Service
D State Servants' PUS
E Goulding
F Post Office PUS

68 The development of Gaeltacht Park. See text for explanation of areas. (Ordnance Survey 1:2500 plan, Sheets 14 XV and XVI, Dublin, 1939 revision.)

storey residential shop, not less than £1500 in value, was to be erected within 12 months, while a lane at the rere was to be transferred to Corporation charge after completion. The other lessees were Mr Patrick Bowler, 2 Lr Ormond Quay; Mr Seán O Ruadhain, 'Iorrus', Nua Gaeltacht, Clonturk; and Mr Seán O'Cuill, 7 Nua Gaeltacht (the same person who had formally objected to the development of the area by non-Irish speakers). Later the Sub-Committee decided to recommend the reserving of eight sites, rather than the original six, and further leases went to Mr Thomas Brendan Herlihy, Araglen, 23 Beaumont Road; Mr Patrick Bowler, 2 Lr Ormond Quay; and two sites to Mr Joseph Rooney, Market House, Balbriggan. Following the disposal of the shop sites at Pairc na Gaeltachta, the remaining ground along the Swords Road frontage and a plot at the rere of the first four shop sites was advertised in three lots for the erection of dwelling houses. Of the four offers received, the highest was received on behalf of Mr Michael Murphy, 21 Shelmartin Avenue, Fairview, and was to involve the erection of ten houses of a value of £1000 each, and three houses valued at £750, within 12 months.

The public utility societies clearly had an important role in the development of 'Gaeltacht Park'. The originators of the scheme themselves formed such a society, while in the Corporation-sponsored development of the area at least four public utility societies built the majority of the houses. The most significant of these was the Civil Service Housing Association, which provided the yard-stick by which the housing standards throughout the scheme came to be judged. The Inquiry of 1939–43 lists the work of 15 public utility societies between 1933 and 1938. In total the Civil Service Housing Association Ltd built 76 houses during this time, the P.O. Public Utility Society erected 116 houses, the St Mobhi Public Utility Society built 32, and the State Servants' Public Utility Society built 12. Therefore, the bulk of their output at that time was at Gaeltacht Park.

Aside from the shops, only two individuals were involved in developing the scheme, Goulding and Murphy, both of whom frequently tendered for sites on Corporation-developed land. Interestingly, Goulding built in the Clonturk area both on his own behalf and for the Civil Service Housing Association Ltd. A Michael Murphy was involved in building at Collins Avenue and Marino. Meanwhile, Joseph Rooney, who developed two shop sites at Gaeltacht Park, also built houses on Griffith Avenue and was the successful tenderer for Section 2 of the Dublin Corporation housing scheme at Ellenfield/Larkhill in 1938.

The layout of the Gaeltacht Park area by the Corporation illustrates the general acceptance of town planning-style layout principles. In addition to the

69 Post Office PUS houses and original Nua Gaedhealtacht houses
(left background). (Photograph by R.McManus.)

use of the cul-de-sac and central circus, the road layout allowed for links with projected later developments. Both Falcarragh and Iveragh Roads were later joined with the extension of Collins Avenue. However, the space left for an extension of Tourmakeady Road was never used, as the adjacent area is used as a sports ground.

The development at Gaeltacht Park provides an illustration of the relationship between Dublin Corporation and the 'semi-private' sector of public utility societies. To the Corporation, the role of land developer rather than builder was attractive. It provided a means of rapidly developing the City Estate at little cost to itself, while incidentally reducing the housing shortage and boosting the City coffers with a steady income from ground rents. The leasehold system of development, as at the 'reserved sites', allowed the Corporation to retain a degree of control over the type of houses being built. Thus, the local authority could ensure that slate roofs were used at Gaeltacht Park, a preference which, due to costs, it was unable to insist upon in its own 'public' schemes.

For the builders who took advantage of serviced sites, the Corporation provided a safety-net in case of mishap. Thus, at Gaeltacht Park, the members of the Nua Gaeltacht society did not lose out when they could not fulfill the terms of the original lease. Instead, the Corporation was able to bail out the society and grant new leases. In addition, the public utility societies could benefit from the reduced costs of serviced sites either by spending the money saved on higher quality houses, or by charging less for its houses than the speculative builder operating on non-serviced sites. Public utility society houses proved to be a better value alternative to 'private' houses, and could remain competitive in the housing market.

Temple Hill, Blackrock UDC

While we have tended to focus on the operations of Dublin Corporation, it must be remembered that prior to 1930 a number of independent Urban District Councils operated in the greater Dublin area, all of which had their own housing policies. One notable scheme, which received considerable attention in the 1920s, is the Temple Hill scheme undertaken by Blackrock UDC which was believed to be unique in Ireland.

In August 1923 it was reported that Messrs T. & R. Macken of Rathfarnham, well-known contractors on Dublin Corporation housing schemes, were developing lands at Temple Hill, Blackrock, on behalf of the Blackrock UDC. Their work included roads, drainage and water mains, as well as building a large scheme of houses to plans by Messrs Donnelly, Moore, Keefe & Robinson. The plans were for six-roomed houses, much larger than the three- to five-roomed Corporation norm of the times, with large gardens both back and front, as well as bathrooms. Irish materials, including Courtown bricks and Drinagh cement were being used as far as possible, while the roofs were to be covered with Major's interlocking red tiles. Major's tiles from Bridgwater were particularly prized, having won an award at the Paris Exhibition in 1900. On the 18 February 1924, the contractors handed over the 20 completed houses at Temple Park to the Council, with a presentation of a golden key by the architect, Mr Robinson to the Chairman of the Council, Mr J.P. McCabe.

The houses built at Temple Park were very different to other houses being completed by local authorities in the Dublin area at this time, in terms of size and general specifications. The houses were being sold, the object being that the occupiers would have an interest in keeping them in good repair. Although tenant purchase of local authority housing was to become a common option after the 1924 legislation was introduced, the Blackrock scheme was different because it had no pretensions that this scheme would assist the working classes of the district. Instead it was reasoned that 40 families would be provided for in the houses on Temple Hill and Seapoint Avenue. Because the Council made a

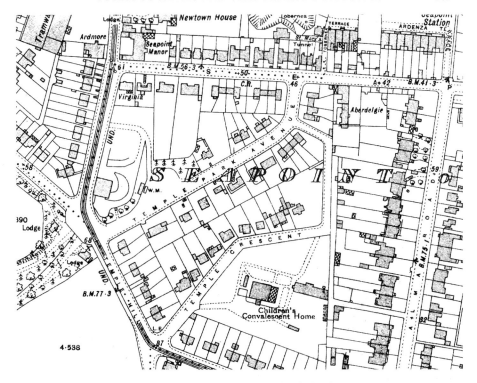

70 Temple Hill / Temple Park, Blackrock.
(Ordnance Survey 1:2500 plan, Sheet 23 VI, Dublin, 1939 revision.)

profit on the development, it would be in a position to build more houses. In
fact, the all-in cost per house was £748 and the scheme catered for middle-
class people who were able to purchase the houses outright.

In addition to the initial 20 houses, by 1924 the Blackrock UDC had
received several applications for sites at Temple Hill from people who
proposed to build houses of their own. Given the shortage of housing for all
classes at this time, as previously discussed, the supply of both quality housing
and serviced sites at this location became quite celebrated. The UDC was
congratulated on the success of the scheme, which cost the ratepayers nothing
(*Irish Builder and Engineer*, 23 February 1924). Again, while Dublin Corporation
instituted a 'reserved areas' policy in the mid-1920s, where it leased plots of land
to private individuals and public utility societies, the Blackrock scheme was
unusual in that it sold sites to private individuals who then built their own
houses. In a sense, then, it provided a taste of the type of semi-private development which was to become so common once the Government embraced new
housing legislation from the mid-1920s.

The Vernon Estate: joint development scheme

The development of Clontarf as a residential suburb is a matter of primary importance to the City, and with this object in mind, negotiations have been carried out with the Vernon Estate with a view to combined action.

(Report 69/1928, p. 249)

The particular circumstances of the joint development scheme undertaken between Dublin Corporation and the Vernon Estate in Clontarf after 1928 appear to have been unique in the history of the Corporation's housing activities. This new departure for the local authority came about in the late 1920s when the Vernon Estate, which owned a considerable amount of land in Clontarf and Killester, wished to capitalize on the area's rapid growth. Rather than incur all of the expense of developing building land, it came to an arrangement with Dublin Corporation, whereby that body would build the new roads through the property, in return for an interest in some of the lands for a certain period of time. Thus, the Corporation assisted a private landowner in site development, and came to act as an intermediary between the land-owner and the builder.

Although the Clontarf Township had been absorbed into the County Borough in 1900, at the same time as Glasnevin and Drumcondra, development had remained confined to the area closest to the city, and much of the ward remained semi-rural. Even in 1920, because it was believed that it would be some time before the district was developed, plans for the erection of houses in unsuitable locations were approved. This included the building of houses in locations where they would interfere with the future extension of roadways (Report 252/1920). However, soon after these short-sighted planning decisions, construction work in the Clontarf area commenced in earnest. This is particularly associated with building by the Ryan Manufacturing and Construction Company at Seaview Avenue, Victoria Park and Haddon Park. The Ryan company was also building outside the city boundary at Crumlin in March 1923, when they ran into difficulties in relation to sewage connections. Of course, the absence of main drainage in the area was one of the deterrents to new building. In Clontarf, application was made for drainage connections to the city sewers for 12 pairs of houses outside the city boundary in late 1921, to be built at Vernon Avenue and Castle Avenue by the Killester Public Utility Society. It was intended that the buildings would form an installment of a

71 Vernon Gardens / Grove, Clontarf.
(Ordnance Survey 1:2500 plan, Sheet 19 V, Dublin, 1938 revision.)

ALL-GAS BUNGALOWS AT VERNON AVENUE, CLONTARF.

The installation in each of these Bungalows is as follows :—

Coke-fired Hob Grate with back boiler to heat principal room and supply hot water ; three Gas Fires ; Wash Copper for laundry work ; and Gas Cooker. An efficient labour and money saving equipment that makes these Bungalows specially attractive homes. Architects and builders engaged in building similar Bungalows or any type of residence are invited to communicate with us before definitely selecting the culinary and heating equipment.

GAS SERVICE DEPARTMENT, 10 HAWKINS STREET, DUBLIN.

72 Advertisement for all gas bungalows at Vernon Avenue, Clontarf.
(*Irish Builder and Engineer*, 25 December 1926.)

73 Vernon Gardens, Clontarf – housing built by the Stewart Construction Company.
(Photograph by R. McManus.)

larger future housing scheme. In the same year, the construction of a new promenade at Clontarf was proceeded with, which would of course have made the area more attractive to prospective new residents.

By 1923, the Streets Committee had recommended the widening of the Howth Road between Castle Avenue and Killester Lane, parts of which were only 40 feet (*c*.12 m) wide, because 'the district is one which is likely to develop rapidly, and the need for a wide approach road will probably be felt in the near future' (Report 40/1923, p. 191). This was a far cry from the decision made just three years previously to allow the erection of houses where they would cut across the line of prospective road extensions. In 1924, plans and specifications were submitted for 30 semi-detached houses at Vernon Avenue and a new road off Vernon Avenue, for the Stewart Construction Company, while an application had already been made by owners and occupiers of houses at Vernon Avenue for the construction of a concrete footpath there, suggesting that quite a degree of development had already taken place. In November 1924 the *Irish Builder and Engineer* reported that the Stewart Construction Company Ltd., Dame Street, was about to build 44 new houses at Vernon Gardens. The same company was also building houses at Auburn Avenue, Donnybrook, at this time. At the request of the Stewart Construction Company, a scheme for the renumbering of houses on Vernon Avenue was approved in the June Quarter, 1925 (Report 178/1926), and by September 1926 it was recommended that the roadways made by the Stewart Construction Company when carrying out their building scheme at Vernon Grove and Vernon Gardens be taken in charge by the Corporation (Report 183/1926). Incidentally, an advertisement appearing in the *Irish Times* for the Alliance & Dublin Consumer's Gas Co., D'Olier Street, used an illustration of the houses in Vernon Gardens which had gas lighting, heating, cooking and hot water (*Irish Times*, 9 April 1925).

Getting the balance right in the speculative building trade was always a tricky process. In the case of the Stewart Construction Company, it was clear that the company had over-stretched its resources and on the 16 February 1926 an Emergency General Meeting adopted a resolution for the voluntary winding-up of the company. In June 1926, the *Irish Builder and Engineer* reported on proceedings in the Dublin District Court concerning an Order to Wind Up the Stewart Construction Company Limited, St Andrew's Chambers, 1 College Street. The company had been incorporated in September 1924 and Mr Stewart and Mr Fitzgerald had commenced business with an 'extensive and costly scheme' at Clontarf. However, the court found that they were unable to complete the scheme and the company was now in a state of hopeless insolvency (*Irish Builder and Engineer*, 12 June 1926).

> Building Sites for Bungalows. The Vernon Estate, Clontarf, Killester, Raheny and Dollymount. No Charge for Sites. Only Small Ground Rents. Builders given every facility for obtaining Government grant. Apply: Estate Office, Franks & Oulton, 21 Lower Fitzwilliam Street.
>
> (Advertisement, *Irish Times*, 12 March 1925:
> Building and Reconstruction Section)

In 1925 the Vernon Estate began to advertise the availability of free building sites. Because of the low site costs, the erection of bungalows was encouraged. In addition, the cheap land (while the sites were free, ground rent was payable on an annual basis) attracted the attention of several public utility societies, who generally built where land was available as cheaply as possible. The advertisement noted that every facility would be given for obtaining the Government housing grant. Thus, Dublin Corporation was not the only land-owner to benefit from Government legislation encouraging private building in the mid-1920s. In the same year, reference was made by Dublin Corporation to a development plan which had been adopted for the Vernon Estate. The plan showed a westerly continuation of Mount Prospect Avenue from the junction of Vernon Avenue, intersecting Castle Avenue near Blackheath, and joining the Howth Road between 'Lauraville' and 'Silver Acre House' (Report 273/1925). All but 100 feet (*c*.30 m) of the new road would run through the Vernon Estate, and it was considered desirable (by Dublin Corporation) to assist the development by acquiring this land, held on lease by Mr Evans. Thus, even before the formal agreements of 1928, Dublin Corporation was assisting the Vernon Estate in its developments. It was probably in connection with this development that new bungalows were approved at Seafield Road and Vernon Avenue in June 1925 (Report 178/1926).

The real alliance between Dublin Corporation and the Vernon Estate began in 1928. In the *Irish Times* of 8 April, the unusual arrangement was reported. In return for the Corporation constructing a new roadway linking up Vernon Avenue and Castle Avenue, and extending Belgrove Road (renamed from Rutland Avenue in 1927) to join this new road, the Vernon Estate had granted a 999-year lease to the Corporation from 2 September 1927 at 1*s*. p.a. of the site of the roads and of building plots (average 300 feet, *c*.91 metres in depth) along the full length of the connecting road on its southern side, and for the

74 Castle Avenue and environs, Clontarf.
(Ordnance Survey 1:2500 plan, Sheet 19 II, Dublin, 1938 revision.)

full length of the extension of Belgrove Road along its Eastern side. The new road was named Kincora Road/Bóthar Cinn Coradh. The benefits to the Corporation were obvious. In the same way that it had leased building plots following road schemes at Griffith Avenue, Mobhi Road and Collins Avenue, it would be able to let these building plots on the new Vernon estate roads and receive income from the ground rents as well as from the rates which would be payable by the new residents.

Meanwhile, the widening of Castle Avenue, which had been under consideration for some time, got underway in August 1928. An illustration of the rapid development of the area is that in order to achieve the required frontage line, it was necessary to acquire varying widths of garden space in front of 20 recently constructed bungalows on the road, running in a southerly direction from Howth Road (Report 164/1928).

The leases of plots on Kincora and Belgrove Roads (figure 75) were for 150 years from 29 September 1928 at a rent equivalent to 4s. 6d. per foot frontage, and were 'subject to the erection to the satisfaction of the City Architect of suitable buildings, which shall be used as residences only, in accordance with plans to be approved of by him and by the Vernon Estate Architects' (Report 22/1929, p. 36). The first leases were granted to Thomas O'N. Gallagher, 16 Drumcondra Park for the erection of one bungalow, and to Mr Victor Scales, building contractor, 11 Rathmines Park for 16 houses on Belgrove Road (east side) (Report 233/1928). According to Report 95/1929, additional land on Belgrove Road was leased to Mr Scales, for use as a builder's yard, and eventually for the erection of garages. Gallagher had been involved in the development of the Mobhi Road 'reserved sites', while Scales had built on Corporation-developed land at Griffith Avenue. Other leases granted that year on Kincora Road included a site for a bungalow for Eugene Casey, Seafield Road East, and one for a two-storey house for the Misses Hunt, Beechview, Glasnevin.

Among those building on Belgrove Road was the Dublin and Rural Public Utility Society, which differed from most of its fellow societies in that it erected bungalows (*Irish Times*, 7 March 1929). This illustrates how close the societies were to the private sector, in most areas, where two-storey semi-detached houses were the norm, the public utility societies built such houses, but in Clontarf, where a large proportion of houses built on the relatively cheap land were bungalows, the public utility society built bungalows. The DRPUS also built houses on Kincora Road and Mount Pleasant Avenue (*Irish Times*, 4 April 1929). Registered in 1927, the DRPUS was criticized by the officials in the Registry of Friendly Societies because 'it would seem that the

75 Kincora Road and Belgrove Road, Clontarf.
(Ordnance Survey 1:2500 plan, Sheet 19, Dublin, 1938 revision.)

houses in respect of which the grants are paid are erected by individual
members of the society and that the grants collected by the society are handed
in cash to the members by whom the houses are built' (RFS R1778, memo
dated 12 January 1933). Thus, the society was a means whereby those building
their own houses could avail of a higher grant than they would otherwise be
entitled to claim as a private individual. This suggestion is borne out by the
decision at a general meeting of the society in January 1934 to wind up the
society as 'no further grants would be payable under the housing acts' (RFS
R1778, AR 1933).

In January 1930, the Dublin Commercial Public Utility Society, Ltd., was
granted a 150-year lease of additional building ground at Kincora Road. This
was its fifth contract and it was intended to build houses of modern design,
'setting an entirely new note in house construction' (RFS R1739, AR 1929).
Some 44 to 46 houses costing at least £958 each were to be built on the 1590
foot (c.485 m) frontage, with the rent payable at 4s. per foot frontage. By June
1932, however, the Society, which had erected 16 houses and started on a

76 Housing on Kincora and Belgrove roads. The upper image shows a bungalow on Kincora Road. The lower image shows more 'traditional' two-storey houses by Victor Scales on the east side of Belgrove Road. (Photographs by R. McManus.)

77 Kincora Road houses designed by J.V. Downes. Built in 1930-1, these are among the first Irish manifestations of the 'International style'. (Photograph by R. McManus.)

further six, 'intimated that, owing to the alterations in the provisions for grants on houses and rates remissions they found themselves obliged to ask to be allowed to surrender the leases of the leases of the three plots on which they had only made preparations for foundations of the houses' (Report 40/1932, p. 210). This change indicates the extreme reliance of public utility societies on Government grants and assistance. Similar difficulties were experienced by the Dublin Commercial Public Utility Society in the Drumcondra area following the introduction of the new legislation.

By the March Quarter, 1930, the Corporation noted that all the sites reserved for building on Kincora and Belgrove Roads had been disposed of. The rents receivable amounted to £371 3s. 6d. for Kincora, and £89 16s. 8d. for Belgrove Road (Report 101/1930). Because of the variety of builders, Kincora Road boasts a variety of house styles. However, it is notable in terms both of the relatively low-density of development, and in the predominance of bungalow-style housing.

Following its close alliance with the Vernon Estate, Dublin Corporation seems to have had a change of heart in early 1931, when, 'on the recommendation of the City Engineer, it was decided that the construction of the proposed new road between Kincora Road and Clontarf Road be left to the Vernon Estate, and that the Corporation proceed no further in the matter' (Report 17/1931, p. 67). However, a 1932 report suggests that the Corporation did become involved in road building there. In connection with the proposed new road at Clontarf from Kincora Road to the sea, involving the free surrender to the Corporation by the Vernon Estate of building ground fronting the new road, it had been arranged to lease this ground back to the Estate for building purposes at a rent of £50 p.a. for a term of 150 years (Report 46/1932). The proposed new road was finally built as Oulton Road, named after the family which owned the Vernon Estate. The difference here was that the Corporation did not concern itself with the individual leasing of building sites on the new frontage, instead leasing the ground back to the Estate at a fixed rent which would provide the remuneration for its road construction work.

By 1932, development in the whole Clontarf area was extensive. In August, shops were proposed at the corner of Hollybrook and Clontarf Roads, while Mr Casey continued to build bungalows along the Clontarf Road. The first mention of Oulton Road occurs during this year, with the erection of seven houses in September, while two pairs of houses were proposed for Beechfield, Clontarf Road. New land had been opened up for development on the Vernon Estate, such as Dollymount Avenue (laid out from c.1933, building until at least 1937), but it seems that infill was occurring in the gardens of large houses as well. Building continued in the Kincora Road, Oulton Road and general Clontarf area during 1933. Houses were built at Hollybrook Park, an old avenue which had led to some of the grand houses of the area, and which now served as the link between Hollybrook Road and the Howth Road. The name Seafield Avenue was adopted for the road running parallel to Seapark Road, from Mount Prospect Avenue to Seafield Road, while building work continued on Seafield Road itself, with Messrs Squire and Company involved in building. By January 1934, both Seafield Road and Seafield Avenue were taken in charge, although building was continuing at Seafield Road in 1939. Planning permissions were granted for two, three or four houses at a time, suggesting that building was occurring on a piecemeal basis.

Between 1935 and 1939, the missing connections in the local system of routeways were gradually filled in, often resulting in the unusual naming of roads (for example, Vernon Avenue is an L-shape, as is Mount Prospect Road). Among the roads planned at this time were 'new roads off Clontarf Road', subject to amendment of layout, to provision of turning place, to provision of a connection to Belgrove Road and the abolition of proposed cul-de-sac and future connection to Belgrove Square – the road connecting Castle Avenue with Clontarf Road to be widened to the requirements of the Corporation (Report 13/1937). Vernon Avenue, one of the major arteries of Clontarf, was continued, with 62 houses, 56 houses, four shops with three flats over, and four further shop dwellings being approved at various stages in 1939. In addition, a new road off Vernon Avenue was named Vernon Park in 1938, with a revised layout plan approved in the following March (Reports 39/1938 and 19/1939). The Mount Prospect area was also developed at this time, with Mount Prospect Park taken in charge in August 1935.

Of course, not all the land in the area was in the hands of the Vernon Estate, although it was probably the development of this large holding which made the development of other land in the area seem an attractive proposition. In March, 1936, the auction of 'Blackheath', Castle Avenue, residence, and 22 acres (*c*.9 ha) of 'valuable building sites' was undertaken by Battersby & Co. on behalf of the estate of the late Mrs Gibson Black (*Irish Times*, 7 March 1936). By July, the new owner had received approval for the proposed layout of the Blackheath Estate, provided space required for widening of Castle Avenue to 40 feet (*c*.12 m) was ceded free to Corporation and to drainage proposals being satisfactory. It seems that one developer was involved, who then leased sites to individual builders. Among the builders involved in the development of the Estate were L. Lane and J. Carabine. By March 1939, some 1224 feet (*c*.373 m) of Blackheath Park was taken in charge, while later that year the new cul-de-sac off Blackheath Park was named Blackheath Drive.

Another of the estates to be opened up for development at this time was that owned by Mr Bradshaw, between the Howth Road and the Malahide Road. The owner of many properties in the area, Bradshaw was resident at Mount Temple, but also owned Croydon Park (which was sold for use in the Marino housing scheme) and Merchamp, a large house at the junction of Seafield and Vernon Avenues. In May 1933, the layout plan for a proposed new road linking Howth Road to Malahide Road was approved, and by October, development was underway. New houses were built on Brighton and Cecil Avenues, Howth Road and Malahide Road. 'Another stage in the development of Clontarf is marked by the announcement that on the Mount Temple site, Malahide Road, houses of seven and nine rooms are to be erected, complete with garage' (*Irish Times*, 8 March 1928). The new link road was named Copeland Avenue, which forms an asymmetrical connection with the publicly developed Griffith Avenue. Apparently Dublin Corporation did not have the power to ensure that the private interests building the new road would align it with the

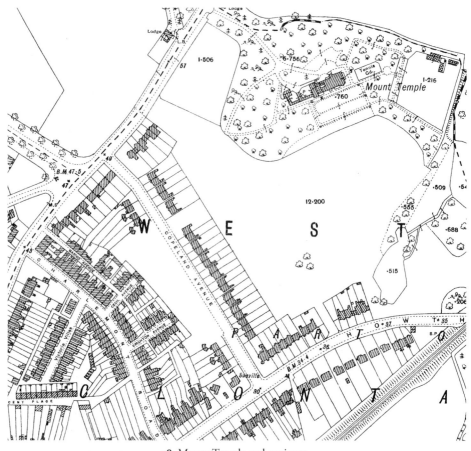

78 Mount Temple and environs.
(Ordnance Survey 1:2500 plan, Sheet 18 IV, Dublin, 1938 revision.)

existing 100-foot (*c*.30 m) wide Griffith Avenue. Among the builders involved
in its development were a Mr Coghlan, E. O'Donoghue and J. Kenny (*Irish
Times*, 7 April 1934).

The development of the Clontarf area in the 1920s and 1930s shows that,
despite some changes, much suburban development was of a piecemeal
nature. The majority of builders lived locally, and concentrated on house
construction in the vicinity. Victor Scales of Rathmines was a notable
exception, building at a number of northside locations at this time. Joseph
McGonagle of 'Lomond', Kincora Road, was involved in private building in
Mount Prospect, Castle Avenue and Kincora Road. Later he built houses at
Furry Park, off the Howth Road. In addition to these local concerns,
McGonagle acquired leases from Dublin Corporation and built houses to

designs by Messrs Higginbotham and Stafford, architects, on Griffith Avenue in the early 1930s.

The development of the Vernon Estate and its surrounds demonstrates the important links between Dublin Corporation and private interests during the period. It also suggests that legislation intending to encourage house building acted as a spur to landowners who developed sites in order to take advantage of the anticipated building boom. Government grants and the availability of cheap mortgages under the SDAA were vital to the success of new building schemes. The reliance of builders, particularly public utility societies, on such incentives is illustrated by the difficulties experienced from 1932 as leases were surrendered following legislative changes.

Importance of public utility societies in Dublin

The scale of building by individual public utility societies may appear relatively small, but in the context of the time their impact was much larger than the modern observer would expect. In the year ended 1929, the Dublin Commercial PUS could report that it had provided 212 new houses since May 1926. Furthermore, it claimed that this total made the society the largest house-building organization in the Free State, with the exception of Dublin Corporation. In its annual report for the year ended December 1930, the DCPUS stressed the importance of a Housing Facilities Act extending over at least five years. This would allow for better planning and the society would be in a position to embark on a four to five year programme of construction, creating building employment for 1000 workers. By the end of 1936, the DCPUS had erected 1047 houses, which (by its own calculations) was by far the largest contribution to the solution of the housing problem by any Free State organization. Such was its success that in 1937 the public utility society was renamed Associated Properties Limited and shortly afterwards was converted into a company under the Companies Acts 1908–1924.

Appendix no. 6 of the Housing Inquiry of 1939–43 provides a list of the number of dwellings erected in the City of Dublin by both private builders and public utility societies from 1933 to 1938. During this period, 15 such societies were in operation in Dublin, building a total of 1878 houses. The most active of the public utility societies was Associated Properties Ltd., accounting for 1296 houses, or just under 70 per cent of the total figure. This society was significant, not only due to the size of its operations, but also because it remained in operation until its eventual liquidation in 1994. It was one of the few public utility societies which rented properties, including houses in Wadelai, which were finally sold off to tenants, presumably in order to take advantage of the 1930s legislation which gave special subsidies to public utility societies providing rental accommodation.

Nine of the societies built fewer than 20 houses each, while the remaining five built between 32 and 160 houses each over the six-year period. These were, in order of magnitude:

> Dublin Building Operatives' Public Utility Society;
> Post Office Public Utility Society;
> Civil Service Housing Association;
> National Housing Society and
> St Mobhi Public Utility Society.

Although it has proven impossible to discover where these societies were building in all cases, some references in Corporation Reports, records of the Registry of Friendly Societies and newspaper articles provide clues. For example, in 1935 the St Mobhi Public Utility Society submitted plans for six houses and three shop dwellings on Sundrive Road, part of the Crumlin Reserved area. A number of public utility societies were building in the general Cabra area. For example, the Economic Public Utility Society built at least four houses on the Navan Road in 1936, while the Celtic Public Utility Society built on Norfolk Road as well as on Collins Avenue and in 1938 the National Housing Society was building at Ardpatrick Road. In 1933 the Post Office Public Utility Society was building houses in Kimmage, while in 1934 it extended operations at Merville Avenue and later in the decade built houses at Lansdowne Park. Also in the early 1930s, the Woodvale Public Utility Society built houses on Mount Prospect Avenue and Conquer Hill Road, Clontarf. The majority of these locations are on the edges of Dublin Corporation's housing areas, on sites which had been serviced as part of the local authority schemes but which had been reserved for better quality housing. Thus, like their 1920s counterparts in Marino, Griffith Avenue and Drumcondra, the public utility societies of the 1930s benefited from the Corporation's housing schemes and were closely linked to them.

For whom did public utility societies cater?

As has already been suggested, many of the public utility societies seem to have consisted of loose groupings of individuals who wished to build their

Table 26 Housing in Dublin city by private builders and
public utility societies, 1933–8.

Public Utility Societies	1933	1934	1935	1936	1937	1938	All
Associated Properties Ltd. (Dublin Commercial PUS until 1937)	66	120	208	376	170	356	1296
Dublin Building Operatives' PUS	20	70	0	12	38	21	160
Post Office Public Utility Society	10	76	14	0	16	0	116
Civil Service Housing Association	36	16	20	25	0	0	97
National Housing Society	0	12	13	14	17	20	76
St Mobhi Public Utility Society	4	12	4	8	4	0	32
Christian Brothers' Past Pupils Union	0	6	10	0	0	0	16
Economic Public Utility Society	0	2	3	7	3	0	15
Tram and Omnibus Workers' PUS	0	0	0	4	6	1	11
St Ultan's Hospital PUS	0	0	14	0	0	0	14
Saorstát PUS	0	12	0	0	0	0	12
State Servants' PUS	0	12	0	0	0	0	12
Holy Child Housing Society	0	0	0	0	10	0	10
Celtic PUS	0	0	0	0	6	0	6
Harold's Cross PUS	6	0	0	0	0	0	6
Totals for Utility Societies	142	338	286	446	270	396	1878
Private Builders	757	964	989	949	660	854	5173
Overall Totals	899	1302	1275	1395	930	1250	7051

(Housing Inquiry, 1939–43, Appendix No. 6.)

own homes. Certainly many of the houses built in the Clontarf area seem to have reflected this goal. We have also seen that public utility societies were sometimes used by private builders as a way of maximizing the grants they could receive from Government, and it is to be assumed that in this case houses were disposed of in the same manner as for any other speculative development.

One notable feature of the public utility societies operating in Dublin is the number of societies which catered for civil servants. This tendency can be traced to the fact that the grants offered by the State gave preferential treatment to civil servants, who were entitled to build larger houses than everyone else (under the 1934 legislation, maximum floor area for houses qualifying for the grants was 1000 square feet (*c.*93 m^2), whereas civil servants could build a 1500-square-foot (*c.*140 m^2) house and still avail of the grants). Thus, at least three societies sought to cater for their needs in the late 1920s and 1930s: the State Servants' PUS, Saorstát Civil Service PUS and Civil Service Housing Association. This preferential treatment was in some measure perhaps seen as a way of making up for less positive changes affecting State employees. In 1924, severe reductions in pay were experienced by civil servants, primary school teachers and members of an Garda Siochána, with further cuts in 1931 (McNiffe, 1997). Providing grants towards housing was at least one way in which the State could hope to offset the negative impact of these wage reductions.

It is clear from the correspondence between the Civil Service Housing Association and the Registrar of Friendly Societies that this society never intended to provide housing for the most needy members of the working classes. Indeed, clarification was sought from the Registrar in relation to whether the society would receive funding if its building programme provided housing for the lower grades of the civil service rather than the poorer classes. All that was required, according to the Registrar, was that they *include* among their objects the provision of houses for the working classes (RFS R1768, letter from RFS to Mr O'Neill dated 29 March 1927). That this was a declared aspiration was enough, irrespective of whether any attempt was ever made to achieve it. The first houses built by the Civil Service Housing Association were at Whitehall, to plans by Rupert Jones who also designed houses in Mount Merrion. The five-roomed concrete houses cost £660 each.

Civil servants could also promise steady employment and guaranteed ability to repay mortgage or tenant purchase agreements. In December 1925 the Civil Service pay scale for unmarried male clerical officers and female clerical officers began at £60 on entry, rising to £70 at 18 years of age and thence by annual increments of £5 to a maximum of £150 per annum. Married men were placed on a different scale, with annual increments of £10 to a maximum of £200 per annum. A lump sum payment was also made on marriage, while allowances were payable in respect of each dependent child up to the age of 16 years. All civil servants were also entitled to a 'cost of living' bonus. Starting wages for a Junior Accounts Clerk were £90, rising to £350 (for women, to £250), while an Assistant Inspector of Taxes started on a salary of £150, the same as an unmarried Junior Administrative Officer. More lowly civil service employees were placed on a weekly rate. Writing assistants in

October 1927 could expect to earn from 17s. on entry to a maximum of 34s. per week. Typists began at 20s. per week for an 18-year old, rising to 30s., while shorthand typists earned an extra 4s. per week in recognition of their additional skill.

A range of occupations was represented among the tenants of other public utility schemes. For example, the occupants of houses in Parnell Road and Arbutus Avenue which had been built by the Harold's Cross PUS included a merchant, brewery official, tailor and civil servant. Some public utility societies were established with the aim of assisting a particular interest group, such as the Dublin Municipal PUS Ltd., R2173, which was controlled by the Irish Local Government Officials' Union, or the Tram and Omnibus Workers' PUS.

A degree of philanthropy was evident in at least some of the public utility societies operating in the 1920s and 1930s, such as the Holy Child Housing Society which built ten flats at Temple Lane/Hill Street. In late September 1924, the Dublin Christian Citizens' Council unanimously approved a resolution proposed by Reverend Hall:

> that this meeting of Dublin citizens calls upon all responsible parties for increased effort in the erection of houses to meet the urgent need of more houses, and to provide more employment; and commends to all employers and investors the appeals of the St Barnabas' Public Society and the Association for the Housing of the Very Poor.
>
> (*Irish Builder and Engineer*, 4 October 1924, p. 858)

It is worth noting that F.G. Hicks was architect for schemes for both organizations, while the architect Mr George Beckett, himself involved in the Bray PUS, presided at the meeting.

Some employers found that assisting in the development of public utility societies was a way of ensuring adequate housing for their workers. Thus, the Linenhall PUS received support from Messrs J. Jameson & Sons and Messrs Maguire & Patterson Ltd., both local firms who were anxious to see their employees properly housed. Among those taking loan stock in the Rathmines PUS were Messrs W. & R. Jacob and Co. and Messrs Robert Roberts and Co. A small number of companies continued to provide workers' housing themselves. For example, in September 1924, the 'married quarters' at Griffith Barracks, Dublin, were acquired by the Greenmount and Boyne Linen Company of Harold's Cross, for the housing of some of their workmen and their families. In all, four blocks were used, in which there were a number of two-, three- and four-roomed flats, each with water and electric light laid on. About 40 flats in all were created, in two-storey blocks, with the top flat being reached by iron stairs from the top of which is a balcony which runs along the whole length of the block. In 1927 the Greenmount and Boyne Linen Company leased a site to Joseph P. Somers who subsequently built 37 houses for the Harold's Cross PUS (discussed below). Provision of housing by employers had been a feature of late-nineteenth-century Dublin, but had become far less common by this time, although the Iveagh Trust continued to build philanthropic housing.

Abuses of the system?

One of the dangers of the public utility society system was that of fraud. In his 1918 report, P.C. Cowan wrote that 'Societies of Public Utility can be formed without any other conditions than registration and restriction of interest or dividends on their capital to a figure not exceeding five per cent' (Cowan, 1918, p. 16). There was no authorized or standard form of society nor any prescribed constitution at that time, and Cowan recommended that conditions should be imposed in order to exclude 'undesirable activities' under the guise of such a society. Although the earliest societies in Ireland used the model rules provided by the Garden Cities and Town Planning Association, while from the mid-1920s the Civics Institute of Ireland provided model rules, there was still considerable scope for deception. For example, in 1925 the Popular Homes Society was cancelled because it was discovered that its registry was obtained by fraud. A Mr J.P. O'Dwyer had been using the names and signatures of a number of people without authority, while a man who had been employed as a canvasser by O'Dwyer wrote to say that none of the people who had bought £1 shares had received share scripts. This was reported by the Registrar of Friendly Societies to the detective authorities and eventually O'Dwyer was charged under the Forgery Act, 1913.

The Harold's Cross PUS, registered in May 1929, also fell foul of the law when it was alleged that the society was being run for the benefit of its officers and not for the members of the society. Further, it was suggested that building grants of £2247 for 37 houses had been acquired by false pretences and were of no benefit to the members of the society. A letter of 1937 addressed to the Registrar of Friendly Societies complained of 'gross irregularities' and 'perfidious conduct' on the part of Mr Erskine and his nominees, who had carried on the business of the society clandestinely and against the registered rules of the society. There was a High Court action in 1941 while in 1948 a High Court Order for the winding up of the society was obtained on the petition of a number of residents at Parnell Road and Arbutus Avenue, and of the builder, Mr Somers. Despite this, a further letter in the files dating from August 1955 alleges 'a shocking and continuous fraud of a criminal character', with Somers continuing to pursue the matter until 1961. The registration of the society itself was finally cancelled in May 1971. Thus, despite apparently clear evidence of misconduct, it was not easy to control the operations of public utility societies.

It is also evident that a number of builders founded utility societies in order to avail of the higher grants afforded to such societies, rather than to individuals. This does not necessarily mean that they were behaving against the spirit of the law. If the Government was concerned to have more houses built, and was willing to provide grants of various types in order to encourage building activity, why should builders not avail of such schemes? Certainly, experienced builders would have brought a level of expertise to an area which was sometimes afflicted by the well-meaning efforts of amateurs. One society which was controlled by a builder was the Whitehall PUS (R1819, registered January 1929). The secretary of the society was Mr Joseph J. Flanagan of Kyle House, Drumcondra, a well-known builder in the area. From December 1930, Flanagan took over all of the assets and liabilities of the society. Even more obvious was the operation of the Blackrock and District PUS, registered in December 1928. A letter of 1934 noted that the society had been formed to facilitate purchasers of houses on a scheme undertaken by Fitzgerald Estates Ltd. at Temple Road and Craigmore Gardens, Blackrock (RFS R1817). The necessary signatories to the rules were people connected with this building company, and then each of the purchasers became a member. However, it seems that the society received the grants from the Government under the housing acts on behalf of the members and paid them out to the builders as the houses were completed and the purchase closed. The bungalows and roadway were mentioned in the *Irish Times*, 8 March 1930 and *Irish Builder and Engineer*, 12 April 1930.

The case of the Frascati PUS (Blackrock) Ltd. is rather less clear. Registered in December 1927, the stated objects of the society were 'to buy, sell, hire, let and develop land; to provide, erect, reconstruct, improve or manage houses for the working classes and others' (RFS R1786, rule book). However, by July 1929 it was noted that 'the society might be considered as owned and financed

79 Charlemont PUS flats, Charlemont Street.
(Photograph by R. McManus.)

by Mr Benjamin McKinley, without interest on the money advanced from time to time by him amounting to £3361 12*s.* 10*d.* at the 31 December 1928 and shown as a loan in the balance sheet'. By the end of 1932, 35 houses had been completed and about 20 more were to be built. In 1933 the Society's auditor wrote that 'Benjamin McKinley is practically the only interested person in the society to all intents and purposes, the only member of the society who is signing cheques, has full control of the funds and carries out all transactions and is independent of any supervision or control of the society' (RFS R1786, letter dated 4 July 1933). The houses were not necessarily cheap, with No. 35 Frascati Park being sold in August 1933 for £950. An internal memo of the Registry of Friendly Societies dated 6 March 1935 stated that it was now clear that the Society had been formed merely with the purpose of securing to Mr McKinley grants under the Housing Acts in excess of the amount which he could have obtained as an individual. However, the same memo concluded that there were no grounds for legal action. In addition, 'on the point of policy under the Housing Acts, it may not make much difference who gets the assistance from public funds, so long as the houses are built' (RFS, R1786).

By the end of 1933 there were 125 registered public utility societies in Ireland. While the total number of houses built by such societies has yet to be identified, especially given the tendency to lump together the efforts of private builders and public utility societies in the official statistics, it is clear that public utility societies made a significant contribution to Ireland's housing stock up to, and indeed after, World War II. In Dublin, during the six years from 1922 to 1927, public utility societies were responsible for building nine per cent of all houses completed in the city at the time, while between 1929 and 1933, Dublin societies belonging to the Federation of Dublin Public Utility Societies built a total of 957 houses.

However, by 1934, Dáil questions were being asked about the extent to which public utility societies were monitored and held accountable for their actions. Mr James Everett, TD for Wicklow, asked the Minister whether he was aware that 'a number of Utility Societies, having abandoned their co-operative characteristics, are earning substantial profits for individual promoters' and that the advantages of the grants payable to such societies were not being passed on to the occupiers of the houses built by them (Dáil Debates, 50, p. 1594, 18 July 1934). Further, where complaint was made to the Registrar of Friendly Societies, the Registrar pointed out that he could not investigate the accusation unless at least ten members complained.

In April 1935 Mr Dillon raised the matter once again, asking whether the Minister could cause strict inquiry to be made into the activities of public utility societies established consequent on the Housing (Financial and Miscellaneous Provisions) Act, 1932, with a view to eliminating those which were functioning for the benefit of their promoters rather than that of their members. Dillon suggested that abuses existed 'on a pretty wide scale in different parts of the country', with numbers of public utility societies being run by building contractors (Dáil Debates, 55, p. 2131).

Once again, in 1938, Mr Everett asked the minister to take steps to secure better supervision over public utility societies. However, Seán T. O'Kelly responded by saying that he was satisfied that public utility societies had played an important part in getting houses erected throughout the country. 'My functions in regard to them are confined to seeing that the houses in respect of which grants are claimed comply with the requirements of the Housing Acts' (Dáil Debates, 70, p. 3).

Conclusion

This chapter has shown that the development process involves not just a simple division between private and public housing schemes, but a much more complex interweaving of relationships. The public utility societies which operated during this time period are a particularly good example of this complex development continuum, although the marriage of public and private elements was not confined to such societies. The blurring of distinctions between public and private housing gave rise to a much wider development role for Dublin Corporation than has been generally acknowledged. As we have seen, the Government was so anxious to have houses built that it tended to turn a blind eye to suspected abuses of the system. The history of the public utility society movement in Ireland is largely unwritten, yet much could be learned from such organizations at this time of renewed interest in public-private partnerships and alternative forms of housing tenure.

Private Developers

Introduction

Thus far we have focused on the role of Dublin Corporation in the development of housing as well as on the nature of the work undertaken by co-operative or public utility societies. However, a very large proportion of the house-building undertaken in Dublin in the early twentieth century was completed by private speculative developers. In the years 1933 to 1938, for example, private builders provided over 8000 houses and paid weekly wages of more than £10,000 (Dublin and District Housebuilders' Association (DDHBA), 1939). As we shall see, their work was influenced by changes in State and local authority policy, particularly through grant availability for particular types of housing. By and large the private builder completed suburban houses for the middle classes. In the earlier part of the century, these houses were often sold to investors for leasing, or even kept by the builder as a source of income. After World War I the tide turned in favour of home-ownership and increasingly the speculative builder provided houses for sale. The style of housing also changed, reflecting societal changes such as the reduction in servant numbers and the increase in motor car ownership, but also in response to the quality of houses being produced by the local authority.

By its very nature, it is difficult to pin down the exact operation of the speculative building process. This chapter and the one which follows attempt to do so by focussing on the development of a particular part of the city, the area of Drumcondra and Glasnevin, and by concentrating on the work of a small number of builders, especially that of Alexander Strain. We shall see the complexity of the building process, the number of actors involved and their varying degrees of influence, the difficulties experienced by Dublin Corporation in attempting to impose order on development, and some of the changes which occurred over time.

The significance of the suburbs

By the last quarter of the nineteenth century, the number of people able to contemplate suburban life had begun to increase significantly. This was due to a steady rise in real incomes, reduced working hours, an increase in the number of administrative, clerical and skilled manual jobs offering good pay and regular hours, and expanded educational facilities allowing more children to reach standards opening the way to white-collar employment. Expansion in the Civil Service, a trade, shipping and overseas investment boom, and the development of joint stock limited liability companies gave rise to a huge increase in the number of clerks, directors, managers and senior officials of all kinds. These desired to climb the social scale, exchanging the congestion, filth and often unpleasant atmosphere of inner area streets for the quiet clean respectability of a new suburb. Other motivations to centrifugal movement, in the case of Dublin and other cities, included the heavier rate burden in the centre, which had already prompted many members of the middle class to move out. The suburban idyll was not easily achieved as the *Irish Builder and Engineer* noted in July 1905: 'It cannot, of course, be expected that when the town invades the country rural beauties can be preserved, for streets be they ever so artistically designed, must inevitably be less refreshing than cornfields and orchards' (1 July 1905, p. 457). Almost 20 years later, the same publication noted: 'Dublin has some of the most beautiful and attractive suburbs in the world, but how many of them are made hideous by the character of the houses built during the last half century? ... With the advent of the wholesale speculative builder, about 50 years ago, began the disfigurement of our beautiful suburbs' (*Irish Builder and Engineer*, 6 October 1923, p. 772)

Although sanitary and building controls were in place, there were no regulations governing the way in which the land in newly-developed areas was laid out, so that suburban growth was generally uncoordinated and haphazard. Land was often used wastefully, with little thought for future requirements. There were many different grades and sizes of houses in the English suburbs, attuned to the many layers of the middle classes, while in turn, variations in architecture and landscaping between different areas enhanced the awareness of class differences (Dyos, 1961). Subtle distinctions were drawn between localities, signifying varying shades of respectability, yet the most desirable areas existed side by side with less favoured districts. Similarly in Ireland, every suburb has unique characteristics resulting from the specific influences acting upon it at particular stages in its development, including local land ownership patterns, national housing policies and economic fortunes. In order to examine the role of the private developer in the evolution of Dublin's suburbs, this study focuses on the area of Glasnevin and Drumcondra, showing how a number of individuals, with or without local authority assistance, shaped the built environment. Foremost among the builders in the area was undoubtedly Alexander Strain, who was active in the early decades of the twentieth century, and his case will be used to illustrate the nature of speculative development at the time.

Introduction to Drumcondra and Glasnevin

The history of the Drumcondra and Glasnevin area has been dealt with elsewhere, and forms little part of this particular story (Cosgrave, 1932; Corpus Christi, 1991; Egan, 1961; Tutty, 1958). However, the role of one significant landowner can be traced back to the twelfth century, when the Anglo-Normans took control of the area, and three home farms were established in the district. With the dissolution of the monasteries at the time of the Reformation, there was a scramble for their lands. The lands of Drumcondra (and Baldoyle) were then granted to the Corporation of Dublin, which leased the land for revenue. The importance of this occurrence to twentieth century suburban development is evident, as the City Estate was to be used as development land in the housing drive of the 1920s and 1930s.

In the meantime, these large tracts of land leased by the Corporation became country estates, occupied by various colourful characters. In the late-eighteenth century, many members of the Protestant nobility and gentry had private residences in the area. Already, however, there was a diversity in the nature of the housing here, since some of the earliest housing in the area was associated with industrial development on the banks of the River Tolka, including linen bleaching and milling of flour and oats. In the early nineteenth century, Drumcondra acquired a reputation for revelry, with tea-houses and places of amusement being established. However, at this stage, Drumcondra and Glasnevin were essentially rural areas, studded with large houses set in parkland and the area, being so far outside the city, became the haunt of highwaymen and other undesirables, as well as a popular location for duels. Maps of the time show narrow roads through rich fields with a few large houses for gentry and some scattered cabins.

The district, within walking distance of the city and on rising ground, would appear to have been ideally suited to take advantage of the nineteenth-century trend for the professional and middle-classes to move from the dirt, disease and high-density city to the suburbs. However, this did not occur. One reason for the delay in development was simply fashion, which resulted in early suburban development becoming concentrated on the south side of the city. Problems related to lack of water, sewage services, the existence of turn-pike roads, and law suits concerning the will of the Earl of Blessington, a major local landowner, were also factors in the late development of the area.

However, the character of the area did change gradually, as many of the large houses were given over to institutional use in the later nineteenth century, while their parklands frequently came to be used for housing. For example, Belvedere House was purchased by the Archbishop of Dublin in 1883 to form the nucleus of St Patrick's Teacher Training College; Drumcondra House has housed All Hallow's Missionary College since 1842; Clonliffe House has been the home of Holy Cross College since 1859; while in 1825 a hospital was established by Dr John Eustace at Hampstead Castle to cater for 'Patients of the Upper Class suffering from mental and nervous diseases'.

In the latter half of the nineteenth century development began to expand beyond the canals which ringed the city, into areas which were outside the jurisdiction of the Corporation of Dublin. Developers in the new suburban areas were left with a decision to be made. Either they could organize to provide services such as running water, lighting and drainage themselves, or they could come under the aegis of the municipal corporation. If they chose the latter route, however, their properties would be subject to the very high city rates, which would fall either to themselves as owners or to their tenants, who might be discouraged from living in the area. Thus, for speculative developers it was important to ensure that rates would be low in order to ensure a good return on their investment. By establishing an authority under their own control, it was possible to charge rates which would be sufficient to improve the living standards in the newly-developing areas, but with a careful eye to the need to avoid excessive taxes. Thus, independent townships were established by private legislation, to be run by a Board of Commissioners. The townships were generally controlled by the largest property owners in the area. For example, the Rathmines township was dominated by businessman and housebuilder Frederick Stokes, Pembroke township was largely controlled by the earl of Pembroke, while the Vernon estate was influential in the setting up of the Clontarf township in 1869.

In the case of the Drumcondra and Glasnevin area, a local Act was passed on 2 September 1878 forming the Township of Drumcondra, Clonliffe and Glasnevin, a move proposed by local property developers and businessmen, but opposed by several major landowners. The township was run by 14 com-missioners, all substantial property owners. They soon formed two distinct and hostile groups, as local landowners and settled residents dominated Glasnevin ward, while property developers and builders held a majority of all seats. The Commission was empowered to levy rates to provide services including water, drainage, road maintenance and general improvements. Rates were kept low, with a maximum possible rate of 3s. in the pound, by economizing on public services. As a result, complaints over sewage and poor drainage persisted well into the twentieth century. Even after the township was absorbed into the city, the influence of builders and developers remained strong, as these parties now had seats on the Dublin Corporation.

The purpose of establishing township status for the area was to encourage residential and commercial development. The existence of a township would increase land values and allow property developers to get a good return on their investment, by increasing the success of speculative developments. Because the development of the northern suburbs had been delayed, the area was at a disadvantage in attracting new residents. The wealthier professionals had already moved out of the city into the southern townships by the time Drumcondra began to develop, so the developers in the north made a conscious attempt to attract artisans and clerks on small salaries (Kelly, 1990). Thus Drumcondra was unique as the only suburb which from the outset aimed to cater for clerical and skilled working class residents. The Township Commission provided a rates remission on all houses valued at £12 or less in order to encourage house building and the settling of well-to-do artizans in the area. By 1884, over 200 houses had already been built under this scheme, and several local Commissioners were among the major beneficiaries, including Mr Butterly, Contractor, Homefarm, Drumcondra, whose houses 'let as fast as they could be built' (the Butterly Estate, it will be remembered, was later acquired by Dublin Corporation for the Drumcondra housing scheme) and Edward McMahon, MP and Member of Dublin Corporation, who built 200 houses for artizans valued at £8 each using money borrowed under the 1866 Labouring Classes Dwellings (Shaftesbury) Act.

In evidence to the 1885 Commission on the Housing of the Working Classes, McMahon described the typical small house rented at 6s. per week to artizans and 'people of small means'. The houses had either three or four rooms, with a frontage of 20 feet (c.6 m) and a depth of 20 feet. At the front, a small hall led to a room of 15 feet 6 inches (c.4.7 m) by about 9 feet (c.2.7 m), which was used either as a parlour or, in the case of large families, as a bedroom. The back portion of the house was divided into a kitchen of 9 feet 6 inches square (c.8.5 m²), and a bedroom of the same size. The 20-foot square (c.37 m²) yard contained a w.c. and a dust-pit, with 'all sanitary arrangements'.

The Township of Drumcondra was probably the one area of Dublin where trams contributed to suburban growth (Daly, 1985). Certainly there was an emphasis on tram access in many of the house advertisements, suggesting that proximity to the tram line was a selling point for houses in much the same way that proximity to the DART is attractive to modern-day house purchasers in the Dublin area. The first horse-drawn trams of the North Dublin Tramway Company began operating in 1875, offering services between the city centre and both Tolka Bridge and Glasnevin. Following the amalgamation of all of Dublin's tram companies into the Dublin United Tramways Company, Drumcondra continued to be well served by this form of transport. This is not surprising, since J.F. Lombard, one of the Township Commissioners and a major housing developer, was also a director of the DUTC.

The success of the trams contrasts with the failure of the railway service in the area. Perhaps the railway came too late to interfere with established tram-going patterns. The Drumcondra and North Dublin Railway Link was established under an 1894 Act of Parliament, but the promoters were forced to incur great expense in the acquisition of land 'the owners of which were not slow to realize its value. Most of the land to be acquired was designated building land and its value was, as a result, enhanced' (Tutty, 1958, p. 95). Two stations were provided at Drumcondra and Glasnevin but were not successful and closed soon after. In the late 1990s Drumcondra station was rebuilt and reopened.

One picture of housing in the township at the end of the nineteenth century is provided by James Joyce in *A Portrait of the Artist as a Young Man*. In early March, 1894, John Joyce was forced to move with his wife and ten children to their seventh home, 2 Millbourne Avenue, Drumcondra. At this time the area had a population of 8000. When the Joyces lived there, Millmount Avenue did not exist, and thus Millbourne Avenue was the first turn to the left after Drumcondra Bridge. In the novel, Stephen crosses the bridge and looks towards the statue of the Blessed Virgin, which stood 'fowl-wise' on a pole in the middle of a ham-shaped encampment of poor cottages. He bends to the left, following the lane which led up to his house. On his way he passes two dairies and a gardener's cottage and smells the rotted cabbages from the kitchen gardens on the rising ground above the river. He thinks of the garden behind his own house and the solitary farm-hand whom the children referred to as 'the man with the hat'. It was a semi-rural area, with many of the neighbours making a living from small dairies and also working as cattle-dealers, farm-hands, and gardeners. Some navvies lived in a row of run-down cottages. The semi-detached Joyce house was known as Holywell

Villas, after the nearby St Catherine's Well. It contained two reception rooms, a kitchen and three bedrooms, and was built for letting in the late 1880s by Mr Butterly. Nearby there were fields and woods and a weir into the River Tolka (Igoe, 1990). In the 1890s Maurice Butterly rented ground in the vicinity of Jones's Road for use as the 'city and suburban racecourse'. The site was also used for soccer and cycling. In 1911, the land was bought by Frank Dineen on behalf of the Gaelic Athletic Association and became known as Croke Park.

Residents: a census picture of Drumcondra and Glasnevin in 1911

Although part of the Drumcondra Township had experienced rapid growth from 1881, large scale suburban development in Glasnevin and Drumcondra awaited the early twentieth century. The 1911 Census of Population provides a snapshot of the area at this relatively early stage of development. As with Dublin's late nineteenth-century suburbs, both Glasnevin and Drumcondra wards had below average percentages of Roman Catholics, with a relatively high proportion of Protestant residents. In Glasnevin, almost one third of the population was Protestant, particularly Church of Ireland adherents.

In both Glasnevin and Drumcondra a large amount of construction work had been undertaken in the ten-year period from 1901 to 1911, resulting in an increase of 510 houses in Drumcondra and 766 in Glasnevin. The relatively high proportion of all housing in the ward still under construction suggested that the boom would continue. Naturally the increasing numbers of houses reflected a growing population. Between 1901 and 1911, the population of Drumcondra ward grew by almost one quarter, while in the same period Glasnevin's population increased by 67 per cent, well above the average increase for the city as a whole, which was under nine per cent. Of course, it must be remembered that the percentage growth is probably a reflection of the fact that the area was starting from a lower base, but equally significant is the fact that it catered for a rapidly growing lower-middle class demand for comfortable, reasonably priced houses. However, despite the construction boom, the housing density (expressed as the number of houses per acre) was low, at 2.5 houses per acre (*c.*6 houses per ha) in Drumcondra, and under 2.2 (*c.*5.5 houses per ha) in Glasnevin. This low-density in the new suburbs did not represent a change in the number of houses being built per acre, but rather reflected the large amount of agricultural or undeveloped land enclosed by the ward boundaries.

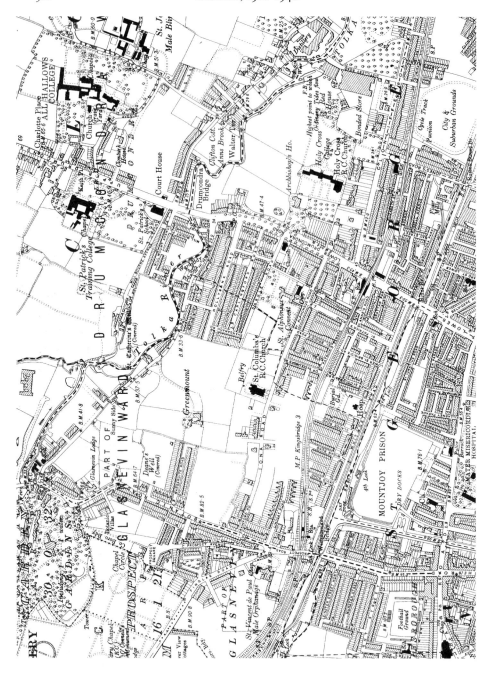

80 Drumcondra in 1912. (Ordnance Survey 1:10,560 plan, Sheet 18, Dublin, 1912 revision.)

Table 27 Housing and population in Drumcondra Township, 1881–1911.

	1881	*1891*	*1901*	*1911*	*1926*
Houses	862	1281	2388	3664	n.a.
Population	4878	7624	13818	20255	23173
Housing change %		48.6	86.4	53.4	n.a.
Population change %		56.3	81.2	46.6	14.4

Statistics for the combined area of the post-1900 Drumcondra and Glasnevin wards, which equates with the Township of Drumcondra, Clonliffe and Glasnevin.

Between 1911 and 1926, when the next census was undertaken, the development of both areas slowed. In both wards the population density (persons per acre) was well below the city mean. This may be partly explained by the effect of mixed residential and farming uses as outlined above, but also reflects the socio-economic profile of the inhabitants, who were in better circumstances than most of the population living within the city boundaries. There was little evidence for overcrowding within individual houses, with an average of under six persons per house, well below the city mean. Unsurprisingly, there were very few sub-divided, multiple-occupancy houses in either Drumcondra or Glasnevin, although there were some poor cabins and cottages.

The results of the 1911 Census illustrate the diversity within a relatively small area which was one of the hallmarks of the speculative development process. As we shall see, the nature of development often resulted in a diversity of housing types being completed within neighbouring streets, with subtle variations in social status. Suburban growth was not uniform, instead the process has been described for English cities as:

> a series of wave-like motions stretching over half a century or more, propelled by the pulse of local or national building cycles, early pockets and islands of higher class settlement becoming in the course of time hemmed in by a rising tide of ... higher density development, or perhaps being overwhelmed by socially inferior infilling ... As a result few areas as large as an entire parish or township experienced a uniform quality of development, and were much more likely to display a mixed social character.
>
> (Thompson, 1988, p. 174)

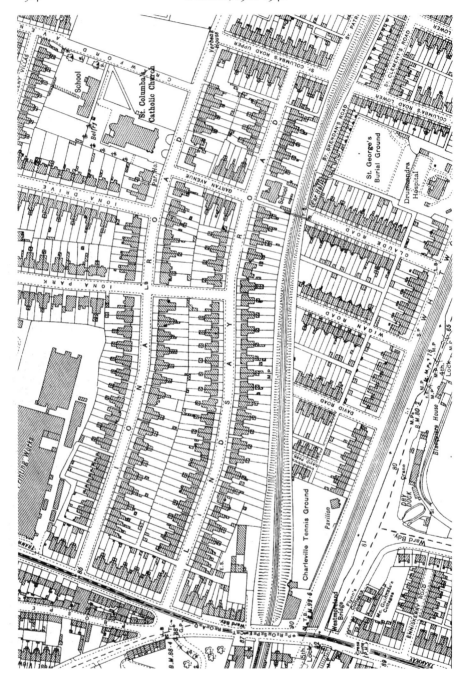

81 General map of the Iona district, Glasnevin.
(Ordnance Survey 1:2500 plan, Sheet 18 III, Dublin, 1938 revision.)
Note the difference in layout and orientation of the streets on either side of the railway.

82 Houses on Iona (*upper image*) and Lindsay roads (*lower image*) by Alexander Strain. (Photographs by J. Brady.)

This same degree of contrast was evident in the suburban development of Dublin during the early twentieth century. By looking at data for a number of streets in the Glasnevin area we can see how this mixed social character had begun to emerge by 1911.

Iona Road was already at the top end of the housing market in 1911. A long road running from a junction with Botanic Road to merge with St Alphonsus Road, there was some variation in the houses built, so that of the 71 houses on the street at the time, 11 were described in census terminology as being first class, the remainder were described as second class. The definitions were based on a count of scores awarded to each house based on the construction materials used, number of rooms and number of windows at the front of the house. Thus, a first class house was likely to be built of brick or stone, have a slate or tiled roof and have more than six rooms. A second class house was generally built of similar materials but may have been smaller, with fewer rooms and windows. Often the distinction between houses within the second class was greater than that between the different classifications. In total, 387 people lived on Iona Road, of whom 299 were Roman Catholic, the remainder belonging to a variety of Protestant denominations. The remainder of the Iona area also included high quality housing. The higher standard of living in this area is reflected by the presence of domestic servants in 12 of the 22 houses in Iona Drive, some having a governess or children's nurse in addition to the 'general domestic'. One feature which we would not tend to associate with better-class housing at this time was the presence of lodgers, but at least four of the houses on Iona Drive had boarders. In fact, the organization of the home focused less on the direct 'nuclear family' during this period, and it was common for households to contain upwards of nine people. For example, the McHenry family of 2 Iona Drive comprised a 63-year-old Customs 1st class Exam Officer (retired), his wife and four adult children, working as shop assistants and clerks. Of 12 children born alive, seven had survived to adulthood. A 68-year old widow from Kerry boarded with the family. Other occupations represented in Iona included the civil service, civil engineering, as well as the assistant superintendent of Prospect Cemetery, supervisor of waterworks in Dublin Corporation, and a railway inspector.

Lindsay Road, which runs parallel with Iona Road, contained 74 inhabited houses at the time of the 1911 Census. The character of this street also varied, as on one side some of the houses back on to the railway line and were therefore considered less desirable. It consisted of second class houses throughout, several of which had fowl houses. The occupants included Mr O'Mahony in number

83 Housing on David Road, Glasnevin. (Photograph by R. McManus.)

47, who described himself as a 'landlord'; Thomas Laurence Duncan, a timber merchant's manager; and James Rowntree from Co. Armagh, manager of a machinery and engineering business.

On the opposite side of the railway line, there was an apparent decline in social status. Although all of the houses on Wigan Road were described as second class in census terminology, the occupants were less well off than those in the Iona/Lindsay area, with far fewer domestic servants. This illustrates the difficulty of relying on census definitions in classifying areas. The houses are more compact than those on Lindsay Road, though still of red brick, and are mostly terraced. Of the 129 people living on the street, 74 were Catholic (57 per cent), showing the relatively higher proportion of Protestants living in this area, compared to Dublin City as a whole. The occupiers included artizans (carpenter, cabinet maker, upholsterer) as well as lesser civil servants (postal sorter, customs service, telegraphist, clerk in the Congested Districts Board) and several drapers and commercial travellers.

North of Iona, off Botanic Road, Marguerite Road was another street of second class housing, with a diversity of inhabitants including Catholics, Protestant Episcopalians, Presbyterians, Methodists, Baptists and others. This street marks yet another social difference, given the multiple occupancy of several houses, including one house containing three families. These were, presumably, single tenants, a step above the common boarder in social standing.

The short terrace of Woodville Road, from Botanic Avenue to the River Tolka, contained eight inhabited second-class houses in 1911, whose occupants included a wine and spirit grocer, a journalist from Tipperary with seven children, a Limerick GPO clerk, and an artificer (silver plateworker). Several of these houses were being purchased under the Small Dwellings Acquisition Acts. One interesting example of an Edwardian household is found at number 7, where an English-born Land Commission surveyor and his Cork-born wife, both Catholics, lived with their three children, plus a cook and nurse.

Nearby St Malachy's Road seems to have represented a slight step down the social scale. Still under construction in 1911, of its 28 houses, seven were inhabited, seven uninhabited and 14 were still building. The seven resident families included Roman Catholics and Protestants, and were also a mixed group in terms of occupation, including a hatters salesman born in Scotland, a brass founder, an unemployed clerk, a superintendent in the Army and Navy Stores, a painting contractor from Waterford, a Leitrim-born telegraph clerk, and a widow with three children.

To the north of the River Tolka, College View Terrace was built on Millbourne Avenue in c.1898/9, together with the cul-de-sac of Millmount Avenue, probably by a Mr Dillon. The houses of the Millmount area varied in size but were terraced and fronted directly onto the street without any front gardens. In the first decade of the century, all were being let to tenants, some on an annual basis. A 1905 advertisement for 6 Millmount Villas, a 3-roomed house (the kitchen/scullery was not counted), with garden, offered it for £28 free of rates, while a 5-roomed house at Millmount Place with a large garden was available at £26 p.a. in 1907, with 6 Millmount Terrace for £20. One Patrick Cotter, 42 & 44 Drumcondra Road, a grocer and 'capitalist', let Nos. 53, 44 and 31 Millmount Avenue at various times. All were four-roomed houses described as being close to the penny tram. The 1911 Thom's directory lists M. Boylan, dairy, at 5 Glenarm Avenue, which was the location for enquiries regarding the letting of another four-roomed house on Millmount Avenue in 1912. This again illustrates the typical background of many small-time landlords. The reports of the Paving and Improvements committees of the Corporation emphasize the lesser social standing of the street, as the condition of the roadway seems to have constituted something of a public nuisance, with frequent references to the filth of the thoroughfare and the need to clean it. In 1916 the Paving Committee ordered the repair and tar spraying of the macadam roadway of

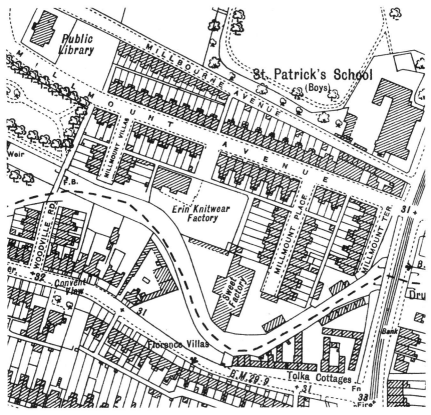

84 Millmount and Millbourne avenues, Drumcondra.
(Ordnance Survey 1:2500 plan, Sheet 18 III, Dublin, 1938 revision.)

Millbourne Avenue, and requested that the Cleansing Committee give greater attention to the cleansing of the roadway (Report 20/1917). A 1918 report refers to repairs made to the roadway at Millbourne Avenue, costing 40 shillings, while in March 1919 it is noted that a large quantity of manure and mud, which had apparently been swept off the road and deposited at the side for a considerable time, was obstructing the work of the Paving Committee employees.

On the southern bank of Tolka, Botanic Avenue contained several terraces of houses built at various times and by different builders, including some of the poorest housing in the area. In this case, later infilling has improved the quality of housing in the area and many of the worst terraces are now gone. The 1911 Census provides details of some of the conditions and occupations of the occupants. Lismore Cottages, (Nos. 86, 88, 90, 92, 94, 96 Botanic Avenue) housed 27 people in 1911, of whom all but two were Roman Catholic. The residents of these third-class houses included a widow and her cycle agent

85 Housing on Millmount Avenue, Drumcondra. (Photograph by J. Brady.)

son; a tailor with his family and elderly mother; a pilot, wife and five children; an unemployed gardener, and several labourers. Similarly, Maher's Cottages, Botanic Avenue 1–10 were all third-class houses which were home to 30 Roman Catholics. Each family occupied one room, with the exception of numbers 2, 9, 10 which had two rooms, number 10 also including a piggery and shed. Number 1 was home to Mrs Mitchell, a 67-year old illiterate widow who earned her living as a charwoman, and by keeping a 60-year old boarder, also widowed. Her neighbour was also a charwoman, with a gardener son. A hackney car driver lived in number seven. Three of the remaining cottages housed agricultural labourers, another a general labourer and one builder's labourer. These houses thus provided accommodation for the poorest classes in the area, many of whom were servants and most of whom were Roman Catholic.

Tolka cottages, mentioned in Joyce's account of the area, built to house workers in one of the mills, were located on a triangle of land bordered by Tolka Bridge and Botanic Avenue. By 1848 there were 22 thatched cottages on the site, the number eventually rising to 42. The area was (and is) subject to flooding and the cramped and insanitary cottages were eventually demolished in 1949 to be replaced by a park. Since 1890 a shrine to Our Lady has stood here, and though the huts are gone, the statue remains.

In the speculative suburbs of the Victorian and Edwardian eras, the new populations tended to provide their own entertainment, based around churches, clubs and societies. From the 1880s, for example, tennis clubs were commonly established on odd pockets of land left by developers. Thus, the Charleville Tennis Club paid rent to Alexander Strain, a local builder. The Church was the key to social contact because, in addition to its spiritual role, it provided a focus for the community, with concerts, outings, talks, lectures, clubs and general companionship. In Dublin the Church was even more significant, since it also provided schooling for the community.

The speculative development process post-1900

In 1900 the Drumcondra Township was included within the city boundary, a necessary step taken by Dublin Corporation in order to increase income from rates in order to extend the city's main drainage and other services, as well as coping with the poor of the city. By 1902 a new Catholic parish was created (until then the population had been served by priests from Fairview) and the existing wooden church enlarged to hold 400 people. In the same year the church of St Aidan (C of I) designed by Caulfield Orpen was opened on Drumcondra Road. A measure of the success of the suburb at this time is the purchase of a 2-acre (c.0.8 ha) site from the sisters in the St Alphonsus Monastery for the erection of St Columba's Church, which was completed by the masterbuilder Thomas Connolly of Hollybank Road in October 1905. When the church was first opened there was no road access, so negotiations were opened with the Lindsay Estate who were the local landowners, and 'a builder', possibly Alexander Strain, to provide both roads and houses. Nine acres (c.3.6 ha) were bought on condition that six of the houses built would have a value of £500 each, an example of how landowners could control the quality of development. Iona Road was thus built, joining Crawford Road (since renamed as part of Iona Road) to St Alphonsus Road (Egan, 1961).

> A small builder often began by putting up less than a dozen houses, using the profits obtained from these to finance a subsequent larger venture, proceeding to something larger still on the third round, and so on. Some would run too fast, having tasted initial success, falling into financial difficulties, their houses standing half finished until another firm came on the scene to complete the estate.
>
> (Jackson, 1973, p. 110)

Prior to the 1914–18 War, building costs were relatively low. In addition, no travelling or subsistence allowance was paid to workers, little overtime was worked, and the trades were subject to one or two hours notice, which meant that in adverse weather conditions employers could lay them off without pay. As the population of Dublin was growing steadily between 1900 and 1911, and house-property was a desirable investment, conditions for speculative development were good. A large number of houses was being built and made available for letting by private landlords to tradesmen and clerical workers. Houses were generally built in small numbers, apparently by small builders, and sold off before the next batch was completed.

Often a builder would reside in one of his houses while building the terrace or street, before moving on again. This could be seen as proof of the quality of the product, and also a convenience when overseeing remaining works. One example is that of Daniel J. Quinn, who lived at number 13 St Columba's Road Upper in 1901. In 1902 he moved to the newly completed No. 35, the only house of the new block (25–35) to be occupied. The small scale of suburban development in the late nineteenth and early twentieth centuries is clear from the street directories of the period. Streets often contained a number of individually-named terraces which, for convenience, had been amalgamated to form one single street. Upper Drumcondra Road, for example, includes Beaumont Terrace, St Michael's Terrace, St Patrick's Terrace, St James's Villas, Charlotte Villas and Clonturk Villas. Each of these terraces would usually have been completed by a different builder, as reflected in the contrasting building styles of the finished houses.

While it is argued that, in general, house building at this time was a small-scale operation conducted by many different builders, it must be noted that the land *developers* tended to think in larger-scale terms. In evidence to the 1885 Housing Inquiry, Edward McMahon, developer and builder in the Drumcondra Township, suggested that, in the event of an extension of the Labourers Dwellings (Ireland) Act, he would undertake to build four or five *thousand* houses.

The actual development process was generally carried out, not by the landowners themselves, but by small-scale speculators. These were either the house-builders or minor capitalists who employed the builders and made money by astutely investing in the development of an area. Because land for building was generally released in relatively small parcels (typically, a few fields at a time), streets were laid out in relation to existing roads, lanes, and the irregular shape of the individual plots. Individual builders might complete only one or two houses per annum, a pattern also seen in Victorian London, where jobbing builders commonly broke off from repairs and alterations to put up a few houses. Therefore, although developments were carried out in a short period, they were far from uniform, with many different builders working within a relatively small area. Even firms which built more than a few houses at a time often had their work scattered, rather than being clustered in the same road.

The most likely purchaser for the pre-World War I speculatively-built house was an investor rather than an owner occupier. This is evident from the way in which contemporary property advertisements were pitched. In 1901, for example, three 'superior private houses' on St Columba's Road were advertised in one or more lots, suggesting that the builder had recently completed these houses and was willing to sell them either to an investor (as a group for letting) or to private individuals as residences. In the same year, number 15 St Brigid's Road and numbers 2 & 4 St Columba's Road were advertised as being 'newly built and let to good tenants', showing that these houses were being sold to investors, probably by the builder who had first let them out. Other houses being sold in twos and threes include 2 & 3 Botanic Avenue, 1 & 2 Woodville Road, and numbers 6, 7 and 8 Prospect Avenue, formerly Cemetery Road. In 1908 an auction notice appeared in the *Freeman's Journal* for Nos. 1, 2, 3, 4, St Michael's Road, lease 245 years from 1906. This was a mortgagee's sale which also included some houses on Claude Road. It would appear either that the builder, or the small-time investor to whom he sold the houses, went bankrupt.

From the census returns and the advertisements discussed above, it is clear that a range of housing was supplied in Drumcondra, from the purpose-built middle class residences of Clonliffe Road, part of Jones Road and some substantial houses in the 'Bishop's Fields', to more modest terraced houses. Smaller houses to cater for tradesmen and artisans, such as the three-roomed cottages on St Joseph's Avenue, were also provided. It would appear that towards the end of the nineteenth century, and in the years prior to 1914, there was a greater emphasis on 'well to do middle class residences'. Some of these were built by Edward McMahon, particularly in the area where St Brigid's and St Alphonsus Road subsequently emerged. Quality housing also dominated Glasnevin, which the builders were starting to exploit around 1914 when the Carroll estate adjoining Botanic Road was opened up.

A survey of newspaper advertisements from 1910 illustrates the variety of houses on offer, as well as the different types of tenure which were available. This included direct sale by the builder, the use of 'house agents' as an intermediary in sales to owner occupiers and the sale or auction of houses in lots for letting as an investment.

- Adjoining Clonliffe Road, modern house, five rooms, hot bath, long lease, sale £230 {owner occupancy}.
- St Michael's Road, Botanic Avenue, Glasnevin. Rent £25, also compact cottage, rent £22— Daly, builder, Botanic Avenue {rental, direct from builder}.
- 36, 38, 40 & 42 Botanic Avenue, Drumcondra. Four compact two-storey dwelling houses (in one lot), close to tramline {investment opportunity}.
- 35 St Patrick's Road, Substantial two-storey, red brick house, Garden, Conservatory, Conveniently situated house, close to penny tram, Lease 900 years at £3 14s 0d {owner occupancy}.
- 19 Home Farm Road, lease 178 years.
- 161 Botanic Avenue, Good shop and house, lease 400 years. In business for a number of years.
- 9 Millmount Place, Administrator's sale. Well-built, modern, two-storeyed house, lease 400 years.

Further evidence regarding the small-scale nature of development, much of it by long-forgotten builders, appears in the Corporation reports. For example, in the June Quarter, 1905, a gravel footpath was laid on Botanic Avenue, opposite six new houses, at a cost of £28. A Mr Lawlor erected Nos. 30 and 32 Lr St Columba's Road, following approval of a combined drainage agreement in 1909. In 1910, the Paving Committee considered projections beyond the building line including the bay windows to proposed houses on St Brigid's Road, Drumcondra for P. Shortall, Esq., while the 1924 renumbering of houses on Fitzroy Avenue included new houses erected by Sir P. Shortall.

One of the more important local builders at this time was Daniel Daly of Hillsboro', Botanic Avenue, who built many of the houses in the area, including parts of St Michael's and St Malachy's roads, Botanic Avenue, Glendalough Road and Hollybank Road, Church Avenue and three quarters of Griffith Park (Sherry FitzGerald, 1994). He was a member of Dublin Corporation and served on the School Attendance Committee and as Chairman of the Cleansing Committee of that body. A 1910 report of the Paving Committee regarding a proposed new road off Botanic Avenue for Mr Daniel Daly makes interesting reading. Although the bylaws required a width of 42 feet (c.13 m), the proposed road of two-storey houses has a width of only 37 feet 6 inches (c.11 m). In addition, footpaths were to be finished with 1 inch (c.2.5 cm) of 1½ to 1 cement compo (that is, composite). The bylaws in this connection specified 1½ inches (c.4 cm) of 2 to 1 compo, but it was agreed to

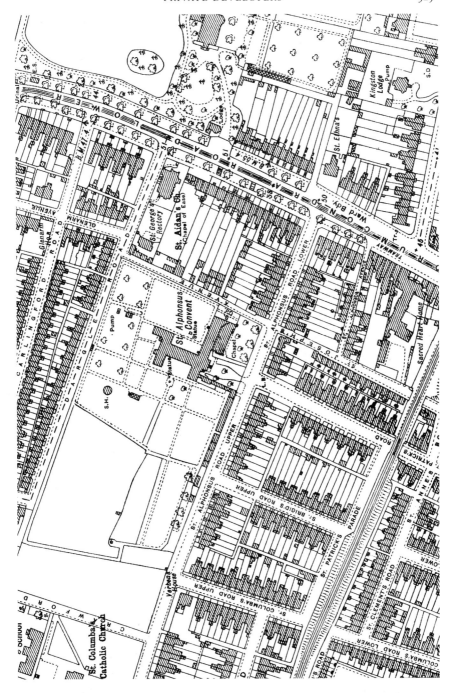

86 St Alphonsus Road and environs, Drumcondra.
(Ordnance Survey 1:2500 plan, Sheet 18 III, Dublin, 1938 revision.)

suspend the bylaws following the report of the Civil Engineer. In support of this recommendation the committee pointed out that the houses to be erected on the proposed new road would be an additional source of revenue to the Corporation! This was probably St Michael's Road, which was taken under Corporation control in the following year. Meanwhile, the same 1911 report also recommends that neighbouring St Malachi's (*sic*) Road, which was constructed by Mr Daniel Daly, be taken in charge of the Corporation, although the road was not made strictly in accordance with the bylaws (since broken black stone was used in its construction instead of broken green stone). One wonders whether Daly's position on the Corporation was a factor in these allowances being made.

Reference has already been made to Mr Dillon, who erected houses at Millmount Avenue in 1909/10. It is likely that this was the same person who owned land on Botanic Road, between 'Fairfield' and 'Glasnevin Lodge'. In 1913 the Paving Committee accepted Dillon's offer to cede to the Corporation a strip of ground adjoining the public footway at this location, on the understanding that the Corporation would concrete the space free of charge to him (Report 233/1913). Councillor John Dillon was a Corporation member for Drumcondra Ward in 1914, living at 17 Drumcondra Park.

The piecemeal nature of housing development in Dublin at this time is evident from an examination of maps, from the Corporation Reports, and from the large variety of house styles within a small area. All of these features suggest that development of this time was largely unplanned. However, by the very nature of the speculative market, it is extremely difficult to trace the individual builders involved in the creation of these suburbs. Few names appear in the Corporation records, and without seeing the lease of each individual house, the identities of the small-scale builders who produced a large proportion of the housing in this area will never be known.

The business of speculative house building

It is not large capitalists that build these houses, but small builders and enterprising industrious artizans. I have had a very large experience of them. When they have a little money, they come to me and get a plot of ground, and I get them a loan of money; and they build houses; and then, when they are built, they are sold to small capitalists, also men with savings of £400 or £500, grocers and butchers, and that class of people.

(Edward McMahon, M.P., Housing Inquiry, 1885, p. 97, para. 24,603)

Edward McMahon and James Fitzgerald Lombard were the two main developers of lower-middle-class housing in Drumcondra Township, providing loans for small builders or artizans to build on their land in the area known as the Bishop's Fields, between St Alphonsus Road and Whitworth Road. A similar form of development, with landowners selling to developers who then sold plots individually to small builders, persisted well into the 1930s in Dublin. In the Mount Merrion area, for example, a middle-man, John Kenny, acquired the land, developed it and then sold leases to private individuals or builders who erected two or three houses each.

The development process described by McMahon was also characteristic of Britain at the same time (Jackson, 1973). The system of building leases which existed at this time could involve as many as eight different roles, from ground landlord to ultimate occupier. The chain might typically consist of ground landlord, speculator, building materials supplier (providing credit), surveyor or architect (the most dispensable, given the widespread availability of pattern books), financier, master builder, sub-contracted journeymen builders and craftsmen from the bricklaying, plastering, plumbing and woodwork trades, and consumer. The final consumer of the finished product might be an investor in houses or the householder who took a monthly or annual lease from the investor or directly from the builder (Watson, 1989).

The ground landlord benefited under the leasehold system, since the land could be developed without the incurring of any personal expenditure, while the landlords received unencumbered title to the developed property on expiry of the lease. Areas of 'ripe' building land were frequently bought up (on building leases or freehold) by speculators, who would then lay out roads and arrange the provision of main services before offering building plots to individual private purchasers, or disposing of groups of plots (or whole sections of the estate) to builders for erection of houses on a speculative basis. We have already seen that Dublin Corporation took on this type of activity from the 1920s, when it developed and serviced land which was then made available to private speculative builders or public utility societies.

The builder often exercised little effective control over development, with the landowner controlling the type of housing to be built by making restrictive clauses in short-term leases, often having laid out the streets already. Bylaws and local board policy could create further restrictions. In Pembroke Township, for example, short leases with restrictive clauses gave rise to an almost uniformly high standard of building. Strict building laws were maintained, with any 'jerry-built' properties being immediately demolished. Occasionally restrictive covenants were included among the terms of sale in an attempt to raise the value of individually-sold building plots.

However, the speculative nature of development could lead to problems, and in the Drumcondra Township many building irregularities were reported at the end of the nineteenth century. Problems associated with this form of development include its piecemeal nature, and the haphazard provision of services. Later infilling could alter the status of the area as, for example, through the erection of smaller houses or even a Fever Hospital. Even more importantly, the lack of building skills in the speculative market led to a dangerous amount of 'jerry-building', in middle-class housing as well as that intended for the working classes. Certainly, small builders and grocers were not generally the most stringent builders, and many would have learned the trade from books. There was a contention that leasehold tenure encouraged jerry-building since there was no benefit to a developer in erecting a house which would outlast the term of the lease. On September 15, 1878, the *Irish Builder and Engineer* reported on the 'New Northern Township' where 'Building speculation is rife ... and we hope it will continue so, and that houses of a better character will continue to be erected than some of those recently raised'. Concern with housing quality persisted. In 1884 it was noted that Drumcondra had 'a large number of jerry-built built structures' and it was hoped that future development would be of improved quality (*Irish Builder and Engineer*, 15 October 1884). The use of breeze blocks made from cinders and gas works refuse gave serious cause for concern, since they were highly combustible. In 1894 one builder was ordered by the Township Commission to demolish five houses which he had built of breeze, while it was claimed that some houses in Carlingford Road consisted of just 4½ inches (*c*.11 cm) of brick facing disguising breeze blocks. As late as 1899 complaints were aired by Township Commissioner Buckly, regarding the use of 'common clay' rather than sand to make mortar for the houses on St Clement's Road (Kelly, 1990). In fact, such breeze blocks were commonly used throughout Drumcondra, where even the garden walls of houses built by a reputable builder such as Alexander Strain comprise this material. The domination of the township by builders and property developers resulted in a policy of non-interference regarding building irregularities, so that, it was claimed, the situation was being talked about all over Dublin (*Irish Builder and Engineer*, 1 July 1894). Of course, not all houses were of questionable quality, but this scrimping on materials reflects the fact that many houses were aimed at the lower end of the market. While sanitary and building controls were in place, there were no regulations governing the way in which the land was laid out, so that suburban growth was uncoordinated and haphazard. Land was used wastefully, with little thought for future requirements.

The arrangement of a speculative building enterprise required financial skill, with careful budgeting to ensure that cash flowed in as fast as it moved out; and the cutting back of activity if sales fell off. It is not surprising, therefore, that many smaller firms stayed in the district they knew best, and where they could form sound judgements of the market. However, some larger builders operated right across the city, especially in the 1930s. There was apparently little difficulty for developers in securing short-term credit from a bank, usually acquiring working capital at 1 per cent over bank rate if the firm was large or old. In the early 1930s in particular, economic conditions made unusually large amounts of capital available for risk investment. Small builders could get financial help from developers selling off plots, and some building societies would provide money for development, while builders' merchants issued large quantities of supplies on a credit basis. In January 1923, the *Irish Builder and Engineer* commented that 'that very useful enterprise, the Irish Civil Service Permanent Building Society', had reported a successful year's activity, notwithstanding the almost total cessation in the building of private houses in Dublin. The hope was expressed that, when the cost of building materials and labour became a little more normal, more active operations of this Society in financing private building schemes would be resumed.

Structure of the Building Trade
In the nineteenth century most building firms were small in size, company organization being discouraged by the easy credit obtainable from builders' merchants, together with the possibility of financing work in progress with advance payments from estate developers. Development was generally on a modest scale, concentrated in one locality at a time. Most builders were content to work under estate companies formed by landowners and entrepreneurs who provided the necessary capital and organization. Alexander Strain teamed up with Walter Kinnear, a civil servant, who financed the purchase of land which Strain would then build upon. Partnerships of this kind were probably common in Dublin.

General contractors held the uppermost position in the hierarchy of the building trade. They engaged in work under contract to sponsors and were directed by professional architects and engineers, their workforces including all the main trades. Regarded as the most respectable firms in the industry, these contractors included companies such as G. & T. Crampton or H. & J. Martin, both heavily involved in Corporation tenders in the early twentieth century. A profile of 'A Progressive Dublin Builder' which appeared in the *Irish Builder and Engineer* on 6 September 1924, gives an indication of the type of work undertaken by a contractor in Dublin at this time. Mr Richard Gough had offices at 1 and 2 Rutland Place and was considered (by that rather partisan journal) to be 'one of the most enterprising and progressive building contractors in Dublin', as well as a large employer of labour. His current contracts included a £3500 extension to the Mater Hospital; St Teresa's Catholic Church, Clarendon Street; a new Catholic church at Lusk, Co. Dublin as well as structural alterations to the premises of Brown Thomas & Co. on Grafton Street. Gough had also erected a new stand for the choir that participated at the Tailteann Games opening ceremony at Croke Park, with seating for 1000. In addition to these large contracts, Gough was also building 26 six-roomed dwellings at Botanic Avenue, Glasnevin 'which will be up-to-date in every detail, and will have large gardens front and rear' (*Irish Builder and Engineer*, 6 September 1924, p. 770). Presumably these were in addition to the 23 houses approved for Gough in May 1923 at Botanic Avenue. These three-bedroomed houses, to plans by Mr Francis Bergin, BAI, of 26 Westmoreland Street, had a livingroom, parlour, bathroom, scullery and gardens front and back.

The wholly speculative builders were below the general contractors in public esteem. They greatly outnumbered the contractors and were generally not much influenced by professional designers. Suppliers and builders merchants were not only wholesale stockists, but also provided a major source of short-term credit for firms on site. Their importance was enhanced by the increasing use of ready-finished components such as prefabricated joinery towards the end of the nineteenth century. With increasing competition between firms of builders suppliers, extensive and profusely illustrated catalogues were an important form of advertisement (Long, 1993).

Conditions in the boom years of the late 1920s and early 1930s favoured the establishment and growth of larger building firms that often undertook every aspect of estate development, although some smaller companies and individuals continued to operate at a small scale. There seems to have been an increasing professionalism in the industry, as seen in the paper qualifications now held by builders. For example, G.M. Linzell was an Associate of the Institute of Builders, a London-based institution which required both practical experience and examinations.

It is difficult to ascertain the extent to which speculative builders utilized the services of architects in designing their houses. It would appear that most speculative builders looked upon an architect as a luxury, and proceeded by practical experience and rule of thumb. The terraced and semi-detached house changed little in basic design, so that only conventional experience was necessary to build them. From the 1850s, the publishers of architectural pattern books began to issue volumes of designs for suburban houses, which often included working drawings, specifications and bills of quantities. Weekly journals such as the *Illustrated Carpenter and Builder* or the *Dublin Builder* (later the *Irish Builder and Engineer*), circulated among small builders and 'superior artisans' and were another source of ideas. In this context, it is interesting to note that the façades of terraces on St Brigid's Road were faced with white enamel brick, but this type of facing not used elsewhere. Such glazed tiles were introduced in England in the 1850s to resist dirt and pollution, but here their use seems purely decorative. This suggests that builders were copying the styles of their British counterparts, probably from pattern books or building journals. If a small developer employed an architect, the former would be at the outset of his career, and the designs, once acquired, would be used over and over again with only the slightest variation. Small-scale builders could gain the necessary experience from practice or could glean it from handbooks, and even into the 1930s it was relatively common for builders to dispense with the services of an architect. Engineers, surveyors and unqualified draughtsmen tried their hands at designing houses, while the *Irish Builder and Engineer* included advertisements for books not only providing 'Lessons in Carpentry and Joinery', but also updated 'pattern books' such as 'Cheap Cottages and Small Houses' by J. Gordon Allen, FRIBA, which contained illustrations of cottages, housing schemes and their plans. While the larger firms employed professional architects, they were rarely named in advertisements. However, in the 1930s the status of the architect was increasing, partly due to professional consolidation, and many more house approvals of the time include mention of the firm of architects involved in the scheme. At the Dublin and District Housebuilders' Association dinner in 1932, one of the speeches stressed the importance of the links between architect and builder.

Catering largely for the middle classes, speculative builders were generally shrewd in their appraisal of their customers' needs. Tastes were generally conservative, with the desire for a well laid-out, well-built and handsome-looking home. The house would symbolize the substance and respectability of the inhabitants, and the names given by the builders or early owners to these dwellings completed the public face of the buildings, revealing the values of the original inhabitants. It appears that speculative developers were influenced by architectural developments taking place in Britain during the nineteenth century. However, what they chose to build was strongly influenced by the conservative nature of the market. Most Irish builders toned down the work of their British counterparts, so that houses built in the late nineteenth century tend to have plainer, less ornamented exteriors than British examples. This seems to be true in all sectors of the market, so that even some of the most expensive houses built in Drumcondra at the turn of the century had relatively subdued exteriors.

That said, speculatively-built housing in Ireland resembled its British counterparts. In the 1870s and 1880s, for example, the better houses built in the Drumcondra Township (and, indeed, elsewhere in the city) tended to conform to the standard English middle-class house. They were terraced, with a tall narrow frontage and a long back addition, with two or more main rooms on the ground floor and three or more bedrooms on the floor or floors above. The degree to which the customer had a direct say in the fitting out of a house depended on the quality of the dwelling, with houses at the upper end of the range generally offering more variety, but also perhaps on the individual builder. For example, we know that Alexander Strain, whose work is discussed in more detail later, offered a menu of extras in his high-quality houses.

The progression from the late Victorian and Edwardian house to that built in the 1920s and 1930s was as evident in external appearance as in decorative features such as stained glass and interior plasterwork. In many ways, the later houses presented a miniaturized, watered-down version of their larger predecessors. The post-war housing shortage resulted in a building boom in the 1920s, encouraged by legislation in both Britain and Ireland. However, housing advertisements from the late 1920s suggest that standards of building fell at this time, and there appears to have been a distrust of the new building materials such as concrete and more light-weight styles. 'All-brick construction' became an important selling point, as was the assurance of 'pre-war standards'. In the rush to build, many houses of the period were of poor quality with leaking roofs, damp and structural defects, while increasing urban sprawl and ribbon development became sources of concern. However, by this time legislation and local bylaws insisted on basic health and safety standards, avoiding the worst excesses of the 'jerry-built' structures of the previous century. The better houses retained the high-quality brickwork of the Edwardian era, presenting a solid, reassuring façade to the world, while the cheaper houses

AN "ALL NOFRANGO" BUNGALOW NEAR DUBLIN

NOFRANGO

AN IRISH INVENTION WHICH SAVES 30% IN HOUSE CONSTRUCTION

The Strength and Waterproof Nature of
NOFRANGO HAS BEEN PROVED

NOFRANGO IS ALSO EMINENTLY SUITABLE FOR THE CONSTRUCTION OF
Paths, Silos, Signposts, Cylinders, Bridge Piers, Stairs
Lining for Lift Shafts, Water Tanks, Bathing Pools, &c.

PROFESSOR STEPHEN M. DIXON, M.A., M.Sc., B.A.I., M.Inst.C.E., of Imperial
College of Science and Technology, City and Guilds (Engineering) College,
London, states as follows :—
   " There is ample ground for having very great confidence in the enduring
   nature of the material. . . The hollow wall will be equally efficient
   in making a cool house in hot climates as a warm one in winter."

Architects and Engineers are invited to communicate with

NOFRANGO, LIMITED

16 MOLESWORTH STREET, DUBLIN

where all information regarding the process can be obtained

87 Advertisement for Nofrango, a 1930s Irish innovation in building technology.

had lost the substantial appearance which characterized earlier middle-class homes. In these houses, the cost of quality facing bricks encouraged builders to resort to the cheapest grades of brick, which would be covered with pebbledash or roughcast, offering barely adequate weather protection. Similarly, the quality of roofing and flooring materials was variable. By 1920 tiles had become virtually universal, and cheap concrete tiles ousted clay tiles and the last of the slates. It is notable, therefore, that Dublin Corporation insisted on the use of Irish slates in the houses built at Gaeltacht Park in the early 1930s. The largely self-taught builders like Strain, however, appear to have continued to use traditional materials with which they were most familiar. Thus Strain used wooden rather than concrete joists in his 1926 houses on Hollybank Road, as well as slate roofing.

Worries about the quality of new houses were picked up in advertisements in the 1920s and 1930s, as for D. Delaney and P. Cronin's houses on Grace Park Road. Patrick Cronin's advertisements emphasized that his semi-detached houses were being built under the practical supervision of 'owner-builder' Cronin, to the designs of Messrs Higginbotham and Stafford, Architects. They were 'built entirely of brick, walls and partitions according to pre-war standard, with red brick fronts, Dublin granite sills and heads to windows, and slated roofs' (*Irish Times*, 3 March 1932).

The speculative builder tended to be seen in a very negative light throughout the period under consideration, as illustrated by the following quote from Page L. Dickinson who was, incidentally, a regular columnist in the *Irish Builder and Engineer*:

> There is still a very large demand for the small house. Numerous builders are doing speculative work in this type of building, and large numbers of these are men with no taste, no tradition of good work behind them; men who are in the work from purely mercenary motives. Profit is their only consideration. Pride in their work counts not at all.
>
> (Dickinson, 1929, p. 144)

A further change in the private speculative building process after World War I was the increasing role of the Government, however indirect. This operated in two ways. Firstly, in terms of subsidies to builders through grants under 1919, 1924 and 1925 legislation and in loans to owner-occupiers under the SDAA, and secondly, more indirectly, through the policy of reserving areas in local authority schemes for development by private interests.

Because the houses built after World War I tended to be smaller and less solidly built than their predecessors, while housing densities were restricted, there tended to be more garden space in houses built after 1920. Front gardens were often larger than those found in many later Victorian and Edwardian lower middle class suburbs, houses took up less of the total plot area, and back gardens were often extremely long. This was certainly the case in many of the Corporation's 'reserved areas' where plot rental was based on length of frontage, not area. In Dublin, where many of the new middle-class suburbanites had migrated from rural areas, gardening was a particularly popular activity in the twenties and thirties.

Among the other leisure activities enjoyed in the new suburbs were reading and the cinema, while tennis and dancing were popular with younger people. In the period after World War I, the cinema became an essential element in suburbia. Initially located in converted church halls, or, in the case of Clontarf, in the old Town Hall, later the cinemas became temples of escapist architecture. The touch of glamour provided by the picture-house, with its exotic luxury and plush fittings, was reflected in majestic names evoking images of wealth and grandeur. Externally, the cinemas were unashamedly modern, contrasting with the 'safe' architecture of the surrounding houses and shops. The 'super-cinemas' of the 1930s contained as many as 1500 or 2000 seats and included a ballroom and café in addition to the cinema itself. The Dolphin's Barn area, for example, had the 1600-seat Rialto Cinema, officially opened in 1936 by Lord Mayor Alfie Byrne (now a motor showrooms), in addition to the Leinster Cinema (latterly an ice skating rink) completed in the same year (Scuffil, 1993). The buildings had to stand out, and in Ireland, the Art Deco and International styles were both applied to cinema architecture, since these new styles were seen as being in keeping with the 'modern' image of cinema (Rothery, 1991).

Selling or renting?

As has been previously discussed, the early part of the twentieth century, roughly up to the end of World War I, lacked the present-day ideology of home ownership. Renting was socially acceptable for all classes, although different grades of tenure, which ranged from weekly tenancies to seven-year leases, were a reflection of class differences (Thompson, 1988). In Britain, due to unfavourable mortgage rates, some 90 per cent of all houses were rented on leases of up to three years (Muthesius, 1982). While comparative figures are not available for Ireland, it is likely that the proportion was similar. Put another way, about ten per cent of all new houses built from 1890 were being bought by owner occupiers, and there was a growing tendency to erect speculatively for sale (Jackson, 1973). Generally, house-ownership was vested in housing landlords, who could own from two to several hundred houses, most often in scattered clutches. Owner-landlords included local tradespeople, shopkeepers, professional people, retirees and widows. Often the builder, having covered his outlays by selling many of the houses he had built, would retain some and set up as a landlord himself. Significantly, Thompson (1988) notes that a builder would often live in one of his own houses as proof of confidence in the product, and as a convenience while building was going on nearby. In the study of Alexander Strain this philosophy will be seen in operation on a grand scale. Incidentally, it is thought that builders sometimes incorporated variations in decorative brickwork for a very specific purpose, so that rent collectors could recognize their clients' houses by these distinctive trademarks.

In the early years of the study, when owner occupancy was relatively unusual, the structure of the rental sector was quite complex. Various rungs existed on the property-owning ladder, which often included the builders themselves. The big-time investors could hold large and varied portfolios of properties, as seen from auction notices, whereas smaller capitalists, including shopkeepers and widows, might own one or two houses which were rented out for specified periods. Among those selling or letting houses in the early years of the century were Patrick Cotter, family grocer, tea, wine and spirit merchant, with premises at 42 & 44 Drumcondra Road, and his neighbour, Thomas J. Lawler, Victualler, of 46 Drumcondra Road. Similarly, Mrs Mary Delany, Fruiterer, of 26 Drumcondra Road, and James Doyle, another grocer, of 17 Denmark Street, invested the profits from their businesses in property. Thus, as is the case in modern-day office developments, building cycles were related not just to demand for houses, but also to the relative merits of other investment opportunities.

Some houses were clearly sold as investments, as in the 1906 sale of a six-roomed, vacant, double-bay window house on St Patrick's Road, with a letting value of £34, leaving seven per cent interest, which was being sold, presumably by the previous investor who lived at 52 St Alphonsus Road, for £310 (*Freeman's Journal*, 14 April 1906). Often groups of houses, rather than single houses, were purchased as an investment. (These might be later auctioned, as in the case of the interest in the lease of 163 and 165 Fane Valley Terrace (Botanic Avenue), two well-built cottage houses auctioned in 1905 (*Freeman's*

Journal, 13 May 1905). The lease was held for 400 years from April 1902 at £10, while the gross rental was £46. Similarly, in 1920 Battersby & Co. offered 16-23 Millmount Place, being 'neat modern houses', subject to £3 each. Holden's Showrooms advertised the auction of three 'nice' houses on Wellpark Avenue, in the *Freeman's Journal* of 18 April 1908, since the owner was going abroad. These were clearly being sold as an investment, with a 102-year lease and a rent of £3 10s. each. When four houses on Susanville Road were being re-sold in 1919, the advertisement specifically appealed to potential investors. The lease was for 390 years from 1915, with a ground rent of £15 for the entire, on monthly lettings of £35 7s. 8d. each (*Freeman's Journal,* 15 March 1919). Presumably the total rent per annum for each of the houses was £35, but the houses were let by the month rather than by the year, suggesting an intermediate status between the lowly St Joseph's cottages, with their weekly tenancies, and the more common annual basis for tenancies.

In 1906, Macarthur & Co. advertised the auction of 44, 45, 46, 47 De Courcy Square, described as being a very desirable investment, consisting of four nice, modern cottages, with a nice outlook, within one minute's walk of the penny tram to the GPO, and each with a garden in front. The houses were constantly let, one at £36 including taxes, the rest at £26, and the lease was for 440 years, with a head rent of £12 (*Freeman's Journal,* 19 May 1906). This example illustrates the structure of the property market, where the landowner had let the land on which the houses were built at £12 p.a., while the occupants of the houses were paying rent to the house-owner, who did not own the land on which the houses were built. Even when houses were sold to owner occupiers, the title of the land was often vested in a ground landlord, so that a small amount of ground rent was paid every year. It was unusual, in the period under consideration, for the land to be held in fee simple by the house occupier. In 1920, however, Battersby & Co. offered the house known as Glenaboy, Botanic Road, for auction. This was an 'excellent semi-detached residence with possession' which would be 'sold free of rent forever' (*Freeman's Journal,* 24 April 1920). In the 1970s, when many ground leases expired, there was considerable controversy over the question of ground rents which eventually led to the outright purchase of many house plots rather than the renegotiation of rents.

Some housing investments were offered through classified advertisements using box numbers, as in the case of two advertisements in the *Freeman's Journal* of 1905. The first offered a terrace of eight substantially built houses, with hot baths and perfect sanitation, in a high and healthy position, '£325 each, pay eight per cent' (*Freeman's Journal,* 20 May 1905). A few weeks later,

88 'The new way', a 1930s advertisement for electricity.

a similar advertisement offered a 'Bargain – Terrace of modern new houses, hot baths, perfect sanitation, producing a profit rent of £208; to prompt purchaser for £2500' (*Freeman's Journal*, 1 July 1905). In the first case, the houses were being offered to potential occupiers, with a built-in loan, while the second was selling the terrace as an investment.

A wide range of housing was available for letting in the first two decades of the century. At the lowest end of the market, a small number of houses were advertised for letting at weekly rents of from 6s. 6d. to 9s. These were among the poorest cottages in the area, and it is a wonder that they were advertised at all. For example, the cottages being let in St Joseph's Avenue for 6s. 6d. per week in 1906 had just three rooms, and 'features' included a yard, w.c., coal

100

Years Ago

The Alliance & Dublin Consumers

GAS COMPANY

was formed and supplied gas within a limited area of the city. Since then the industry has made tremendous strides and steadily increased its radius of distribution.

To-day the Gas Service Department supplies "fuel on tap" for Lighting, Heating, Cooking and Power over an area of 35 square miles, through 700 miles of pipe-line from Dollymount on the north of Dublin to Bray on the south and inland to Castleknock and Foxrock.

It is one of the largest Irish Industries, and in view of the increasing popularity of Gas for industrial and domestic use is growing to still larger proportions.

Offices: D'OLIER STREET, DUBLIN.

Showrooms and Distribution Offices:

10 HAWKINS STREET, DUBLIN

89 'The traditional way', a late 1920s advertisement for gas.

vault, sanitation, Vartry (water) and gas. For an extra shilling per week, a four-roomed cottage on the same street and 'newly done down' could be had. Nine shillings per week paid the rent of 2 Lismore Terrace, Botanic Avenue, a four-roomed dwelling with pantry, coalhouse, w.c., gas, close range, which, like its 8s. p.w. neighbour, boasted good gardens and penny tram to the pillar.

Monthly rental was relatively unusual, based on a survey of newspaper advertisements, but was mentioned in a number of advertisements in 1919.

The first of these was a portfolio of rental property being sold by the executors of the O'Hanlon Estate, which included 'eight neat modern houses' in Carlingford Road, of which three were let on monthly tenancies at £28 15s. p.a., while the remainder were let on weekly tenancies from £27 6s. to £28 15s. p.a. The ground rent was £4 4s. for each house, while the lease was for 450 years. The auctioneers notice appeals to investors, stating that 'the situation is select and convenient, where houses are much sought after. This sale, therefore, should appeal to buyers of best class medium-sized property'. Huggard & Co. offered a well-furnished house on Iona Road, with nine apartments and every convenience for £12 12s. monthly or £8 for half a house. This advertisement shows how expensive houses had become, since £60 p.a. was the asking price for other Iona Road houses in 1914 and again in 1917.

Frequently, advertisements for houses 'to let or sell' were placed in newspapers by the builders, such as Daniel Daly's Hollybank Road houses built in 1905 which cost £38 to rent, or £312 to purchase, for a 'compact house, six apartments, hot bath, perfect sanitation and good garden' (*Freeman's Journal*, 22 July 1905). In the same year, Molloy's 'nice terrace of two storey houses' at Wellpark Avenue, which also boasted six rooms and hot and cold baths, in addition to being 'up to date', with bay windows, a splendid high and healthy position, sanitary certificate and College Green tram direct, cost £34 per annum rental, or 'will be sold reasonably' (*Freeman's Journal*, 20 May 1905 and 1 July 1905). However, even as early as 1911, some builders seem to have abandoned the option of letting, and tended to sell all of their houses. One such builder was Daniel Daly of Botanic Avenue, who was selling two 'substantially well-finished houses with up-to-date improvements, electric light, perfect sanitation' on Iona Road in 1911 for an undisclosed sum (*Freeman's Journal*, 15 April 1911). As the trend towards using house agents continued, however, some houses on Iona Road continued to be advertised to be let or sold. In 1914, James H. North (Auctioneer) offered 'one of these favourite houses', containing two reception, four bedrooms, hot bath, servant's room, electric light, large garden and side entrance, for £60 p.a. rent, landlord paying taxes, or for sale at £660 (*Freeman's Journal*, 7 March 1914). After this date, there appear to be very few advertised examples of the 'let/sell' option, although some houses continued to be sold specifically as investments. The builder of St Michael's Terrace, Upper Drumcondra Road, offered one or more of his double bay window villas, which possessed every modern improvement, in addition to large gardens, for sale in 1908. These were, importantly, described as 'suitable for own occupation', showing that Whelan was appealing to both the investor and owner occupier (*Freeman's Journal*, 14 March 1908).

The 1908 seller of a 'nice modern three-storey house' offers one possible reason for a builder to avail of the anonymity of a box number. In this case, there is a 'large reduction', while other examples noted that a prompt sale was sought. A builder who was in financial difficulties, or having trouble off-loading houses, would not wish to advertise the fact. Similar reasoning would have encouraged builders like Alexander Strain to make their sales through a third party, increasing the difficulty of discovering the identity of many of the builders working at this time.

This gradual trend towards ownership from the 1910s was strongly encouraged by Irish Government policy post-independence, while the declining economic returns to be gained from landlordism when compared to other forms of investment led to a decrease in the availability of houses for letting. Part of the reason for this change can be traced to World War I. At the end of the war it cost at least four times as much to build a small house in London as it had done in 1914, due to increases in the cost of materials, labour, high interest rates and the demand for higher standards of amenity (Jackson, 1973). Even in 1922, building costs in Ireland were three times what they had been before 1914. As a result, the economic rent was beyond the reach of those for whom the houses were designed. In this situation investors deserted the housing market. Up to 1914 private development had been mostly restricted to properties for renting, the incentive for developers and builders lying in the profits to be secured by building on relatively cheap land on the suburban fringe, using capital provided by building societies, landowners, trust funds and banks, and selling the houses as an investment ('as safe as houses'). The money thus obtained was used to finance further developments. Now in the post-war period, many of those who would at one time have invested in rental housing probably deposited their money in building societies, thus exchanging one form of housing investment for another.

References to 'possession' begin to appear in advertisements from about 1912, and over the next decade or more the trend towards sale of houses to owner occupiers becomes increasingly apparent, so that by the mid-1920s almost all newspaper-advertised houses were for sale. Many builders advertised that a portion of the purchase money might remain outstanding, thus, in effect, offering a loan facility to prospective purchasers. Of course, it took a long time for the changeover from private rental to owner occupation to be completed. As late as 1931, Mr Casey's advertisement for a new house at Mount Prospect Avenue illustrates that, while owner occupancy was now increasingly common, builders would provide various options for their clients.

His house cost £1000 (18s. 4d. or to let at £120) (*Irish Times*, 28 March 1931). In general, these Mount Prospect Avenue dwellings were at the upper end of the middle-class market, offering maid's rooms as well as garages, representing the old and new status symbols.

In both Britain and Ireland, home ownership became more common from the 1920s, and houses were now built for mortgage rather than for rental. The structure of housing ownership thus became less complex than previously. However, the large-scale conversion to owner-occupation was not necessarily a deliberate choice, as recognized by the Housing Inquiry of 1939-43. The report claimed that if white-collar families wanted a new house, they had virtually no alternative but to buy. Although purchase was becoming more common, three-quarters of civil servants still rented accommodation in 1932 (Farmar, 1995). Private building in the 1920s and 1930s focused on the provision of middle-class suburban dwellings. There was a general increase in the size of developments, and a greater tendency for speculators to plan their activities at the start of building operations. Thus, layout plans would be submitted to the Corporation covering a complete estate, although that estate might be built over five or six years. Houses in the 1920s generally conformed to certain size restrictions which allowed the builder to benefit from Government grants, so that there was a general lack of variety in suburban housing built during the period. During the 1930s, it would appear that the market for houses was becoming saturated, and builders had to work harder to sell their wares. As a result, there was an increase in advertising, and many more speculators offered purchase rental arrangements on new private housing. The average density of suburban housing estates conformed to the 'garden suburb' norm of 12 houses per acre (c.30 houses per ha), while there was a limited awareness of tree preservation and cul-de-sac planning among speculators. However, most speculative housing schemes remained unimaginative in layout, with long straight streets, while private gardens rather than public open space was preferred.

Owner occupation was facilitated by a piece of 1899 legislation, the Small Dwellings Acquisition Act, which was introduced by the British Government to encourage home-ownership, as discussed previously. Under the Act, the local authority, in this case Dublin Corporation, could provide loans enabling people to acquire the ownership of small houses in which they intended to reside, or actually did reside. By the time of publication of the *Civic Survey* (1925), just over 25 years later, it was being suggested that these loans were particularly availed of by Dublin's middle classes, at a time when speculative building operations were widespread, and the cost of building low.

Prior to 1914, just over 300 loans were made by Dublin Corporation under this Act. The interest charged was 4 per cent p.a. on up to 75 per cent of the value of the houses. Since the maximum value of the houses for which loans could be granted was £400, this meant that anyone who could afford a £100 down-payment was in a position to purchase their own home (later amendments increased the maximum house value). As with all mortgages, once the loans were fully paid, the interest in the premises would be transferred to the new owners. However, if borrowers failed to pay their instalments, the houses purchased would revert to the Corporation. Advances made for the purchase of houses under the Small Dwellings Acquisition Act of 1899 were noted in the Estates and Finance Committee's accounts for each quarter. A selection from the Drumcondra area for 1912 and 1913 shows that loans of between £132 and £300 were granted on properties in Millmount Avenue, St Anne's Road, Claude Road, Arran Road, Iona Crescent, Drumcondra Park, Wigan Road, Home Farm Road, Lindsay Road, Clare Road, some of which were quite substantial houses. Numbers 2 and 3 Woodville Road had been bought under the SDAA, but by 1912 both had reverted to the Estates and Finance Committee and were later resold (Report 274/1912, Report 141/1913).

Speculative builders naturally took advantage of the SDAA, and probably priced their houses accordingly. In 1905, a 'superior house' on Botanic Road was advertised for sale. It had seven rooms, hot bath, comfortable garden, and offered 'sound value' at £390, on a 999-year lease, subject to £5. In addition, it was noted that this house could be purchased under the SDAA. The advertisement could have been placed by an owner, but it seems more likely that this was a builder. Similarly, an advertisement placed in 1911 for a house in Upper Drumcondra, notes that it 'could be bought through Corporation' (*Freeman's Journal*, 22 April 1911). The price of £260 seems rather low for a five-bedroomed house which also boasts a parlour, kitchen, servant's room, hot and cold bath, in addition to a healthy position and green fields at the back.

From the late 1920s until the loans were stopped in 1938, the Small Dwellings Acquisition Act became an increasingly important means by which families could buy their own homes. The mortgages between 1925 and 1930 were for up to 75 per cent of the value of the houses, with a maximum term of 40 years, but later advances were for up to 80 per cent of the market value. The high number of loans made to purchasers at this time is a reflection of the building boom under the 1920s Housing Acts. Middle-class private housing was now within the reach of many, as local authorities and the Government provided loans to builders and potential owners, fuelling a large increase in building, often by public utility societies. However, as previously discussed, by the end of the 1930s, the SDAA had become extremely unpopular within the Corporation, which felt that its role was to house those who could not afford to pay a deposit on a house. By this time, it was claimed that anyone with £50 was in a position to get accommodation from a public utility society or a housing society.

While Dublin Corporation was one source of loans for house purchasers, it is thought that at least three-quarters of new houses bought in the 1920s and 1930s were obtained by building society mortgage.

> Buy your home and pay for it with the rent through the unique house purchasing scheme of the Munster and Leinster Assurance Society.
>
> *Irish Times*, 9 March 1929

> House Purchase loans from Irish Civil Service Permanent Building Society. Established over 75 years. Repayments 5 to 20 years. No Waiting List.
>
> *Irish Times*, 20 September 1943

The initial cash deposit assumed less importance in the 1930s, and above all the prospective purchaser had to be able to maintain regular payments. Building societies developed a 'safe rule' that total outgoings on house purchase, including local rates, should not exceed a quarter of the net income.

Sometimes loan facilities were made available through the builders, as seen in the advertisements mentioned in the previous section. Meanwhile, other means were also available for house purchase. For example, members of the Amalgamated Engineering Union, headquartered in London, could avail of a Superannuation Reserve Fund which provided loans to facilitate house purchase.

Physical planning and provision of infrastructure in private schemes

> Deliberate planning rarely intervened to spoil the variety and unpredictability of the process. The one universal characteristic was wasteful use of land.
>
> (Jackson, 1973, p. 116)

For the private developer operating in the early twentieth century, the above quotation generally held true, with little apparent foresight in laying out developments. In Glasnevin, for example, one of the link roads between Iona and Lindsay Roads has no name and no houses, just dead space (figure 101). In many cases, roads followed less-than-direct paths. This could be due to the fragmented nature of land-holdings or to restrictive clauses in the leases of building ground. Sometimes they simply followed the meanderings of old farm tracks. This had the effect of making access difficult and also sometimes encircled backland under separate ownership, making its subsequent development more difficult. Unfortunately, the issue of layout was one over which the local authority had very little control. As long as plans accorded with bylaw regulations the Corporation had no powers (other than persuasion) to prevent development prior to the 1934 Town and Regional Planning Act.

Lack of spending power was (and remains) a restrictive factor influencing what planning can achieve. Because planners must rely on the private sector and other local authority spending departments for the execution of plans, they are in a weak position in relation to development interests, especially during slump periods in the housing construction industry. Political pressure at such times weighs heavily in favour of getting any development going for the sake of employment in the construction industry. In addition to high unemployment in the 1920s and 1930s, the Corporation was faced with a shortage of housing, and thus saw the need to encourage building at almost any cost, while any addition to the Corporation's income from rates was also welcomed. Even before the advent of a Planning Act, the Corporation enjoyed an element of control over development through its bylaws, but all too often the bylaws were put aside for the reasons referred to above. Unless it was prepared to take what the developer was willing to offer, sometimes with token adjustments, the Corporation ran the risk of a scheme being abandoned altogether.

Sometimes, in any case, the bylaws were over-stringent. In the case of proposed new roads and cottages at Fassaght Lane, Phibsborough for the Dublin United Tramways Company, the Paving Committee recommended the suspension of the bylaw requiring a 42-foot ($c.13$ m) wide roadway on the three new roads. Firstly, the 27-foot ($c.8$ m) width was deemed ample with regard to the height of the 33 one-storey cottages; the roads, being culs-de-sac, were unimportant as regards traffic; the scheme would provide employment; and the scheme would result in increased revenue to the Corporation in the form of rates (Report 150/1912).

In Autumn 1907, Alexander Strain had submitted plans for five new streets to the Improvements Committee for consideration. The plans were approved with the exception of the proposed extension of Hollybank Road. Here Strain proposed a width of 42 feet ($c.13$ m), whilst the width of the existing road was

90 Hollybank Road was eventually completed by the addition of a block of shops.
Note the width of the road. (Photograph by J. Brady.)

55 feet (*c*.17 m), and he also requested that the Corporation should extend the
existing sewer, at an estimated cost of £40. Neither of these proposals was
accepted. The narrowing of the extension as proposed was not recommended
on the grounds that it would completely destroy the building line; while the
Corporation wished to avoid the expense of extending the sewer (Report
235/1907). By 1913, Strain had altered his plans somewhat, agreeing to make
the Hollybank Road extension 52 feet (*c*.16 m) wide, still three feet (*c*.1 m)
narrower than the existing roadway. As a result, the Paving Committee was
favourably disposed towards suspending the bylaws in the case of Strain's
proposed two new roadways off Iona Crescent, the total widths of which
would be 36 feet (*c*.11 m) rather than the bylaw minimum of 42 feet (*c*.13 m)
(Report 114/1913). Strain's extension of Hollybank Road was intended to be
one of the main arteries connecting Drumcondra Road with Botanic Road,
but this was never built. In fact, the continuation of Hollybank Road was not
undertaken until the 1920s, the last work completed by Strain in his Iona
development. It seems likely that this delay was due to failed negotiations
between Strain and the Carroll Estate over the acquisition of the land on
which two factories were soon to be built. As a consequence, Hollybank Road
is one of the widest in the district but is truncated by a row of shops at its

western end. Traffic must come to a halt (often screeching) before turning left into the much narrower Iona Crescent or going right into the narrower-still lane leading to Mannix Road.

On the other hand, in some cases, the bylaws were not strong enough to prevent unwise development. In 1915, J.J. Flanagan submitted plans for new houses at Wellpark Avenue and Arran Road (figure 92). The awkward angle of Wellpark Avenue is explained by its previous incarnation as 'Watery Lane', a farm laneway. Three months later the City Engineer brought the plans lodged by Mr Flanagan before the Paving Committee, for consideration in regard to the questions of widening Wellpark Avenue and the desirability of continuing Arran Road out to Wellpark Avenue, instead of making it a cul-de-sac as proposed. However, the Law Agent had considered whether the Committee had the power to compel Mr Flanagan to carry out the Engineer's suggestions, and advised that if the proposals shown on the plans were in accordance with the bylaws the Corporation could not refuse its approval. Mr Flanagan could not be compelled to continue Arran Road to Wellpark Avenue, as compulsory purchase was 'at present out of the question'. This case underlines the extreme limitations of the bylaws as a planning too.

Even where the Corporation refused permission on the grounds that a development failed to comply with bylaws, there was no guarantee that development would not take place anyway. In the early 1920s, the City Architect reported that the Ryan Manufacturing and Construction Co. had proceeded with the erection of new buildings at Seaview Avenue, Clontarf, despite the fact that he had disapproved the plans, for the reason that the method of construction of the houses did not comply with the Corporation bylaws. The Company was informed that it was proceeding with the building at its own risk. When the same Company submitted a block plan for the erection of houses and bungalows at Victoria Park and Haddon Park, Clontarf, the plan was returned with a notice of disapproval (Report 36/1921). However, the construction company clearly appealed to a higher authority, the Local Government Board, since, by the time of the next breviate, a communication had been received from the Local Government Board Housing Department, intimating that they had approved of the 'Orion' form of construction as defined in the documents lodged with them by the Ryan Manufacturing and Construction Co. Ltd. Not only was the Corporation thwarted in its attempts to prevent this form of building, but the LGB noted that the Company was entitled to full grants under the Housing (Additional Powers) Act, 1919 (Report 56/1921).

The Corporation had a blind-spot about the building of industry in the midst of a developing residential area. The Carroll Estate (Prospect), Glasnevin was situated on Botanic Road, Glasnevin, bounded by Iona Road, Iona Park, Marguerite Road and Botanic Road. Reference has already been made to 1914 plans for the development of the Carroll Estate with three new roads and over 100 houses. However, the proposed residential scheme was never built, and the road connection from Botanic to Drumcondra Road proposed by both Strain and Bradbury was never made. The next reference to the site is made in the March Quarter, 1918, when Messrs Alexander Thom & Co. Ltd. communicated with the Paving Committee regarding a proposal to erect a printing factory similar to the one formerly in Middle Abbey St (destroyed in 1916) on the 'O'Carroll Estate' (Report 98/1918). They required to know whether any difficulty would be placed in their way by the Corporation as regards facilities for constructing and running the factory. The decision not to build houses on the land was probably for financial reasons. Perhaps Thom's offer for the site was too attractive to refuse, while the cost of road building was probably a discouragement to residential building. It appears that the Corporation did not obstruct this development although it took a full two years before plans and specifications for the proposed new printing works were submitted. The Thom's printing works was soon joined by Messrs Player & Sons who erected a cigarette factory. Suburban locations were increasingly being chosen by new industry, beginning a process that has continued to the present. In addition to their use of prime building land for the factory, Players were responsible for the erection of houses for their employees and managerial staff. The better houses were built on the Hollybank Road extension, probably by George Wearing, with the houses for workers on Botanic Avenue.

J.J. Flanagan, Kyle House and the Corporation

Joseph J. Flanagan was a contemporary of Alexander Strain's who built in the Drumcondra area for at least 30 years. His building activity is remarkable in its apparently confined range, since all known construction work by Flanagan was undertaken within a radius of less than half a mile (0.8 km). He is typical of the old-style builder, in that his style of house changed little over the period in which he worked. The earliest houses by Flanagan were on Wellpark Avenue and St Mary's Road (now Home Farm Road), built from c.1906. These houses are extraordinarily similar to Strain's Iona houses, including all of the features which make the latter's houses so desirable, such as bay

91 The impressive facade of the Player's factory on Botanic Road.
(Photograph by J. Brady.)

windows, granite sills, tiled porches and interior plasterwork. The land on which he built was owned by the Butterly family, and the Achill and Arran Road junctions with Home Farm Road were laid out prior to development. In 1912, Mrs E. Flanagan lived at Coolmount, 20 Achill Road, presumably one of the builder's own houses, but the family soon moved to nearby Drumcondra Road.

Unlike Strain's land acquisition in the 1890s, it appears that Flanagan obtained his building land in a very piecemeal fashion, described below, although he eventually built up most of one section of Drumcondra Road. Much land in the Drumcondra area was vested in Dublin Corporation, and in late 1912 the Estates and Finance Committee decided to offer the premises known as Kyle House for letting by public auction. The auction of Kyle House was finally held in July 1915, offering a 150-year building lease, with an expenditure of £1400. J.J. Flanagan offered a rent of £29, which was considered excellent given that the existing structure was of very little value and the greater part would have to be taken down (Report 205/1915). The site had a frontage to Drumcondra Road of 99 feet (*c.*30 m), with an average depth of 200 feet (*c.*61 m), and presumably Flanagan intended to use the land for building purposes. In the meantime, however, the urban/rural mix in the

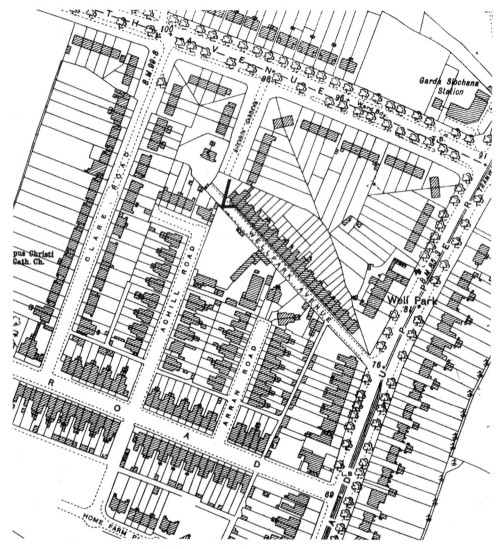

92 Layout of Clare, Arran and Wellpark roads, Drumcondra.
(Ordnance Survey 1:2500 plan, Sheet 18 III, Dublin, 1938 revision.)

suburb is emphasized by his 1916 plans for a new house and *cow shed* at Kyle House (Report 20/1917). When the lease on a portion of the City Estate adjoining Kyle House expired in 1918, the occupying tenant, Mr James D'Arcy, applied for a building lease of the holding, having arranged with Mr Flanagan that they would jointly build on the site.

In addition to his interests on Drumcondra Road, Flanagan maintained an interest in the Wellpark Avenue and Arran Road area, lodging plans to build new houses there in September 1915. The City Engineer suggested that Wellpark Avenue should be widened, and that Arran Road should be continued out to Wellpark Avenue, but in fact, the Corporation was unable to insist on good planning in this case. Similarly, when the City Engineer considered Flanagan's plans for ten houses on Arran Road in March 1916, he found that two of them (Nos. 26 and 28) had the building face of houses placed at an angle between the houses No. 23 and 24 but, as there was no properly defined building line, the Paving Committee decided to approve the plans (Report 108/1916). Thus the houses at the end of Arran Road presented a crooked face to the world, and prevented the joining of Arran Road to Wellpark Avenue.

In September 1920, J.J. Flanagan submitted plans for the erection of eight additional houses on Arran Road. Four were on the west side at the end of the road, two faced directly south, closing off the northern end of the road to Wellpark Avenue, and two more were facing south-west, with reres also extending to Wellpark Avenue. Flanagan proposed applying to the Government for a grant in aid under the 1919 Housing (Additional Powers) Act towards the cost of the new houses. The City Engineer suggested (once again) that Arran Road should be carried through to Wellpark Avenue, which would necessitate the abandonment of the proposed houses closing off the northern end of Arran Road. However, the need for houses was considered more pressing than planning considerations, as the Local Government Board was prepared to approve the erection of all eight houses, making a grant of £260 per house towards the cost of building.

> We referred the question to the Inspection Committee, who reported that they did not consider the connecting of Arran Road to Wellpark Avenue of greater importance than having houses built at the present juncture, when there is such a scarcity of housing accommodation. They were also informed by Mr Flanagan that there was a clause in his lease forbidding him to build any houses facing Wellpark Avenue. They accordingly recommended that his plans be sanctioned …
>
> (Report 252/1920, p. 550)

Flanagan was still building on Arran Road as late as November, 1924, when plans for a 'villa' and garage were approved.

The Corporation was not entirely ineffectual. The terms of its leases could also be used to discourage development. Joseph J. Flanagan had held a plot with a 110-foot (c.34 m) frontage to Drumcondra Road between Kyle House and Ivy House since 1917, but because this was a yearly tenancy, only one cottage stood on the plot. In 1926, following negotiations with Flanagan, the Finance and General Purposes Section of the Corporation finally recommended that the plots adjoining Kyle House be let on a 150-year lease at a rent of £50 per annum. The lease was granted subject to the erection on the site within one year of four shops with dwellings over, in accordance with plans to be approved of by the City Architect. A strip of ground along the frontage, having an average depth of *c.*30 feet (9 m), was reserved from letting, in connection with the contemplated widening of Drumcondra Road (Report 217/1926).

In July 1928 a further plot of ground on Upper Drumcondra Road which had been acquired by the Corporation from All Hallows College in connection with the widening of the thoroughfare was leased by Dublin Corporation to Mr J.J. Flanagan. The plot on the eastern side of Upper Drumcondra Road running north from Charlotte Place contained a frontage of 930 feet (*c.*283 m), which was 200 feet (*c.*61 m) deep. Again the Corporation used the terms of the lease as a way of controlling development. In this case, the 150-year lease was granted at a rent of £220 per annum, over and above rates and taxes, on condition that Flanagan would build 24 two-storeyed semi-detached houses, for use as residences only, and two residential shops costing £1000 each. The two residential shops were to be built on the portion of ground immediately adjoining Charlotte Place.

The above examples illustrate the absence of planning control in Drumcondra into the mid-1920s. Bylaws proved ineffectual as a means of control, and the Corporation generally seems to have taken an over-liberal stance regarding the operations of private builders. Of course, the Corporation, like the Township Commission which preceded it, stood to gain by rapid development of the area, which would increase the revenue from rates. The builders were, by nature, opportunists, who would tend to make decisions based on business rather than planning considerations. In the context of the time, it is not surprising that the Corporation allowed builders to behave in such a hap-hazard manner, but for the present-day observer it is easy to criticize the lack of planning in the area, the intermixing of industrial and residential uses which has become a headache for present residents, and the absence of key road connections, especially in the case of Hollybank Road/Iona Crescent.

Role of the Catholic parish in development

Dublin experienced noticeable demographic changes in the nineteenth century. Population was both attracted to the urban area and at the same time withdrawing from its centre, preferring to settle in the expanding suburbs. Population moving from the city core gave rise to the need for new suburban parishes which were themselves subdivided later as they continued to grow (O Fearghail, 1992). The parish provided an administrative network for the Church, but also formed a framework for a complex mesh of Roman Catholic institutions whose influence permeated the very fabric of society. Nowhere is this more evident than in the Drumcondra and Glasnevin area. Lay support and involvement in such institutions and associations produced social and spiritual integration of the parish communities, while the parish came to have some importance as a spatial unit, being used by sporting associations such as the GAA clubs, while Catholic-run schools and parish halls became centres for all sorts of social activities.

An account of the development of the parish of St Columba illuminates an issue of some note in the area. A conversation with Father John Byrne, priest responsible for the erection of the church on Iona Road, costing over £20,000 and with seating for 1250 people, in 1905 is reported: 'Father Byrne was asked by a friend one day – "What do you want such a large church for, Father? Where are the people to come from?" He replied – "The day will come when it will not be large enough"' (Egan, 1961, p. 8). These remarks are significant given the predominantly Protestant nature of development in the area. The impression given is of an aggressive Roman Catholic approach, with the building on high ground of a very large and imposing church visible for considerable distances (as was Corpus Christi church further north), Roman Catholic schools and even plans for a Catholic University in the heart of this Protestant area. The name originally proposed for Crawford Avenue was, reputedly, Protestant Row, an indication of the importance of religious affiliation in the developing area.

The local clergy also had an impact on the shape of development in the area. In the December Quarter, 1914, a proposal was submitted to the Corporation by Venerable Archdeacon Gorman, Parish Priest of Drumcondra-Glasnevin for the construction of a short length of new road from Crawford Avenue to Iona Road, along the convent wall. The new road would greatly convenience the residents of Drumcondra, as it would link up Crescent Villas with Iona Road, and thereby facilitate traffic from Hollybank Road and district to St Columba's Church. Archdeacon Gorman agreed to provide the land free of cost, and to dedicate the road to the use of the public when completed, if the Corporation would undertake to construct the road. Legally, however, the Paving Committee could not undertake to do this, but it was empowered to provide the materials

93 Church of St Columba, Iona Road. (Photograph by J. Brady.)

to make the road, which it hoped would be constructed by the Distress Committee. Some £330 was to be provided to pay for the cost of materials and labour for the new road (Report 229/1915).

In the March Quarter, 1916, Mr Alexander Strain made a proposal to have the new road recently constructed connecting Crawford Avenue and Iona Road continued on a portion of *his* ground. For this purpose, he expressed his willingness to hand over the necessary ground to Dublin Corporation free of charge. The Corporation agreed to the proposal, on the understanding that Mr Strain would bear the cost of concreting and kerbing the footways on the extended portion of the road. The cost to the Corporation would be £60. In the June Quarter of the same year, the Paving Committee agreed to Archdeacon O'Gorman's suggestion that the new road from Crawford Avenue to Iona Road be named Gartan Road, after the birthplace of St Columba. Thus, Church, Corporation and private developer (and a Protestant at that!) had worked together, for different reasons, to complete one road.

Further clerical intervention, aimed at improving access to the church, was recorded in later Corporation reports. In 1926, Michael Nugent of Greenmount handed a portion of his land over to the Corporation to form a 60 yard (*c*.55 m) passage connecting Marguerite Road with Iona Park, to accommodate persons attending St Columba's Church and schools. The roadway was constructed under the Unemployment Relief Grant, 1925–26, and an expenditure of £20 1s. 10d. was incurred in the purchase of a fence. However, this fence was considered unsuitable by Mr Nugent, and a more expensive one supplied, the extra cost being borne by the Revd Fr Nolan, Parish Priest of St Columba's, Iona Road (Report 4/1928). In 1929, the same Revd Fr Nolan proposed the construction of a pathway connecting the overhead bridge at Claude Road with St Brendan's Road, which was carried out at the expense of the parishioners (Report 22/1930).

Taking in charge of roads

In the earlier part of the study period, the making of both roads and sewers was the responsibility of the builder, a point emphasized by Edward McMahon in his evidence to the 1885 Housing Inquiry. When a road was completed (that is, when it was fully built upon), it could be taken in charge by the local authority, after which time that body became responsible for its upkeep. Local bylaws meant that a road would not be taken in charge unless it was completed to certain specifications, and had been fully built upon. In addition, the Corporation would charge the occupiers for any costs incurred in making a road fit to be taken in charge, although sometimes these charges were waived where the local residents were thought to be unable to pay, as in the case of frontagers – a term used by the Corporation to refer to people with property that fronted onto a road – of St Brigid's Road Upper, St Clement's Road and St Columba's Road in 1916.

The requirement that the road be completely built upon caused difficulties for many builders who tended to build slowly over a prolonged period. In 1914, a report considering the taking in charge of three roads in the Iona area (Iona Crescent, from Iona Drive to No. 44, Crescent Villas, from Iona Crescent to Crawford Avenue, Crawford Avenue, from No. 2 to No. 20 inclusive) noted that the roads were in all respects in a fit condition to be taken in charge of the Corporation, with the exception that in one case the road was not fully built upon (Report 143/1914). It was argued that it would be a great hardship to the owner of these roads if they were not taken in charge, since the houses to be built on some of these roads were proposed to be sold under the provisions of the Small Dwellings Acquisition Act, under the terms of which the Corporation was deprived from advancing loans in relation to houses on roads which were not in charge of the Corporation. It was felt that the

Corporation's action in refusing to take the roads in charge would actually tend to retard the building of houses.

In the case of the neighbouring Carroll estate, the question of taking the new roads in charge before all the houses were built on them arose again. Plans for the development of this estate were received in 1914, for the construction of three new streets and the building of about 106 houses. Fourteen of the new houses were to front onto Botanic Road, which the Committee saw as an excellent opportunity to achieve an increase of about 14 feet in its width, with the surrender of a triangular piece of ground by Mr W.A. Carroll. The cheques were signed in 1915 and the work was duly undertaken (Report 26/1916). A letter from Mr Edwin Bradbury, Architect, quoted in the report, illustrates the state of mind of the builder at this time:

> My client proposes to construct new roads at his own expense in order to develop ground so that houses may be built upon it. It might be several years, say ten years, before the last plot in the estate were built upon; or it might even happen that some odd plots might not be built upon for very many years, and moreover, unless the roads are taken over by the Corporation on their completion, I understand that likely purchasers of the houses to be built would find it practically impossible to obtain loans under the Small Holdings Act or from Building Societies …
>
> (Report 263/1914, p. 531)

The argument advanced in this letter is a further reminder of the nature of timescales which operated under the speculative development process. The builder was setting out to construct over one hundred houses, but it was likely that this could take anything up to ten years, depending on various factors.

A particular bone of contention was road 'X', a proposed continuation of Iona Crescent linking up with Botanic Road, which would form a considerable avenue of traffic between Drumcondra and Glasnevin districts. The responsibility of Mr Carroll to maintain this road 'for an unascertained and possibly lengthy period' would be onerous, and was likely to cause the deferral of its completion and linking up with Iona Crescent until the last possible moment. Indeed, this Corporation regulation was likely to deter builders from undertaking work altogether, a fact which was used to pressurize the local authority, as in the letter on behalf of Mr Carroll:

I may add that your Committee's proposal as regards the taking over of the roads by the Corporation ... if insisted upon, will probably make it incumbent upon my client to reconsider the advisability of carrying into effect the proposal for the construction of public roadways.

(Report 263/1914, p. 531)

In 1920, representations were made to the Improvements Committee of the Corporation, urging the carrying out of such improvements as were necessary to render Wellpark Avenue fit to be taken in charge. These included the construction of a macadam road, insertion of two new gullies, repair of concrete pathway and construction of manhole in existing sewer, costing an estimated £340 in total. In March 1925, the Streets Section recommended that Glendalough Road be taken in charge of the Corporation, although the street was not in good repair. The cost of macadamizing the roadway, constructing a concrete footpath, inserting two gullies and erecting a lamp, was estimated at £380.

Prior to the 1920s, the builder had to incur all costs involved in road building, and the road would be taken under Corporation control only after all houses had been built on it and if it was in a fit state. However, the attitude of the Corporation had gradually softened over time, as the desire to encourage building led to the waiving of this regulation in certain cases. Now, from the first of January, 1924, a special scheme was to operate for three years, by which the roads would be provided by the Corporation where schemes of sufficient size contained houses under a certain valuation. By the time of the Corporation's Drumcondra Housing Scheme, road construction and taking in charge of roads was viewed in a completely new light. In 1928, when the first leases were granted for private building in the 'reserved area', all roads and underground services were constructed by the Corporation free of expense to the lessees (Report 41/1928). Indeed, one of the main incentives to erect houses in the Corporation-sponsored schemes was the provision of roads and their taking in charge, thus guaranteeing the sale of houses to owners availing of the SDAA.

The organization of supplies of electricity and gas for private development is unclear, although once again, the Corporation's role was important, since its Electricity Department owned the generating capability for the city. Gas was mentioned in most of the house advertisements in the first decade of the century, most of which also showed the prevailing importance placed on hot and cold water supplies and modern sanitary facilities. Although these were Victorian innovations, they were not yet to be taken for granted. The earliest advertisements for houses with electricity appear *c.*1914, when an advertisement for the letting of 70 Drumcondra Road mentioned electric light among the amenities on offer (*Freeman's Journal,* 28 March 1914). In the following year, the *Freeman's Journal* carries an advertisement for Beechmount Villas, two new seven-roomed houses with electric light and bells as well as gas and hot presses. Gradually from the early 1920s, the supply of electricity, at least for lighting purposes, became more common. However, although the Corporation's houses at Marino were wired for electricity, gas was provided for cooking and lighting, and a battle was waged between gas and electricity suppliers throughout the 1920s and 1930s (figures 88 and 89).

In April 1925, over 1000 people visited three demonstration houses equipped by the Gas Company at Marino, including builders and architects as well as prospective tenants (*Irish Times,* 9 April 1925). In 1926, an increase in the use of gas was reported, while advertisements for 'all-gas' houses, such as those at Temple Park, Blackrock, were carried in the *Irish Times.* Experimental 'all-gas' homes were featured on the House Builders' page of the *Irish Times* in the 1930s, while advertisements in 1935 for the Westfield Estate, Harold's Cross boasted that these were 'all electric model residences'.

By the late 1920s, the area supplied by the City of Dublin Electricity Department was 13 square miles (*c.*34 km^2), from Clontarf to Inchicore, and from Rathmines to Glasnevin. As a result of the Corporation building scheme and private enterprise in Drumcondra, it was argued that approximately 1000 additional customers would be provided for the Electricity Department, so it was agreed that the cost of the electric cables for the scheme (estimated at £6450) would be charged against the funds of the Electricity Supply Department, thus reducing the costs of the scheme somewhat (Report 26/1928). The use of electricity was promoted at the electric showroom at 39 Grafton Street, which demonstrated the home comforts to be secured by a more general use of electricity. The showroom included model kitchen, diningroom, drawing room, bedroom and bathroom. In the 1930s, the ESB began to follow the Gas Company's lead, and in 1936 it had demonstration houses at Tyrconnell Road, Home Farm Park, and Greenfield Road, Mount Merrion.

Legislation and private housing schemes

We believe, in general, more houses could be got for the money available by subsidizing private builders than by subsidizing local authorities.

(Ernest Blythe, Minister for Local Government and
Public Health, 20 June 1923)

It is gratifying, in these days of socialism, to find the head of State disassociating himself from the foolish notions that some have, that the whole of such vast problems have only to be made a Government concern to be solved …

(Irish Builder and Engineer, 8 March 1924, p. 169)

The Government and local authority finance available to speculative builders has already been briefly considered. The impact of the 1919 Housing (Ireland) Act, as the first to acknowledge the importance of the private builder, was discussed, along with the series of legislative changes in the 1920s and 1930s which had a large impact on house-building by all sectors of the construction industry. Throughout the 1920s in particular, there was a recognition that the housing shortage was unlikely to be solved without the co-operation of private enterprise. The 1919 Act allowed the Government to make grants of up to £260 per house in the hopes that the measure would ease the immediate housing shortage following World War I, and both builders and private individuals benefited. However, the attempt to kick-start building operations was not entirely successful, and private development was slow to resume, particularly in the fraught conditions of the War of Independence and Civil War periods.

Thus, when the new Free State Government came to power, it persisted in its attempts to get private building started again, making State grants of between £60 and £100 per house available under the Housing (Building Facilities) Acts. From 1925 these grants applied to people building houses for sale or letting, as well as to those building houses for their own use, or public utility societies building houses for their members. Grants were occasionally transferred, as was the case when an application was received from the Saorstát Civil Service Public Utility Society for a subsidy under the 1925 Act, in respect of 19 houses on Clare Road, in lieu of a grant provisionally made for 19 houses at Cabra Road (Report 230/1926). Similar applications were approved for the transfer of grants provisionally allocated in respect of the building of a house on Home Farm Road, to a site on Old Finglas Road, and to the Civil Service PUS in respect of two houses, from Clare Road to Old Cabra Road (Report 269/1926).

The 1924 Housing (Building Facilities) Act, was designed to facilitate the provision of houses and to ensure the supply of building materials at reasonable prices. By now the housing problem had become even more acute, affecting 'the comfort, the health and the morale of the working and lower middle classes' *(Irish Builder and Engineer,* 17 May 1924, p. 429). Thus, the new Act was 'intended to transform the erection of small dwellings into a business proposition for landlord and tenant, builder and purchaser; it is neither a sop to greed, not does it connote charity'. The Act had many perceived benefits. The speculative builder could sell a house for £450 and still take a profit of £50. The local authority would, through the generosity of its rates remissions, in the long term see an increase in the rateable valuation of the district. The Government could see a family comfortably housed with a State grant of 20 per cent of the actual cost of building. A potential occupier who built a five-roomed house for £500 would receive 20 per cent as a free grant from the State, his ground rent would not exceed £5 per annum, and the rates over 20 years would average just half the normal rates. In addition, the local authority might grant him an additional 20 per cent of the cost, lend him 40 per cent of the cost, give him a site, or provide roads, sewers and other works of development free of charge. 'The keynote is the substantial inducement to a man with small capital, or who can raise a loan, to build and thus save himself the unproductive payment of annual rent; to a speculative builder to develop large areas and thus merge small individual profits into a not inconsiderable sum.' (Oculus, *Irish Builder and Engineer*, 17 May 1924, p. 429).

Main provisions under the Housing (Building Facilities) Act, 1924.

- Free grant to persons building for their own occupation, or for sale or letting, at £100, £80 and £60, for 5-, 4- and 3-roomed houses, respectively, less £10 per house when sewers and watermains are not available.
- Limitation of profits if a house, erected under the scheme, is sold. The maximum selling price of the three classes of houses is £450, £300 and £270, respectively.
- Limitation of ground rents to £1 per room.
- Limitation of rent on letting to eight per cent on the maximum permissible selling price, the tenant paying the rates.
- Remission of rates by the local authority to the extent of from 19/20ths in the first year to 1/20th in the 19th year.
- Limitation of size, thus ensuring that expenditure under the Act will benefit only those for whom its provisions are intended, while securing that reasonable accommodation will be provided. Minimum floor area = 520 square feet (*c*.48 m²), Maximum floor area = 1000 square feet (*c*.93 m²), extracted to 1500 square feet (*c*.139 m²) in the case of permanent civil servants who may wish to build.
- Provisions aimed at the prevention of profiteering in materials.

- Also opportunities for local authorities to assist further those intending to build:
    - free grant not exceeding amount of Government grant.
    - loan not exceeding twice amount of Government grant, repayable within a period not exceeding 15 years, with interest at the rate of ½ per cent above the rate at which the authority can borrow.
    - a grant or lease of a site.
    - works of development connected with the site.

In 1924 the amount of private speculative building being undertaken, especially for lower-middle-class occupation, remained small. According to the *Irish Builder and Engineer,* the limited success of the State-aided building scheme could be attributed to the 'unfair terms and conditions' under which the building owner was permitted to sell. Because the margin of profit was considered too low to cover the risk and loss of time involved, the scheme had not attracted speculative builders. Instead, the scheme had attracted a limited number of people who wanted a house for their own occupation and had enough capital to build it with the help of the State grant.

However, by the end of 1924 there were signs of a general revival in the building trade with the restoration of law and order. Several terraces of houses for selling and letting were being built in Dublin's suburbs by the end of the year. Among the largest of these were the 60 houses being erected by Mr Frank Manning of Rathgar in Castle Avenue, Clontarf, the 75 houses built by Messrs Stewart at Vernon Avenue, Clontarf (although as was shown, this proved to be overconfident, and the business floundered) and the 60 houses by Messrs Bailey, Son and Gibson at Sandford. Meanwhile, Alexander Strain, Mr Boyd and Mr John Dillon were building in the Drumcondra area. All of these houses were being quickly disposed of at satisfactory terms, whether bought or rented. However, these were some of the few developments being undertaken, as in general the speculative development which had ceased at the outbreak of World War I had yet to resume. The *Irish Builder and Engineer* considered that the Government's scheme of grants towards private building were 'almost useless' because of the restrictions on sale price. A five-roomed house that might cost £600, £700 or even more to build, must be sold, if placed in the market for sale, to the first bidder of £450, 'all for the sake of a Government grant of £100' (*Irish Builder and Engineer,* 27 December 1924, p. 1090).

Despite these complaints, the 1924 Act was significant in accepting the principle of State promotion of (and grants for) private speculative building.

It was also important in that five sets of house plans were issued in association with the legislation, influencing the appearance of houses built by both private builders and by local authorities. The plans were generally based on existing schemes. For example, type C7 was the design to which the first houses constructed under the 1922 Million Pound Grant were built, in Waterford. The dwellings at Marino by Mr Hicks, at Donnelly's Orchard by Messrs McDonnell & Dixon, and at Fairbrother's Fields by H.T. O'Rourke, were based on types D8 and D9. It is noteworthy that the plans included bungalow designs (Type 6D). As previously discussed, such bungalows became particularly common in the Seafield Road area of Clontarf, where many individuals built houses under the Act.

Table 28 House plans issued in connection with the 1924 Housing (Building Facilities) Act.

Book	Number of Designs	Type
A	3	Three-roomed dwellings
B	3	Four-roomed, parlour-type dwellings
C	8	Four-roomed, non-parlour type cottages
CL		Four-roomed dwellings in areas where sewers and water mains are unavailable
D	9	Five-roomed cottages, parlour-type.

(Department Local Government and Public Health, 1925, House Designs prescribed by the Minister for Local Government under the Housing Act, 1924.)

The extent to which Government grants were instrumental in the building of private housing schemes cannot be underestimated. In October 1938, for example, the existing provisions in regard to rates remissions on new houses expired. In November, Mr Dockrell asked the Minister, 'Does he realize that all transactions in housing are held up pending the introduction of this measure? I suppose there are some hundreds of houses stopped, and the employment that would be given on their construction is stopped also' (Dáil Debates, 73, p. 642). The position was that no purchaser would buy a house without knowing where they stood as regards the remission of rates, while no builder would commence a house without some idea of the likely arrangement of terms, not unlike the recent position with 'Section 27' assistance.

Whereas it has been shown that builders before World War I (with a small number of notable exceptions) generally operated on a small scale in a fairly

94 Housing at David Park, Glasnevin. (Photograph by R. McManus.)

localized area, the picture began to change in the late 1920s. Of course, some builders like Phillips (see page 410) continued to operate on a small scale, but many more, encouraged by the security afforded by Government grants and the availability of serviced sites on Corporation-owned land, began to extend activities into other parts of the city. Almost all of the land available for building in that part of Drumcondra and Glasnevin nearest the city had been developed, and, as elsewhere in Dublin, house construction activity moved further out into the countryside. Some infill development also took place, such as David Park, a tiny cul-de-sac of ten terraced houses off David Road, Glasnevin, approved for development in early 1932. The houses, described as 'attractive' and 'compact', were sold for £500 each, and included a rates remission. With their pebble-dashed exteriors, they are markedly different from the red-brick late-Victorian and Edwardian houses in neighbouring Whitworth and David Roads.

Meanwhile, some builders in the Drumcondra and Glasnevin area appear to have been confronted with the lack of availability of building land in the immediate surrounds. This was not because the area was built-up. In part, the shortage was due to the Corporation's activities, since it had acquired large tracts of land in association with the development of both Griffith and Collins Avenues, effectively creating a northern barrier to the spread of speculative development. Much land was also in the hands of religious institutions. These maintained large urban estates, some of which have been developed for housing only within the past decade. Thus builders like Linzell and Ritchie began to extend their activities to the southern suburbs, both building houses in the Merrion/Ailesbury area in the early 1930s. Some continued to reside in the Glasnevin area, while others, following the practice of earlier years, moved with their work.

Other builders from Drumcondra and Glasnevin began to erect housing in areas such as Terenure and Rathfarnham in the 1930s. For example, in 1933, particulars regarding the newly-built semi-detached three-bedroom houses at Butterfield Park, Rathfarnham were available from Webb, 10 Cremore Park. These houses were fully decorated, supplied with both gas and electricity, and had 'power plugs'. The fact that the houses were open daily until 9.00 p.m. suggests the lengths which were now necessary in order to sell in what was, increasingly, a buyer's market. Webb also appears to have worked with Alexander Strain at Old Finglas Road. In 1934, R.A. Harrison of 65 Iona Road was selling 'desirable semi-detached villas' on Fortfield Road and Drive in Terenure. Like many schemes of the 1930s, a purchase scheme had been arranged.

In the 1930s there was a housing 'boom', accompanied by a huge increase in the population of Dublin. At this time, there were also greater strictures regarding development, particularly as awareness of planning and environmental issues increased with the introduction of the first town planning bill. More detailed conditions for development were set out by the Dublin Corporation, some examples of which are provided below. In addition, areas further outside the city, both on the south side and, to a more limited extent on the north side, were being developed. There appears to have been an increasing commercialism in construction circles, and a tendency of builders to group together. Among the builders who have been followed in the study, there was a notable increase in the areas covered by their activities, which were now less localized. The houses being built were more likely to be described as 'Estates', and sold in a new way. Despite these changes, the building scene in Dublin remained relatively small-scale. Builders still tended to cover all aspects of the business, with Kenny running his own concrete tile factory in the 1930s, as Strain had made his own bricks just after World War I. Public utility societies remained important, while the Irish Sailors' and Soldiers' Land Trust was still providing ex-servicemen's houses, often on Corporation-developed land (such as the Cabra area, developed from 1932). Building could still be relatively slow, as at the Rise, Glasnevin, which was started in 1932 and still

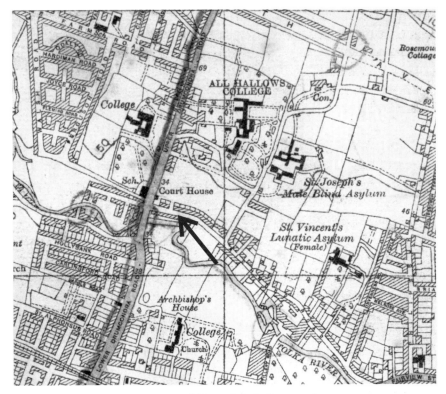

95 Environs of Clonturk Park, Drumcondra.
(Ordnance Survey 1:25,000 plan, sheet 265B, Provisional Popular Edition 1933.)

being built in 1939, while piecemeal development remained a feature, although less prominently than in the past.

The rural-urban mix characteristic of a new suburb was very much a feature of the Drumcondra and Glasnevin area as late as the 1930s, when cattle were still being kept in the locality. Patrick Geraghty rented fields from Mr Butterly which he used to graze his cattle awaiting export to Britain, though the cattle were continually frightened by the footballers from the newly formed Home Farm Football Club. As late as 1934, the rural aspect of the area was being used to good effect in housing advertisements. Michael J. Murphy's houses on 'Whitehall Road', Drumcondra, were in this 'healthiest and brightest suburb', overlooking the grounds of High Park Convent, with a 'guaranteed country aspect'.

In 1934, development continued on Home Farm Road, most of which had been acquired by the Corporation for lease to individuals and public utility societies. However, one of the fields off that road had remained in the hands of the Butterly Estate and had been used, for a time, by the local soccer club.

In November, probably encouraged by the considerable development in the area, permission was sought and granted to develop this field as a 48-house estate. Work proceeded relatively slowly, with two sections of the new Home Farm Park being taken in charge in March, 1937. In the same year, the original proposal which had included two shop dwellings was altered, with two houses substituted. These houses were approved by the Corporation under the condition that the frontage would match the design and colour of the existing houses in the scheme, an illustration of how the local authority had begun to pay more attention to the architectural details of housing schemes (Report 2/1937).

In February 1932, approval was given to plans for the development by the Royal Bank of Ireland of portion of the Clonturk Park Estate, and in March 1933, the proposed 64 houses at Clonturk Park were approved. This tract of land was one of the largest (in private hands) to remain untouched at this relatively late date. Interestingly, before the laying out of Clonturk Park, which runs at right angles to Drumcondra Road, roughly *parallel* to Richmond Road, several maps show a road running from Richmond Road parallel to Drumcondra Road to Ormond Road, through the area where Clonturk Park was subsequently built. The possibility that a road was originally intended to be built here is reinforced by the gap in the frontage along Richmond Road, shown in the Ordnance Survey's Provisional Popular Edition 265B (1933) and in the 25" (1:2500) map of the area and which still persists (figures 95 and 96).

Louis P. Kinlen, the builder of Clonturk Park, was already involved in development in the area, having taken leases of ground at Griffith Avenue. His operations were not restricted to Drumcondra, however. One of the few recorded private building operations being undertaken in the troubled year of 1922 was by Kinlen & Co. of Airfield House in Rathgar. It was reported in the *Irish Builder and Engineer* that eight semi-detached houses in Vernon Grove, Rathgar, were being completed in July 1922. According to the paper, they differed from the usual type in being 'of artistic design', constructed of concrete blocks on the Australian system, pebble-dashed outside and roofed with red Somerset tiles. Nor was the company restricted to house building, for in December of that year, the company was building a red brick motor garage for Mr Carton of Aylesbury Park, to designs by Messrs Jones & Kelly, as well as new dressing rooms and lavatories at Clontarf Rugby Club. Kinlen did not just undertake new build projects, for in September of 1923 his company was involved in alterations and repairs to 53 James' Street for Messrs Byrne Brothers. In 1926, Mr Louis P. Kinlen was erecting houses at Dolphin's Barn, while in the following year he lodged plans for the erection of eight houses at nearby Church Avenue, South Circular Road. Meanwhile, Kinlen extended his activities to the north side of the city, having plans approved for combined drainage of houses on Griffith Avenue in early 1928, where he planned to build 62 houses. He continued working here in tandem with his building work on the south side of the city, and had further plans approved in 1930 and again in 1932, when the layout plan for 56 houses was approved. Interestingly, Clonturk Park is the only estate which Kinlen built in this period on privately-owned land, the remainder of his activity apparently being confined to land leased by the Corporation, on Griffith Avenue and also on the south side of the city. In June 1929, for example, he acquired the lease of two sites at Bulfin Road, Inchicore, for the erection of six residential shops. One adjoined the South Circular Road, the other adjoining the Kehoe Square area. The two sites had been advertised for letting on lease, but the only offer had been received from Louis P. Kinlen, 17 Vernon Grove, Rathgar at 7s. 6d. per foot frontage for the former site and 5s. per foot frontage for the latter. The leases were for 150 years and 94 years respectively. However, a surrender of the lease granted to Kinlen for land on Bulfin Road adjoining Bulfin House was accepted in 1930. It had been discovered that the site was unsuitable for the purpose, since building would involve abnormal costs and was therefore an uneconomical proposition (Report 124/1929 and 124/1930). In 1930, a further plot of ground on Bulfin Road was leased to Louis Kinlen of 3 Rathgar Avenue, at £12 p.a. Once again the site had been advertised but only one offer was received (Report 13/1930). The above discussion also highlights another feature of Kinlen's activity which he had in common with other builders of the period, the fact that he frequently changed address. In Kinlen's case, most of the locations mentioned were in the Rathgar and Rathfarnham areas.

The lease of one of the houses in Clonturk Park illustrates the layers of ownership involved in the property. The first lease, registered in July 1934, was between the Royal Bank of Ireland, as lessor, and Kinlen and Co. Ltd, Darwin Hall, Rathfarnham, the lessee. The 420-year lease was dated from March 1933 at a specified ground rent, payable half yearly, and covered plot 5 of the development, or house numbers 34 to 48. Kinlen, as builder, had, with the agreement of the lessor, granted a lease of 44 Clonturk Park at £800 to a Christopher Toal of Lower Dorset Street. Toal had then applied to the Corporation for an advance of £580 under the provisions of the SDAA 1899/1919 and the Housing (Miscellaneous Provisions) Act, 1931, and had paid the balance of £220 to Kinlen. The lease specified that the Corporation's £580 advance with interest at £5 10s. per cent per annum was repayable by 140 equal

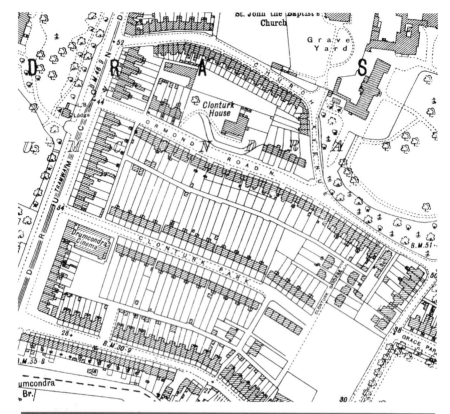

96 Layout of Clonturk Park and Ormond Road, Drumcondra.
(Ordnance Survey 1:2500 plan, Sheet 18 III, Dublin, 1938 revision. Photograph by J. Brady.)

quarterly payments of £9 8s. 1d. each of principal and interest combined. Payments were due to begin on the first of January 1935, continuing until January 1970. Toal's lease ran from May 1934 for a period of 418 years, with an annual ground rent of £9. Kinlen was paying ground rent of £49 10s. 6d. p.a. to the Royal Bank, and erected eight houses, whose occupants would all have been paying a similar ground rent of c.£9. Therefore, in addition to paying off his own dues, Kinlen was making a profit not just on the sale of the houses, but also had a regular income from the ground rents each year.

The map accompanying the lease was provided by Donnelly, Moore & Keatinge, Architects. The houses were typical of many three-bedroom dwellings of the 1930s, with mass concrete walls rather than the increasingly expensive brick. While the houses were terraced, and no garages were provided, an access lane to the rear of the extremely long back gardens (average c.185 feet; 56 m) allowed for parking. Conditions of the lease included the use of the premises as a private dwellinghouse only, and for no other purpose. For the term of the Corporation advance, the house and messuage were to be insured against loss or damage by fire in the sum of £900.

In May 1935 approval was given to the naming of the two new roads at Clonturk as Clonturk Park and Gardens. The Clonturk Park scheme was notable in that it included proposals for a cinema and shops on the Drumcondra Road frontage of the scheme, including a petrol station (Report 67/1933). Developers were becoming aware of the need to provide amenities for their clients, and were also eager to cash in on higher ground rents from shop premises in a developing area with a 'captive' market. The suburbs became increasingly important to retailers in the 1920s and 1930s, as housing developments were built on a larger scale, and at a greater distance from the city centre. In response, builders began to incorporate the 'parade', a self-contained row of essential shops, into their developments. In Dublin, such blocks of shops, described as 'shopping centres', were generally built in the same style as the housing development with which they were associated.

Development now extended well into the countryside, with G.M. Linzell's Hampstead Hill Estate, which is discussed further in association with the work of Alexander Strain. The area around the Ballymun Road was slowly being built on, as ribbon development stretched the built-up area of the city. In 1934, Vartry water supplies were granted to Denis Delany, 23 St Canice's Road, Ballymun Road, previously involved in the development of Grace Park Road and a member of the Dublin and District Housebuilders' Association, while Messrs Maher and Murphy were also building at Walnut Grove, Ballymun Road. On Ballymun

Road itself, houses were being built throughout the period from 1934 to 1939, some by Linzell and others by Messrs T. & T. Wharton, Glasnevin.

The opening up of Griffith Avenue by the Corporation, together with incentives for private housing in the form of lump-sum grants, encouraged the development of privately held land in the area, such as the Rosemount Estate and Calderwood Avenue. In October 1934, the layout of Rosemount Estate, Griffith Avenue was approved, subject to certain amendments in accordance with a plan prepared by the Housing Architect's Department. The names Glandore, Carbry and Muskerry were later approved for three new roads on the estate. In keeping with the changing times, in March 1936, the *Irish Times* reported the approval of 168 houses and garages at the Rosemount Estate, Griffith Avenue, for Patrick Cronin. This is typical of private developments of the time, in that the whole estate was planned at the outset, rather than developed in a more haphazard way. The scale of development had increased, with one builder developing the whole estate. These changes were in part due to Government policy, with the effects of the 1934 Planning Act being experienced on a small scale. Only one month later, in April 1936, Cronin was advertising his Rosemount Estate houses on Calderwood Road. These three- and four- bedroom brick houses were 'skillfully planned, solidly constructed and tastefully decorated' and occupied an 'unrivalled position 100 feet (*c.*30 m) over sea level' (*Irish Times*, 9 April 1936). Plans also included eight shop dwellings on Glandore Road. Again, it seems that Cronin was involved in building in other parts of the city at the same time, including two shops on Rathfarnham Road in 1934 (*Irish Times*, 5 March 1934) and houses on the nearby Grace Park Road (*Irish Times*, 12 March 1936).

The development of Rosemount, Calderwood and Clonturk Park shows how private speculative building practice had changed in the 1930s. Each estate was more or less fully planned before building began, and the Corporation had a greater interest in, and control over, the planning of new housing schemes.

Dublin and District Housebuilders' Association

Another indication of the increasing scale and profession-alism of the speculative house-building industry is the formation of the Dublin and District Housebuilders' Association. The first reference to the DDHBA appears in late 1931, when a deputation from that body requested information regarding the provision of grants in aid under

the terms of the new Housing Bill (Report 59/1931). It was decided to recommend that the Council provide £3000 in the Estimates, thus supplying a grant
of £20 per house in respect of 150 houses. The Bill provided that the State
would make similar grants to those provided by the local authority.

The advent of the DDHBA illustrates an important change in the building
industry. Although there was some formal organization of developers prior to
1931, with the Dublin Master Builders' Association and the National Federation
of Building Trades Employers of Great Britain and Ireland, for example, and
much informal contact, the DDHBA appears to mark a change in internal
relations within the industry. The organization was specific to builders of
houses, rather than general contractors, and suggests that the builders were
now coming together to form an oligopoly. Indeed, their success was such that
allegations of a cartel were made at the 1939–43 Inquiry. A photograph of the
members of the Association in 1932 (figure 97) provides one of the few
available pictures of the men who were building Dublin's suburbs at this time.

The Association had premises at 16 Dawson Street, and employed P. Deey,
FLAA, ACWP as Secretary. It is notable that Deey had also been secretary of
the Dublin Brick Company Limited. Of the members in the photograph, no
information is available about E. Kearon, James A. Kyle, William Kyle and
J. O'Connell. Of the remainder, Strain and Linzell are discussed in depth later
in this work. Louis P. Kinlen has already been mentioned as builder of
Clonturk Park and much of the 'reserved area' at Drumcondra and Griffith
Avenue, while Delaney was noted as builder of houses on Grace Park Road in
1930 and St Canice's Road in 1934. P. Cronin also built houses at Grace Park
Road and Rosemount. Many of the remainder also had interests in the
Drumcondra area. Gough had premises in Rutland Place and was involved in
developments on Botanic Road and Mannix Road. Cowell lived in Old
Finglas Road and was selling houses in Glasnevin in 1930s. G.F. Byrne was
building off Shandon Road, Phibsboro. In November 1924, 17 houses on
Shandon Road were approved for Byrne. These houses were of a high
specification. First quality Bridgwater red facing bricks were specified for the
facing of the front walls and chimneys, best quality close-grained red deal was
to be used for sashes and frames and doors, while all floor joists, rafters etc.
were to be made of best-quality imported spruce. It seems that Byrne was also
involved in building in the Mount Merrion area. P.L. O'Brien was possibly
involved in building at Fairfield Road. R.G. Kirkham was building shops on
Grattan Crescent, Inchicore in 1926 (relatively close to Strain's Inchicore land)
as well as shops on Phibsborough Road including nos. 53/54 in 1929.

97 Dublin Housebuilders' Association prior to their 'smoking dinner' at the Dolphin Hotel in 1932. This photograph appeared in the *Irish Builder and Engineer*. Reading from left to right, the names are: -sitting: Messrs. J. O'Connell, G.M. Linzell, Alexander Strain (chairman), L.P. Kinlen (vice-chairman), G.F. Byrne, James A. Kyle, William Kyle. Standing: Mssrs. R.G. Kirkham, J. Townley, P.J. Whelan, J.P. Somers, P. Cronin, R. Gough, E. Kearon, P.L. O'Brien, R. Cowell, P. Decy (secretary) and D. Delany.

J. Townley had premises at Millmount Terrace, 1929. He was involved in building at Butterfield Drive, Rathfarnham in 1934. P.J. Whelan lived at 1 Iona Villas, Finglas, in 1908 and was possibly involved in building in the Finglas area. J.P. Somers was building at Sandford Avenue, Merton Park in 1927. This was part of the Fairbrother's Fields area. Indeed, Report 216/1930 notes that due to the failure of Somers to fulfill the covenant in his lease of a plot in Merton Park, Fairbrother's Fields, requiring the erection of three houses on the plot, proceedings for possession were being undertaken. He was also involved in the development of Hazelwood, Dundrum.

Other members listed in Thom's directory in the period to 1941 included Charles Archer, R. Crighton, R E. Stringer, J.S. Pickering (23 Rostrevor Road, Rathgar), M.P. Kennedy, H. Delany, Thos. Corless and Ernest Webb. Pickering and Son built in the area around Cowper Gardens in Rathmines during the late 1920s and early 1930s. Houses in Cowper Gardens were advertised in the *Irish Times* on 25 April 1931. An advertisement for one of their Park Drive houses which appeared in the *Irish Times* on 12 March 1932 illustrates the high quality of these houses, reflected in the relatively high cost:

'New semi-detached, all-brick, slate roofs, well finished and equipped. Two reception, four bedrooms, bath, *two* inside w.c.s, kitchen, pantry, cloakroom, *garage, rates remission*'. The cost was £1200. In September 1933, Cowper Drive was adopted as the name for a new road off Cowper Road, having been suggested by its owner (Report 47/1933). In April 1936 it was decided that the cul-de-sac formerly known as Cowper Grove and Park Drive would now be called Park Drive (Report 31/1936).

The Stringer name is one of the best known in the estate agency business. Like 'Strain-built', the Stringer tag is important in house sales to this day. At a time when almost no private building was being undertaken, in August 1921 it was reported that Mr Thomas Stringer was erecting two dwelling houses at Orwell Park, two-storeys high and faced with Courtown brick. By 1925, Stringer was building new houses at Orwell Road, Rathgar, on land leased by Messrs Dockrell Ltd. (*Irish Times*, 26 March 1925). An advertisement for houses on Orwell Road in 1932 reveals a two-way thought process by the builder. On the one hand, he looked to the past with the inclusion of a maid's room in addition to the four bedrooms, at a time when the 'servant problem' had become acute, on the other he included all the latest conveniences, including two w.c.s, garage, electricity etc. (*Irish Times*, 23 April 1932). Incidentally, not all of the houses on Orwell Road were built by Mr Stringer. In April 1931, F. Morton, builder, was advertising houses in Braemor Road, Dodder Road and Orwell Road, Rathgar.

The Association appears to have been intended as a lobby group, aimed at strengthening the position of private builders at a time when the security which had been afforded by the 1920s Government and Corporation policies was being eroded. As the emphasis of housing policy shifted to slum clearance in the early 1930s, private builders had to fight to retain the privileges which had been secured in the previous decades. One of the most important factors for private builders was, apparently, the existence of the SDAA which encouraged home-ownership. Therefore, the DDHBA lobbied strongly for its retention in the 1930s. In March 1934, for example, the DDHBA proposed that the Small Dwellings Advances be continued so as to provide for houses costing *c*.£500 (Report 16/1934). This proposal coincided with the exhaustion of the existing £250,000 which had been raised for the purpose of making advances under the Acts, and at a time when the City Manager considered that the demand for houses costing from £800 to £1000 was practically satisfied. The Dublin and District Housebuilders' Association, however, hoped for a reduction in the cost of houses eligible under the scheme, and that the Corporation would bring them within the means of the better-off working

A RECORD OF PRIVATE ENTERPRISE

HOUSE BUILDING
IN DUBLIN

During Six Years 1933—1938

Private Builders Provided

New Homesteads for more than

THAT ENTERPRISE INVOLVED :

1. PAYING OVER £10,000 WEEKLY IN WAGES.

2. ENSURING AN ULTIMATE ADDITION OF OVER £200,000 YEARLY TO DUBLIN'S RATE REVENUES.

FORTY THOUSAND CITIZENS !

3. PROVIDING MANY MILES OF NEW ROADS, SEWERS AND WATER SERVICES FREE OF COST TO RATEPAYERS !

If you are interested please read on—

98 Extract from promotional pamphlet *8,000 New Homesteads in Six Years* produced by the DDHBA (1939).

classes by advancing 90 per cent of the market value instead of the present 80 per cent. In fact, the conditions were not altered, but the lending operations of the Corporation were continued until 1938.

The building boom ended in 1938/9 and the subsequent slump was attributed by the builders to the cecession of advances under the SDAA from November 1938. In November 1939, the DDHBA informed the Housing Inquiry of 1939–43 that due to the war emergency the previously restricted credit facilities for house purchase had almost ceased to be available, and that within a few months 95 per cent of their members would be completely closed down. However, the Corporation considered that the main reason for the slump was that the pent-up demand by purchasers who were able to deposit the average 30 per cent required by the lenders had been satisfied, so that in 1939 many of the speculative builders had houses on their hands unsold.

The report promised that operations under the Acts could be resumed in the future, when the Corporation had overtaken its arrears and the resources of the building industry could safely be diverted from the work of slum clearance. This would be done in order to meet the needs of 'those persons to whom house-ownership is a desirable objective and whose economic circumstances are suitable' (Report of Inquiry, 1939–43, p. 184, para. 539). The wording of this statement reflects the prevailing ideology of home-ownership and social engineering.

Planning in the 1930s on private estates

It took some time before the ideals expressed in the Tudor Walters Report in Britain filtered through to the planning and layout of privately-developed schemes in Ireland. Among the objectives of the Report were the design of the town plan in relation to the distinctive natural features of the site, the provision of an interesting outlook for each house, with as much natural light as possible, and a standard of no more than ten to 20 houses to the acre (*c*.25 to 50 per ha). Privacy and seclusion were to be enhanced by tree planting, while houses were carefully grouped in culs-de-sac or facing gardens and greens. However, most of the low-density private housing estates built in the 1920s and 1930s were little more than haphazard accretions of residential roads around a main thoroughfare.

From the early 1930s, Dublin Corporation began to have a greater involvement in the physical planning of new housing estates. Whereas speculative builders had previously been treated almost with kid gloves, the local authority now took a tougher line. The detailed specifications of a given scheme were required to be submitted at the outset of development, and the Corporation made frequent amendments and required, rather than requested, these changes before building could begin. In part, this change seems to have reflected greater cohesion within the building industry itself. It appears that builders were more likely to plan the whole development at the outset than previously, while estates were now completed more rapidly than in the past.

The development of Furry Park, off the Howth Road, illustrates the level of detail which the Corporation now required in new housing schemes. In April 1936, two layouts were approved for the development of Furry Park, from two separate developers. The first was for J. McGonagle (involved in the development of Griffith Avenue and the Vernon Estate), subject to a large number of conditions relating to the drainage of the scheme, road width, and the setting back of houses from the roadway (Report 31/1936). In the same report, Mrs Davies' amended layout was approved, subject to provision being made for a further widening of Howth Road to 50 feet (*c*.15 m), to the omission of a proposed island site and to the space included in this site being incorporated in the front gardens of the houses.

It seems likely that one or both of these applicants leased sites on their estates to other builders, since one of the earliest applications for ten houses at Furry Park, Howth Road came from T. Caffrey in July 1936. In October of that year, plans for the site were still under consideration, with approval for

99 Development underway at Furry Park, Clontarf.
(Ordnance Survey 1:2500 plan, Sheet 19 I, Dublin, 1938 revision.)

proposed roads subject to further alterations. These included an insistence on
the preservation of an existing grove of trees, an aspect of planning which had
been important in 'Tudor Walters' town planning in Britain, but which seems
to have previously been neglected by Dublin Corporation. In addition to its
required alteration to road junctions, and to new roads having carriageways
20 feet (*c*.6 m) wide and two footpaths eight feet (*c*.2.4 m) wide, the
Corporation ordered that the proposer hand over to the Corporation, free of
cost, sufficient ground to enable Howth Road to be widened to 50 feet (*c*.15
m) along the frontage of Furry Park Grounds (Report 71/1936). Again this
shows that the Corporation was becoming more involved in development and
exhibiting a greater degree of foresight in its development policies. By January
1937, the layout had been finalized, and plans for 80 houses were approved,
subject to variation of frontage line of blocks of houses and to combined drain
agreement. Large numbers of houses continued to be erected throughout 1937

and into 1938, with the amended drainage plans for 136 houses being approved in February 1937, while applications for small numbers of houses, some with garages, continued to be received into 1938.

Another example of the extent to which estates were fully planned at the outset is that of L.C. Ritchie's development at Nutley Park, Donnybrook. In July 1935, approval in principle was given to the amended layout plan for the proposed development, subject to the following reservations (Report 43/1935, p. 192):

(i) pending further information as to the development on the Nutley Lane frontage, no sanction is given to the proposed buildings on the four sites on each side of the proposed new road at its junction with Nutley Lane or on the frontage facing Stillorgan Road adjoining Nutley Lane;

(ii) the proposed right angle bend in the main road of the scheme is sanctioned as the plan shows the ground adjoining set aside for golf links. In the event, however, of this ground being developed for building the right angle bend is to be abolished and central road continued;

(iii) the substitution of a properly constructed and lighted, etc., pedestrian passage instead of vehicular traffic road as shown on plan over new main sewer and approx. parallel to Nutley Lane and

(iv) the corners of this passage and also of the new road to the south of the site should be well splayed for visibility in connection with traffic on Stillorgan Road.

By September 1935 the drainage plan for the Nutley Estate Development was approved, while in November, authority was granted for a 150 yard (c.137 m) extension of the water main to supply the building site for Mr L.C. Ritchie. The amendments required by Dublin Corporation at Nutley Estate illustrate the changing nature of public intervention in the private housing sector in the 1930s. Good planning was now demanded in all new housing developments, and the local authority now took a more serious view of the development process than was evident in its treatment of earlier cases.

The new interest in town planning exhibited by Dublin Corporation in the 1930s extended to a greater awareness of the importance of housing density. In January 1938, for example, permission was granted for the erection of a 'private housing scheme' on the Howth Road, provided frontages were set back to an amended line and the density reduced to six per acre (15 houses per ha). It is noteworthy that this is the first time a Corporation report specifically referred to a scheme as 'private' (Report 10/1938).

Whereas in the development of Drumcondra in the 1920s, first J.J. Flanagan, and then the Saorstát Civil Service Public Utility Society evaded the issue of joining Clare Road to Achill Road, Dublin Corporation began to insist on properly planned road connections in the 1930s. In some cases, this led to the local authority building the roads itself, rather than relying on private speculators. For example, in early 1934, the Corporation purchased the leasehold and fee simple interest in an area on Howth Road, adjoining Silver Acre, 'for the purpose of making a connection at some future date' between Howth Road and Castle Avenue (Report 21/1934). However, Dublin Corporation generally ensured that the land was ceded free of charge, rather than paying compensation to land owners as had previously been the case.

One unusual feature of Dublin Corporation policy in the 1930s is its attitude to retail facilities. While even speculative builders were becoming more aware of the need to provide shops in their new schemes, their proposals were frequently turned down by the local authority. In the development of Calderwood Road, off Griffith Avenue, the shops planned were omitted as (according to the Corporation) there were sufficient shopping centres approved in the vicinity, while a proposed cinema was also omitted (Report 55/1938). Similar plans were rejected in other areas with the explanation that over-provision of such services was feared. This stance seems surprising, but may perhaps be linked to the City Architect's antagonism to the Gaeltacht Park scheme for the building of shops in a residential area.

In the late 1920s, Dublin Corporation had specified the quality and cost of housing being built on the 'reserved areas', land leased by the local authority for building by others. It seems that, in the 1930s, the Corporation began to insist on specific quality and cost of housing even in areas where it was not the ground landlord. Thus, in December 1938, approval was given to the erection of a house on Eglinton Road, subject to its value being not less than that of the houses on the opposite side of the road (Report 1/1939). In this case the builder is not known, though it may have been Crampton or even Linzell. This whole Eglinton/Ailesbury area seems to have experienced infill development in the 1930s. In 1932, 'on the request of the builders who constructed the thoroughfare', a new road was named Eglinton Park (Report 29/1932), while in 1936, two houses were being built on Eglinton Road (Report 58/1936).

Despite these changes, with increased planning, larger scale private schemes and more rapid building, the piecemeal nature of development was a persistent feature in much of suburban Dublin. In the Vernon Estate, while leasehold tenure ensured some measure of control by the Estate, there were many individual builders involved in the building up of each road. On Mount Prospect Avenue, off Vernon Avenue, the builders included Joseph McGonagle of Lomond, Kincora Road (also building on Kincora Road, Castle Avenue and later at Furry Park), Woodvale Public Utility Society (also building on Conquer Hill Road), Mr Fitzpatrick and Eugene Casey of nearby Seafield Road East (also building bungalows on Kincora Road in 1929):

> Attractive semi-detached two-storey houses, Clontarf. Two reception, four bedroom, garage, ideal situation, low ground rents, remission rates, price moderate, extended payments. Fitzpatrick, 'St Kilda', Mount Prospect Avenue.
>
> (*Irish Times*, 17 March 1932)

In the following year, a similar advertisement emphasized the small deposit payable, the balance to be paid as rent.

Mount Merrion: a private garden suburb

The development of Mount Merrion is interesting for a number of reasons. It was billed as a 'garden estate', illustrating how the concept had gradually diffused from local authority housing as at Marino to more expensive private housing for owner occupation by the 1930s. In some ways, the development illustrates continuity with the type of processes which we have seen already in Drumcondra and Glasnevin. A large number of builders was involved, yet piecemeal development could no longer occur, as the layout plans for the estate had been formalized in advance of building work. The architectural style of the scheme also owes much to 'modern' influences which were being imported, largely from Britain.

The story of Mount Merrion began in 1918 when land belonging to the Pembroke Estate was purchased by Thomas O'Neill, who later sold it on to T.J. Wilson, the first developer of the area. Wilson's company, Mount Merrion Estates (later part of the British Housing Corporation) began building in 1926, while an attractive brochure promising amenities such as tennis courts and a swimming pool was produced. In an advertisement appearing in the *Irish Times* of 13 March 1926, sites at Mount Merrion were being sold through Battersby & Co. as 'exceptionally attractive Building Sites, Stillorgan Rd, Foster Ave, Mt Annville; drainage and water laid on; minimum site ½ acre; special facilities to builders'.

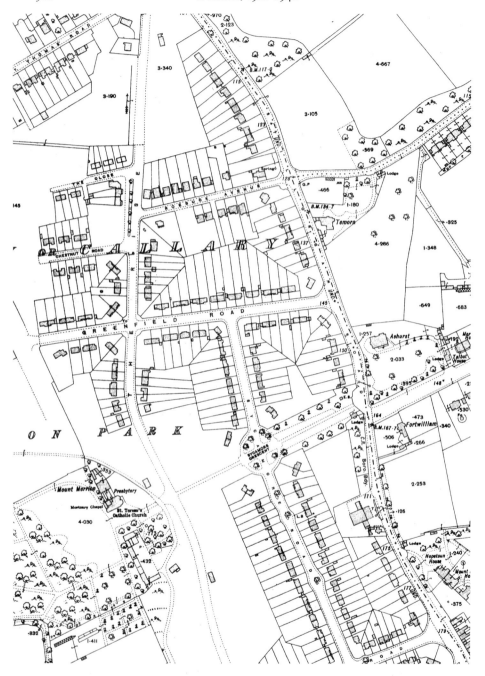

100 Layout of part of Mount Merrion.
(Ordnance Survey 1:2500 plan, Sheet 23 V, Dublin, 1939 revision.)

However, due to slow sales, Wilson mortgaged much of the property, which was eventually taken over by John Kenny of Irish Homes Limited, with the help of the Trade Loans Act. In 1933 building began at Greenfield Road. The houses were varied in style, while intelligent preservation of trees (following Tudor Walters principles) enhanced the appearance of the new roads and avenues. The roads built at this time included Sycamore Road, Greygates, Trees Road, The Rise, The Close and Chestnut Road, together with a shopping centre on the Rise, including a sub-post office.

Typical mentions of the Mount Merrion estate in the Corporation reports include references to extensions of the mains to provide water supplies for building purposes. In June 1935, for example, a ½ inch (c.1.2 cm) building supply was granted for a dwelling house at Plot 271, Foster Avenue for Mr G. Byrne, while two ½ inch connections were approved in November for new houses at Plot 170, St Thomas's Road for Mr G.C. Marsh. Marsh's name reappears in connection with the erection of a house on the same road, this time as Messrs Marsh and Maharry, in March 1936, and it seems that many builders specialized in building on these developed sites in the same way that others focused on Corporation-provided sites. Other builders involved in the Mount Merrion development included J.J. O'Hara, J.P. du Moulin, and Messrs Henly at Woodlands Park and Mount Merrion Avenue. Marsh seems to have had a number of different associates, since in January 1935, approval was been given to the erection of houses at Henley Park, Churchtown by Hodgins, Marsh and Waters (Report 5/1935).

Messrs John Kenny and Sons, like Alexander Strain, were involved in the production of building materials for their own use. In November 1935, reference was made to the company's concrete tile plant at the Rise, Mount Merrion Park. Because development took place over a relatively long period, rather than leaving the land idle, Kenny seems to have continued operations as a farmer for some time. In November 1935, a ½ inch (c.1.2 cm) water supply was arranged for a cattle field at Seafield, Mt Merrion, for Messrs John Kenny & Sons, and as late as 1939 water supplies for cattle use were being provided for Messrs John Kenny & Sons at the Mount Merrion Estate. This arrangement harks back to the earlier part of the century in Drumcondra, where J.J. Flanagan kept cattle on his building land.

By the mid-1930s, the advertisements for Mount Merrion had become more sophisticated, partly in response to greater competition from subsidized suburban schemes. In March, 1935, John Kenny's Irish Homes Company was making cars available to drive prospective purchasers to the estate, described in the advertisement as a 'Garden City'. More in tune with 1990s advertising than that of its contemporaries, Irish Homes stressed environment and amenities in its advertisements: 'First things First: Consider Choice Environment' (*Irish Times*, 30 March 1935). The first new 'shopping centre' had been completed, while a 1936 advertisement also refers to the kindergarten available on the estate. These 'Ideal Homes' at Mount Merrion Park offered 'Sunshine, Good Sanitation, Health, Happiness' (*Irish Times*, 9 April 1936). There was a wide range of house designs on offer (Rupert Jones was the architect), while the houses were decorated to the purchaser's specifications. Costs varied from £850 up to £1200. In 1937 the advertisements again stressed how different this development was from its contemporaries: 'unlike any other, this estate is being developed on modern town planning lines-wide roads, spacious gardens and, to avoid dull monotony, various types of houses have been constructed' (*Irish Times*, 15 April 1937).

Development came to a halt with the six-month long building strike in 1939, although Kenny did his best for his house purchasers, and in cases where houses were completely built but not decorated, he handed them over to the purchasers with a generous allowance to complete the decoration. However, following the strike and World War II, Kenny got into financial difficulties, and the remainder of development in the area took place on a piecemeal basis after 1947, when various parcels of land were taken by a number of different building contractors.

Kenny's development at Mount Merrion shows some of the changes experienced by the house-building industry in the 1930s. In particular, it was one of the earliest speculative schemes to apply the principles of modern town planning and which fully advertised the fact. However, within Kenny's overall plan, there were many different builders engaged in house-building on the estate. Thus, the piecemeal nature of development, involving various builders, was being focused through the intervention of a developer with an overall plan. The Estate also shows the newly important role of the architect, whose name is now mentioned in advertisements.

Some final comments

In the area of Glasnevin and Drumcondra selected for more detailed study, it is clear that there was a gradual transition from a rural to a suburban environment. The study has shown the degree of complexity within a small area, with many different builders and investors erecting houses in various styles and for various grades of occupant. The photos throughout the chapter illustrate the variety of house styles used within this relatively small area. It is notable, too, that most of these houses could have been photographed anywhere in Britain or Ireland. There was little truly distinctive architecture, and builders (even those employing architects) appear to have copied British styles.

The private middle-class housing built in the period to 1940 reflects societal changes, as house size tended to decrease with a drop in middle-class family size, there were fewer maids' rooms, and garages became a more common feature as car ownership became more widespread. Owner occupancy was becoming a reality even for the less affluent lower middle-classes. There was thus a decreasing complexity in house ownership structure, as the landlord system was gradually dying out, but a corresponding increase in the importance of Dublin Corporation and other lending institutions who made cheap mortgages available.

Dublin Corporation was also important to the builders in its changing attitudes to bylaws, the taking in charge of roads, planning and zoning. The area along the Tolka was specifically mentioned in Abercrombie's 1914 competition plan, and it is interesting to note that his suggestions were applied in the development of Mobhi Road, but not in the provision of a link road between the Drumcondra Road and Botanic Road. While many examples of suspension of bylaws and lack of planning have been shown, it is notable that Dublin Corporation began to take a more active role in the planning process in the 1930s. This had little effect on the Drumcondra and Glasnevin area, most of which had been built up by this time, but impacted on the builders from the area who had extended operations to the south side of the City. By this time, the Dublin and District Housebuilders' Association had accepted the need for planning, and indeed John Kenny began to use the planned nature of his Mount Merrion estate as an important advertising feature. Dublin Corporation and the private speculative builders had a diverse series of relationships, which were constantly in flux. Despite differences over bylaw regulations, in general there was a degree of symbiosis in their relations. It suited the builder to avail of serviced sites along newly-completed roads such as Griffith or Collins Avenue, and it also suited Dublin Corporation to have someone else undertake construction and add to the rate-paying base of the city. Similarly, land swaps between the local authority and the private speculator generally worked to the benefit of both parties. At times the Corporation reports show the degree of haggling which took place, as a speculative builder would agree to cede a portion of land to the Corporation for the making of a footpath, on condition that the Corporation would undertake to extend services such as lighting or sewers. In one case in the Clontarf area, a builder even arranged to 'borrow' items of plant from the Corporation. When Dublin Corporation agreed to build roadways or provide services free of charge to the builder, this was of enormous assistance to the speculator, enabling him to complete houses more speedily and at lower cost. Sometimes even the promise that the Corporation would take roads in charge before they were fully built on had huge consequences for the builder. Without this undertaking, the prospective residents of the new houses would be unable to avail of cheap loans under the Small Dwellings Acquisition Act (provided through Dublin Corporation, yet another bonus to the developer). Thus, by taking the roads in charge, the Corporation ensured that the houses built there would be more readily sold by the speculator. In many ways, therefore, the operations of Dublin Corporation and the private speculative builder were closely entwined. This was not simply the case where a 'private' builder chose to build on the 'Reserved Areas' close to Corporation schemes, but also related to the ways in which Dublin Corporation operated bylaws and embryonic planning practices. The Corporation also had an important role in operating the Small Dwellings Acquisition Acts which promoted the purchase of speculatively-produced houses among the lower middle-classes. Few, if any, 'private' housing projects could have occurred without some form of intervention from the local authority, to a greater or lesser degree. The chapter has thus shown the complex nature of private housing development, how it changed over the period in question, and the extent to which, like other forms of development, it had come to be influenced by Dublin Corporation.

Alexander Strain: profile of a builder

This chapter focuses on the operations of one particular speculative builder, Alexander Strain. In doing so, we can further explore the complex nature of the development process during the early-twentieth century. It is possible to illustrate the interrelationships between the various actors in the building process, including the many links which existed between various builders, as well as between this particular private speculative builder and the local authority. Strain was a well-known builder in the early decades of the twentieth century, whose name (along with those of contemporaries Kenny and Crampton) is still used by estate agents wishing to denote the particular quality and charm of dwellings which he built. What is known of his story may be considered representative of a reasonably well-established builder working in Dublin in the late-nineteenth or early-twentieth century.

Alexander Strain, who built much of Drumcondra and Glasnevin, was born in Markethill, County Armagh, eldest son of another builder, Robert Douglas Strain from Cremore, Armagh. He came to Dublin in 1893, initially working as a timber traveller and living in Rathmines. The Strain family moved to Glasnevin in about 1902, and Alexander spent the rest of his life there. Following his retirement, he made a permanent home at the Cremore estate, but during his working life Alexander Strain always moved his family to wherever he had houses under construction, a fact which must have been tiresome for his wife Kathleen, involving at least ten different addresses within the district. The Strains were respected members of the Presbyterian community, attending and later endowing the Abbey Church in Parnell Square, a background reflected in Alexander's dedication to perfection in his building, and high standards of ethics in business dealings. While Strain was not an extremely wealthy man, almost all of his money being tied up in property, it is clear that he was well-esteemed in social circles. When his youngest daughter, Dorothy, married Mr William A. Murison on 3 June 1935, her marriage was listed among the *Irish Times*' 'principal weddings of 1935' (28 March 1936).

Because he operated over a long period, Alexander Strain's work is of particular interest. He was building during a time of profound change within the housing industry, as Government and local authorities became increasingly involved in the planning of the building process, while economic and societal

101 The street with no name. Lying between Iona and Lindsay roads, the development
potential of this street was lost. (Photograph by J. Brady.)

changes resulted in changing demand for housing. There was a trend towards
owner occupation, with smaller families and fewer servants, which is reflected
in the changing style of Strain's houses. Although it is evident that Strain was
a highly-respected and affluent member of society, it is clear that the nature of
building operations necessitated a large amount of his capital being tied up in
property. Thus, the leases of the houses built by Strain on the south side of
Hollybank Road in the late 1920s show that he built and sold a house approximately every two months. The money from this transaction would then finance
the next house to be built, and so on. Such a 'hand to mouth' existence was
characteristic of the building trade at this time. One benefit of the relatively
small-scale nature of development was that the builder was able to 'personalize'
each house. Thus, for example, the railings around neighbouring gardens were
customized to suit the requirements of the individual purchaser.

   The question as to whether a builder such as Strain had an overall vision
for his development is a vexed one. He acquired a large tract of land early in
his operations but 30 years later he was still building on it. His developments
were piecemeal and jumped around the area. This might suggest a lack of
vision but it might also simply reflect the nature of the building trade and the
opportunities (and finance) available to a small builder. The road network that
emerged is less than ideal and it is hard to believe that he planned the wasted

street frontage in the in the un-named street between Iona and Lindsay roads for example. This was valuable real estate and the usual procedure would have been to shorten the gardens of the nearby houses on Iona and Lindsay roads to accommodate perhaps four houses on the cross road. That this did not happen suggests that, overall vision or not, he did not have the resources to control the development process in the locality. It is interesting too that, despite the apparently unplanned nature of Strain's housing developments, in his capacity as Chairman of the newly formed Dublin and District Housebuilders' Association in 1932, Alexander Strain emphasized the important future role of town planning in developing new residential areas. To Strain, planning would be beneficial both to builder and inhabitant of the new suburbs.

Another point to note is the relationship that Strain had with Dublin Corporation. While largely a speculative builder, nonetheless the grants offered by the Corporation were vital to his success, while he was happy to do deals with the Corporation to the benefit of both parties.

Residences of Strain and Family

Robert Douglas Strain, father of Alexander, was listed in Thom's Directory from 1907, when he was living at 'Cremore', 75 Iona Road, named after his home in Co. Armagh. From 1909, he lived at 9 Iona Drive, while in 1912 he was living at 6 Iona Crescent. It seems likely that Strain Senior was involved in building houses in the area, probably in partnership with his son. At the time of the 1911 Census, the household living at 9 Iona Drive included the 65-year old widowed builder, his unmarried daughters Belinda (34) and Caroline (32), and Mary Carolan (28), their Roman Catholic Cavan-born servant. In 1913 and 1914, R.D. Strain lived at 23 Ballymun Road, probably in a house he himself built, since there are references to houses built by him on 'Claremont Road', presumably referring to this section of Ballymun Road. The last houses built by Robert's son Alexander at Cremore were close to this area.

In 1901 Alexander Strain and his family were living at 1 York Road, Rathmines. At the time, Alexander was a 27-year-old timber traveller, his Dublin-born wife, Kathleen, was 22, and they had a one-year-old baby daughter June. Alexander's 21-year-old brother Samuel, unmarried and in the building trade, was also present in the house on census night, and probably lodged with the family. Thom's directory also listed an Alexander Strain living at this address in 1904, but from 1905 he lived in Drumcondra, with a first address at 25 Drumcondra Road Lower. In 1891, this same house had been

102 Residences of Alexander Strain.

occupied by Thomas Wall, Builder, suggesting that this was a business address. Indeed, in 1907 Alexander Strain Esq. resided at 'Dunallen', Iona Road, while the Drumcondra Road premises was still listed in the name of A. Strain. Between 1908 and 1912, Alexander Strain, builder, had at least three different addresses: 2 Iona Park (1908), 8 Iona Drive (1909) and 76 Iona Road (1912).

By the time of the 1911 Census, the family had moved to 76 Iona Road, a 12-roomed first-class house which he had built. Now listed as a house builder, the 37-year-old Alexander and his wife had been married for 13 years, and had four children: June (11), May (8), Madge (7) and Dorrie (4). Clearly well set-up in life, the family also had a domestic servant, Daisy Watson, an 18-year-old Methodist. The family remained at 76 Iona Road until 1922, when the Strains moved to 34 Iona Road. According to Thom's Directory, Mrs Kathleen Strain lived at 2 Cliftonville Road in 1926 and 1927, but moved to number 46 in 1928, while Martin Leslie Atock, a civil engineer, future husband of Madge Strain, and a partner in the business, was living in number 2. From 1931 to 1943, Mrs Strain lived at 24 Cremore Park, but was also listed as the occupant of 46 Cliftonville Road, suggesting that the Cliftonville Road house was not sold until some time after the Strains had moved.

Iona and Lindsay Roads

In 1896, some three years after his arrival in Dublin, Alexander Strain, Contractor together with Walter Samuel Kinnear Esq., Financier, became registered owners of lands in Daneswell/Cross Guns North amounting to 10 acres, 3 roods and 17 perches (c.4 ha). While some of this land was built upon from about 1904, when Strain began work on Iona and Lindsay Roads, he did not undertake the extension of Hollybank Road until the late 1920s. The land formed part of the Bishop of Kildare's estate, sold by his descendant Lt Col. Sir Henry Gore Lindsay.

Although it has become fashionable and financially sensible to attribute the houses of Iona and Lindsay to Strain, creating difficulties for the researcher, in fact he did not build all of them. The houses at the top of both roads were in place before Strain came to Dublin, while his rival Thomas Connolly, Masterbuilder, was also building houses on Iona Road. Connolly, incidentally, claimed to have built better houses, his walls being a half an inch thicker. Little information has been found regarding the Connolly construction 'dynasty', although it is known that in 1890, contractors Thomas and James Connolly were living at Fernville, Drumcondra, while William Connolly, also

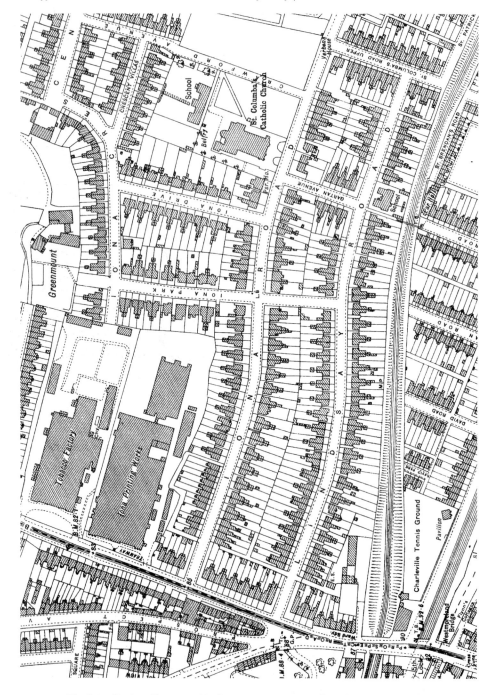

103 The Iona district, Glasnevin. (Ordnance Survey 1:2500 plan, Sheet 18 III, Dublin, 1938 revision.) Note the location of St Columba's church and the factories on Botanic Road.

104 Housing on Iona Park. (Photograph by J. Brady.)

a contractor, resided at Roseview. It is evident that the Connolly family was heavily involved in development in the district, and as late as 1932 a 'desirable residence with garden, tennis court, garage, electric light etc.' was being sold, with possession, by Connolly of Fernville (*Irish Times*, 26 March 1932).

In terms of style, the type of houses built by Strain in the first decade of the twentieth century reflect many of the changes which were occurring in terms of housing style in Britain as well as Ireland. The fairly solid, unpretentious late-Victorian house tended to be quite dark and built to a high density, with 'tunnel backs' for kitchen, scullery and other necessary facilities. From the 1870s, however, there had been an increase in the amount and variety of external materials and decoration used, while the new Edwardian-style houses being built from the turn of the century tended to be of lighter construction and more cheerful appearance than their Victorian counterparts. Fixtures and fittings included wood, marble, slate and cast iron. Red-tiled roofs with irregular patterns of window and gable were the norm. Outside walls were of light red bricks or covered with cement or rough-cast, while there was much outside woodwork (usually white) including balconies with wood palings.

105 Detail on housing in Iona. Note the tiling in the porch and the granite lintels
(Photograph by J. Brady.)

Now casement, rather than sash, windows began to predominate, and the bays
were of lighter construction, whether timber on a brick base, or tiles hung on
a timber frame, instead of brick and stone throughout. Strain's early houses
with their many 'extras' conform to this model.

This new ideal home of the early-twentieth century reflected the growing
importance attached to health and convenience, responded to the appeal of
individuality, flexibility and informality in the home, and sought an atmosphere of cosy homeliness and modesty. The new standard house reflected the
preference for one-family occupation and the smaller average family. The
house was squarer and more compact in plan, with a general reduction in the
number and size of rooms, fewer corridors and no back addition. Even so,
before 1920 rooms were still of generous proportions, and it was common to
have many more rooms, with a morning room as well as a sitting-room and
dining-room, and a separate scullery in addition to the kitchen. With the
elimination of long, dark and draughty passages, the house became brighter
and airier, in response to the Edwardian aspiration of the healthy home, while
the front garden was an important indication of status.

The houses in Iona and Lindsay are probably Strain's finest achievement as
a builder. Quality was the key to his approach. Although at first glance the

streets present an impression of uniformity, with red brick facades, granite sills, lintels and cornerstones, interlinking wrought iron railings and an even roofline, they are all different from each other. The houses in Lindsay Road were at the upper end of the range of dwellings built in the area. These red-brick houses 'both looked well and were extremely well-equipped and comfortable, with the added luxuries of a bathroom ... and indoor lavatory' (Gumley, 1982, p. 95). They had gardens front and back, and the fittings included marble fire-places, excellent kitchen ranges which provided hot water, and handsome stained glass transomes and doors. Many optional extras were offered to Strain's purchasers, including an additional stairway to a converted attic, while a façade of glazed brick (e.g. 66 & 68 Iona Road) was available, the bricks costing an extra half-penny each. Number 23 Lindsay Road, a three-bedroomed red-brick terraced house, was typical of the houses built by Strain. Although it was relatively small, details included decorative fireplaces, ceiling plaster-work, bathroom fittings and maid's room. Built in 1907, it had remained in the same family, almost unchanged apart from rewiring, until its auction in 1994, when it was sold for £105,000, a very high price for the time. More recently, houses in the area have been selling for anything from £300,000 to £660,000, depending on size and conditions. Indeed, such is the reputation and prestige of Strain-built houses that prices regularly outstrip those for similar homes on the southside of Dublin. Interestingly, many houses which have recently come on the market have done so for the first time since their initial purchase early in the twentieth century, having been passed down through the same family. Gumley (1982, p. 95) has suggested that the inhabitants of Lindsay Road had purchased their own homes, 'either with ready cash or cheap loans provided by the Dublin Corporation or building societies. Each dwelling cost anything from four hundred and twenty five pounds to about five hundred, if the attic was made into another room'. In early 2001 the story of a house on Iona Road which was up for auction came to the surface. Number 42 was one of three houses on the road which had been bought by Mary Jane Clarke directly from Strain, reputedly intended as dowries for her three daughters. This certainly suggests that the occupants of Strain's houses were fairly well off in the main.

The development of the roads can be traced in requests made by Strain to have various sections of new roads taken in charge by Dublin Corporation. By December 1911, Iona Park (from Lindsay Road up to and including the portion opposite 7 Iona Park), Lindsay Road (from Upper St Columba's Road to Gartan Avenue), and Gartan Avenue (from Iona Road to Lindsay Road) were ready to be taken in charge. Within two years, Strain had completed

Lindsay Road (from Iona Park to Gartan Avenue), Iona Park (from No. 7 to Iona Crescent), Iona Crescent (from No. 4 to and including the portion of the Road opposite Iona Drive), Iona Drive (from and including No. 15 to Iona Crescent).

A small portion of the plot acquired by Alexander Strain for house-building on Lindsay Road faced Prospect Road, opposite the Orphanage, now demolished and redeveloped for housing as Dalcassian Downs in the late 1980s. Having completed work on Lindsay, Strain turned his attention to this 'spare' land, and in 1919, plans were submitted to the Corporation for four new houses and shops at Prospect Road, between Lindsay Road and Whitworth Road, for Mr A. Strain. However, the projection was not approved, as the new houses were to be built on a line seven feet in advance of that of the adjoining houses, although the Paving Committee intimated that approval would be given if the existing building line was respected. Strain clearly put the Prospect Road plan on hold, because the next reference does not occur until June 1921, when the Paving Committee again directed that the new buildings be kept back to the frontage line of adjacent houses. As late as 1925, the Streets Section made reference to the proposed houses at Prospect Road, in connection with the proposed widening of that road, which had yet to be undertaken (Report 205/1925).

Strain, the Corporation, and interests outside Drumcondra/Glasnevin

Strain also had investments outside the Drumcondra/Glasnevin area. One such investment property was damaged during the 1916 Rising. In late 1918, the Paving Committee Accounts noted that Mr Alexander Strain had questioned an account of £15 18s. 5d., charged against him in connection with the pulling down of Nos. 18, 19 and 20 Lr Sackville Street, on the grounds, as he alleged, that certain work was included therein which was more for the protection of the adjoining buildings (Report 49/1918). A sum of £10 was offered in full settlement and, on the advice of the Law Agent, was accepted by the Corporation.

Strain was also active in the Inchicore area. In 1913 Dublin Corporation considered a suggested exchange of land at Inchicore, adjoining the Corporation dwellings there (Reports 287/1913 and 288/1913). This land was right at the edge of the city boundary at that time, and the exchange would straighten the existing irregular boundaries between the property in the county area, which had been purchased by Alexander Strain from the Lansdowne Estate, and the city. In all, 1 acre 2 roods 12 perches and 11 yards (c.0.4 ha) would be absorbed by the Corporation, in exchange for 1 rood 12 perches 7 yards (c.0.1 ha). The difference in value between the two areas of ground being £329, that sum was offered to and accepted by Mr Strain. Thus an area of building land slightly over one acre (c.0.4 ha) in area was valued at £329 in 1913. A boundary wall costing c.£390 would have to be erected, with Mr Strain undertaking to contribute one-third of the expenditure, on condition that he be allowed to erect the wall himself. The alteration of the boundary would place the Corporation in a position either to extend its existing building scheme at Inchicore or to let the additional land to private builders. This consideration is particularly interesting, suggesting that even at this early date, the Corporation was interested in the prospect of co-operating with private builders, although the 'reserved areas' system apparently did not come into operation until the 1920s.

In February 1914, the Housing Committee outlined the proposed exchange of land at the city boundary at Inchicore which, in addition to securing a uniform boundary, would enable the Corporation to erect about 50 additional working-class houses (Report 68/1914). Since the initial considerations, Mr Strain had acquired Lord Lansdowne's interest in this ground and negotiations were pursued with him. In addition to obtaining agreement from Strain, the Law Agent of Dublin Corporation needed the consent of both Dublin County Council and the South Dublin Rural District Council to the proposed annexation to the city of the ground situated within their district. In return for their non-opposition to the proposal, they suggested that the Corporation should afford sewage disposal and water supply facilities to the inhabitants of the houses which Mr Strain intended to erect outside the city boundary at Inchicore (such facilities would normally be the responsibility of the County Council and RDC). However, the Law Agent reported that he could not advise the Corporation to agree to such terms (Report 68/1914). In any case, the proposed exchange of land, and the resultant annexation of some further ground to the city area, were subject to the sanction of the Local Government Board. In 1915 the deal fell through, as the Local Government Board had been advised that it did not have the power to grant a Provisional Order for the proposed extension of the city boundary (Report 195/1915).

Undaunted, however, in the March Quarter, 1917, the Improvements Committee referred to another proposal involving an exchange of land at the Oblate site, Inchicore between Strain and the Corporation which was under consideration. This exchange would allow for the widening of the approach to the scheme at Ring Street, and would provide space for 20 additional working-class dwellings. However, these additional dwellings would be liable to the Rural District and County Council rates, which would come against the profits (or indeed increase the losses) on the building scheme. The Corporation

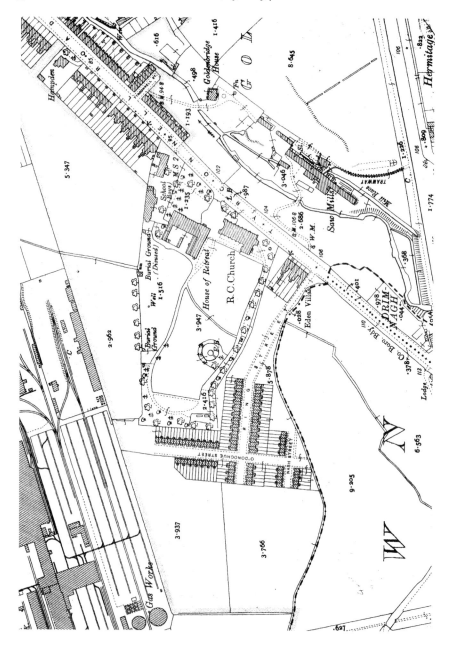

106 Development in Inchicore between 1907 and 1943. Note the western extension from
Ring Street in Dublin Corporation's 'Oblate' scheme and the new Jamestown road in the
plan on the right. The allotments were referred to in the Corporation's Land Cultivation

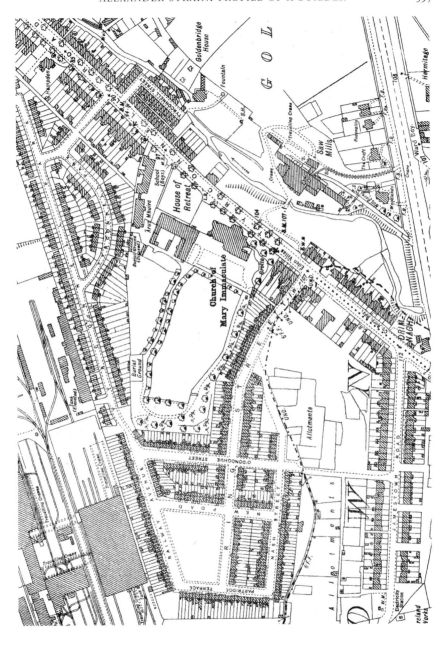

Committee reports as 'Strain's Fields'. Note also the SIAC site.
(Ordnance Survey 1:2500 plan, Sheet 18 IX, Dublin, 1911 and 1938 revisions.)

would have to expend £1133 on the erection of a boundary wall, give a piece of land in exchange and would have to take into the city drainage scheme at a fixed rate the drainage of any houses to be built by Mr Strain in the locality. The Committee thus agreed with the Law Agent's suggestion that negotiations should be confined to the acquisition of sufficient land to widen the entrance to Ring Street. Six months later, the Housing Committee noted that Mr Strain was willing to give sufficient land to enable Ring Street to be enlarged at its entrance, the Corporation assigning to him in return the angular plot near Tyrconnell Road. Strain also proposed that some exchange should be made which would render the angle of land held by the Corporation between Ring Street and Mr Strain's property available for building. The Corporation thus made plans to purchase his land, providing room for 25 or 26 additional houses on Ring Street (Report 278/1917).

The proposed exchange of land at Inchicore between the Corporation and Mr Strain was again under consideration in 1918. The original proposal (discussed in 1914) was that the Corporation would annex c.1½ acres (c.0.6 ha) of Strain's land, and hand over to him a ¼ acre (c.0.1 ha) of city property, thus straightening the city boundary and providing space for 50 additional working-class dwellings. The new plan involved diverting the stream in an open cutting through Mr Strain's lands, which were in allotments, on the agreement that, whenever Mr Strain required to build upon that portion of his land, or use it for purposes other than general agriculture, the Corporation would fill in and pipe the cutting (Report 189/1918).

While Strain did not begin building on this land for some time, in October 1919 he wrote to the Corporation, intimating that he had made arrangements for the manufacture of bricks at Inchicore and would probably be able to turn out from 80,000 to 120,000 per week (Report 110/1920). The City Architect welcomed the move, since some healthy competition would reduce the currently high prices, while this source of supply would be useful when the work on the Fairbrother's Fields area began. One imagines that the latter advantage had not been lost on Mr Strain!

It was not until the summer of 1925 that Strain apparently began building houses at Jamestown, Inchicore. At this time a drainage connection was approved 'provided the South Dublin Rural District Council enter into an agreement with the Corporation for the drainage and for payment of the Main Drainage and Sewers rates on each of the houses in question' (Report 178/1926, p. 493). It is notable that these houses were being built at a time when new legislation was providing grants for builders.

In the mid- to late-1930s, the Tyrconnell Road/Jamestown Road area was developed further. In May, 1934, revised drainage plans for 160 proposed houses on Tyrconnell Road were approved, while 12 houses were to be built there in the following year. Among the builders involved in development at Tyrconnell and Jamestown Roads was W. Kennerk, who may have been operating on Strain's land. Other builders mentioned in connection with housing on Jamestown Road included Thomas Gallagher, possibly the same man who built extensively on 'reserved sites' at Mobhi Road/Griffith Avenue and in the Vernon Estate, and A.E. Dunn. Development in this area continued at a rapid pace in the late 1930s, and in April 1936, numbers were allotted to 12 houses and two shops on Tyrconnell Road. Although the precise details are not available, it seems likely that this development involved land owned by Alexander Strain. In November 1938, reference was made to the extension of the 4 inch (c.10 cm) main to supply houses on the 'Shannon and Strain Estate', Jamestown Road, Inchicore. It seems unlikely that Strain himself was building here, since none of the houses have the characteristic 'Strain' quality, but he was acting as a developer, leasing sites to others. It is interesting to note that the general impression is of poorer class houses than those built by Strain in the Drumcondra and Glasnevin area. Also, the reference in the report to the Shannon and Strain estate may refer to W.J. Shannon, Strain's solicitor, and a possible co-financier. Hunter (1981) notes that builders or speculators often raised capital from a solicitor who would have the small savings of his clients to invest.

In Alexander Strain's will, it is shown that he held the fee simple to five statute acres (c.2 ha) in undeveloped land in Jamestown, leased from September 1913. In addition, a corrective affidavit to the will shows that he had shares in the Leinster Brick Company, while part of the premises was let to the South of Ireland Asphalt Company (SIAC), which has dominated Irish road-building since the 1920s, when the company was the sole concessionary and contractor for Trinidad Lake Bitumen and Limmer Asphalt Products. SIAC Construction Ltd. still operates a depot from Jamestown Road, Inchicore.

Cliftonville, Fairfield and Daneswell: developments from the late 1920s

It is likely that Strain had some sort of overall scheme of development in mind for the land that he had purchased in 1896. We saw in the previous chapter that he had planned to extend Hollybank Road to connect with Botanic Road but this had never happened. Following this failure, the unbuilt land north of

107 Cliftonville and Marguerite roads, Glasnevin.
(Ordnance Survey 1:2500 plan, Sheet 18 III, Dublin, 1938 revision.)

Marguerite Road was developed by a number of interests in the mid-1920s. In a report on the construction of new roads at Glasnevin, proposals for the development of the land lying between Botanic Road, Botanic Avenue and Hollybank Road submitted by Messrs Charles J. Reddy and Sons and by Mr Alexander Strain were approved in general terms by the Commissioner (Report 27/1924). Mr Strain was to build 46 houses on a new road to be named 'Cliftonville Road', while Messrs Reddy were to erect a number of houses on a new road to be constructed off Botanic Road at Fairfield. Six houses had already been completed and the rest were in course of construction. Charles J. Reddy and Sons of 35 Westland Row were involved in the sale of several houses on Iona Road in 1918. While acting as solicitors in several cases where houses were sold by auction, there is no doubt that, in 1930, Reddy acquired the fee simple of land at the junction of Mobhi Road and Fairfield Road, where he later built four shops. Perhaps, like Mr Shannon, Reddy was a solicitor who acted as investor in construction projects.

Both Reddy and Strain had applied for benefits accorded by the City Council's resolution of 29 October 1923 as amended by the resolution of 14 April 1924, namely 'that where the owners of land on which a sufficient number of houses of a PLV not exceeding £22 each have been built request the Corporation to construct the necessary streets, and convey to the Corporation free of cost the land necessary for such purpose, the Streets Committee shall, subject to the prior approval of Council, and the sanction of the Minister for Local Government, construct such streets as may be considered advisable- this offer to hold good for three years from 1 January 1924' (Report 27/1924, p. 89). By March 1925, the works at Fairfield and Cliftonville Road had been carried out with the approval of the Government under the Unemployment Relief Grant (Report 202/1925).

The plans for Strain's houses at Cliftonville Road were prepared by Mr John Butler, architect, of 1 Percy Place. The specification for the 46 houses provided for the superstructure of the outside walls to be built in County Dublin brick, the interior walls to be of breeze concrete, and the window-sills to be of granite or concrete. The roofs were to be covered with asbestos slates or Penrhyn slates, supported by the best white spruce.

Meanwhile, the *Irish Builder and Engineer* reported that plans for about 70 semi-detached, two-storey houses on Fairfield Road (Reddy Estate) had been completed for Messrs Chas. Dillon & Co. by the end of May 1924 (*Irish Builder and Engineer*, 31 May 1924). Messrs Geo. Dillon and Co., presumably the same firm, lodged plans for new roads and houses at Fairfield, Botanic Road, which were examined by the Commissioner for the Streets Section in the Quarter ended 30 June 1924. He sanctioned the erection of 14 houses on the new road, as he was satisfied that these houses would not interfere with the future development of the area, or the construction later on of a new road connecting Botanic Road with Ballymun Road. An application was also included to have the roads on Fairfield Estate constructed at the Corporation's expense (Report 52/1925).

The Imperial Tobacco Co. (Messrs John Player and Sons) offered to sell to the Corporation the land necessary for the construction of a road and sewer for £190, consisting of 1 rood 14 perches (*c*.0.1 ha). Due to the conformation of the land, it was necessary to drain some of the houses on the new roads

108 Housing in Cliftonville Road (*above*) and Marguerite Road (*below*).
(Photographs by J. Brady.)

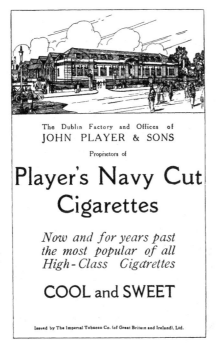

The Dublin Factory and Offices of
JOHN PLAYER & SONS
Proprietors of

Player's Navy Cut Cigarettes

*Now and for years past
the most popular of all
High - Class Cigarettes*

COOL and SWEET

Issued by The Imperial Tobacco Co. (of Great Britain and Ireland), Ltd.

109 Advertisement for
Players cigarettes.

being built by Strain and Reddy off Botanic Road into a sewer in Botanic Avenue. For this reason, a drain was to be laid in the land adjoining Botanic Avenue which was formerly owned by Mr Maher and acquired by the tobacco company for the erection of houses for their employees (Report 69/1925).

Cliftonville and Hollybank Roads, c.1926

Strain began work on Cliftonville Road in 1926. Housing requirements changed after World War I, with the desire for smaller, more convenient houses reflecting smaller family sizes and the lack of servants. In Britain, housing architecture generally promoted an escapist image, with mock-Tudor styles aspiring to the security of a long-gone age. Builders in Dublin included some of the features of these British houses, using half-timbering (mock beams), bays hung with tiles, leaded lights, red brick or pebble-dash, fancy brickwork and gabled roofs. The attempt to evoke a 'rural idyll' resulted in a haphazard combination of architectural details in many semi-detached houses. Strain's post-World War I houses reflect the changing demands of the time but in a more sober style. Maid's rooms and butler's pantries were no longer required, since servants were no longer freely available, and in general houses had to be

110 Imperial Tobacco Co. houses on Botanic Avenue. (Photograph by J. Brady.)

more manageable and easy to heat. Provision for garaging took the form of a laneway to the rear, although as yet few motorcars were in private hands. However, despite the changes, these terraced houses feature many of the embellishments of Strain's earlier houses, with high ceilings, bay windows, leaded glass hall doors, granite sills and lintels. Apparently when Strain was building these houses at Cliftonville Road the first owners were given the option of having either two storeys or three, which explains why the landings on Cliftonville are very tall and wide to allow for the building of another staircase going up to the large attic. The style of the Hollybank Road houses, built at about the same time, is similar, though less well specified, despite the fact that here Strain opted for a semi-detached type. As at Cliftonville Road, the Hollybank Road houses were designed by J.M. Butler. The *Irish Builder and Engineer* noted that the plans for the eight new houses about to be erected at the top of Hollybank Road by Strain at the end of 1924 provided for the erection of a garage in each case, still an unusual feature at the time.

In most of Strain's activities in the Drumcondra and Glasnevin area, he acted as a builder on land either acquired on a long building lease or purchased in fee-simple from a local land-owner. However, in at least one instance, there is evidence that Strain acted as a developer of land which he

111 Strain houses (*above*) and Wearing houses (*below*) on Hollybank Road.
(Photographs by J. Brady.)

then sold to another builder for the erection of houses. Like many small transactions of this nature, this would probably have remained undiscovered but for a chance legality which was duly recorded in the Dublin Corporation Reports. This might indicate that Strain could not afford to retain lands that he was not then in a position to develop. Why sell to Wearing when he could have built himself?

In June 1926, Mr G.B. Wearing applied for a Corporation grant of £75 per house in respect of six houses in course of erection at Hollybank Road. These houses, some, at least, intended for managers in the Player's factory, are situated opposite Strain's houses. Because it was originally intended that Dublin Corporation would carry out the road construction in connection with these houses, charging it against the sum provided in the Estimates for such work, the Scheme was not scheduled for grants under the Local Assistance Scheme. Subsequently, however, Mr Strain, owner of the site, intimated his intention of carrying out the road work himself, and it was accordingly decided to give Mr Wearing the appropriate grant. But for Strain's intervention, the existence of this extra link in the development chain would never have come to light. Mr Wearing himself lived at 53 Marguerite Road in 1930 and may have been involved in construction on that street.

Cremore Estate

The Cremore Estate was named after the birthplace of Alexander Strain's father, Robert Douglas Strain. In June 1928, Alexander Strain applied to the Streets Section to extend the sewer on Old Finglas Road to include 52 recently constructed new houses, presumably part of the Cremore area. Six months later, sanction was given to plans lodged by Strain for the construction of 26 houses at Cremore Avenue and Cremore Road, subject to the position of Cremore Avenue being altered to a site ten feet (c.3 m) further north. One of these houses, 4 Cremore Park, a semi-detached house, was auctioned in October 1994 for £130,000, a very considerable amount at the time. The unusually long garage was built to accommodate the original owner's Daimler, another example of the personalized touch to Strain's houses, while other features included picture rails, ceiling mouldings, leaded and stained glass panels, and a small built-in unit by John Hicks. In 1930 the Strains made their final move, to 24 Cremore Park, while Alex built Cremore House for his newly-wed daughter Madge and Martin Atock, the civil engineer who had joined him in the business some years earlier. Another daughter, Dorothy, was positioned by Strain in a corner house on Cremore Road, opposite his own. An 'attractive new house' at Cremore Park cost £1000 in 1932, with rates remission. The house had two sittingrooms and three bedrooms, and all modern conveniences, including a garage. Prospective purchasers were invited to apply directly to Strain, 24 Cremore Park (*Irish Times*, 9 April 1932).

Again the style of the houses built by Strain in the Cremore area reflects many aspects of changing house style in the inter-war period. The bay window, often over two storeys, was the most standard feature of these inter-war houses, in Ireland as in Britain, while a porch was generally considered to be essential, to frame and emphasize the front door. Bay windows were an almost obligatory feature, partly because they were rarely included in local authority houses, but also because they made the room appear larger and brighter. Mass-produced joinery for bay and other windows was one of the few advances in building methods adopted in the boom of the late 1920s and 1920s. While steel-framed windows were introduced about 1919, they were not widely used until the mid-1930s. Usually the hall was lit by an extra window to the side of the front door, often an oriel or porthole design in stained glass.

Interior plasterwork remained extremely popular, using mass produced cornices and ceiling roses, while stained glass featured on front door and bay window panelling. These details were one of the means used by builders to make their private houses distinctive from neighbouring local authority estates of a similar high quality, thus justifying the additional cost incurred. Thus, houses on Jamestown Road, Inchicore adjoining the 'Oblate Site' Corporation dwellings included expensive granite lintels, to distinguish these as private homes. A new-style internal layout, as advocated by the Tudor Walters Report, became the norm in the 1920s, as it was recognized that maximum floor space could be afforded by the elimination of passages and waste spaces. More light and air were achieved by leaving out the 'back addition', but rooms became smaller with lower ceilings. Most builders of cheaper houses adopted a basic rectangular plan which kept construction simple and costs at the minimum. There were four main rooms of more or less equal size, with the third bedroom and kitchen squeezed into the remaining space. There was very little variation in interior arrangement in these houses. The entrance hall stood in front of a kitchen which was much smaller than its pre-1914 equivalent, just managing to accommodate a cooker, gas washing boiler, wringer, sink, hot water boiler and storage cabinet. The dining-room was at the back, alongside the kitchen, and often with a serving-hatch, and French doors giving access to the garden. The stairs were parallel to the side wall of the house, leading to a

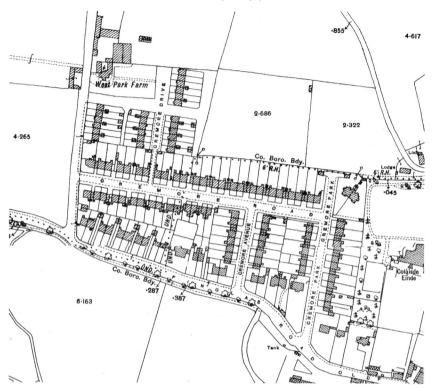

112 Layout plan of Cremore estate, Glasnevin and Alexander Strain's house at 23 Cremore Park. (Ordnance Survey 1:2500 plan, Sheet 14 XV (1939) and 18 III, Dublin, 1938 revision. Photograph by R. McManus.)

tiny landing serving the two main bedrooms directly above the living-rooms, also the bathroom and w.c. over the kitchen, and, at the front of the house, the third bedroom or 'boxroom'.

Only the most expensive houses built after 1920 contained any provision for servants, and 'labour-saving' was the catchword of the period. Many houses now had some tiling in bathrooms and kitchens and even the cheapest houses had some form of fitted kitchen furniture. Most post-1919 construction had indoor toilets, or at least a w.c. near the back door of the house and houses were generally fitted with a hot water system operated either by a back boiler in the living-room fireplace or a slow combustion stove or gas circulator in the kitchen. Although electricity was available, its use was confined to lighting, irons and small fires. For those who had lived in older accommodation without bathroom or inside w.c., heated by coal fires, and lit by gas, oil lamps and candles, the new suburban homes and estates invariably brought dramatic improvements in standards of hygiene, health and well-being. Indeed, the improved heat, lighting, plumbing and sanitation meant that, by the 1930s, services in housing had grown in complexity and cost, comprising up to one third of the total cost per house (Powell, 1980).

Mobhi Road (Dean Swift Avenue)

Mobhi Road (also spelt Moibhi) runs parallel to the Drumcondra road as an important routeway to the city centre. It acts as a boundary to the Iona district. A plot of ground on the west side of what was then called Dean Swift Avenue, Drumcondra, was leased jointly to Alexander Strain and G.M. Linzell, Strain's son-in-law, in 1929. The plot, comprising approximately 1022 feet (312 m) frontage, formed part of a Corporation 'reserved area' for letting to private builders and public utility societies. Strain had applied for leases of ground for the erection of 28 dwelling houses at a cost of from £800 to £1000 each. A 150-year lease was offered at a rent of 4s. per foot frontage, on condition that houses were erected within 12 months of the date on which the letting was sanctioned (a common stipulation at the time). Strain was clearly adept at negotiations, because the report noted his acceptance of the conditions, subject to the ground being demised in two leases, and to a period of two years being granted in which to complete the buildings, with the customary remission of one year's rent to be made, provided that the buildings were completed within two years. It seems that Strain acquired further building sites on Mobhi Road at a later date, since No. 161 St Mobhi Road, a recently-

113 Home of Samuel Philips, Ormond Road. (Photograph by R. McManus.)

sold four-bed semi-detached house, described as Strain-built, is at the opposite end of the road to the above-mentioned houses.

Associates of Alexander Strain

In looking at Strain's associates, we can build up a picture of the networks which existed in the building profession during the first half of this century. In many ways, Strain can be seen at the centre of a building dynasty for, although he had no sons to carry on his work, his daughters married members of the building trade.

Samuel Phillips, who married Rita Strain, was involved in building in the Church Avenue/Ormond Road area during the 1920s. At all times, he appears to have been a small-scale builder, with four or five houses approved at a time. In 1926 he lived at 9 Church Avenue, but later moved to Ormond Road. A Patrick Kerr was living at No. 13, and in 1925, Messrs Phillips, Wilson and Kerr were granted permission to build five houses on Ormond Road. However, in the 1930s, there is some evidence that Phillips had extended his activities outside the Drumcondra area. In January 1930, for example, it was noted that Phillips was erecting two semi-detached houses on the Stillorgan

Road, while in July 1933, a Mr S. Phillips was building flats and offices at 21 & 22 Lr Dorset Street. Finally, in 1939, Phillips' quote for the erection of a concrete boundary wall at St Joseph's Blind Asylum, Drumcondra, was accepted, being the lowest suitable tender. This is the only indication that he undertook any public works.

Among the other builders who erected houses on Ormond Road were Messrs Pigott and O'Brien in 1925 and Mr Daly in 1929, while P.T. Gallagher, another builder, lived, and probably built, on the street. The road was built in dribs and drabs, with two to four houses being approved at a time. Sewer reconstruction work at Ormond Road, costing £45 was approved in the June Quarter, 1929, while in July 1932, S. Phillips of 2 Ormond Road was erecting a pair of two-storey semi-detached houses on Ormond Road to plans and specification prepared by Messrs McDonnell, Dixon and Downes, Ely Place. As late as 1940, Phillips was listed as a building contractor in Thom's Directory, and was still living at 2 Ormond Road, Drumcondra. His situation contrasts with that of his brother-in-law, G.M. Linzell, who, although still a building contractor at that date, had moved his home and business to the Donnybrook area. While Linzell apparently prospered, the position of Phillips was less secure, particularly as Strain worded his will so as to exclude Phillips in the event of his daughter Rita's untimely death!

Boyd, the supposed partner and Ritchie, another 'successor'

In 1923, Thomas J. Boyd was listed in Thom's Directory as the occupier of 52 Iona Crescent (built in 1921), and 'successor to Strain & Boyd, Building Contractor'. It seems strange that Boyd was advertising himself as the successor to the business, given that Alexander Strain was still building in Hollybank Road in 1927, and was involved in developments at Mobhi Road well into the 1930s. Perhaps Boyd was referring to Robert Douglas Strain, who died c.1915. Apparently, Strain and Boyd built houses on Hollybank Road together. In 1921 Boyd was living at 62 Lindsay Road, one of Strain's houses, but in 1926 he moved to the newly completed 135 Hollybank Road, beside his offices. This may have been one of the houses which he built in association with Strain. Meanwhile, in several 1930 editions of the *Irish Builder and Engineer*, an advertisement was carried for the firm Thomas J. Boyd, with L.C. Ritchie, Builder and Contractor listed as proprietor. The premises were still at Iona Crescent, Glasnevin, Phone Drumcondra 159, and free estimates were promised.

T.J. Boyd built at a number of locations in the city, as evident from a notice in June 1923, stating that the following contracts were being carried out: two

Telephone : Drumcondra 159.   ESTIMATES FREE

THOMAS J. BOYD

(Successor to STRAIN & BOYD).

BUILDER and CONTRACTOR   -

Alterations, Shop Fitting, Sewerage

Painting, Etc. -   -   -   -   -

VILLAS AND BUNGALOWS BUILT TO ORDER.

IONA CRESCENT, GLASNEVIN, DUBLIN

114 Advertisement for Thomas J. Boyd of Iona Crescent (Hollybank Road).

shops on Rathmines Road for the NKM Co., shop in Killester for Mr Ging (who was previously seen to be involved in development on Dublin Corporation 'reserved areas'), return building 18 Lr Drumcondra Road for Mr P. Fitzpatrick, two houses at the head of Hollybank Road, Drumcondra. By August, plans were being prepared for a further eight houses at Hollybank Road. In addition, he carried out structural improvements at 7 Liffey Street. In August 1924, Boyd had plans prepared by J.M. Butler (the architect used by Strain at Cliftonville and Hollybank) for two new houses at Crescent Villas.

As available building land in the Drumcondra and Glasnevin areas became increasingly scarce in the 1930s, builders began to migrate southwards, as previously mentioned, concentrating on erecting high quality housing in the southern suburbs. As early as June 1932, the *Irish Builder and Engineer* reported that Mr L.C. Ritchie of Iona Crescent, Glasnevin had commenced work on the erection of 'a further series of houses' at Aylesbury Park, Merrion Road to plans by Mr Hicks, 86 Merrion Square. Ritchie became involved in the development of the Nutley Estate, Stillorgan Road soon after, and in 1937 the name Nutley Park was approved for the new road. An advertisement of 14

March 1936, for Nutley Park Estate, 'adjoining the Elm Park Golf and Sports Club and within ten minutes bus ride of the city centre', provided a description of the housing type utilized. In fact three different types of houses were on offer, all of 'sound solid construction' and costing from £1150 each. The three bedroom, semi-detached homes featured two reception rooms, a maid's room (unusual at this late date), large hall, bathroom, lavatory, kitchen, scullery, outside w.c., coalhouse, gardens, electricity, gas and a coke boiler. In addition, the advertisement noted that 'should you wish to erect a house to your own plans, a site with any frontage can be leased on a long term at a reasonable rate', another example of how the builder-developer could be flexible in their operations.

In October 1937, Wilton House, Merrion Road, was recommended for a building development. This was built through 1938 and into 1939, the new roads being named Merlyn Road and Drive. This infill development was close to Ritchie's houses at Ailesbury Park, and may have been built by him.

Linzell: The Rise, Glasnevin and Ailesbury Road areas

Having built houses jointly with his father-in-law on Mobhi Road in the late 1920s, G.M. Linzell had a larger scheme at Hampstead Hill approved in February 1932. The layout plan was approved subject to roads and sewers being constructed to Corporation specifications. The architect used was Mr Harold Greenwood of London, who designed a series of terraced and semi-detached houses at Hampstead Hill as well individual houses on Ballymun Road, such as that built for J.G. Wilson, Esq. Some of his houses were used in a 1932 advertisement for Snowcrete White Portland Cement. Building must have begun almost immediately, since by October, a collection of domestic refuse once per week was approved for the new houses in Hampstead Avenue, Ballymun Road. Linzell did not ignore the need for services for the occupants of his new houses, and by March 1933 had received permission for the erection of four shop dwellings. By October, approval was given to a proposal to have grass plots and shrubs in the concrete footpath facing the new shops, provided that the owner erected a railing around these plots or, alternatively, to fix seats in the concrete (Report 62/1933).

A typical lease for one of Linzell's houses is that of the 'leasehold estate in the dwellinghouse and premises known as Baravore, 104 Ballymun Road', dated the 1 June 1933. The lessor was one Henry Sinclair Jermyn, who had previously lived at 43 Marguerite Road, not too far away. The house was

115 Linzell's 'Wendon', off Mobhi Road, Glasnevin. (Photograph by J. Brady.)

purchased for £999, while the lease of the ground rent was for the term of 999 years from the 1 May 1933 at the yearly rent of £9. Jermyn purchased the house through the Guinness Permanent Building Society over a period of 21 years. The lease was signed in the presence of Shannon & Co., 19 Ormond Quay, the same firm of solicitors as used by Alexander Strain. Given that Strain was a governor of the Adelaide Hospital, it is interesting to note that by the 1970s, before it was finally purchased outright, the ground rent on the property of 104 Ballymun Road was being paid to the Adelaide Hospital, Peter Street, Dublin 8.

George Malcolm Linzell, like his father-in-law, came from a building background. In his case, Linzell followed in the footsteps of two generations of builders, but rather than being self-taught, he also took courses of training in architecture and town planning. Linzell illustrated his interest in the new architectural styles not only by building a new style of speculative housing, but also by choosing to live in a 'modern' architect-designed house named 'Wendon'. Linzell was described as 'a man whose imagination and capacity to handle infinite practical detail made life really worth living for a few refreshing and stimulating hours' (*Irish Builder and Engineer*, 13 August 1932, p. 735). Wendon illustrates that great imagination, as an extraordinarily pure 'modern' style house which included a loggia and sleeping-porch. Up-to-date materials

MODERN ARCHITECTURAL DESIGNS

in brick, concrete or concrete units are a feature of both the cheapest and most luxurious houses in all schemes by

G. M. LINZELL, A.I.O.B.

WENDON, BOITHRIN MOIBHI, GLASNEVIN, DUBLIN, N.W.3

The roofing tiles and bricks used in the construction of the houses illustrated below and on page 25 are manufactured by

Concrete Products of Ireland L<u>td.</u>

at their DUBLIN works [6a DOLPHIN'S BARN] to pass all Government and Building Research Board Tests

116 Advertisement for Linzell featuring 'Wendon' and for Concrete Products of Ireland. (*Cautionary Guide to Dublin*, 1933, p. 39.)

117 House by Linzell at the corner of Hampstead Avenue. The lower image shows houses on The Rise, Glasnevin. The house on the left has its orginal windows.
(Photographs by R. McManus.)

were used, including pre-cast concrete blocks for the walling, using a 2.5 inch cavity to provide insulation. Wendon was considered to be 'the last word in artistic comfort in Ireland' and was also admitted by visiting architects to be the equal of anything of its type in England or elsewhere. Hidden in a small side road off Moibhi Road, renamed and now the location of the Central Fisheries Board, little of the original style of Wendon is now evident to the passer-by.

In 1935 Linzell was advertising 'Suntrap' houses at The Rise, Glasnevin. At the same time, however, he had clearly begun formulating plans for his next major development, this time on the south side of the city in the prestigious Ailesbury area, close to L.C. Ritchie. 'Suntrap' houses were in vogue because of a then current concern with a healthy environment and a new craze for sunbathing. The house was a watered-down version of the Modern movement in architecture with horizontal windows and a lack of mouldings and ornament but still with a hipped roof and door canopy, unlike the 'pure' form with a flat roof. Porthole windows, flat and curved surfaces and the use of white paint were other features.

In March 1933, approval was given for an amended layout plan for Alpha Close and The Rise, Hampstead Estate, but alterations continued as late as 1936. In November 1936, some 700 feet (*c.*213 m) of the Rise was taken in charge, and by April 1937 the entire road was in charge of the Corporation. In August 1937, 22 houses were approved off The Rise, subject to the maintenance of the 'island' feature to the satisfaction of the Corporation and in September, Linzell was given the go-ahead for a central island in the layout at Hampstead Close, while approval was given in December 1938 for houses at Hampstead Park, the Rise, subject to conditions including a combined drain agreement, specifications re road/paths, sewers and manholes (Reports 40/1937, 48/1937, 1/1939). In June that year, it was noted that approval for the 21 houses was given subject to the lower part of the flanks of the end houses being brick faced to match the fronts (Report 30/1939). Finally, in July 1939, plans for eight garages at The Rise, Hampstead Park were approved.

Development in the Ailesbury Road area began in the early 1930s, when infill development occurred on the grounds of several large houses. Plans for 'Ailesbury House Estate Development' subject to acceptance of Corporation's requirements regarding sewers, width of roads etc., were agreed in early 1931, and by November a numbering scheme for four new houses on Ailesbury Road was adopted. Further references to the Ailesbury House Estate Development were made that December, when a proposed eight houses were approved.

Linzell and his wife eventually moved to Ailesbury Drive, so it is likely that the houses being built here from January 1934 were built by him. By April 1939, 100 yards (*c.*91 m) of Ailesbury Drive from Angelsea Road were fit to be taken in charge. Meanwhile, development at the St Anne's site, a large house on Anglesea Road, Donnybrook, began from about 1936. Approval was given to the building development at St Anne's, subject to a number of conditions which illustrate the impact of the Town Planning Committee on the work of the Corporation. In addition to concerns that the frontage on Anglesea Road would be set back to allow for future widening to 50 feet (*c.*15 m), and to the building line on side roads being 35 feet (*c.*11 m) from back of footpath, there was a greater concern with the layout and architecture of the houses. Thus, it was required that the houses fronting on Ailesbury Road would be of red brick, while the houses on remaining frontages were to be of brick or stucco, but laid out in balanced groups (Report 31/1936). The same report notes the approval of the layout of 2–14 Ailesbury Grove, St Anne's (*sic*) Development Scheme. In May 1938, approval was given to a house at the corner of Ailesbury Drive and Eglinton Road, and to a house at the corner of Brookvale Road and Eglinton Road. It appears, therefore, that Linzell was involved in building on both roads.

In March 1937, the Ailesbury Grove Development was advertised, with show houses on view daily. The houses had two reception, five bedrooms (unusually large), large garages, out-offices and garden, with 'all brick construction of superlative quality'. Not surprisingly, the price of £1765 was a reflection of that high quality and unusual size. Interested parties were requested to apply to St Ann's Development Co. Ltd. Wendon, Boithrín Mobhi, Glasnevin (*Irish Times*, 27 March 1937). Thus Linzell, Strain's son-in-law, had extended his movements to the southside, again focusing on high quality housing. It is interesting to note that the building trade had now developed to the extent that, rather than operating as an individual, Linzell had formed a limited liability company to undertake development at this estate.

The great interest taken by the Corporation in the development of this area reflects a generally heightened official interest in the ideas of town planning. It also seems likely that the Corporation hoped to retain the high status of the area, ensuring high rateable valuations on the houses. Thus, as late as 1939, as work continued on the St Ann's Estate, Ailesbury Road, plans for a 'residence' were approved by the Corporation subject to there being no departure from the layout plan already approved and to the colour of roof tiles being altered to comply with the scheme already approved for the general development of the estate (Report 12/1939).

The Dublin and District Housebuilders' Association
and town planning

Although Alexander Strain can be shown to have operated in a small way, in that he built only a few houses at a time, it seems likely that he had a broader conception in mind. That in 1896 he acquired such extensive lands, some of which were not developed until some 30 years later, suggests a degree of forethought, if not conscious planning, on the part of the builder. But what of the connection with formal town planning? Did builders of this time have much awareness of the debates going on regarding housing and town planning? While articles in the *Irish Builder and Engineer* show that information was available to them, how many builders actually concerned themselves with issues beyond financial gain? Here the researcher is particularly fortunate, because Alexander Strain was a man of action. As chairman of the Dublin and District Housebuilders' Association, records survive of the speech made by Strain on the occasion of the association's 'annual supper and smoking concert' in October 1932. The following lines provide the only surviving clear, direct view of the man and his opinions.

> There is so much that could be said about the city of Dublin, its history, architecture, and the culture of its people, and I feel all I can do is to confine myself to an aspect with which I have been associated for the best part of my life- that is, the development of its suburbs. The suburbs of Dublin compare, I think, very favourably with those of any of the great cities of England. But neither in Dublin nor in any of the cities of England have the suburbs been developed on a pre-arranged plan. The result is ribbon development, depreciation of good-class housing owing to the construction in recent years of houses of lesser value and schemes of artizans' dwellings in their immediate vicinity; and other defects. The opportunity was not taken, I am sorry to say, of lining the main roads leading from our city with houses having some pretence to beauty and surrounded with spacious gardens. This cannot now be remedied, but there is no doubt that during the last ten years or so there has been great improvement in the development of the suburbs. There is more variety in design and layout and larger gardens are being provided. It is hoped that the promised Town Planning Bill will very soon become a fact and that it will be drafted in such a way as

to encourage those who have the beauty of our city at heart and make it difficult for those who have not to continue in their old ways.

(Alexander Strain, quoted on the occasion of his speech
to the Dublin and District Housebuilders' Association,
Irish Builder and Engineer, 22 October 1932, p. 962).

Clearly, here was a builder who was very much aware of the need for town planning. His early developments were hardly innovative, Iona and Lindsay roads are conventional through-streets, but though conservative by nature, nonetheless clearly he had been convinced by the town planning movement. He was critical of past developments and hopeful for a better future, when town planning, better design and site layout would result in a more beautiful city. Naturally, as a speculator, he was concerned at the way houses depreciated in value but more surprising was the support given to the ideals of the town planning movement.

At the same meeting, the views of other prominent members of the building and allied trades were heard. Louis P. Kinlen, as Vice-Chairman of the Association, spoke of the intentions of the body to improve the standard of building in Dublin in terms of design, material, construction and possibly price, in order to make Dublin a model for other Irish towns. H.M. Dockrell, TD, spoke at length about the new Town Planning Bill while Mr G.F. Beckett, president of the RIAI, was concerned with the need for close co-operation between builders and architects, reminding his audience to retain a common goal, of building better and more beautifully. Mr Thomas O'Donnell, BL, toasted 'The Association' before turning to discuss the numbers of families living in one-room tenements. He also urged members to use Irish building materials wherever possible.

Will of Alexander Strain

Alexander Strain died in 1943. Various pieces of information relating to property holding and management can be gleaned from his will. Much of his money was clearly tied up in property, and upon his death No. 28 Wicklow Street, premises in the Rise, Cremore Road, Cremore Drive and Cremore Park were sold. The fact that houses in the Rise were sold suggests either that Strain built some of these houses (thus explaining the stylistic differences between houses on the north and south sides of the road), or that Strain financed Linzell's building operations here. The building works at 52a Iona Crescent,

No. 3 Iona Crescent and Hollybank Works were also sold. He received rent from Charleville Lawn Tennis Club and held the fee simple to five statute acres (*c.*2 ha) of undeveloped land in Jamestown, leased from September 1913. As befits a builder, Strain had shares in the Leinster Brick Company, as well as in the Phoenix Oil and Transport Company. Alexander Strain died very suddenly on 18 September 1943 at his home in Cremore Park and was buried at Dean's Grange.

An obituary in the *Irish Times* recorded some of Strain's charitable work in later years, including involvement as chairman of the Drumcondra Hospital Managing Committee, Governor of the Adelaide Hospital, keen supporter of the Marrowbone Lane Fund and trustee of the Abbey Presbyterian Church, in addition to his position as a well-known builder. Indeed, his obituary in the Abbey Church Magazine noted that Alexander Strain 'was known far beyond the bounds of the Abbey congregation, and in many homes, of other communions as well as our own, his passing has caused keen regret … We know something of his generous gifts to our congregation, but we know little of his private munificence in a multitude of ways, especially to folk in difficult circumstances without inquiry as to their faith'. In the address at Strain's funeral service, his generous nature was remembered, as were 'his freshness and buoyancy, his sense of humour, his delightful smile, everything about him, quite unspoiled by his success in life … an inspiration to us all'.

Conclusion

The story of Alexander Strain and his many connections illustrates the nature of Dublin house-building industry in the early part of this century. Generally small-scale, relatively-unplanned, although this gradually changed in the years preceding the World War II, the housing built in this period was the work of a relatively small, close-knit community. The fact that at least three of Strain's four daughters married builders indicates the close ties between the contractors socially as well as professionally. The discussion of the Dublin and District Housebuilders' Association shows how these informal contacts were strengthened in the 1930s, as pressures on the private sector developers grew.

This chapter has focused largely on the experience of one particular builder, Alexander Strain, whose work was typical of speculative building operations for the middle-classes at the time. His experience illustrated the piecemeal nature of development by speculators, but also showed the degree to which the local authority could influence private decision-making. Private speculative builders like Strain were reliant on the availability of mortgages under the Small Dwellings Acquisition Act in order to secure relatively rapid sale of their houses. As owner occupancy became increasingly important from the late 1920s, so too did the reliance by private speculators on the local authority.

The speculative builders operating in Dublin at the time appear to have formed a closely-knit group, as suggested by the web of interests surrounding Alexander Strain. These links were evident in the establishment of a lobby group to look after building interests in the 1930s, and in the suggestions made to the 1939–43 Housing Inquiry of a cartel controlling tendering. However, the nature of building operations changed during the study period. Builders in the generation after Strain, including Linzell and Ritchie, tended to operate on a more 'professional' basis. In the case of Linzell, this is seen in the limited company which he established to develop land in the Ailesbury area. Similarly, the Belton family who built housing in the Donnycarney area formed Irish Developments Limited. Architects were now being used more frequently, and housing styles and the scale of operations began to change. In addition, there was greater local authority control over development and planning of new schemes.

This chapter, and those which preceded it, attempts to show the importance of the suburbs which emerged in the first 40 years of the twentieth century. The houses built at that time are a legacy of this period of great change. By understanding the background to the housing activity of the period we can better understand how the city evolved. In understanding the past, it is also to be hoped that we can learn from both the mistakes and achievements of our predecessors, to develop a city which truly provides for all of its citizens.

The background to modern town planning and suburban development

RUTH McMANUS

The issues which concerned Dubliners in the early twentieth century, such as insanitary housing conditions, were not unique. Throughout the nineteenth century, in both Britain and Ireland, there had been a change in attitudes, as the defects of the *laissez-faire* philosophy were gradually recognized while State intervention came to be acceptable. This was a time when modern town planning can be said to have gradually evolved as a new and distinctive approach to the ordering of the urban environment. This new movement was quite complex, embracing civic design, housing improvements and social reform, and it stemmed from a context of economic, political and social factors as discussed by planning historian Gordon Cherry (1974). Those interested in town planning aimed to accomplish the deliberate physical ordering of towns or parts of towns in order to make them function more efficiently and equitably as both economic and social entities. Part of the goal was also to create an aesthetically pleasing environment. In Britain and Ireland the new discipline of town planning was closely associated with housing reform, and was perceived almost exclusively as a logical approach to the problem of the slums. In Continental Europe, planning had different roots, emerging from the Baroque tradition of monumental city design. It was the ultimate fusion of architecture and design elements, largely drawn from Continental Europe, with aspects of housing reform and legislative control, a feature of British and Irish cities at this time, which gave birth to modern town planning.

The nineteenth century saw profound economic and social changes, one of which was the increasing concentration of population in industrial towns and cities. The segregation of the rich, living in suburban villas, from the poor or 'working class' who lived close to the factories, has been amply described in the novels of Dickens and Zola, the political tracts of Engels, and by many modern researchers. A new buffer between the extremes, both physically and socially, was formed by the 'middle classes' of artisans, traders and clerks which emerged to serve the bureaucratic needs of the entrepreneurs. This separation of the classes in the cities was something new and perplexing for Victorian observers. The industrial and business core of the city was encircled by the poor housing areas of the mass of workers, while the homes of the wealthier classes were as far as possible from the noise, smells, squalor and disease of the central area.

At the beginning of the nineteenth century, the huge increase in wealth generated from industry was reflected in the building of large numbers of new houses for the middle and upper classes, causing rapid growth in the fashionable areas of English and American cities. New ideas concerning the layout of these areas were developing at the time. For example, when Britain's official royal architect, John Nash (1752–1835), began to prepare a plan for a large tract of undeveloped Crown land in London in 1811, he moved away from the repeating pattern of streets and squares which was characteristically urban. Instead, Nash created a large park, like the grounds of a country estate, with over 50 villas half hidden in groves of trees, a decorative lake and a new church. Although the plans for Regent's Park were not completed as originally intended, the plan was one of the first suggestions that the pattern of suburban development might be significantly different from that in the urban centre. Nash's Park Village was the first example of what, in the mid-nineteenth century, became a broader trend, as an increasing number of 'villa residences' and mansions were built around Britain for the newly affluent. Following the Romantic revolt against order, the house, plot and garden were deliberately de-formalized, and straight lines were avoided in laying out streets. Often described as 'arcadian' or 'romantic' suburbs, examples include Victoria Park, Manchester (1837), Prince's Park, Liverpool (1842), Joseph Paxton's Birkenhead Park (1844) and Llewellyn Park, New Jersey (1857). These low-density developments were often heavily landscaped in a picturesque manner. Access was generally controlled by gated entrances, and dwellings were uniformly detached or semi-detached villas, ensuring privacy for the family both indoors and in the garden.

As cities became increasingly less pleasant and transport possibilities increased, it became the fashion to live in the country. The dilemma of the middle-classes, who wanted to escape the city, but, in order to continue enjoying the benefits of industrialization had to accept it as their work-place and source of their wealth, was solved by the suburban concept. Successive waves of house building engulfed the rural fringe, and by the end of the nineteenth century, the most rapid growth was occurring in the suburbs of the large cities, pointing to a transfer of population from inner to outer areas. The growth of the suburbs signalled an increased actual distance between, and growing

118 The crowd illuminated. (*The Graphic*, 6 March 1873.)

contrast in, the meaning of home and workplace. The home was increasingly seen as a refuge from the stresses of life in the world outside, and the preference for the detached or semi-detached house, screened off with gardens, hedges, walls blinds and lace curtains from neighbours and passers-by, was a reflection of the emphasis on the single family unit and the domestic ideal of protection and privacy (Long, 1993). The private home became an important vehicle for both achieving and expressing individuality, character and personal fulfillment, projecting an image of prosperity and self-sufficiency to the world. The rise of the suburb thus coincided with the rise of the middle class as a dominant force of economic and political life. As the middle classes have continued to grow in the twentieth century, so too have the suburbs which house them.

As British towns and cities continued to grow during the nineteenth century due both to natural increase and in-migration from impoverished rural areas, fears were raised regarding the unmanageability of such large, ever-growing metropolises.

One extremely influential and commonly held belief was that the growing concentration of population in unhealthy cities was leading to dangerous social unrest and to the physical and social degeneration of the nation (Wohl, 1983). The growth of cities accelerated rural depopulation, threatening a way of life which was believed to be healthier, more wholesome and which enshrined the best moral and social values. Country-bred people were often seen as inherently superior to city-dwellers in health, strength, temperament and morals. For example, Dublin's Metropolitan Police were almost exclusively recruited from the countryside, where superior diet and fresh air produced taller, stronger and healthier physical specimens. As the level of urbanization increased in Britain, there was a strengthening in pastoral nostalgia among many city-dwellers, particularly among the middle and upper classes. It was fashionable to love the countryside and believe that, given a free choice, most people would live there, a view which is still heard.

As the wealthy moved to semi-rural retreats, in many cases, the former houses of the rich were subdivided and downgraded to become tenements for the poor, as was the case in Dublin. Alternatively new houses were built by private speculators (the 'jerry builders') with quality based on the worst that working-class families would put up with. Victorian growth depended on cheap casual labour. Rents were closely linked with wages, themselves the minimum compatible with the survival of the worker, so that profits could be realized on housing only by reducing the outlay and building houses of the lowest possible quality. In fact, Dyos suggests that 'slums were necessary so as not to dissipate too many resources in housing, and … while labour was abundant, cheap, and docile this was economically justifiable. The logic of this, tacitly accepted at the time, is that the slums helped to underpin Victorian prosperity' (Dyos, 1967, p. 27). As the population of the towns swelled, increasing demand for accommodation resulted in the over-occupancy of the existing housing stock and the development of back-land which lacked the most basic amenities (in Dublin, courts and mews). Thus, the slums were often out of sight behind the main thoroughfares along which the wealthy travelled, and the grim reality of the industrial city was hidden by shops from the ruling classes. Most towns relied on the private sector to supply public services such as drainage, water supply, street lighting and scavenging, and lacked effective building regulations. The 'market' was the dominant force in the supply of housing and other basic amenities. In any case, the rapid growth of cities, especially in the coalfield areas of Britain, stretched the existing infrastructure to its limits, and overwhelmed any existing public services.

The prevailing ideology of the time was one of *laissez-faire* and unfettered 'free enterprise'. Short (1984) has commented that this gave the majority of the population the 'freedom' to live in squalor. The slums were crowded, damp, filthy and insanitary, and became breeding grounds for diseases such as cholera. The death rates spoke for themselves, the industrial city was a dangerous place in which to live. In fact, despite the large numbers of children born to the working classes, natural increase of the poor was low. The high birth rate was matched (and in times of epidemic, exceeded) by the high death rate. It is not surprising that slums were often described at the time as 'rookeries', 'fever-dens', 'little hells', 'devil's acres' and 'dark purlieus'.

Contemporary observers were shocked by the apparent breakdown of societal norms in these places and many influential figures became highly critical of the industrial city. The pressure for change came from many sources, revealing many inter-related areas of concern. Novelists and men of letters, clergymen and moralists, doctors, political agitators, artists and aesthetes, economists and land reformists all exhibited an anti-industrial and anti-urban sentiment. Thus, despite many improvements towards the end of the nineteenth century, informed (mainly middle class) opinion held the view that the city was undesirable due to poor living conditions, its economic inefficiency caused by congestion, and its possibilities for civil unrest.

In Britain, sanitarians like Edwin Chadwick, who was appointed Inspector of the Poor Law Commission in 1830, introduced measures providing proper water supplies and sewerage, minimum construction standards and appointing medical officers of health. Philanthropists like George Peabody built experimental working class dwellings in British cities, while optimists like James Silk Buckingham devised utopian cities. Private individuals like Octavia Hill (discussed below) demonstrated that poor properties could, with proper upkeep and supervision, be improved to the advantage of both landlord and tenant. Paternalistic employers built model villages for their workforces, while members of all these groups joined in the formation of the National Association for the Promotion of Social Science.

Various utopian socialists and anarchist groups attempted to establish small, self-contained communities away from the metropolis, in the belief that planning must start again from scratch. Robert Owen who is associated with New Lanark, Frenchmen Claude-Henri de Saint-Simon, Charles Fourier and Godin, who created the familistière at Guise, adhered to this view. Meanwhile, reformers considered the problems of the industrial city to be soluble within the existing society and aimed to tackle the technical needs connected with the growth of the industrial town, curing its individual defects. Among the most influential of British reformers was Anthony Ashley Cooper Shaftesbury, 7th earl of Shaftesbury, who was a tireless campaigner on behalf of the working classes. He strongly supported the Ten Hours Act of 1847 and other factory legislation, including the 1842 Act forbidding the employment of women and children underground in mines. He was also associated with the movement to provide free education for the poor, and was responsible for two housing Acts in 1851. In addition, he persuaded George Peabody to establish a housing trust to provide 'affordable' housing for rent. Thus, in order to maintain the system it was gradually seen as necessary for the State to become involved in laying down and enforcing minimum standards of public health, sanitation and housing.

Stenhouse (1977) has suggested that two factors made housing reform a matter for 'respectable' concern: moral health and epidemics. While tuberculosis, smallpox and diphtheria, symptoms of overcrowding, could be ignored as irrelevant by the ruling classes, the epidemics of typhoid and cholera, no respecters of class distinctions, meant that it was in the interests of the upper classes to support housing reform. There was a serious outbreak of Asiatic Cholera in Dublin in 1832–3, with further outbreaks in 1866 and 1884, while typhoid recurred regularly in the late 1870s and 1880s, including one outbreak in the 'respectable' Pembroke township in 1879.

Meanwhile, many well-intentioned Victorians turned their reforming zeal upon the 'loose morals' of the working classes. Statistics showed high rates of illegitimacy, prostitution and criminal activity in the cities. The perceived drunkenness and lack of respect for marriage among the poor was seen, in a deterministic view, as the outcome of severe overcrowding where privacy was impossible. However, according to Wohl (1977, p. 42), 'the very concept of overcrowding, and the desire for fresh air, ventilation and space, were basically middle class; among the working classes there were many complaints about high rents and sanitary conditions, but almost none concerning the lack of room space.' Of course, if you cannot afford even the poor conditions that you live in, it might seem pointless to dream about open space and fresh air.

The concentration of population in urban areas had other implications, economically, politically and socially. The problem of municipal government and national power and stability, the distribution of wealth and employment, the organization of labour in towns, the threat to agriculture, and soaring land values in the centre of large cities were all important. So too was the fear for community life, since an urban way of life was thought to promote individualism and anonymity. A mixture of individual agitation and public pressure ultimately resulted in the introduction of various Public Health Acts in Britain. These legislative measures were intended to combat the growth of disease and poverty caused (according to popular belief) by lack of adequate sanitation and poor housing standards. They began with the Public Health Act of 1848 and included various Building Acts which regulated the width of streets and back lanes, and dealt with the provision of open space at the rear of buildings. However, until quite late in the century these Acts were operated on an arbitrary, patchy basis. Most legislation of the Victorian era, whether related to public health, building or slum clearance, was either a response to an existing situation or an attempt to cure an existing ill. The cholera epidemics of the 1840s, for example, motivated legislation at a time when few members of the ruling elite were willing to consider more than the containment of the existing situation with the minimum amount of interference. The legislation of this era was simply an attempt to prevent town growth from becoming worse than what had previously been built, rather than an attempt to formulate a policy for town expansion and growth. The primary concern of the legislation was with hygiene and sanitation, rather than equity and increased opportunity for the working-classes.

The introduction of the Common Lodging Houses Act and the Labouring Classes Lodging Houses Act (Shaftesbury Acts, both 1851) gave local authorities the power to build and maintain public lodging houses. The first laws which directly tackled housing conditions were the Artizans' and Labourers' Dwellings Act (Torrens Act, 1868) and the Artizans' and Labourers' Dwellings Improvement Act (Cross Act, 1875) which were particularly concerned with slum clearance. Finally it came to be recognized from about the 1870s that a more active municipal initiative was necessary in order to secure more acceptable standards of housing and street layout. At first, local authorities systematically purchased and demolished slum areas, to be resold and redeveloped by private speculators, but eventually the municipal authorities began to build dwellings for artisans on their own initiative. The desirability of subsidized municipal housing in urban renewal schemes was finally recognized by parliament in the 1880s.

With growing awareness of the plight of the working classes, the middle-class conscience was stirred to charitable enterprise. The housing reform movement, which gradually gained respectability, consisted of many diverse elements with varying interests and objectives. One of the most famous of all housing reformers was Octavia Hill (1838–1912), who restored and managed 15,000 properties over 50 years. Her work is an example of the 'character building' attitude towards the poor, with an insistence on homes rather than houses and family life rather than bricks and mortar (Wohl, 1977). Hill's work inspired efforts in Dublin by groups including the Alexandra Guild Tenements Co. Ltd. and the Social Services (Tenements) Co. Ltd. Various philanthropic bodies also began to build artisans' dwellings. One of the best known of the philanthropic enterprises was that financed by George Peabody, who had been persuaded by Lord Shaftesbury to invest his private fortune in a trust providing 'affordable' housing for rent. His half a million pounds allowed the trust to build 5000 solid and utilitarian flats over 30 years. In themselves, however, the housing societies including the Peabody Trust and Waterlow's Improved Industrial Dwellings Company could only scratch the surface of an enormous problem. Although profits were kept to a minimum (giving rise to the comment 'five per cent philanthropy') the very poor could not afford to rent the new accommodation, while the scale of building was too small to contribute much to central renewal, and indeed accusations were often levelled that these enterprises merely exacerbated the problem, because it was impossible to rehouse all those displaced by their schemes. The tendency was to build flats, which were bleak and barrack-like, attracting severe criticism from contemporaries and reinforcing in the public mind the notion that flats were inferior to one-family houses or cottages. 'It was one of the few aspects of their housing on which the poor made their voices heard, and in every case it was to decry the barrack-like, Bastille-like, grim and unadorned façades of the model dwellings. They looked too much like the dreaded workhouses for comfort' (Gauldie, 1974, p. 223). Indeed, the general dislike of the exteriors of the model dwellings probably played a part in bringing about the romantic movement in housing reform which took up the Garden City idea with such enthusiasm.

Harrison's (1966) discussion of the concept of philanthropy in the nineteenth century raises several further questions. Firstly, because of the residential isolation of rich from poor by the mid-Victorian period, it was difficult to sensitize wealthy districts to the needs of the slums. Philanthropists generally preferred to see the effects of their donations in their own localities rather than in the slums where it was most needed. In addition, Harrison suggests that nineteenth-century philanthropy helped to preserve the unjust status quo, since it 'helped to validate existing social institutions by highlighting the generosity of the rich and the inadequacies of the poor' (Harrison, 1966, p. 368). Contemporary accounts tended to laud middle class benefactors while ignoring the widespread generosity of the poor to their relatives and friends. Often the philanthropic organizations of the time demoralized the poor. They tended to concentrate only on those who they defined as the 'deserving, or respectable, poor' and did not always give their beneficiaries what they wanted. Harrison, in common with other writers, raises the question as to the extent to which philanthropic zeal was linked to the Victorian fear of insurrection, 'better housing as a bulwark against revolution' (Wohl, 1977, p. 64).

After about 1850, there was a more environmentalist attitude towards the slums. It became increasingly admitted that the best means to achieve character building and moral improvement of the poor was by improving their physical environment, although many were hostile to the theory that it was environment rather than character which led the poor into reckless and indolent lives. As the environmentalist theories began to take hold, housing improvement became advocated as the cure-all for all types of social ills. Thus, effective education, the reduction of drunkenness, crime and mass protest were all thought to be dependent upon improved housing.

Changing attitudes during the Victorian era resulted in a 'softening' of the *laissez-faire* approach to economics, and resulted in an increasing tendency towards intervention. From the 1860s philanthropic housing schemes, modelled on those in London, were built in Dublin, while there was a gradual increase in the level of public involvement in housing, with slum clearance policies from the 1870s and the first local authority housing in the 1880s. Increasingly, however, it came to be realized that the piecemeal, uncoordinated attempts at municipal improvement often exacerbated the situation. Thus the new ideas of town planning were generally welcomed.

Searching for Utopia, Ebenezer Howard and the Garden City movement

Legislation relating to town planning was gradually enacted in Britain as a response to existing urban conditions. This was the reactive and pragmatic element in planning. However, there was more to town planning than a purely practical response to the nineteenth-century city. It was also based on utopian idealism, the search for an ideal city in physical terms, and the ideal community (Cherry 1988). While there is a streak of the utopian in every town planner, a small number of idealists and visionaries inspired the modern profession with their single-mindedness and audacity.

While reformists like Edwin Chadwick (1800–90) and Lord Shaftesbury (1801–85) pressed for better national controls of living conditions in the nineteenth-century British city, other individuals became convinced that

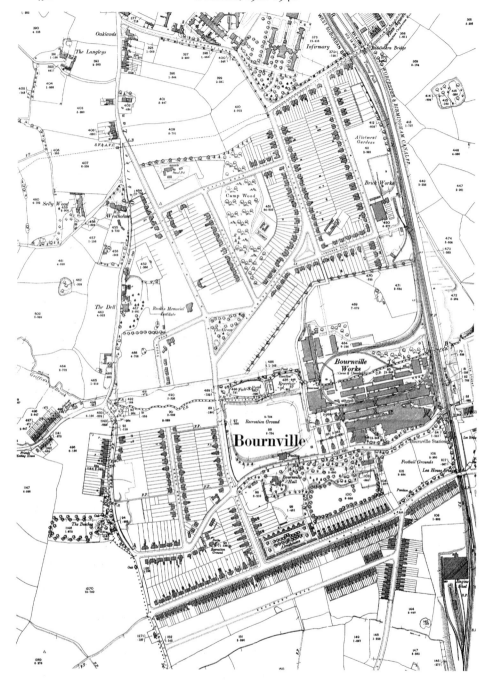

119 Layout plan of Bournville, Birmingham.
Note the size of the plots and the street layout in the upper part of the plan.

improvements would be best organized at a local scale, within small communities. Among those who concentrated on the development of separate new communities outside urban areas were Owen, Buckingham, Salt and Cadbury. Their localized developments include the 'model industrial villages' which became a feature across Europe in the nineteenth century. One of the most influential of these early 'benevolent industrialists' was Robert Owen whose promotion of his socialist ideas led to international knowledge of the scheme at New Lanark. Arthur Vandeleur, a landlord, was greatly influenced by Robert Owen's (New Lanark) socialism and established a community on his property at Ralahine, Co. Clare with the aid of Thomas Craig from Manchester, a follower of Owen. The Ralahine Agricultural and Manufacturing Co-operative Association began in 1831 with rules emphasising mutual assistance, common capital and the mental and moral development of its members but failed in 1833 when Vandeleur became bankrupt. John Richardson built the Quaker community at Bessbrook, Co. Armagh in 1846. The year 1854 saw the foundation of two model villages in Britain, Price's Candle Works, Bromborough which includes open spaces and gardens for workers, and Saltaire, the textile community founded by Titus Salt (1803–76). This was also the year that the first Society for Improving the Dwellings of the Labouring Classes was established. Continental Europe also had its share of company towns, such as the Krupp family's settlements around Essen completed between 1863 and 1875 (Westend, Nordhof, Baumhof, Kronenberg) or M. Degorge's village of Gran-Hornu in Belgium, begun as early as 1825.

Later schemes at Port Sunlight (1888) and Bournville (1879/1895) set new standards, with housing that was of a better quality and design than most middle class dwellings elsewhere (Stenhouse, 1977). Together they were to have a huge impact on the fledgling town planning movement. The new Cadbury suburb of Bournville, built by Quaker brothers George and William Cadbury, is significant in the realms of 'company towns' in that it was open to all workers, irrespective of their place of employment. The houses were well spaced, with large gardens, and an initial density of six houses to the acre (15 houses per ha).

At Bournville the layout techniques employed gradually introduced the curve, as a response to the topography and micro-climate rather than as an end in itself. The initial architect for Bournville, W.A. Harvey, first considered the detail design of the house, its aspect and prospect; only then did he proceed from the individual unit to its setting and, within the total architectural climate in which he operated, he began to produce a concept of housing

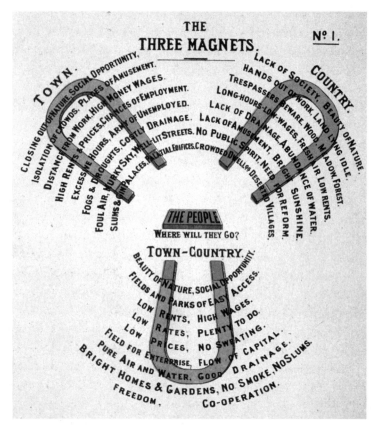

120 The three magnets. (*Tomorrow. A Peaceful Path to Real Reform*, 1898.)

which broke the whole bylaw development. The layout for Bournville grew as the village gained in momentum. Its form is probably best, if lavishly, described as a 'deft and sensitive weaving of roads and house plots onto a piece of gently moulded and contoured open countryside' (Tarn, 1980, p. 89). Thirty years after its inception, the Cadburys renounced all financial interest in the town and transferred ownership of land and housing to an independent body, the Bournville Housing Trust, which agreed to use all profits for further improvement of the village.

These schemes are significant in that they produced integrated settlements. In addition to above average (for the time) housing, the plans included churches, schools, clubs, washhouses, parks, hospitals and even art galleries (at Lever's Port Sunlight). The model industrial villages show employers accepting a degree of responsibility for the living conditions of their workers, a principle far ahead of the prevailing ideology of the period. The development and appreciation of these model villages encouraged the progress of town planning in its broadest sense, relating both to physical surroundings and to the growth of community spirit. Not all philanthropic developers detached themselves from their creations and there was a price to be paid for living in many such communities. In Pullman's towns in the USA, for example, adherence to a sober and moral lifestyle was required and the inhabitants were monitored to ensure compliance.

Ebenezer Howard (1850–1928) attempted to incorporate the best of utopian ideas into a *practical* urban solution, first published as '*Tomorrow: A Peaceful Path to Real Reform*' in 1898, reprinted in 1902 as '*Garden Cities of Tomorrow*'. His aim was the marriage of town and country, the integration of what was best in both urban and rural life to create a new form of settlement, the 'garden city'. The model proposed by Howard influenced most of the designs for towns which followed, even to the present day, a remarkable achievement. Indeed, George Bernard Shaw said of Howard that 'he was one of those heroic simpletons who do big things whilst our prominent worldlings are explaining why they are Utopian and impossible' (quoted in Creese, 1967, p. 37).

The Garden City movement can be seen as the culmination of a century of both anti-urban writings which were a reaction against the conditions of nineteenth-century industrial cities, and of the schemes such as Saltaire which attempted to improve the housing and moral standards of the working classes. Rather than being anti-urban in general, Howard hoped to improve on the specific evils of the city in his time. Howard's Garden City was to be a compact town of 1000 acres (*c.*400 ha) which would accommodate 30,000 people, while a further 2000 would live in a 5000-acre (*c.*2,000 ha) rural hinterland. Central to Howard's principles was the ownership and administration of the town by the people who lived in it. The town would be financed by rents alone which would firstly pay off the debts incurred in its foundation and then fund municipal functions. These funds would be managed by a Central Council in whom were vested the rights and powers of the community as sole landlord of the Garden City. This allowed for greater control over land-use, in particular the prevention of suburban development on the fringe. Howard spent more time in his book discussing this aspect of the town than on urban form and he would have undoubtedly regretted the emphasis that came to be placed on physical planning to the neglect of governance.

Basic functional zoning was to be used within the town, with industrial and commercial subdivisions. Around the central park the public buildings and places of entertainment were to be arranged within an inner 'ring park'

420 feet (*c*.130 m) wide. A 'Crystal Palace' in the intermediate space was a precursor of the modern shopping centre, housing all the shops of the city, while electrically-powered factories, railways and sidings would be located at the edge. Six boulevards divided the area into six residential zones of 5,000 strong communities composed of a mix of social groups, a forerunner of the neighbourhood unit idea.

In Howard's garden city, the houses would be of varying sizes, but all would have gardens and be within easy reach of all facilities and of the open country-side. Howard's plan thus dealt with personal lives, not just bricks and mortar, and was a 'brilliant exposition of the need for a balanced urban environment' (Gauldie, 1974, p. 194). In particular, he emphasized the importance of planning a whole community at the outset of the development.

He also placed great importance on limiting the size of the urban area, providing for the foundation of new communities once the initial target population was reached. Howard proposed that the population size of his garden city would be limited. Growth would be by means of the creation of new, separate garden cities, linked by a transport network to form a regional unit known as the Social City. This would bring at least ten garden cities, with a total population of 300,000, into a single organized system, allowing for the support of functions which required a larger population base (e.g. symphony orchestra, university, hospital). The regional system would be focused on a larger mother city with a population of *c*.58,000. Howard expected that the population of existing cities would thin out as more and more garden cities were built. Eventually the old cities would be reorganized and, since they could no longer pay their debts, property values would fall and the remaining population would move into the best houses, leaving the slums to be replaced by gardens. His proposals offered a comprehensive vision of social and political reform which would involve the gradual transformation of the existing con-centrated cities into a decentralized but closely interrelated network of garden cities. Thus he was advocating 'nothing less than the total reorganization of the entire country as something quite feasible and practical, in fact almost inevitable' (Barnett, 1986, p. 66).

Howard, therefore, was more interested in social change than in physical form. The garden city was intended as a vehicle of fundamental social trans-formation, although these socio-political ideas have been little understood, or put into effect. His proposed new settlements would offer a greatly improved quality of life, including housing, work and leisure conditions, but also with transformed social relations and even religious sensibilities. Howard envisaged a third socio-economic system superior to both Victorian-type capitalism and bureaucratic centralized socialism. Both capitalism and co-operation would flourish, as the garden city would work on the basis of 'associated individualism', made up of voluntary, semi-co-operative, self-governing communities rooted in the land. Thus Howard aimed to reconcile two opposing social philosophies as well as the best qualities of town and country. In effect, basic social changes would emerge in a new physical environment produced by planning. Howard was not a lone prophet but a spokesman for many late-Victorian reformers. He moved in the circles of radical liberal and socialistic reformers, including the Cadburys, W.H. Lever, Alfred Marshall, Alfred Russel Wallace, G. Bernard Shaw and Sydney Webb. He was dedicated to social reform through peaceful methods and hoped to reconcile individualism and socialism in the new environment of the garden city.

Garden Cities and Garden Suburbs

As a tireless worker and effective public speaker, Howard, unlike many utopian reformers, succeeded in attracting a core of skilled and influential followers which crystallized in the Garden City Association (forerunner of the Town and Country Planning Association) formed in 1899, with the intention of putting his theories into practice. In 1901 and 1902 the Association held annual conferences in Bournville and Port Sunlight respectively. In 1903 the Garden City Pioneer Company (registered 1902) bought a site of 3900 acres (c.1500 ha) at Letchworth in Hertfordshire, 35 miles (c.56 km) north of London. Shares in the First Garden City Limited were sold, with dividends limited to five per cent, the remainder of the profits to be reinvested in the project.

Tomorrow had been largely concerned with the practicalities of developing and administering the garden city, but dealt very briefly with the physical environment of the town, using highly simplified diagrams. Indeed his illustrations were marked 'Diagram only, plans can not be drawn until site selected'. Therefore, when Raymond Unwin (1863–1940), who was to be so influential in Dublin, and brother-in-law Barry Parker (1867–1947) were commissioned to design this first garden city they had the opportunity to give the garden city a definitive physical form. Some 1500 acres (c.600 ha) were available for buildings, roads and urban open spaces, around which a permanent green belt was located. Unwin and Parker came up with a pleasant, informal layout, basing site design decisions on topography, prevailing winds and existing vegetation. The styles of building were varied to cater for different people, including a

121 An early plan for Welwyn Garden City, London by Louis de Soissons (*c.*1921).

range of terraced, semi-detached and detached housing (a lesson from which latter-day local authorities could learn!), while the architecture was clearly influenced by the Arts and Crafts movement. The groups of cottages and houses were designed to create architecturally related groups. All houses had ample gardens, resulting in an average density of 6 to 12 houses per acre (15 to 30 houses per ha). The road reserves were of generous width (40 to 100 feet, *c.*12 to 30 m) and liberally planted with trees and grass verges, while mature trees and parkland were retained. A formal shopping centre, social buildings, schools, churches and clubs were all included in the plan. Following the initial 'new town blues' and slow growth, Letchworth was successful both financially and socially, and due to its balanced employment and population structure, did not suffer in the Depression of the 1930s. Welwyn Garden city followed in 1919 to which Howard moved and where he lived until his death in 1928. However no other garden cities were built in Britain and it was not until 1947 that a programme of new town building was undertaken. These towns were not garden cities as Howard would have wanted them, though the influence of the movement on them was clear. In the short term, at least, the garden city was transformed into the garden suburb.

The immediate design context of Unwin and Parker's Letchworth plan was the revival of vernacular architecture in the late nineteenth century. Having published two books which revealed a reformist interest in improving the architectural vernacular and restoring the virtues of village life, the two architects set to work applying their ideas at Letchworth.

Letchworth was considered something of a social experiment in the early years, and images of free thinking, vegetarianism, co-operative housekeeping and pursuit of the 'simple life' encouraged Edwardian amusement. However, the increasing involvement of influential business interests in the Garden City Association and Letchworth brought respectability to the movement as well as more tangible assets such as money and organizational skills. George Cadbury and *Daily Mail* proprietor Alfred Harmsworth helped to establish a bridgehead of middle-class tolerance and sympathy. In addition, the buildings of Unwin, Parker and the other architects provided an image of a quality residential environment which had much to offer middle class suburbanites. However, this widening base of support and the articulation of the physical form of the garden city intensified the emphasis on the environmental dimension, bringing further movement away from Howard's original conception. The lovingly executed site and residential planning ideas of Unwin and Parker began to acquire an identity of their own, especially since these environmental aspects were far less problematic to private capital and respectable middle class opinion than Howard's larger social reformism. Thus the garden city idea began to be fragmented:

> Ebenezer Howard's writings and tireless promotional efforts made the concept of the garden city internationally known, but the image of the garden city was established by Unwin and Parker, and it is much more the image of Hampstead Garden Suburb than it is of Letchworth. Hampstead was more accessible; it had a superior site plan, which created architecturally defined spaces; and with its greater range of incomes, it had far more distinguished architecture.
>
> (Barnett, 1986, p. 75)

122 Howard's home at Welwyn Garden city, London (1920–9).
(Photograph by R. McManus.)

Early town planners, while referring to their designs as 'garden cities' or
'garden suburbs', were generally influenced by Unwin and Parker's plans, rather
than the writings of Howard himself. In many ways, Hampstead Garden Suburb,
designed by Raymond Unwin from 1905, illustrates how Howard's original
ideas had degenerated so that the picturesque element of design, and the anti-
city aspect of the project were emphasized to the exclusion of the social theory
and other factors which rendered it unique. However, the urban design elements
first employed at Hampstead were to have an immediate and lasting impact
on both public and private housing development in Britain and Ireland.

The suburb was established through the inspired efforts of Henrietta Barnett,
a social reformer, who envisaged a landscaped settlement of houses, cottages
and flats, each with a garden, where all classes from artizan to upper middle
'would live together under the right conditions of beauty or space'. Barnett
raised enough capital to see the Hampstead Garden Suburb Trust safely
launched in March 1906, and in the following year the trust bought 243 acres
(c.100 ha) for £112,000. While the Barnett's original aspiration was for a community of all classes, viewpoints and incomes living 'in helpful neighbourliness', in
fact Hampstead remained predominantly middle class. The original plan had
the most expensive houses (up to £3500 leasehold) grouped around the newly

123 Housing at Hampstead Garden suburb. (Photograph by R. McManus.)

acquired Hampstead Heath Extension (southern end of the site) with middle value ones (from £425 upwards) at the western end of the land. Revenue from ground rents of these houses was to subsidize the ground rents of 70 acres of workmen's cottages to the north, to be erected by Hampstead Tenants' Ltd, operating on co-partnership principles, while a portion of the overall revenue was allocated to upkeep and amenity of the estate. Despite its democratic intentions, however, few workers remained in the suburb.

Protected by its own legislation, the trust which controlled the development of Hampstead was able to over-ride local bylaws forbidding culs-de-sac and streets less than 50 feet (*c*.15 m) wide, and undertook that the overall density would not exceed eight houses to the acre. This enabled Raymond Unwin to 'indulge his theory that T-shaped closes and culs-de-sac, and blocks of houses grouped around little 'commons' were a more economical and more spacious form of layout than an extravagant number of bylaw streets set in rows' (Jackson, 1973, p. 79). A hierarchy of streets was created, by distinguishing between streets providing access to individual dwellings and those that carried traffic. Walkways were designed for pedestrians, many of which are short cuts away from roads. In addition, many open spaces were provided behind houses for allotments, tennis courts and children's areas.

HOUSE IN MEADWAY, HAMPSTEAD GARDEN SUBURB
M. H. BAILLIE SCOTT, Architect

A CHARMING HOUSE, Designed by T. L. DALE,
to stand at the corner of Hampstead Way and Willifield Way,
Hampstead Garden Suburb

124 Housing designs for Hampstead Garden suburb.
(*Garden suburbs – Town planning and modern architecture*, 1910, p. 116.)

Unwin acted as resident partner and supervising architect until 1914 while, in his capacity of 'expert-advisor', Lutyens (1869–1944) contributed some of the larger buildings, including those in the Central Square – the Anglican and Free Churches, the Institute and two schools. Although purchasers of plots were allowed to employ their own architects, designs had to conform with the general scheme, the objectives of which were to retain as close a harmony with nature as possible and to create a mood of rural peace and security. Hampstead

little or no co-ordination between the different activities, and no integrated plan of improvement. The concept of providing an integrated approach to development and improvement was particularly relevant in the context of rapid nineteenth-century urban expansion. Modern town planning was thus a concept which fitted well into the context of the times. Because it seemed to offer a logical approach to the city's problems, it was greeted with considerable interest, and a broadly based international town planning movement was firmly established within a short number of years. This movement was to prove influential in Dublin's early-twentieth-century development.

By the early twentieth century, the housing situation in Dublin was recognized as a crisis. As Allan has suggested, 'the boundaries of the problem of slum clearance are constantly receding (because) when the worst slums are removed the next worst properties become the worst and formerly acceptable standards become unacceptable (Allan, 1965, p. 598). Perhaps actual conditions, though bad, had improved but public opinion had begun to see the situation as unacceptable. In addition, much of the housing stock was now on the point of collapse, and in some cases fatalities were recorded, such as the 1902 collapse of a tenement house in Townsend Street which killed one person. At the same time, there was increasing pressure on public schemes due to rising interest charges, while the Dublin Artizans' Dwellings Company (DADC) actually ceased building in 1907. The population began to rise, which combined with economic recession led to worsening unemployment and pressure on living standards. At the time of the 1911 Census, Dublin's population had reached 304,802, an increase of almost five per cent on 1901. The average annual birth rate had reached 31.9 per 1000, compared to an average for Ireland as a whole of 23.1, and the marriage rate was also above the national average. Some 9617 persons were receiving relief under the Poor Law System, of whom 5602 were in the workhouse. Meanwhile, there were increasing calls for State intervention in the housing crisis, while public bodies began to show more interest in the situation. The prospect of Home Rule and the labour unrest of 1913 increased the political importance of housing.

Dublin was not immune to what was going on across the Irish Sea. The work of the Garden City movement was known and admired and many had read about, if not seen, the developments in Hampstead Garden Suburb. As Brady (2001b, p. 269) has pointed out, William Pickering, a builder with an address at Richmond Avenue, Palmerston Park, promoted his Cowper Garden Building Estate at the International Exhibition of 1907. In an advertisement in the *Irish Times* (3 August 1907) he described it as a development of villas in country surroundings with 'all the advantages of both town and country within easy reach of Dublin … Within an unobstructed view of the Dublin mountains, these houses enjoy the advantages of the most advanced civilization, combined with all the scenery and associations of primitive country beauty'. In 1911 Geddes brought his Town Planning Exhibition to Dublin, and there was a surge of interest in town planning over the next few years (Bannon, 1985). Soon he and Unwin were to become important promoters of town planning in the city as well as offering concrete plans for garden suburbs. Town planning seemed to offer a means of achieving orderly development of the city and amelioration of slum conditions. Therefore, the concept of modern town planning became closely associated with efforts to improve housing conditions in Dublin.

A brief guide to maps of Dublin in the first half of the twentieth century

JOSEPH BRADY

Maps are the essential tools of any geographical investigation and it would have been impossible to complete this volume without making extensive use of them. That said, the variety of maps available to the researcher of the early-twentieth century city is probably less than is the case of the nineteenth century. This is compensated somewhat by the quality of what was produced, particularly by the Ordnance Survey of Ireland (OSI).

Major revisions were undertaken of the 1:10,560 series (6 inch), and the 1:2500 series (25 inch) around 1910–12 and again in second half of the 1930s. This was quite fortuitous because maps *c*.1910 provide a view of the city before the major process of suburbanization had begun. The late 1930s represent a good point to take stock. Many of the major developments were in place by this time and their effect on the landscape was clear. A revision between these two dates would have been useful but it is easy to understand why it did not occur in the circumstances of the time. Some sheets were partially revised again in the mid-1940s to reflect major changes. Thus earlier in this book it was possible to show the development of Crumlin between the late 1930s and early 1940s. The 1:2500 was a particularly good scale, providing a welcome balance between detail and utility. The greater detail provided by the modern 1:1000 sheets comes at the cost of utility; there are too many sheets to manipulate.

The OSI began to produce a street map in the 1930s at a scale of 1:25,000. A provisional issue bears the sheet number 265B and the date 1933. This became known as the Dublin Street Guide or Popular Edition and is perhaps the best known and most used of all maps of Dublin. At a scale of 1:25,000, more recently 1:20,000, it is very useful in tracing the developing spatial footprint of the city. This is particularly so for the latter decades of the twentieth century when it was regularly revised. At this scale, the individuality of streets and housing developments is lost but a sense of the overall urban environment is gained.

Thom's street directories were invaluable as a nineteenth-century resource; all the more so because they included a map of the city at 1:10,560 which was regularly updated. By World War I, the practice of including map was at an end and, though the directories remained an invaluable resource, the loss to the researcher was significant. This makes the Civic Survey of 1925 all the more important. As a prelude to what they hoped would be the production of a town plan, a twenty-two member Civic Survey committee, drawn from the professions, the Civics Institute, voluntary associations and local authorities was established in 1923 and the survey published in 1925. Its coverage was comprehensive involving questionnaire surveys, air photography and traffic counts for the Dublin region. The results were presented under seven headings; Archaeology; Recreation; Education; Hygiene; Housing; Industry and Commerce and Traffic. A series of magnificent maps were used to display the spatial distributions of the data and were also published as a separate supplement. These are very important statements of the character of the city particularly in the area of housing and transportation.

As in the nineteenth century, maps continued to be included in the guides produced both by the city authorities and commercial companies. Ward Lock updated their guide to Dublin on a regular basis and included a number of maps, including one of the city and another of the environs. However, as with most of these maps, the coverage does not stray much beyond the city centre and it is in the suburbs that much of what is of interest was occurring. Maps were also produced independently of guides. The Bacon company produced a pretty but generalized plan of the city and suburbs which was marketed by Eason's and Fred Hanna. This was at a 6-inch scale but without the fine detail of the OS maps. Nonetheless the fact that they are available for the early 1930s makes them useful. The Browne and Nolan company printed *Browne's Map of Dublin and Suburbs* costing 1s. in the paper version. Likewise the Geographica map company produced maps of the city, very similar to the OSI's Popular edition, at a variety of scales though most deal with a later period than the focus of this book. One annoyance with these commercial maps is the problem in dating them. They do not, as a rule, carry revision dates and it is often not easy to work it out. For example, Geographica maps generally carry a letter code that can be cracked only by the initiated. This omission was for sound commercial reasons. The 'shelf life' of the map was greatly increased if customers were unaware of just how up-to-date it was. Of course, this limits the value of these maps as a means of dating developments.

The fire insurance plans produced by the Charles E. Goad company were updated on a regular basis. Detailed mention was made of these in volume 1 of this series but essentially the need of fire insurance companies for maps to assist them in the calculation of risk was met from 1885 by Charles E. Goad. His company's plans show by using colour and symbols, *inter alia*, the size and location of individual buildings, the broad land use, the number of storeys and the nature of the roof. An initial atlas was issued for each town, concentrating on the commercial centre of the city and this was updated at regular intervals. It is this updating which has caused the plans to be very rare. The Goad Company had a policy of only leasing the maps to insurance companies. The atlases were returned to Goad when updates were available; this happened on a regular basis. Fortunately there is a good, though not complete, set available for the centre of Dublin in the late 1920s.

The 31st International Eucharistic Congress resulted in the production of a number of maps of the city and of the Phoenix Park. For example, a large plan prepared in 1932 by the organizing committee in Lower Abbey Street provides details of the management of the accommodation for the Congress as well as being surrounded by a large number of very informative advertisements.

In 1939, Dublin Corporation commissioned Professor Patrick Abercrombie to produce a sketch development plan for the city of Dublin. The plan was not as comprehensive as the one he had produced in 1914, it was after all only a sketch development plan, but it covered many aspects including metropolitan development, transportation and future growth. The Corporation never intended to implement the plan as an entity. They noted that:

> while endorsing in most cases the recommendations of the Consultants, the Town Planning Committee is aware that the heavy expenditure on buildings and compensation involved in some of the proposals, is an obstacle to their being undertaken for years to come. It is therefore suggested that the General Purposes Committee should first consider the various proposals in principle, merely. From the proposals that meet with their approval, a selection can be made by the Town Planning Committee, of a restricted number of proposals for which, it is hoped, the necessary money will be forthcoming in the near future ... This is not to say that the other proposals will be abandoned. They will, so to speak, be kept in reserve.
>
> (Abercrombie, 1941, pp 9–10)

This is by way of introduction to a map. Abercrombie produced a map to accompany the report. While the report may be readily obtained, the map is quite rare probably because it had to be purchased separately but also because it being during the Emergency, it was printed on quite flimsy paper. It was printed in colour by the Dollard printing company at a scale of 1:20,000 and could be purchased for 1s. which seems rather good value. It offers a fascinating vision of the city that might have been and bears comparison with the equally wonderful, but smaller scale maps, that were included in Abercrombie's first attempt to plan for the city. This was his prize-winning *Dublin of the Future*, published in 1922 by the Civics Institute.

Advertisements and the like are very important in developing a picture of the city and helping to add an additional dimension to the two-dimensional surfaces of maps. The Ward Lock guides to Dublin have been mentioned above. There is an edition for 1918 and another for 1932 and 1936 and to those can be added the guides produced by the City of Dublin on an irregular basis during the first decades of the twentieth century. Dublin Corporation, for example, produced an *Official Guide to the City of Dublin* in 1926 and 1928. In 1929, *A Book of Dublin*, edited by Bulmer Hobson appeared with a second edition in 1930. There was a variety of special printings for important international gatherings over the next few years. For example, one such was the handbook produced for the annual conference held by the Royal Institute of British Architects in Dublin in 1931. The Irish Tourist Board produced a guide to the city for 1933 and also in the early 1940s though these also suffer from the same lack of copyright dates mentioned above. In 1942 and again in 1944, the Corporation produced *The Lord Mayor's Handbook*, a municipal annual with reports on the activities of the Corporation. These guides vary in the detail they provide and in their orientation but they contain a variety of essays, commentary, practical information for the visitor as well as advertisements that are immensely useful is coming to understand the city as it was experienced by those of the time. Particular mention must be made of the two handbooks that were produced in 1927 and 1929 for Civic Week. These are especially fine productions.

The Eucharistic Congress also led to the production of guides to Catholic Dublin. That produced by Gill and Co. in 1932, *Gill's Guide to Catholic Dublin* was excoriating in what it saw as the anti-Catholic bias of other guides and is all the more interesting for that.

Finally we come to visual images. The heyday of the postcard was over by the 1920s and there is not the variety of images, especially of less tourist-oriented locations, that was available in the nineteenth century. Many variants were produced nonetheless and they make real the data that can be obtained from the map and guides. A good selection is available for the city centre and some of the suburbs. Photographic guides to the city were also produced for the visitor and some comprised pasted-down photographs. This was the case with Eason's *Rebellion in Dublin*, a guide to the impact of the 1916 rising in the city and with Hely's *Guide to the Sinn Fein Rebellion*. The Wilson Hartnell company, publisher of many guides to the city, produced a guide to *Old Ireland in Pictures* (1922) that contained many images of the Civil War in the city. Eason's, for their part, printed a folder containing 24 views of the city and environs for the early to mid 1920s and one with 21 views for the late 1920s/early 1930s.

So all in all, there is a good variety of maps and ephemeral material to help the researcher put flesh on dry statistics. Some suffer from the problem of not being specifically dated but this difficulty can be overcome. Much of this range of data was employed in producing the re-creation of the character of the city centre in the pages that follow.

Some specific references

Abercrombie, P., Kelly, S. and Kelly, A. (1922) *Dublin of the future – the new town plan.* Dublin: Civics Institute of Ireland and Liverpool University Press.

Abercrombie P., Kelly S. and Robertson, M. (1941) *Dublin – Sketch Development Plan.* Dublin: Dublin Corporation.

Civic Week Council (1927) *Dublin Civic Week Official Handbook.* Dublin: Civic Week Council.

Civic Week Council (1929) *Dublin Civic Week Official Handbook.* Dublin: Civic Week Council.

Dublin Corporation (1926) *Dublin–Official guide.* Dublin: Wilson Hartnell.

Dublin Corporation (1928) *Dublin–Official guide.* Dublin: Wilson Hartnell.

Dublin Corporation (1942) *Lord Mayor's handbook – Dublin municipal annual.* Dublin: Dublin Corporation.

Dublin Corporation (1944) *Lord Mayor's handbook – Dublin municipal annual.* Dublin: Dublin Corporation.

Eason and Co. (*c.*1916) *Rebellion in Dublin.* Dublin: Eason.

Eason and Co. (1920s) *Dublin and District.* Dublin: Eason.

Gill and Co. (1932) *Gill's guide to Catholic Dublin.* Dublin: Gill and Co.

Hobson, B. (1929–30) *A Book of Dublin.* Dublin: Kevin Kelly by permission of Dublin Corporation.

Irish Tourist Board (*c.*1933) *Dublin-Official guide.* Dublin: ITB.

Ward Lock (1918) *Guide to Dublin, Kingstown, Bray.* London: Ward Lock. Numerous editions of this guide were produced during the twentieth century.

Wilson Hartnell (*c.*1922) *Old Ireland in pictures.* Dublin: Wilson Hartnell.

Some aspects of the geography of the city centre in the early twentieth century

JOSEPH BRADY

As we have seen in this volume, the County Borough of Dublin, the area under the control of Dublin Corporation, experienced considerable spatial growth as a result of boundary changes. In 1900, the northside townships and the Kilmainham township were absorbed into the city. The Corporation failed to get control over the Pembroke and Rathmines townships which would have been a valuable prize. At the 1901 census, the population within the County Borough was enumerated at 290,638. This had grown to 304,802 by 1911 with a further 37,840 people in Rathmines and 29,294 in Pembroke. The next census was not taken until 1926 and showed a modest increase in the County Borough to 316,693. The city's area expanded considerably in 1930 when the Rathmines and Pembroke urban district council areas (the townships) were absorbed into the city along with such areas as Rathfarnham, Terenure and Kimmage on the southside. To the north of the city was added several areas from Cabra to Killester including Raheny village and the area along the sea from Clontarf to the boundary with Howth. This increased the area of the city from 8172 acres (3307 ha) to 18,776 acres (c.7600 ha) and would have had a population of 404,078 in 1926. The gave the city a greater spatial coherence than had existed for over a century but it was not the ideal solution. Instead of amalgamating the coastal townships into the city they were formed into the Borough of Dun Laoghaire. Howth was left as a separate UDC (Urban District Council) and the remainder of the county of Dublin came under the jurisdiction of Dublin County Council. It was clear that the County Borough was going to outgrow its boundaries before too long but the arguments adduced in respect of separate boroughs won the day. There was a recommendation that a 'Great Council' be set up to administer common services in the metropolitan area but nothing came of this. The administration of the city was streamlined, however, by adoption of the 'city manager' system whereby the day-to-day running of the city was in the hands of an appointed manager and his administration.

The metropolitan area

Issues of administrative efficiency and boundaries were revisited in Local Government (Dublin) Tribunal set up in 1935 and whose report was published in 1938. This inquiry highlighted a remarkable lack of interest by Dublin Corporation in unified services across the various local authorities in County Dublin. They recognized the need for what they referred to as a certain limited type of co-operation between adjoining authorities such as in housing areas which were split between Corporation and Council areas. They were not in favour of co-ordination, their term for a unitary body, preferring instead to be under the direct control of the Minster only. This rather isolationist policy was manifest in their attitude to town planning. The Town and Regional Planning Act (1934) came into operation in November of that year. Under the Act, the Corporation became the statutory regional planning authority for the counties of Meath, Kildare and Wicklow as well as Dublin. Though they adopted the required Town Planning Resolution under the Act in 1936, they chose not to act as a regional authority but to limit themselves to the County Borough area. Not everyone within Dublin Corporation agreed with this, as the evidence to the local government tribunal makes clear, but this isolationist stance obviously commanded sufficient support and the evidence to the tribunal also contained complaints from other authorities of unhelpfulness. The tribunal's report shows a realization that it made no sense to have multiple uncoordinated authorities managing a growing urban area. 'The town planning service cannot, in our opinion be properly administered within the existing County Borough as a unit; it is essential to have a common administration of this service for the City, County and Borough' (para. 366, p. 103). They came to the view that what was needed was to place the entire county under the control of a single authority.

> We recommend the constitution of a new authority, to be called the Dublin Metropolitan Corporation, to administer a unified Dublin Metropolitan Borough, bounded by the present Dublin County Borough, the Borough of Dun Laoghaire, the Urban District of Howth and the Dublin County Health District.
>
> (para. 468, p. 131)

The borough would have an urban part and a rural part which would share common services as well as having services particular to each. All would be under the control of an elected Metropolitan Council and an appointed Metropolitan Manager on the lines of the City Manager. Interestingly, they were of the view that the Council should be kept small with few electoral areas to preclude the possibility of representation in any area being restricted to specialized interests. This report went the way of all such reports, pieces of it were implemented and although even the current system of local government provides for a metropolitan council, it has yet to make any impact. So at the end of the 1930s, we had a rapidly growing city but a less-than-efficient system of metropolitan governance and a less-than-complete acceptance of the need for regional planning. The population of the County Borough in 1936 stood at 472,912 with another 7724 being described as living in the north city suburbs and a further 11,017 in the south city suburbs. Some 46,422 lived in Dun Laoghaire and its suburbs, giving a total for the 'Dublin Conurbation' of 538,075.

Growing pains

The growth of Dublin had many consequences both major and minor. By the late 1930s, parking had become a problem in the city centre. There were approximately 870 official parking spaces but people were used to other unofficial locations too. Controls were introduced in 1937 under two sets of by-laws. These by-laws were quite permissive by the standards of today but they were seen at the time to be quite punitive. In his notes to a guide to the new parking regulations, the editor wrote that 'it is necessary that all concerned should be enabled to apprehend the drastic departures from previous conditions and habits which are now imposed…' (Kenny, 1938, p. 5). Waiting time was now limited to 20 minutes on many streets and prohibited on others. Some streets were now one-way while on others waiting was permitted only on one side of the street which alternated on odd and even days of the month. Heavy vehicles and horse-drawn traffic was restricted in some streets as was the transport of ordure, dung and farmyard manure.

The controlled zone was very similar to that of today. It was bounded by Parnell Street, Gardiner Street, Tara Street, Kildare Street, St Stephen's Green North, South Great George's Street, Lord Edward Street, Parliament Street and Capel Street. The following gives a flavour of the restrictions, which were complicated by parking alternating from one side of the street to the other on different days and streets changing from two-way to one-way at different times of the day. Henry Street was one-way from O'Connell Street with parking on the north side of the street on even dates and *vice versa*. No waiting was permitted

125 O'Connell Street in the early 1930s. Note the availability of parking spaces.

on Nassau Street from Dawson Street to Grafton Street or from Dawson Street to Leinster Street on the TCD side. Horse-drawn traffic was restricted on Grafton Street from Nassau Street to St Stephen's Green between noon and 6.30 p.m. The street was one-way from Nassau Street to St Stephen's Green during the same hours but two-way at other times. Parking also alternated on odd and even dates, it being on the east side on even dates. There was no waiting permitted along the streets from Nassau Street to College Green. There was a certain innocence about the regulations and their practicality was somewhat dubious, particularly the notion of switching streets from one- to two-way and alternating the side of the road on which parking was permitted. Nonetheless, these restrictions marked the arrival of the motor car as a major issue in the management of the city of Dublin.

The transport network

By the end of the 1930s, public transport had kept up reasonably well with the process of suburbanization. The network had always stretched beyond the city along the main arterial routes, even in the early years of the century, to reach

126 The era of the tram. A view from Nelson's Pillar.
(*Dublin by Day and by Night*, 1939, p. 27.)

places such as Howth and Dun Laoghaire. This relatively simple network had now been filled in and the 1940 map accompanying the Dublin United Tramways Company (DUTC) street guide showed a quite dense network serving such new suburbs as Marino, Fairbrother's Fields, and Kimmage. In some parts of the city, such as Drumcondra, the service was denser than it is today but there were also gaps where service was inadequate. West Cabra was isolated with buses serving only the Navan Road and Fassaugh Avenue while newly-developed Crumlin needed additional services. This bears out the point that the transport system tended to follow development rather than determine it. The density of the service was the legacy of competition. There had been an explosion of private bus operators during the 1920s and the DUTC's network was an attempt to counter this. By the early 1930s, Thom's Directory had two pages of listings of private operators – some limited companies but others one-person businesses. The buses had names. There were many saints among them but much more evocative were services such as 'Adaline' that plied between Eden Quay and Walsh Road or 'Blue Prince' that ran to Dollymount. However these services ended when the DUTC was able to compulsorily acquire them under the 1933 Transport Act.

The trams were rapidly being replaced by buses. In their timetable for 1939, the DUTC listed 15 tram routes and some 66 bus services. The network stretched out in the countryside. There were buses to Portrane (1s.), Malahide (8d.), Howth (6d.), Bray (1s.), Delgany (1s. 8d.), Maynooth (1s. 3d.) as well as to Baldonnel Airport (10d.). There were two daily services to Baldonnel; one from O'Connell Street at 11.15 a.m. to be in time for the arrival of the London flight at 12 noon and the second at 12.15 p.m. to be in time for the 1 p.m. departure to London. A trip-time of less than 45 minutes, allowing for boarding etc., is a clear indicator of one major difference between then and now. Services began earlier compared to the 1910s (see volume 1, p. 248). At that time, most services from the city began after 8.00 a.m. and Howth could only be reached after 9.00 a.m., though you could get into the city somewhat earlier with services from Clonskeagh and Clontarf at around 7.30 a.m. By 1940, many services left the city centre before 7.30 a.m., including the number 31 to Howth, and services in the opposite direction were equally early. The practice of having early special cars on some routes continued. It was possible to get from Donnybrook to Nelson's Pillar at 5.30 a.m. every morning and there were special cars from Dalkey (4.45 a.m.) and Terenure (5.30 a.m.). Not all services woke up so early. For example, the first Sunday service on the 24 route from the new suburb of Marino did not begin until after 10.10 a.m. The system began to shut down after 11.30 p.m. but there were routes that offered

He was patently concerned that development could run out of control to the detriment of the urban environment. Running though the introduction, one senses that the author lacked faith in the ability and/or the willingness of those responsible for growth to exercise the necessary restraint. And so his appeal was to the public. The aim of the guide was to educate the public in what should be avoided and in the threefold aims of town planning – beauty, health and convenience. A particular bone of contention was public advertising which had grown in recent times to be a blight. Much of the guide is taken up with contrasting examples of bad and good advertising. The advertisement for David Allen and Sons in the guide, obviously good advertisers, spells out the concerns. The hope of the guide was to mobilize public opinion and to build civic spirit so that it would not be possible to contemplate bad practice.

> Without a sound public opinion our position will be without hope, since no legislation can instill a cultural attitude of mind, neither can we expect our Local Authorities to exert adequately any powers of control that may be conferred upon them if they know that they electorate is indifferent or hostile to any restraint exercised for the public good.
>
> (Robertson, 1933, p. 5)

Suburbanization

At the beginning of the twentieth century much of Dublin's industry was located in the central area close to the retail and commercial areas. There was little heavy industry, but there were a number of distinctive industrial zones. The most imposing, at least in spatial terms, was the brewing and distilling companies that located in the south-western sector of the city. The Guinness brewery occupied a huge block that stretched from the quays to the far side of James' Street. The Anchor brewery was located not far away on Usher Street on a site of seven acres (2.8ha). A third major brewery, in the same general vicinity in Ardee Street was that of Watkins, Jameson, Pim and Co. Limited whose speciality was 'foreign export stout'. The brewing industry was complemented by the distilling industry. There were six large distilleries in the city in the early years of the century. There was the 'big four' of John Jameson, William Jameson, John Power and George Roe, the Scottish Distillery Company and a private company that operated a distillery on the River Tolka, near Jones' Road. The businesses of the Roe Family, William Jameson and the Jones' Road distillery had amalgamated in 1891 to form the Dublin Distillers'

AN EXAMPLE OF MODERN POSTER ADVERTISING

The activities of the legitimate Billposter who appreciates and conforms to the amenities of his City must not be confused with indiscriminate "flyposting" and enamel sign advertising.

By discriminating in the choice of sites and erecting planned structures as illustrated above—there are no finer advertising structures in the world—a National advertising need is combined harmoniously with the aesthetic demands of the inhabitants of a beautiful city.

A well planned advertising display pleases the Public and promotes sales, thereby serving the advertising purpose of the Nation's producers.

David Allen & Sons Billposting L^{td.}
40 PEARSE STREET, DUBLIN

127 Advertisement for the David Allen Company.
(*Cautionary Guide to Dublin*, 1933, p. 46.)

Company. As with the breweries, the south-western part of the city was the most important location. The Roe family had their operation at Thomas Street on a site of over seventeen acres (6.9ha) and buildings of up to four storeys in height. The (William) Jameson Distillery was not far away and also occupied a large site of some fifteen acres (c.6 ha). John Power provided the fourth element in a large distilling/brewing complex that reached along Thomas Street as far as Steeven's Lane and included the Watkins and Guinness breweries. The John's Lane distillery was also large, about six acres (2.4 hectares) and like the others it was a self-contained enterprise with workshops, cooperage, sawmills and, of course, stables. In contrast, the distillery of John Jameson was located on the northside of the Liffey near Smithfield. By the 1920s, this industry was in terminal decline. Prohibition in the USA had finished the US market and high tariffs and duties imposed after Independence had ruined the British market. Exports of whiskey fell from 1,097,908 gallons (49,912 Hl) in 1924 to 199,133 gallons (9053 Hl) in 1929. It never recovered and by the middle 1950s, exports of whiskey were less than 150,000 gallons per year. By 1923, the Dublin Distillers' Company had rationalised their production by closing two distilleries and more closures followed. Brewing also became more concentrated during this period with amalgamations amongst the smaller firms. It was not a sudden end, the business petered out, the buildings were gradually demolished, some of the Thomas Street operation was amalgamated into the Guinness site while other parts were used for local authority housing between the 1930s and 1950s. The Guinness brewery extended its dominance both in employment terms with over 5000 on the company's books in 1935 (including pensioners) and in spatial terms with its 24ha site. However despite the impact of Guinness on the landscape, this industrial zone was well into a process of contraction by 1930. So as older industry was becoming less of a feature of the central city landscape, suburban locations were being chosen for new operations.

New industries had developed during the 1920s, particularly in response to the policy of industrial protection, essentially import substitution, whereby it was financially expedient for international companies to locate branch plants in Ireland. The WD and HO Wills cigarette company located on the South Circular Road, John Player built in Glasnevin, and the Gallagher Company built on East Wall. The docklands had seen a general decline in manufacturing activity by the end of the 1920s and a consequent greater concentration on warehousing and storage, especially the tank farms for oil storage. The main advantage was that land there and in the suburbs was easy to obtain and extensive plants could be laid out. Other companies took the same path such as Alex Thom

128 1920s advertisement for Capstan Navy Cut cigarettes.

and Co., the printers of the eponymous directory, who shared a little industrial estate with the Player Company in Glasnevin. This is not to suggest a wholesale flight from the city. Industry continued to be located in the city centre for many years to come but it marked the beginning of the decentralization process. It was not just people who were moving from the city centre.

The city centre

At the beginning of the twentieth century Dublin had extensive commercial and retail sectors. The commercial sector with a strong emphasis on the legal, insurance and banking activities was centered on College Green and Dame

129 Redevelopment was a feature of the city even in the nineteenth century. (Postcard.)

Street and spread into nearby streets such as Suffolk and Nassau streets. Along the quays, particularly Ormond Quay, were concentrations of lawyers and associated professions. Commercial offices were now being increasingly housed in 'chambers'. These were purpose-built multiple occupancy buildings but still on too small a scale to be called 'office blocks'. On the whole, they fitted in well into the existing streetscape and, by now, they were everywhere in the city. For example, the block between Middle Abbey Street and Sackville Place now housed the American Chambers and Unity Chambers, which is still there. These took up most of this block with the Hibernian Bank on the strategic Abbey Street corner.

There were two retail cores, one on either side of the Liffey. The greater of the two, both in spatial terms and probably status, was focused on Grafton Street. It reached to George's Street on the west and Dawson Street on the east where it blended with commercial activities. The northside core was more linear. The main axis was along Henry Street into Mary Street on the west and then across Sackville Street into Earl Street and Talbot Street on the east but with little expansion into the adjoining streets. Retailing was also important on Sackville (O'Connell) Street but it did not dominate and did not rival Henry Street. The second decade of the century was quite traumatic for the city. During the 1916 Rising every building on the east side of Sackville street

130 Upper O'Connell Street reconstructed. (Postcard.)

from Eden Quay to Cathedral Lane was destroyed while much of the north side of Lower Abbey Street was partially destroyed. Clerys and the Imperial Hotel were reduced to ruins and so were landmark buildings such as the Dublin Bakery Company (DBC) restaurant and Hopkins and Hopkins, the noted jewellers. Towards Eden Quay, the destruction was more extensive and most of the block between Sackville and Marlborough streets was destroyed. The west side of the street fared better. By some miracle, with the exception of the corner site, the buildings from Bachelor's Walk to Middle Abbey Street survived with minor damage. Most of the block to the north of this, between Sackville Street and Liffey Street, containing the GPO as well as the Hotel Metropole was gutted. However the imposing premises of Arnott and Co. escaped with relatively minor damage.

The Civil War almost completed the ruin of the street. On 5 July 1922 the east side of upper Sackville Street from Nos. 9 to 28 and some houses on the west side were destroyed by fire. Amongst the buildings lost were the Gresham Hotel and the Hammam Hotel, remarkable for its Turkish bath which gave it its name. In an earlier advertisement, the owners claimed that this was the largest and loftiest in the Kingdom and that 'the hygienic and medical advantages of Turkish Baths are very great, and the advantage of having them in connection with a first-class hotel cannot be over-estimated'.

Reconstruction took time and it was really the end of the 1920s before all, or almost all, of the scars had healed. The destruction in Sackville Street and elsewhere offered an unexpected opportunity to remodel the city centre and there was much debate and suggestions about how this might be done. Ruth McManus has discussed this process earlier and it will suffice now to say that few opportunities were taken. Some minor alterations were made to the street line, Cathal Brugha Street was cut through to O'Connell Street for example, but the streetscape that re-emerged was not unlike what was there before. Granted the architectural style was more modern but the overall impression was of reconstruction rather than redevelopment. So what then of the character of the revivified city centre? We will now attempt to recreate the city centre of Dublin in the late 1920s.

Grafton Street and Environs

Grafton Street was the pre-eminent shopping street in Dublin in the late 1920s or so the Grafton Street Association said in their advertisement in the handbook for Civic Week 1927.

> It is in Grafton Street that one finds revealed the latest concepts of Fashion, the greatest variety of goods for every purpose and that standard of Quality which is the deciding factor in Value. These remarkable shopping facilities are supported by courtesy, promptitude and efficiency.

The street still catered for those who could afford a gracious lifestyle. This was in spite of a downturn in retail sales. Arnotts on Henry Street had seen sales fall from a post-war high of £933,000 in 1920 to around £600,000 in 1925 (Nesbitt, 1993, p. 86). There were three large stores on the street in close proximity and these were a powerful magnet for shoppers. Brown Thomas and Millar and Beatty on the lower part of the street faced Switzers. The latter had prospered over the years and since 1911 had absorbed its next-door neighbour to obtain the corner block that they still occupy. Millar and Beatty declared themselves in 1927 to be complete house furnishers and boasted that 'their stock is of a distinctly superior class to that of most other houses without being any higher in price'. This was exactly the same boast that they had made in their advertising in 1911. All three stores managed to survive into the late 1940s and two into recent times.

Clothing shops and particularly women's clothing shops dominated the landscape. There were ladies' tailors, costumiers, furriers, hosiers and hatters. Slyne and Co. were costumiers and Vard's offered furs.

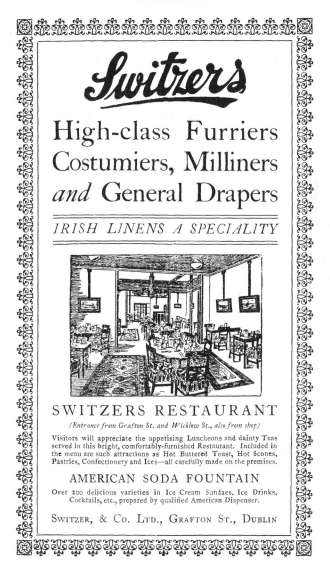

131 Switzers of Grafton Street. Note the American Soda Fountain.

Francis Smyth and Son offered umbrellas, parasols and fancy sticks and Robert and Co. advertised themselves as drapers and milliners, lace and boot and shoe merchants and importers of furs. They claimed that the 'ever changing decrees of Fashion are always faithfully reflected in every department ... but there are three fashions which never change in their warerooms – courtesy, efficiency and value'. At 24, W. Leon offered exclusive models in coats, costumes,

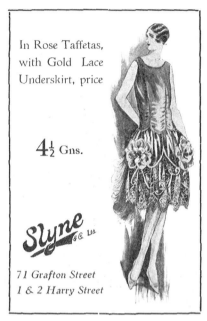

In Rose Taffetas,
with Gold Lace
Underskirt, price

$4\frac{1}{2}$ Gns.

Slyne & Co. Ltd.

71 Grafton Street
1 & 2 Harry Street

132 Advertisement for Slyne.

evenings and afternoon gowns. Newells Ltd had two stores on the street, at 63 and 76 and had the proud, though intriguing boast, that 'exclusively engaged in UNDERWEAR, buying and selling, our staff attains a degree of efficiency which is reflected in the styles and in the prices'.

Men were not neglected. For more than seventy years E. and W. Seale had been men's outfitters at 97–9, close to Switzers. They modestly claimed to be Dublin's 'Premier Outfitting Establishment' and could offer a 'Happy Medium' made-to-measure suit which embodied both machine and hand labour and so could be sold for the modest sum of six guineas. Unfortunately, by the end of the 1920s, E. and W. Seale were no more and W.J. Kelly then operated a large tailoring and outfitting shop from the same location. Shoe shops such as Tyler's Fashion Shoe Shops and the American Shoe Company complemented the clothes shops.

However it seems that both the number and elegance of shops had decreased since the early years of the century. Forrest and Sons Ltd, with large premises at 100–101 Grafton Street as well as 4,5 and 9 Wicklow Street had once advertised their Royal appointment as silk mercers to Her Majesty Queen Alexandra but although they were still advertising their extensive range in the handbook for Civic Week 1927, by 1930 they had been replaced by Britain's, the automobile agents and assemblers.

Gone also or going were the military tailors and colonial outfitters such as Jeffrey Brothers and Coldwell Ltd. The former was replaced by an iron-mongers while the latter premises were absorbed into an expanded drapery store run by Robert and Co. The court costumiers were also of a by-gone age and there were fewer stores advertising themselves as milliners or shirt makers. In the early years of the century Alfred Manning of 102–3 Grafton Street had operated a Magasin de Nouveatués which catered to the quality end of the market. There was no garment which could not be manufactured and the client could be assured at everything was á la mode, the costume specialists being 'conversant with every phase of modern fashion and anticipating correctly all its possible and probable permutations'. This had now become

133 E. and W. Seale Ltd of Grafton Street. Note the 'six guinea suit'.

FORREST'S
ATTRACTIVE DISPLAY OF
AUTUMN NOVELTIES

A Charming Selection of Millinery, Costumes, Three-piece Suits, Knitted Wear, Evening Gowns, Smart Coats for Autumn Wear, Fashionable Crepe-de-Chine Scarves and Neckwear, the latest designs in Gloves and Coloured Hosiery, Dainty Lingerie, and a magnificent range of the very latest in Overshirts, : : Jumpers and Sleeveless Cardigans. : :

Sole Agents for
ELIZABETH ARDEN
TOILET PREPARATIONS

100 & 101 Grafton St., 4, 5 & 9 Wicklow St.
DUBLIN

134 Advertisement for Forrest's Autumn Novelties.

the premises of West and Son, the jewellers. In number 9 there had been a hat manufacturer with a court dress manufacturer overhead. Number 11 had been a trunk and portmanteau manufacturer. By the late 1920s both had been absorbed into an expanded Mitchells restaurant and tearooms. So while clothes retailing remained vital to the street, it cannot be said to have had the same style as in the pre-war days.

Nonetheless a great variety of goods and services were available. There were jewellers, opticians and pharmacies. Combridge and Sons were booksellers, stationers and picture framers. There were hair dressers (and hair specialists – presumably more expensive) and Dr Scholl offered 'foot comfort services' at no. 11. In addition, there was a generous distribution of tobacconists, florists and fruiters, though James Thornton had closed. Those with a sweet tooth were well catered for, particularly at the St Stephen's Green end where Noblett's and Maison Philippe were side by side and near Switzers was Fullers, the 'American Confectioners'.

Retailing had become more international and mass-market oriented by the end of the 1920s and this was evident on Grafton Street. Woolworth's now had a store there at 64–6 replacing a number of individual shops. Burton's outfitters were a direct challenge to the bespoke tailors such as Seale and Co. offering off-the-peg clothing for men. Across Britain and Ireland, they characteristically occupied corner sites and on Grafton Street they were located on the corner of Duke Street. Bernardo's Furs, the previous occupant was displaced but they retained their less central location on the other side of Suffolk Street. Bewley's Oriental Cafes had expanded onto Grafton Street and now occupied 78–9 where once had been Manfield and Sons the boot manufacturers, thus complementing the long-established Bewley's on George's Street.

Although Grafton Street extends across Suffolk Street towards College Green, then, as now, it became a somewhat different street. This is where the commercial and retailing spheres overlapped and this was reflected in the use of the buildings. It was not a clean transition, retailing and commerce were intermixed. The first three units (107–9) were occupied by Hamilton Long, Bernardo's furriers and Barrett's silversmiths but closer to College Green were the premises of James North estate agents, Dudgeon and Sons government stockbrokers and the Northern Bank. Northern Bank Chambers was home to a variety of uses but was dominated by solicitors. All was not lost to retailing though. The prime locations at the corner of College Green were occupied then as now by Kapp and Peterson, Thomas Cook and James Fox. The combination of a pipe manufacturer and tobacconist, a cigar merchant with a travel agent was an interesting mix.

South Great George's Street
At the beginning of the twentieth century, George's Street was an important retailing centre and so it remained by the end of the 1920s. It might not have had the elegance of Grafton Street but it had large, imposing and important stores. The existence of two strong parallel retail streets was important for the cross streets and Wicklow/Exchequer Street benefited as a result. The key to under-standing the success of George's Street was the presence of Pim's department store which had been an important landmark since the middle of the nineteenth century. It had grown in size and occupied almost the entire western side of the street from Exchequer Street to Dame Street. At the other end of the street was Thomas Dockrell and Sons; a large houseware department store that opened onto Drury and Stephen's streets and was an important draw in its own right. Clothing stores and, to a lesser degree, food and drink stores dominated the retail landscape. In addition to Pim's there was the large drapery store of David Kellett, across the street at 19–21a as well as on Exchequer Street which emphasised value for money. They promised that:

> to retain the confidence of the public is our first consideration and we
> endeavour to study their interests in every way ... To be well dressed

need not necessarily be an expensive matter. To a great extent the solution rests with a lady herself, for it is not always a question of means, but simply a wise discrimination in the choice of her shopping centre.

Further up the street at 69–71 was the multifaceted store of W. Holmes who were milliners and furriers, costumiers, silk mercers, glovers and general drapers. In 1913, they had advertised that 'doing so large a business, the stock is constantly being renewed and patrons are assured that they will at all times be able to secure the latest styles'. And in particular:

> for all who desire to achieve success in their dress, it is evident that to obtain the best results for their gowns they must use corsets which are in harmony with the gown of the moment. Messrs Holmes … have always a fine display of their very latest models.

They must have done well in the intervening years because by 1929 they had expanded into No. 69, previously a tea merchant. Food retailing was to be expected given the presence of the City Markets and food wholesaling on the minor streets around. There were poulterers and butchers and general provisions suppliers. Eastmans and Hafner's would have been well known throughout the city, the former having a large network of suburban branches.

There had been changes to the composition of the street but its essential character had not changed since 1911 and the familiar names were still there. Gibson the tailors were still at 15, Winstanley shoes still occupied 18. One could buy tea from Becker Bros and wines and spirits from Mrs Bolger and Sons or instead from the Home and Colonial Tea Stores at no. 40.

By the late 1920s the National Bank had opened a branch at 64–5, previously a drapers, mantle and costume manufactory. Burtons had opened a store at the corner with Dame Street; the third such location they occupied. The fact that they chose to locate there in addition to their stores on O'Connell, Henry and Grafton streets emphasises the continuing importance of George's street at this time. Comparing Grafton Street and George's Street the impression is one of a gap having been narrowed somewhat. Grafton Street was still a superior shopping street to George's Street but it had lost some of its elegance and exclusivity while George's Street, never quite as fashionable, had not lost out as much.

The streetscape of the eastern side was given additional character by a unified building style for the two main blocks, that from Exchequer Street to

OUR TEAS

Are the pick of the Market
Are unvarying in quality
and give universal satisfaction

Prices from 1/4 to 3/2 per lb.

BECKER BROS., Ltd.

8 SOUTH GREAT GEORGE'S STREET and   **DUBLIN**
17 NORTH EARL STREET   Telephone 156

135 Becker Bros Tea – still an important feature of the city in the 1920s.

Dame Street and the immensely impressive edifice of the City Market. Food retailing and wholesaling was still important in the central or Market Arcade. Fruit and flowers, fish, poultry and game were on offer but intermixed with paper merchants and a furniture merchant. Several units were vacant. The units on the outside of the markets were very varied and included retailing, services (quite a number of plumbers), manufacturing (the Central Tie Company on Drury Street for example) as well as a laundry and hotel. These were clearly secondary streets undoubtedly because they did not lead directly to Grafton Street and were thus less valuable locations.

Exchequer and Wicklow streets were more important and valuable because of their role as cross-streets but they were not of the first rank. Therefore more space-demanding land uses were found there and commerce could not be kept out by high rents as was the case on the main retail streets. On Exchequer Street there were hotels, the Central Hotel occupying the key location, a house furnishing department of Pims and a business chambers. However, here also were clothing stores, Nicholls, milliners and tailors, had large premises. Wicklow Street, being closer to Grafton Street was given over to clothing retailing to a greater extent. The same range as offered on Grafton Street was available here. There were drapers, milliners, mantle makers, tailors, shoe shops, furriers and costumiers but with a greater variety of other landuses.

These included commercial chambers, a dairy, hairdressers, and, interestingly a number of dentists. Nonetheless the impression is of an overwhelmingly retail street of good quality. There is no direct route to George's Street at the northern end of Grafton Street and consequently no street mirrored the character of Wicklow Street. Chatham Street was interesting because of the preponderance of high quality food shops. Of the 14 shops up to the junction of Clarendon Street, there were three fish merchants, three victuallers, one dairy produce supplier, one fruiterer and one general provision merchants as well as Thomas Neary, wine and spirit merchant. Such a concentration of complementary uses is unusual, especially as they serviced the upper end of the market – both Lawson-Powell (No. 2) and Sawers (No. 3) offered fish, oysters, game and venison.

O'Connell Street and environs

The northern alternative core was centered around O'Connell Street, as it is today. It was an awkward shape, roughly cruciform with the short axis being formed by Henry and Mary streets on the western side and Earl and Talbot streets on the east. Henry Street was, by far, the most important shopping street and, for all its great length and width, O'Connell Street would have had relatively little to offer but for the presence of Clery's. That said, Clery's were happy to talk-up the street and refer to it in the advertisement below as the 'finest and busiest street in Ireland'.

Clery's gave structure to the street and ensured that flows of shoppers were attracted to the east side. It was generally understood that southsiders did not cross the Liffey to shop. The duplication of outlets by so many retailers in both shopping districts would tend to give weight to this assertion. North and south were seen as two different and distinct shopping centres rather than a single elongated unit.

The damage to the district between the 1916 Rising and the later Civil War had been considerable but thought there were some changes both to form and character, what emerged from the reconstruction process was not different in kind to what had been before. There had been changes in emphasis. Compared to the beginning of the century there had been a shift on O'Connell Street to commercial uses at the expense of retailing. There were now fewer hotels but a mass-entertainment sector had emerged and become important.

The upper and lower parts of the street had different characters at the beginning of the century and so it remained. Upper O'Connell Street was an

CLERYS DUBLIN

IRELAND'S GREATEST STORE
and one of the most beautiful in Europe, situated in the centre of the finest and busiest street in Ireland

136 Clery's department store, the key anchor for O'Connell Street.

interesting mix of land uses – retailing, commercial, manufacturing and leisure. Some, such as Laird's chemists, at the corner of Henry Street, and nearby Noblett's the confectioners were well-known landmarks. Thwaites continued to manufacture mineral waters from their premises at 57, demonstrating the continuing centrality of manufacturing industry while Gilbeys, wine and spirit merchants, had their bottling store at 46–7. Other uses were new arrivals. There were two additional cinemas, the Pillar Picture House (No. 62) and the Carlton Cinema which replaced a wine merchants. The Temperance Hotel had been lost and there was a new bank (the Provincial) on the corner with Parnell Street. While the eastern side of the side had been badly damaged by the civil war, not all had been destroyed. Findlater's had the headquarters of their wine and spirits chain at 28–30 and from no. 39 Kelly Brothers offered fine Burgundy wines such as Moulin à Vent 1918 for 54s. a dozen in 1926. Reconstruction was far from complete by this time. On the block from Cathedral Street to Findlater Place only the Gresham Hotel and Mackeys

Stephen's Green Turkish Baths

OPEN DAILY   -   7.30. a.m to 9.30 p.m.
TURKISH BATHS   7.30. to 4   3/-
                            4 to 9.30   2/6

WARM, SULPHUR, ELECTRIC AND SALT BATHS

127 STEPHEN'S GREEN, DUBLIN

137 Stephen's Green Turkish Baths.

(seed merchants) had been rebuilt. Four year later progress had been substantial with only two plots (17 and 18) still incomplete. A commercial development with offices above and shops below had replaced the Hammam Hotel. It was a substantial block with a unified façade that was not unattractive. While the loss of the Turkish bath in the Hammam was a matter of regret, it is comforting to note that this did not deprive the city completely of this service. There was another at 127 St Stephen's Green which offered a variety of baths, Turkish, warm, sulphur, electric and salt baths for 3*s.* between 0730 and 1600 hours and for 2*s.* 6*d.* between 1600 and 2130 hours.

Other small hotels on the street had also disappeared leaving the Gresham Hotel as the only hotel of substance. Underneath the offices in Hammam Buildings was a variety of retail units that included two drapers, a jewellers and Keys, the tobacconists. These might have been expected to prosper because the newly-built Savoy Cinema would draw a considerable passing trade to this part of the street. There were now two large cinemas opposite each other on O'Connell Street and others were added elsewhere. The

HOPKINS & HOPKINS

MANUFACTURING JEWELLERS
AND SILVERSMITHS

OPPOSITE O'CONNELL MONUMENT

DUBLIN

ESTABLISHED 1787.   REBUILT 1922

We manufacture reproductions of
Antique Celtic Art Jewellery on
the Premises, also Crosses, Medals
and Badges in beautiful Patterns

HOPKINS & HOPKINS

AGENTS IN IRELAND FOR THE
PERFECTED AMERICAN WALTHAM WATCHES

Opposite O'Connell Monument,
DUBLIN

138 The restored façade of Hopkins and Hopkins, O'Connell Street.

provision of these cinemas might be seen to be a distinctive moment in the story of the street since it moved its character firmly towards mass-market entertainment. It would not be long before ice cream parlours became an additional element, there was already one on Lower O'Connell Street.

By the late 1920s, Clerys, the Hotel Metropole and the GPO had been rebuilt and thus the major elements of the lower part of the street were restored. Hopkins and Hopkins (jewellers) were at the junction with Eden Quay as they had been for many years but there had been significant changes too. The Dublin Bread Company (DBC) had been replaced by the Grand Central Cinema and the Grand Hotel and Restaurant was now the Broadway Soda Fountain. There were more banks and commercial offices. The Ulster Bank, The Munster and Leinster Bank, The Hibernian Bank and the Bank of Ireland had branches on the east of the street. The block between Middle Abbey Street and Sackville Place had been rebuilt as commercial chambers. The ground floor of these chambers was given to retailing and there was a fruiters, a chemist and a boot company. The impression is of a different character of retailing to what had been there before when there was a gents' outfitters, a naval and military tailor, a ladies' and children's outfitting warehouse as well as the imposing sounding City of Dublin Drug Hall.

The nature of these commercial activities had evolved to reflect the changing world. The oddly-named Pratts petrol, the brand name of the Irish American Oil Company, had their offices at 1–2 O'Connell Street. Further up the street, the company of Siemens-Schuckert offered demonstrations of their new electric polishers and vacuum cleaners. They noted in their advertising that 'in these days of servant problems the housewife must not become a drudge'. This both indicated the growing availability of household electrical appliances as well as the changed nature of households in the post-war period as servant numbers declined, though there were still over 10,000 at the 1926 census. Though there were more companies concerned with consumer products on the street, the prices, twelve guineas for a vacuum cleaner, meant that they were still not mass-market appliances.

The west side of the street showed the same pattern of continuity and change. Elverys, famous for outwear with its distinctive elephant trademark, Easons and Lemons (confectioners) were where they had always been. Frewen and Ryan were still hosiers, glovers and waterproofers but Chancellor and Son, the photographers were gone while Kapp and Peterson, the pipe makers and tobacconists, now occupied the corner site with Bachelor's Walk in place of Kelly, Martin and Son who had been fishing tackle manufacturers and gunpowder importers; perhaps too explosive a land use. Some activities had changed location on the street. This is a normal occurrence in the operation of the property market but the redevelopment of the street must have enhanced this process. Thus Hamilton Long, apothecaries and mineral water manufacturers, had premises at 3 lower Sackville Street in 1911 but by the late 1920s were at No. 5. Ulster Bank Chambers, another purpose-built commercial building with the bank occupying the ground floor, now occupied their original location. The True-Form Boot company crossed from one side of Sackville Place to the other while Kapp and Peterson moved from the corner location on Princes' Street. Meanwhile Burtons, the outfitters, had taken its trademark corner site on Earl Street.

Henry Street and environs

Henry Street, and its extension, Mary Street, recovered well from the damage of the 1916 Rising. In the late 1920s, there were three anchor stores just as there had been at the turn of the century. Arnotts, then as now, was a large department store mid-way down Henry Street while Todd Burns was at the

Todd Burns & Co. *Ltd.*

The Leading Drapery *and*
House-Furnishing Establishment

HIGH CLASS GOODS
At MODERATE PRICES

Mary Street, Dublin

139 Todd Burns at the corner of Mary and Jervis streets.

junction of Mary Street and Jervis Street. Todd Burns was particularly important in that it occupied two sites on Mary Street, a little like Pims on a smaller scale, and gave a boost to quite a long linear shopping street. It brought shoppers to that end of Mary Street who might otherwise have not crossed Liffey Street. By 1930, The Henry Street Warehouse Company, across the road from Arnotts, had become Roches Stores. The presence of these three large quality stores ensured the necessary throughflow of customers to sustain a range of uses. This included a large array of clothing stores of various kinds, jewellers and opticians. The variety of stores paralleled that on offer in Grafton Street, though the street was probably closer in status to George's Street. This is not to say that the shops were downmarket. Sydenham of 30 Henry Street,

140 Leon of Henry and Grafton streets.

on the corner of O'Connell Street, offered exclusive styles at popular prices. However the 'Fifty Shilling Tailors' at no. 50, complemented further down Mary Street by the 'Two Guinea Tailors' probably appealed to a different market. The reduction in the price of a suit as one travelled down Henry Street might be a good status indicator and may be contrasted with that of Seale's 'modest' suits available on Grafton Street.

The presence on Henry/Mary Street and on O'Connell Street of many stores that also operated in Grafton and George's Street indicates the storekeepers saw themselves as servicing two distinct shopping districts. There were northside branches of the Singer Sewing Machine Company, Hafner's the butchers, F. & W. Woolworth, Tylers Shoes, Burtons outfitters, Hayes Conyngham and Robinson, the chemists and Findlater's to name but some.

Retailing continued into Capel Street though the junction with Jervis Street marked the end of the core area. On the other side of O'Connell Street, the eastern arm of the cross led from Earl Street into Talbot Street. Here too, retailing was largely linear. Marlborough Street, parallel to O'Connell Street provided local services and some commercial buildings but tenements were a major feature. Earl Street is quite a short street but it was home to a number of important city landmarks. Downes bakery had its shop on the street and its production in a large premises along Earl Place behind Clery's. Boyers and Hickey's were popular general drapers and equally well-known was the Home and Colonial Tea Stores on the corner with Marlborough Street. Tailors and other forms of clothing stores occupied the greater part of the remainder of the street but there were no major anchor stores. Talbot Street was predominantly retail all the way down to Amiens Street with its railway station. The retailing was unremarkable, however, with many local services – butchers, dairies, family grocers and the like. Nor was a particular gradient in types of shop evident as one travelled towards Amiens Street. Rather it was a well-supplied secondary shopping street. The best known unit on the street would have been that of the Varian Brush Company, about half way down on the southern side of the street.

While the retail cores discussed above were distinctive, there was not a sharp boundary between them. Quality retailing was important on the streets between them, though not as dominant. Dame Street had many interesting and important shops as did Westmoreland Street though not D'Olier Street to the same degree. The important factor was the passage of people. Intermixed with insurance companies and banks on Dame Street were stores such as T.J. Callaghan, the outfitters, Siberry, 'the tailor who never sends you a bill' and Edmondson, bulb and seed merchants.

Concluding Comments

This has been a brief attempt to give a flavour of the city centre at the mid-point of the period discussed by Ruth McManus. It was a prosperous, well-supplied city with a well-developed system of public transport that was reasonably priced. There were probably sub-surface tensions, however, arising from Independence and the assertion of a Catholic identity. It is interesting to note, for example, the company of Williams and Sons who were at 2 Dame Street and who described themselves as 'naturalists'. They offered a specialised service in animal mounting. Horns and hoofs mounted as trophies was a particular speciality as was fish mounting. In 1929 they still felt comfortable in describing themselves as 'naturalists to the Lord Lieutenant'. Contrast this with an advertisement three years later on the occasion of the Eucharistic

141 Retail activity beyond the core – Kenny and Owens.

Congress for The O'Hanrahans, gramophone specialists of 33 Upper O'Connell Street. The advertisement, reproduced below as figure 142, speaks for itself.

Gill's Guide to Catholic Dublin is just as forthright. It begins by noting that 'This [guide] has the exact purpose and scope indicated by its title. Many alien, intrusive, anti-Irish institutions and buildings, persons and events occupy the foremost place, and fill almost all the space in the usual Guide Books to the Metropolitan Region'. The guide singles out *A Book of Dublin* for particular comment.

> Yet the forces of ignorance, bigotry and servility die hard. Most tenacious of all is their grip on Modern Irish History and on the Civic History of Ireland's Capital. One recent instance of the perversion of our Civic History, a gross instance, may here be cited as a specimen of these influences in action. Within the past four years, at the expense and in the name of the Catholic City of Dublin and its Catholic

142 Advertisement for the O'Hanrahans. (Congress Committee, 1932, p. 120.)

Corporation – fraudulent claims in each case – a mendacious work called The Book of Dublin has been compiled, published twice, and circulated over the world as if it was a genuine civic publication... It treated to pride of place the English Protestant and Puritan Academy, called legally, 'The College of the Holy and Undivided Trinity of Queen Elizabeth near Dublin, as being the University of the city.

(*Gill's Guide to Catholic Dublin*, 1932, p. vii)

Some specific references

Brady, J. and Simms, A. (2001) *Dublin through space and time.* Dublin: Four Courts Press.

Civic Week Council (1927) *Dublin Civic Week 1927 Official Handbook.* Dublin.

Civic Week Council (1929) *Dublin Civic Week 1929 Official Handbook.* Dublin.

Congress Committee (1932) *The Thirty-First International Eucharistic Congress. Advance Programme.* Dublin: Congress Committee.

Gill and Co. (1932) *Gill's Guide to Catholic Dublin.* Dublin: Gill and Co.

Kenny, K.M. (ed.) (1938) *Dublin's New Traffic and Parking Bye-Laws.* Dublin: The Traffic and Safety First Association of Ireland.

Local Government (Dublin) Tribunal (1938) *Report of the Local Government (Dublin) Tribunal.* Dublin: Stationery Office.

Nesbitt, R. (1993) *At Arnotts of Dublin.* Dublin: A. and A. Farmar.

Robertson, M. (1933) *Cautionary Guide to Dublin.* Dublin: The Royal Institute of the Architects of Ireland.

Stratten and Stratten (1892) *Dublin, Cork and south of Ireland: A literary, commercial and social review.* London.

Bibliography

The information available to the researcher interested in development in the early twentieth century is quite varied. Official reports and documents generally provide a good outline of public housing activity, from which some suggestions relating to private speculative undertakings and the activities of public utility societies can sometimes be gleaned. Tracing the work of private developers is more difficult, often relying on chance finds and snippets of information from newspapers, street directories, wills, leases and other contemporary sources. Valuable documents for the history of the city are kept in the City Archive, South William Street, in the National Archives, Bishop Street and the Gilbert Library housed in the Public Library, Pearse Street. Other useful locations for specific information include the Religious Society of Friends Historical Library and the Church Representative Body Archive.

There are two housing inquiries that are relevant to the discussion. The first report was published in 1914 as the *Report of the Departmental Committee Appointed by the Local Government Board for Ireland to inquire into the housing conditions of the working classes in the city of Dublin*, British Parliamentary Papers c 7273. The second report, the *Report of the Inquiry into the housing of the working classes of the city of Dublin 1939/43*, took longer to complete and is dated 1939–43. These are referenced in the text as Housing Inquiry (1914) and Housing Inquiry (1939–43) respectively.

The volumes of Dáil Debates give some indication of the political debate surrounding various housing initiatives. The index volumes are most helpful in locating references to particular aspects of speculative housing, the question of public utility societies and new housing legislation. These are referenced in the text by volume number and page number, e.g. Dáil Debates, 14, p. 325.

The annual reports of the Department of Local Government and Public Health provide tables covering housing grants provided by county for both local authorities and private building. Unfortunately, the actual numbers of dwellings built are often difficult to ascertain, in that the private building and public utility society activity is generally amalgamated under one heading.

The reports of the Housing Committee of Dublin Corporation appear in the annual compendium of *Dublin Corporation Reports and Printed Documents*. For brevity, in the text these reports are listed as Report number/year e.g. Report 29/1928. The records of Pembroke Township and Rathmines and Rathgar UDC are also housed in the City Archives.

Public utility societies were registered under the Industrial and Provident Societies Act of 1893 and subsequent amending legislation. Under this legislation they were required to register with the Registrar of Friendly Societies and to submit copies of their rules for approval. Audited annual returns and a triennial return which listed all of the members of the society and their shareholding were also required, with threats of prosecution for failure to submit these documents. The records of the Registry of Friendly Societies are located in the National Archives, Bishop Street. An index lists organisations by their registered number, so that housing organizations will be listed with turf co-operative societies and creameries. Information sourced from these records is referenced in the text as follows: RFS, followed by the registered number of the society and a brief description of the source, for example, RFS, R2173, letter.

Unfortunately, the official purpose for which the data in the returns was required limits the information which can be derived from the official records. For example, the annual returns provide a balance sheet of activities, but need not specify the location or nature of building activity. Sometimes the returns suggest that no building activity took place, whereas in fact building by the organization is recorded in the *Irish Builder and Engineer* or another publication. However, other societies, particularly those with a more philanthropic bent, often lodged information in excess of that which was legally required, such as their own annual reports, which provide the researcher with additional detail. The file for each public utility society was divided into two parts, one containing the official returns and the other containing correspondence. Additional information can often be gleaned from the correspondence between the Secretary or Chairman of the society and the Registry of Friendly Societies, though more often than not the correspondence file consists of copies of reminders to submit returns and threats of prosecution. Therefore, when using the returns of public utility societies it is important to bear in mind the official function for which they were compiled and, where possible, to qualify information obtained through the use of other sources. It is worth noting that the Registrar of Friendly Societies also produced printed annual reports which outline activities and provide useful general statistics.

Other documentary sources include wills, such as that of Alexander Strain, which are available from the National Archives. In order to locate a will, it is necessary to have a good estimate of the date of death of the person, because they are listed according to the year in which probate was granted. Within each annual volume, the entries are arranged alphabetically by surname.

Much useful information on all aspects of the building trade may be gleaned from the *Irish Builder and Engineer*, established in 1859. The paper was published on alternate Saturdays and cost just 3*d.* in 1930. In addition to its head office at 54 Upper O'Connell Street, it had a London office, and following the emergence of the Irish Free State it remained an all-Ireland publication, with specific articles from Belfast. Each edition had roughly 36 pages, with a mixture of editorial and news snippets, correspondence, sections on roads and roadmaking, building news, the building market (listing current prices for building supplies), an engineering section, reviews, advertisements and contracts. With features on architecture, town planning, and even topics such as 'Early Church Art in Northern Europe' (*Irish Builder and Engineer*, 4 January 1930), the *Irish Builder and Engineer* was an indispensible periodical for all builders, whatever the scale of their operations. It lists applications for new houses and other building work, sometimes providing additional detail such as the type of building materials or architect being used.

In tracing the development of a given area over time, one of the most valuable sources of information is *Thom's Official Directory* which has been produced annually since the middle of the nineteenth century. Detailed information is provided on a range of matters, including statistics of Ireland, parliamentary and ecclesiastical directories, trades directories among others. Most useful in charting the growth of the suburbs is the Dublin city and county directory which gives a street-by-street breakdown of the land use of the city. The name of the person(s) occupying each building is given as well as the nature of any commercial activity. This is extremely useful in determining the general timing of particular developments, although it should be noted that the directory has its limitations and an annual updating cannot be guaranteed. In addition, it can be inaccurate, with misspellings occurring relatively frequently. It should also be recognised that houses on individual streets were sometimes renumbered as additional plots were built up or terraces were renamed and numbered within the overall street pattern. The user should also beware of misspellings of names and incorrect initials, which can be confusing. However, despite these shortcomings, Thom's provides a great level of detail and, when used in conjunction with other sources, can be extremely useful. The directories of trades and professions should also be mentioned, in which the location of various commercial activities is listed under a quite detailed classification. This is a useful source for information about builders suppliers, some of the contractors and their locations.

Newspaper advertisements provide an impression of the nature of the property market at a given point in time. The *Irish Times* also ran a fortnightly 'Building and Reconstruction' section which covered both public housing schemes and some of the larger new speculative developments. Photographs are sometimes included. The reader is directed to an extensive review of newspapers, directories and gazetteers as data sources in Horner, A. (1998) *Irish Towns – A Guide to Sources*. Dublin: Geography Publications, pp 147–62.

The journal of the *Statistical and Social Inquiry Society of Ireland*, formerly the Dublin Statistical Society, is a useful source on the housing question in Dublin during the late-nineteenth and early-twentieth centuries, while interesting articles may also be found in *Studies* and *The Bell*.

To understand fully the background to the housing problem and the development of Dublin, it is necessary to look back to the nineteenth century which is unfortunately beyond the scope of this book. The first port of call should be the first volume in this series, *Dublin though space and time* (2001), edited by Joseph Brady and Anngret Simms. Aalen has produced a considerable corpus of research dealing largely with philanthropic approaches, while Jacinta Prunty's text (1998) on Dublin Slums focuses on three particular strands: contagious disease and public health, sanitation and the housing challenge, and vagrancy and poor relief. Other useful texts include those by O'Brien (1982) and Daly (1984).

The bibliography also suggests some more general background reading relating to suburbs, such as Harris and Larkham (1999), the British experience of slums and suburbanization, including pioneering work by Dyos (especially 1961) and reading relating to the history of modern town planning, especially work by Cherry (1974).

Aalen, F.H.A. (1984) Approaches to the working class housing problem in late-Victorian Dublin: The DADC and the Guinness Trust. *In:* Bender, R.J. (ed.) *New research on the social geography of Ireland, Mannheimer Geographische Arbeiten*, 17, Mannheim, pp 161–90.

Aalen, F.H.A. (1985) The working-class housing movement in Dublin, 1850–1920. *In:* Bannon, M.J. (ed.) *The emergence of Irish planning 1880–1920*. Dublin: Turoe Press, pp 131–88.

Aalen, F.H.A. (1987) Public housing in Ireland, 1880–1921, *Planning Perspectives*, 2, pp 175–9.

Aalen, F.H.A. (1988) Homes for Irish heroes: housing under the Irish Land (provision for soldiers and sailors) Act 1919 and the Irish sailors' and soldiers' land trust, *Town Planning Review*, 59(3), pp 305–23.

Aalen, F.H.A. (1990) *The Iveagh Trust: the first hundred years, 1890–1990*. Dublin: Iveagh Trust.

Aalen, F.H.A. (1992a) Health and housing in Dublin c.1850–1921. *In:* Aalen, F.H.A. and Whelan, K. (eds) *Dublin city and county*. Dublin: Geography Publications, pp 279–304.

Aalen, F.H.A, and Whelan, K. (eds) (1992b) *Dublin city and county: from prehistory to present.* Dublin: Geography Publications.

Aalen, F.H.A. (1992c) English origins. *In:* Ward, S.V. (ed.) *The Garden City; past, present and future.* London: Spon, pp 28–51.

Aalen, F.H.A. (1992d) Ireland. *In:* Pooley, C.G. (ed.), *Housing strategies in Europe, 1880–1930.* Leicester: Leicester University Press, pp 132–63.

Abercrombie, P. (1942) The Dublin town plan (with comments), *Studies*, 31, pp 155–70.

Abercrombie, P., Kelly, S. and Kelly, A. (1922) *Dublin of the future: the new town plan.* Liverpool: University Press of Liverpool.

Abercrombie, P., Kelly, S. and Robertson, M. (1941) *Dublin sketch development plan*. Dublin: Dublin Corporation.

Allan, C.M. (1965) The genesis of British urban redevelopment with special reference to Glasgow, *Economic History Review*, 18, 2nd series, pp 598–613.

Aldridge, H.R. (1915) *The case of town planning- a practical manual for the use of Councillors, Officers and others engaged in the preparation of town planning schemes*. London: National Housing and Town Planning Council.

Anon. (1937) Book review of slum clearance in Dublin, 1937, *Dublin Magazine*, 12 (3), p. 92.

Anon. (1942) Book review of Dublin town planning report, *Dublin Magazine*, 17 (4), p. 57.

Archer, J. (1988) Ideology and aspiration: individualism, the middle class, and the genesis of the Anglo-American suburb, *Journal of Urban History*, 14 (2), pp 214–53.

Artifex (1930) Greater Dublin: complexities and possibilities, *Dublin Magazine*, 5(1), pp 37–43.

Baillie Scott, M.H. *et al.* (1910) *Garden suburbs, town planning and modern architecture*. London: Fisher Unwin.

Bannon, M.J. (1978) Patrick Geddes and the emergence of modern town planning in Ireland, *Irish Geography*, 11(2), pp 141–8.

Bannon, M.J. (ed.) (1985a) *The emergence of Irish planning, 1880–1920*. Dublin: Turoe Press.

Bannon, M.J. (1985b) The genesis of modern Irish planning. *In:* Bannon, M.J. (ed.) *The emergence of Irish planning, 1880–1920*. Dublin: Turoe Press, pp 189–260.

Bannon, M.J. (1988) The Capital of the new State. *In:* Cosgrave, A. (ed.) *Dublin through the Ages*. Dublin: College Press.

Bannon, M.J. (ed.) (1989a) *Planning: the Irish experience, 1920–1988*. Dublin: Wolfhound Press.

Bannon, M.J. (1989b) Irish planning from 1921 to 1945. *In:* Bannon, M.J. (ed.) *Planning: the Irish experience*. Dublin: Wolfhound Press, pp 13–70.

Barnett, J. (1986) *The elusive city: five centuries of design, ambition and miscalculation*. New York: Harper and Row.

Barrett, H. and Phillips, J. (1987) *Suburban style: the British home 1840–1960*. London: Macdonald & Co. Ltd.

Behan, B. (1963) *Hold your hour and have another*. London: Hutchinson.

Behan, D. (1965) *My brother Brendan*. London: Leslie Frewin.

Bell, C. and Bell, R. (1969) *City fathers: the early history of town planning in Britain*. London: Barrie & Rockliff.

Bender, R.J. (ed.) *New research on the social geography of Ireland, Mannheimer Geographische Arbeiten*, 17, Mannheim.

Benevolo, L. (1967) *The origins of modern town planning*. Cambridge, Mass: MIT Press.

Bolger, D. (ed.) (1988) *Invisible cities, the new Dubliners: a journey through unofficial Dublin*. Dublin: Raven Arts Press.

Bowley, M. (1945) *Housing and the State 1919–44*. London: Allen & Unwin.

Boydell, B. (1984) Impressions of Dublin 1934, *Dublin Historical Record*, 37 (3/4), pp 88–103.

Brady, J. and Parker, A.J. (1986) The socio-demographic spatial structure of Dublin in 1981, *Economic and Social Review*, 17(4), pp 229–52.

Brady, J. and Simms, A. (eds) (2001) *Dublin through space and time*. Dublin: Four Courts Press.

Brady, J. (2001a) Dublin in the nineteenth century – an introduction. *In:* Brady, J. and Simms, A. (eds), *Dublin through space and time*. Dublin: Four Courts Press, pp 159–65.

Brady, J. (2001b) Dublin at the turn of the century. *In:* Brady, J. and Simms, A. (eds), *Dublin through space and time*. Dublin: Four Courts Press, pp 221–81.

Brady, J. (2001c) The heart of the city- commercial Dublin c.1890–1915. *In:* Brady, J. and Simms, A. (eds), *Dublin through space and time*. Dublin: Four Courts Press, pp 282–340.

Brady, J.V. (1917) *The future of Dublin- practical slum reform.* Dublin: Dollard.

Burnett, J. (1978) *A social history of housing 1815–1970.* London: David & Charles.

Butler, R.M. (1916) The reconstruction of O'Connell Street, *Studies,* 5, pp 570–6.

Butler, R.M. (1927) Dublin past and present. *In: Dublin Civic Week Handbook.* Dublin: Civic Week Council, pp 26–33.

Cameron, C.A. (1904) *How the poor live* [pamphlet, private printing].

Cameron, C.A. (1913) *Reminiscences.* Dublin: Hodges, Figgis & Co.

Cameron, C.A. (1914) *A brief history of municipal public health administration.* Dublin: Hodges, Figgis & Co.

Cherry, G.E. (1974) *The evolution of British town planning.* Leighton Buzzard: Hill.

Cherry, G.E. (1988) *Cities and plans.* London: Edward Arnold.

Chesterton, G.K. (1936) *Autobiography.* London: Burns, Oates & Washbourne Ltd.

Citizens' Housing Council (1937) *Interim report on slum clearance in Dublin 1937.* Dublin: Citizens' Housing Council.

Citizens' Housing Council (1938) *Report on slum clearance in Dublin, 1938.* Dublin: Citizens' Housing Council.

City of Dublin Vocational Education Committee (1993) *The old township of Pembroke 1863–1930.* Dublin: City of Dublin VEC.

Clout, H. (ed.) (1991) *The Times London history atlas.* London: Times Books (Harper Collins).

Cooke, P. (ed.) (1989) *Localities: The changing face of urban Britain.* London: Unwin Hyman.

Corden, C. (1977) *Planned cities: new towns in Britain and America.* London: Sage Publications.

Corpus Christi Parish (1991) *Golden Jubilee 1941–1991* [private publication, no details]

Cosgrave, A. (ed.) (1988) *Dublin through the ages.* Dublin: College Press.

Cosgrave, E. and Strangways, L.E. (1907) *Visitor's guide to Dublin and neighbourhood.* Dublin: Sealy, Bryers & Walker.

Cosgrave, D. (1932) *North Dublin- city and environs.* Dublin: Gill & Son (2nd edition).

Cowan, P.C. (1918) *Report on Dublin housing.* Dublin: Cahill & Co. Ltd.

Craft, M. (1970) The development of Dublin: background to the housing problem, *Studies,* 59, pp 301–13.

Craft, M. (1971) The development of Dublin: the southern suburbs, *Studies,* 60, pp 68–81.

Creese, W.L. (1967) *The legacy of Raymond Unwin: a human pattern for planning.* London: MIT Press.

Curriculum Development Unit (1978) *Divided city, portrait of Dublin 1913.* Dublin: O'Brien Educational.

Daly, M.E. (1981) Late nineteenth and early twentieth century Dublin. *In:* Harkness, D. and O'Dowd, M. (eds), *The town in Ireland.* Belfast: Appletree Press, pp 221–52.

Daly, M.E. (1984) *Dublin: The deposed capital, a social and economic history 1860–1914.* Cork: Cork University Press.

Daly, M.E. (1985) Housing conditions and the genesis of housing reform in Dublin 1880–1920. *In:* Bannon, M.J. (ed.) *The emergence of Irish planning 1880–1920.* Dublin: Turoe Press, pp 77–130.

Daunton, M.J. (1983) *House and home in the Victorian city: working class housing 1850–1914.* London: Edward Arnold.

Daunton, M.J. (1988) Cities of homes and cities of tenements: British and American comparisons, 1870–1914, *Journal of Urban History,* 14(3), pp 283–319.

Dawson, C. (1901) The housing of the people with special reference to Dublin, *Journal of the Statistical and Social Inquiry Society of Ireland,* 11, pp 45–56.

Dawson, C. (1913) The Dublin housing question- sanitary and insanitary, *Journal of the Statistical and Social Inquiry Society of Ireland,* 13, pp 91–5.

Dawson, W. (1912) My Dublin year, *Studies*, 1, pp 694–708.

Dennis, J. (1989) From 'rookeries' to 'communities': race, poverty and policing in London, 1850–1985, *History Workshop*, 27, pp 66–85.

Department of Local Government (1948) *Housing- a review of past operations and immediate requirements*. Dublin: Stationery Office.

Department of Local Government and Public Health [various] Annual Reports, Dublin, Stationery Office.

Dickinson, P.L. (1929) *The Dublin of yesterday*. London: Methuen & Co.

Dillon, T.W.T. (1945) Slum clearance: past and future, *Studies*, 34, pp 13–20.

Dix, G. (1978) Little plans and noble diagrams, *Town Planning Review*, 49(3), pp 329–52.

Dix, G. (1979) Patrick Abercrombie: pioneer of planning, *Architectural Review*, 990, pp 130–2.

Dublin and District House Builders' Association (1939) *The contribution of private enterprise to Greater Dublin's needs* [pamphlet]. Dublin: Sackville Press.

Dyos, H.J. (1961) *Victorian suburb: a study of the growth of Camberwell*. Leicester: Leicester University Press.

Dyos, H.J. (1967) The slums of victorian London, *Victorian Studies*, 11 (1), pp 5–40.

Dyos, H.J. & Wolff, M. (eds) (1973) *The Victorian city*. London: Routledge.

Eason, C. (1899) The tenement houses of Dublin, their condition and regulation, *Journal of the Statistical and Social Inquiry Society of Ireland*, 10, pp 383–98.

Edwards, A.M. (1981) *The design of suburbia*. London: Pembridge Press.

Egan, M.J. (1961) *The parish of St Columba, Iona Road, Glasnevin* [private publication].

Electricity Department [no date] *City of Dublin electricity department 1892–1928*. Dublin: Cahill & Co. Ltd.

Fishman, R.L. (1984) The origins of the suburban idea in England, *Chicago History*, 13(2), pp 26–35.

Fitzpatrick, D. (ed.) (1986) *Ireland and the First World War*. Dublin: Trinity History Workshop.

Fraser, M. (1966) *John Bull's other homes: State housing and British policy in Ireland, 1883–1922*. Liverpool: Liverpool University Press.

Friendly Societies (1923) Registrar of Friendly Societies for Saorstát Eireann to the Minister for Finance for the year ending the 31st day of December, 1923 (presented to the Oireachtas pursuant to Section 6, Friendly Societies Act, 1896, and Section 17, Trade Union Act, 1871). Dublin: Stationery Office.

Garrett, A. (1970) *From age to age, history of the parish of Drumcondra, North Strand, St Barnabas*. Dublin: Blackrock Printers.

Garvin, T. (1996) *The birth of Irish democracy*. Dublin: Gill and Macmillan.

Gaskell, S.M. (ed.) (1990) *Slums*. Leicester: Leicester University Press.

Gaskell, S.M. (1987) *Model housing*. London: Mansell.

Gaughan, J.A. (ed.) (1981) *Mount Merrion, the old and the new*. [no publisher], Naas.

Gauldie, E. (1974) *Cruel habitations, a history of working class housing 1780–1918*. London: Allen & Unwin.

Greater Dublin Commission (1926) *Report of the Greater Dublin Commission of Inquiry*. Dublin: Stationery Office.

Guild, R. (1989) *The Victorian house book*. New York: Rizzoli.

Gumley, F.W. (1982) Remembering … *Dublin Historical Record*, 35(3), pp 95–8.

Hall, Revd D.H. (1919) unpublished letter to Mr. Whitehead of 22 Haddon Road, Clontarf, dated 13 January 1919, held in the CRB Archive.

Hall, Revd D.H. (1920) The Church and housing, *Church of Ireland Gazette*, 26 March 1920, p. 196.

Hall, Revd D.H. (1924) The need for houses, *Church of Ireland Gazette*, 8 February 1924, pp 86–8.

Hall, P. (1985) The rise and fall of the planning movement: a view from Great Britain, *Royal Geographical Society of Australia, South Australian Branch, Proceedings*, 85, pp 45–53.

Harkness, D. and O'Dowd, M. (1981) *The town in Ireland*. Belfast: Appletree Press.

Harris, R. and Larkham, P.J. (eds) (1999) *Changing suburbs: foundation, form and function*. London: E & FN Spon.

Harrison, B. (1966) Philanthropy and the Victorians, *Victorian Studies*, 9, pp 353–74.

Hobson, B. (ed.) (1929) *A book of Dublin*. Dublin: Corporation of Dublin (1st edition).

Hobson, B. (ed.) (1930) *A book of Dublin*. Dublin: Kevin J. Kenny (2nd edition).

Horner, A.A. (1985) The Dublin region 1880–1980. In: Bannon, M.J. (ed.) *The emergence of Irish planning, 1880–1920*. Dublin: Turoe Press, pp 21–76.

Horner, A.A. (1992) From city to city-region – Dublin from the 1930s to the 1990s. In: Aalen, F.H.A. and Whelan, K. (eds), *Dublin city and county*. Dublin: Geography Publications, pp 327–58.

Horsey, M. (1990) *Tenements and towers*. Edinburgh: Royal Commission on the Ancient and Historical Monuments of Scotland.

Houghton, J.P. (1949) The social geography of Dublin, *Geographical Review*, 39, pp 237–77.

Housing and Public Health Committee (1937) *London housing*. London: King and Staples Ltd.

Howard, E. (1898) *Tomorrow: a peaceful path to real reform*. London: Swan Sonnenschein.

Housing Inquiry (1885) *Report of the Royal Commission appointed to inquire into the housing of the working classes*. Minutes of evidence etc., Ireland, British Parliamentary Papers, cd. 4547, London.

Housing Inquiry (1914) *Report of the Departmental Committee Appointed by the Local Government Board for Ireland to inquire into the housing conditions of the working classes in the city of Dublin*. British Parliamentary Papers, Vol. 19, 1914, cd.7272/7317–xix, London.

Housing Inquiry (1939–43) *Report of inquiry into the housing of the working classes of the city of Dublin, 1939–43*. Dublin: Stationery Office.

Hubbard, E. and Shippobottom, M. (1988) *A guide to Port Sunlight*. Liverpool: Liverpool University Press.

Hughes, J.B. (1914) Poverty in Dublin, *Irish Messenger Social Action Series*, 13. Dublin: Irish Messenger Office.

Hunter, M. (1981) *The Victorian villas of hackney*. London: Hackney Society.

Igoe, V. (1990) *James Joyce's Dublin houses*. London: Mandarin Paperbacks.

Jackson, A.A. (1973) *Semi-detached London: Suburban development, life and transport, 1900–39*. London: Allen & Unwin.

Johnston, J.H. and Pooley, C.G. (eds) (1982) *The structure of nineteenth century cities*. London: Croom Helm.

Johnston, M. (1985) *Around the banks of Pimlico*. Dublin: Attic Press.

Jordan, T. (1857) The present state of the dwellings of the poor, chiefly in Dublin, *Dublin Statistical Society*, 2(1), pp 12–19.

Kelly, J. & MacGearailt, U. (eds) (1990) *Dublin and Dubliners*. Dublin: Educational Company of Ireland.

Kelly, P. (1990) Drumcondra, Clonliffe and Glasnevin township, 1878–1900. In: Kelly, J. and MacGearailt, U. (eds), *Dublin and Dubliners*. Dublin: Educational Company of Ireland, pp 36–51.

Kennedy, T. (ed.) (1980) *Victorian Dublin*. Dublin: Albertine Kennedy Publishing.

Killen, J. (1992) Transport in Dublin: past, present and future. In: Aalen, F.H.A. and Whelan, K. (eds) *Dublin city and county*. Dublin: Geography Publications, pp 305–25.

Knox, P.L. (1982) *Urban social geography, an introduction*. London: Longman.

Lawless, P. and Brown, F. (1986) *Urban growth and change in Britain: an introduction.* London: Harper & Row.

Leonard, H. (1979) *Home before night.* London: Penguin.

Leslie, Revd Canon J.B. (no date) *Fasti of Christ Church Cathedral, Dublin* [copyright Representative Church Body]

Lincoln, C. (1992) *Dublin as a work of art.* Dublin: O'Brien Press.

Local Government (1938) *Report of the Local Government (Dublin) Tribunal.* Dublin: Stationery Office.

Long, H.C. (1993) *The Edwardian house.* Manchester: Manchester University Press.

Lord Mayor's Handbook (1944) *Dublin Muncipal Annual.* Dublin: Parkside Press.

Luddy, M. (1995) *Women in Ireland, 1800–1918, a documentary history.* Cork: Cork University Press.

Lynch, K. (1990) *City sense and city design.* Cambridge, Massachusetts: MIT Press.

Markus, T.A. (1985) *Visions of perfection: the influence of utopian thought upon architecture from the middle ages to the present day.* Glasgow: Third Eye Centre.

May, S. (1944) Two Dublin slums, *The Bell,* 7(4), pp 351–6.

McCarthy, T. [no date] Outcast Dublin, *Labour Museum Pamphlets,* 3, Dublin.

McCullough, N. (1989) *Dublin: an urban history.* Dublin: Anne Street Press.

McGrath, F. (1931) The Sweep and the slums, *Studies,* 20, pp 529–54.

McGrath, F. (1932) Homes for the people, *Studies,* 21, pp 269–82.

McGrath, R. (1941) Dublin panorama: an architectural review, *The Bell,* 2(5), pp 35–48.

McKenna, L. (1916) School attendance in Dublin, *Studies,* 5, pp 109–18.

McKenna, L. (1919) The housing problem in Dublin, *Studies,* 8, pp 279–95.

McKeon, J. and Jennings, R. (1978) *Public subventions to housing in Ireland.* Dublin: An Foras Forbartha.

MacLaren, A. (1993) *Dublin, the shaping of a capital.* London: Belhaven Press.

McManus, R. (1996) Public Utility Societies, Dublin Corporation and the development of Dublin, 1920–1940, *Irish Geography,* 29(1), pp 27–37.

McManus, R. (1998) The Dundalk Premier Public Utility Society, *Irish Geography,* 31(2), pp 75–87.

McManus, R. (1999) The 'Building Parson' – the role of Reverend David Hall in the solution of Ireland's early twentieth-century housing problems, *Irish Geography,* 32 (2), pp 87–98.

McNiffe, L. (1997) *A history of the Garda Síochána.* Dublin: Wolfhound Press.

Meghen, P.J. (1963) *Housing in Ireland.* Dublin: Institute of Public Administration.

Meller, H. (1990) *Patrick Geddes, social evolutionist and city planner.* London: Routledge.

Mikhail, E.H. (ed.) (1982) *Brendan Behan.* London: Macmillan.

Miller, M. (1989) Raymond Unwin and the planning of Dublin. *In:* Bannon, M.J. (ed.) *The emergence of Irish planning, 1880–1920.* Dublin: Turoe Press, pp 189–260.

Miller, M. (1992) *Raymond Unwin, Garden Cities and town planning.* Leicester: Leicester University Press.

Mingay, G.E. (1986) *The transformation of Britain, 1830–1939.* London: Routledge.

Ministry of Local Government (1925) *House designs.* Prescribed by the Minister of Local Government under the Housing Act, 1924. Dublin: Stationery Office (5 volumes).

Moody, T.W. & Martin, F.X. (eds) (1967) *The course of Irish history.* Cork: Mercier Press.

Mumford, L. (1961) *The city in history.* London: Penguin.

Municipal Boundaries (1881) *Report of the Municipal Boundaries Commission (Ireland).* British Parliamentary Papers, Vol. 50, c.2827, Dublin.

Murphy, F. (1984) Dublin slums in the 1930s, *Dublin Historical Record,* 37 (3/4), pp 104–11.

Muthesius, S. (1982) *The English terraced house.* New Haven: Yale University Press.

National Economic and Social Council (1981) *Urbanisation: problems of growth and decay in Dublin.* Dublin: NESC.

Nowlan, K.I. (1989) The evolution of Irish planning, 1934–64. *In:* Bannon, M.J. (ed.) *Planning: the Irish experience.* Dublin: Wolfhound Press, pp 71–85.

O'Brien, J.V. (1982) *Dear dirty Dublin, a city in distress, 1899–1916.* Berkeley: University of California Press.

O'Brien, M. (1950) The planning of Dublin, *Journal of Town Planning Institute,* 36(6), pp 199–212.

O'Connell, J.R. (1913) *The problem of the Dublin slums.* Dublin: Irish Catholic [pamphlet].

O'Connor, D. (1979) *Housing in Dublin's inner city.* Dublin: Housing Research Unit, School of Architecture, UCD.

O'Connor, L. (2000) *Can Lily O'Shea come out to play?* Dingle: Brandon.

O'Dwyer, F. (1981) *Lost Dublin.* Dublin: Gill and Macmillan.

O Fearghail, C. (1992) The evolution of Catholic parishes in Dublin city from the sixteenth to the nineteenth centuries. *In:* Aalen, F.H.A. and Whelan, K. (eds) *Dublin city and county.* Dublin: Geography Publications, pp 229–50.

Ó Maitiú, S. (1997) *Rathmines Township 1847–1930.* Dublin: City of Dublin Vocational Education Committee.

O'Rourke, H.T. (1925) *The Dublin civic survey.* Liverpool: University Press of Liverpool.

Oliver, P., Davis, I. and Bentley, I. (1994) *Dunroamin: the suburban semi and its enemies.* London: Pimlico (Random House).

Olsen, D.J. (1976) *The growth of Victorian London.* London: Penguin.

Orbach, L.F. (1977) *Homes for heroes, a study of the evolution of British public housing, 1915–1921.* London: Seely, Service.

Owen, D. (1965) *English philanthropy, 1660–1960.* Cambridge, Massachusetts: Harvard University Press.

Peters, A. (1927) *Dublin fragments, social and historic.* Dublin: Hodges Figgis and Co.

Pevsner, N. (1968) Model dwellings for the labouring classes, *Architectural Review,* 93, pp 119–28.

Pooley, C.G. (1984) Residential differentiation in Victorian cities: a reassessment, *Transactions of the Institute of British Geographers,* 9(2), pp 131–44.

Pooley, C.G. (1985) Housing for the poorest poor: slum-clearance and rehousing in Liverpool, 1890–1918, *Journal of Historical Geography,* 11(1), pp 70–88.

Pooley, C.G. (ed.) (1992) *Housing strategies in Europe, 1880–1930.* Leicester: Leicester University Press.

Pooley, C.G. and Lawton, R. (1992) *Britain 1740–1950, an historical geography.* London: Edward Arnold.

Powell, C. (1974) Fifty years of progress, *Built Environment,* 3(10), pp 532–5.

Powell, C.G. (1980) *An economic history of the British building industry, 1815–1979.* London: The Architectural Press.

Power, A. (1993) *Hovels to high rise: State housing in Europe since 1850.* London: Routledge.

Prunty, J. (1998) *Dublin slums 1800–1925, a study in urban geography.* Dublin: Irish Academic Press.

Prunty, J. (2001) Improving the urban environment. *In:* Brady, J. and Simms, A. (eds), *Dublin through space and time.* Dublin: Four Courts Press, pp 166–220.

Rahilly, A.J. (1917) The social problem in Cork, *Studies,* 6, pp 177–88.

Rapoport, A. (1990) *The meaning of the built environment: a nonverbal communication approach.* Tucson: University of Arizona Press.

Ratcliffe, J. (1974) *An introduction to town and country planning.* London: Hutchinson.

Ravetz, A. (1974) From working class tenement to modern flat. *In:* Sutcliffe, A. (ed.) *Multi-storey living.* London: Croom Helm, pp 122–50.

Rockey, J. (1983) From vision to reality: Victorian ideal cities and model towns in the genesis of E. Howard's Garden City, *Town Planning Review,* 54(1), pp 83–105.

Rosenau, H. (1983) *The ideal city, its architectural evolution in Europe.* London: Methuen, 3rd edition.

Rothery, S. (1991) *Ireland and the new architecture, 1900–1940.* Dublin: Lilliput Press.

Scott, W.A. (1916) The reconstruction of O'Connell Street, Dublin: a note (including sketch), *Studies,* 5, p. 165.

Scuffil, C. (ed.) (1993) *By the sign of the dolphin: the story of Dolphin's Barn.* Dublin: Dolphin's Barn Historical Society.

Shaffrey, M. (1988) Sackville Street/O'Connell Street, *GPA Irish Arts Yearbook,* Dublin, pp 144–56.

Sheehan, R. and Walsh, B. (1988) *The heart of the city.* Dingle: Brandon.

Sies, M.C. (1987) The city transformed: nature, technology and the suburban ideal, 1877–1917, *Journal of Urban History,* 14(1), pp 81–111.

Simms, A. and Fagan, P. (1992) Villages in County Dublin: their origins and inheritance. *In:* Aalen, F.H.A. and Whelan, K. (eds) *Dublin city and county.* Dublin: Geography Publications, pp 79–119.

Simpson, M. and Lloyd, T. (eds) (1977) *Studies in the history of middle class housing in Britain.* England: Newton Abbot.

Skilleter, K.J. (1993) The role of PUSs in early British planning and housing reform 1901–36, *Planning Perspectives,* pp 125–65.

Slater, T.R. (ed.) (1990) *The built form of western cities.* Leicester: Leicester University Press.

Spence, N. (1982) *British cities: an analysis of urban change.* Oxford: Pergamon Press.

Stedman-Jones, G. (1971) *Outcast London: a study in the relationship between classes in Victorian society.* Oxford: Clarendon Press.

Stenhouse, D. (1977) *Understanding towns.* Hove: Wayland Publishers.

Stevenson, J. (1984) *British society, 1914–45.* London: Penguin.

Sutcliffe, A. (1972) Working class housing in nineteenth century Britain: a review of recent research, *Society for the Study of Labour History,* Bulletin 24.

Sutcliffe, A. (ed.) (1974) *Multi-storey living: the British working-class experience.* London: Croom Helm.

Sutcliffe, A. (ed.) (1980) *The rise of modern urban planning, 1800–1914.* London: Mansell.

Sutcliffe, A. (1981) *Towards the planned city: Germany, Britain, The U.S. and France, 1780–1914.* Oxford: Basil Blackwell.

Sutcliffe, A. (ed.) (1981) *British town planning: the formative years.* New York: St Martin's Press.

Swenarton, M. (1981) *Homes fit for heroes.* London: Heinemann.

Tarn, J.N. (1973) *Five per cent philanthropy.* Cambridge: Cambridge University Press.

Tarn, J.N. (1968) Some pioneer suburban housing estates, *Architectural Review,* 143, pp 367–70.

Tarn, J.N. (1980) Housing reform and the emergence of town planning in Britain before 1914. In: Sutcliffe, A. (ed.), *The rise of modern urban planning, 1800–1914.* London: Mansell, pp 71–98.

Thackeray, W.M. (1985) *The Irish sketch book 1842.* Belfast: Blackstaff Press.

Thompson, F.M.L. (1988) *The rise of respectable society: a social history of Victorian Britain 1830–1900.* London: Fontana Press.

Thompson, F.M.L. (ed.) (1982) *The rise of suburbia.* Leicester: Leicester University Press.

Thrift, N. and Williams, P. (eds) (1987) *Class and space: the making of urban society.* London: Routledge.

Townroe, B.S. (1924) *A handbook of housing.* London: Methuen.

Tudor Walters Report (1918) *Report of the committee appointed by the President of the Local Government Board and the Secretary for Scotland to consider questions of building construction in connection with the provision of dwellings for the working classes in England, Wales and Scotland.* London: HMSO.

Tutty, M.J. (1958) Drumcondra, *Dublin Historical Record,* 15 (3), pp 86–96.

Unwin, R. (1912) *Nothing gained by overcrowding.* London: Garden Cities and Town Planning Association.

Unwin, R. and Parker, B. (1909) *Town planning in practice* (1994, reprint). Princeton: Princeton Architectural Press.

Vitaliano, D.F. (1983) Public housing and slums: cure or cause? *Urban Studies,* 20(2), pp 173–83.

Ward, D. (1984) The progressives and the urban question: British and American responses to the inner city slums, 1880–1920, *Transactions of the Institute of British Geographers,* 9(3), pp 299–314.

Ward, S.V. (ed.) (1992) *The Garden City; past, present and future.* London: E &FN Spon.

Watchorn, F. (1985) *Crumlin and the way it was.* Dublin: O'Donoghue Press International.

Waterman, S. (1981) Changing residential patterns of the Dublin Jewish community, *Irish Geography,* 14, pp 41–50.

Watson, I. (1989) *Gentlemen in the building line: the development of South Hackney.* London: Padfield Publications.

Whitehand, J.W.R. (1987) The changing face of cities: a study of development cycles and urban form, *IBG Special Publications, 21.* Oxford: Basil Blackwell.

Whitelaw, J. (1805) *An essay on the population of Dublin, being the result of an actual survey taken in 1798 with great care and precision, to which is added the general return of the district committee in 1804, with a comparative statement of the two surveys, also several observations on the present state of the poorer parts of the city of Dublin, 1805.* Dublin. Reprinted as *Slum conditions in London and Dublin* (1974). Farnborough, Hants: Gregg International.

Wohl, A.S. (1977) *The eternal slum, housing and social policy in Victorian London.* London: Edward Arnold.

Wohl, A.S. (1983) *Endangered lives: public health in Victorian Britain.* London: Dent.

Yelling, J.A. (1982) LCC slum clearance policies, 1889–1907, *Transactions of the Institute of British Geographers,* 7(3), pp 292–303.

Yelling, J.A. (1992) *Slums and redevelopment: policy and practice in England, 1918–45.* London: UCL Press.

Illustrations

Tables

Index

Italic page numbers refer to illustrations

499